CONECUH PEOPLE

CONECUH PEOPLE

Words of Life from the Alabama Black Belt

WADE HALL

Foreword by Thomas D. Clark

BLACK BELT PRESS

Montgomery

Black Belt Press
P.O. Box 551
Montgomery, AL 36101

ISBN 1-881320-25-1

*The Black Belt, defined by its dark, rich soil, stretches across central Alabama.
It was the heart of the cotton belt. It was and is a place of great beauty, of
extreme wealth and grinding poverty, of pain and joy. Here we take our stand,
listening to the past, looking to the future.*

For

My Parents and Grandparents—

With Pioneer Names Like Hall, Waters, Grider, Rollo, Allen—

Indeed, All the Families Who Have Called Bullock County, Alabama, Home

Even Before It Was a County

CONTENTS

Sing them over again to me,
Wonderful words of life;
Let me more of their beauty see,
Wonderful words of life.
Words of life and beauty,
Teach me faith and duty:
Beautiful words, wonderful words,
Wonderful words of life.

—P. P. Bliss

There are all those early memories;
one cannot get another set . . .

—Willa Cather

FOREWORD

THOMAS D. CLARK

Historians of the South in large measure have failed to fill in the human interstices of the region. Always there has existed that large segment of humanity which has been treated as little more than a digital blip in the statistical abstraction of Southern history. Since the days of Anglo-American settlement beginnings, there has lived and labored in the South a population element which met eternal challenges under a dimming pall of isolation, environmental influences, and political neglect. Nevertheless, this groundrail of the population formed a veritable phalanx of adventurers who helped to open frontiers, claim the land, open fields and meadows, and planted myriad communities along the way. They did this while living at the lowest subsistence level of human existence. Across the South they planted their unsophisticated institutions to fulfill their basic cultural needs, and economically they looked to the land to sustain them.

In his seminal study, *Plain Folk of the Old South*, Frank L. Owsley has come closest to plowing the fertile soil of basic human history in the region. The people Owsley dug out of the mire of myriad statistical sources and from random family papers and those interviewed by Wade Hall introduce to modern readers a sense of a vital segment of the human past. They present an intimate glimpse of the survivors of an ever-nagging environment, of progenitors and at once preservers of a varicolored heritage and of an unrelent-

ing attachment to a highly circumscribed place. They were at once rowdy and bumptious on one hand and gracious and hospitable on the other. In the waning years of the twentieth century there are few more than a corporal's guard of us who can say, "I was there once, and not only understand the language and spirit of a simple, unsophisticated, land-bound people, but I could sense the nuances and emotions of their deeply felt sentimentalities for their way of life."

Fortunately, over a span of years Professor Wade Hall was able to elicit from elder survivors in his native Bullock County, Alabama, interviews in which individuals looked back into their pasts. Skillfully, he was able to set the subjects of his interviews at ease and extracted from them more meaningful statements than if they had attempted to write memoirs. In fact, there is a documentary significance in the fact of informality of the interviews.

The Black Belt land of Bullock County exacted heavy tithes from its occupants, tithes which were paid in kind of arduous labor, of seasonal frustrations, of adverse weather conditions, short crops, and, always, with low expectancies. Clearly, the subjects of these interviews had, in their simplistic approaches, a sense of history, a warm human concept of the past.

Many of the persons interviewed by Professor Hall recalled in vague memory that their forebears had come to Alabama at an early date from "Old" South Carolina. They had been tolled westward by desires to find fresh virgin lands. They had been propelled along the way in that tide of humanity which swarmed into freshly vacated Indian lands like a plague of Biblical locusts. The famous old emigrant road which sliced diagonally across Georgia, Alabama, and Mississippi channeled a mighty horde of human beings into the region, emigrants who fetched along a generous baggage of cultural folkways, a

Tombstone in Liberty Cemetery.

loyalty to simple institutions, to fierce religious beliefs, and, above all, an unrelenting sense of social homogeneity.

Again, the history of both the vibrant folk movement across the South and the type of civilization it planted in the region at the ground level of a yeoman people still awaits serious comprehensive and integrated treatments by historians and sociologists. These Alabama interviews will prove highly palatable grist for such an undertaking.

One reads the transcribed sagas of Beansie Hall, Martha Hall Driggers, Estelle Cope Campbell, Frances McLendon White, Luke Mariner, and others with realization that they were reliving in spirit and in fact a past which had assumed a tolerant if not rosy glow. There runs through the collective interviews a common bindage of individual experiences. In each interview there was expressed a tender recollection of the past and its human associations, and an inseparable attachment to place. Although many of the persons interviewed had lived at or below the poverty level, there was little expression of dissatisfaction or anger. For human beings conditioned to a set way of life in a demanding land, there were snatches of pleasures in community gatherings, in family associations, in church meetings, and even in the mere matter of neighborliness. Always there prevailed, if as a hallmark, a folk code of dignity and civility, expressed frequently in terms of simple hospitality and human compassion. In every instance the person interviewed expressed respect and appreciation for central community figures such as a doctor, a teacher, a storekeeper, or a minister.

Earlier historians of the westward movement viewed the opening of new lands as a social and economic safety valve helping to reduce the rising stresses in old communities. In the instances of rural Southern communities, like Bullock County, there was some safety valve effect within the tight bindings of isolated provinciality itself.

So far as most of the subjects of these interviews knew, all across the continent rural people lived on a common level of human relationships, of family, of community, and of the county. Seldom did they venture much out into the state, or cross its boundaries into other areas. There prevailed, however, within the unrelenting bounds of Bullock County provinciality, a spirit of gentility and general hospitality which rural Southerners knew how to extend with utmost sincerity and a timely grace.

An abandoned Bullock County farmstead, 1995.

surviving neighbors in Bullock County is a rich and penetrating documentation of a way of life and a heritage which can be passed on in the sounds of human voices and in script for future generations to vicariously re-enter the past. It was fortunate that Professor Hall could persuade so many people to look back into their past and explain how they made the necessary compromises of life to exist within the contexts of place and time. In many respects these journeys back in time and place fall little short of being a signing off of the past of a bygone rural South *sine die.*

In the South's advancement into a modernizing industrial-commercial-social reform era, there took place a monstrous erasure of ancient landmarks of the earlier ways of life. Old homesteads either melted into the dust of decay or were left ghostly shells devoid of all the spirit of human occupancy. No country stores stood at cross roads, schoolhouses surrendered to consolidations, and country churches were remodeled in imitation of those in towns. "Good roads," automobiles, and pick-up trucks obliterated provincial barriers. There no doubt remained in Bullock County, as all across the rural South, one virtually untouchable monument to the past—the cemeteries. Rows of simple stone tablets stand in upright phalanxes in unrelenting defiance of change. They do that and more. Inscribed on their faces is perhaps the only creditable documentation that the person lying beneath once walked the face of the land and enjoyed such fortunes as it was willing to award him or her.

Wade Hall's incisive interviews with kinsfolk and

I can vouch first-hand for the authenticity of the spirit of these interviews. In my early life in rural Mississippi I was present in such a social, economic, and geographical setting as a member of a family whose roots were back in "Old" South Carolina. We lived on and off the land in a comparable social and cultural setting. As simple and unsophisticated as most of these interviews are, they must survive as the testimonials of people who endured and survived the vagaries of land and time within the comfortable cocoon of their place and station in the fabric of American life.

A PERSONAL PREFACE

WADE HALL

In September of 1950, when I was sixteen, my mother drove me from our Bullock County farm down to Troy, Alabama, to live with my Great Aunt Emma Grider O'Steen on South Brundidge Street and to enroll as a freshman at the nearby teachers college. I did not know what it meant to go to college because, except for my teachers, I'd never known any college graduates up close. Indeed, I knew very few people who had ever completed high school—certainly, no one in my own family.

The Inverness Consolidated School, which I had attended from the first through the twelfth grades, never had more than one section of any class. I, therefore, did not know what class registration was all about. While my mother waited in our Ford pick-up truck in

The author's great-aunt, Emma O'Steen.

the hot late summer sun outside Bibb Graves Hall, the administration and main classroom building, I hurried inside to tell someone I had arrived and was ready for classes. I said to my mother that I should be back in five or ten minutes. It never occurred to me that it would take any longer to say, "Hey, I'm Wade Hall, and I'm ready to start to college."

When I was able to disentangle myself from the registration procedure some three hours later, I ran outside to see about my mother. I knew that this shy, inexperienced country woman would never have thought to seek out a cool place in the library, nor would she have known about the college canteen, where she could go for a sandwich and a soft drink. Sure enough, she had not set foot outside the truck and was still waiting patiently for me in the cab.

Such was my rude, sweaty baptism into the new world I had chosen to enter. It was scary. A few minutes later my mother left me at Aunt Emma's, and I felt utterly alone and bereft. As she backed down the driveway, I wanted to cry out for her to stop and take me home; but I knew what I had to do. I had to tough it out and stay at Troy, this strange new country not more than twenty-five miles from where I was born but light years distant in every other way. It was the only ticket I had out of Bullock County, out of the family and community I so desperately wanted to flee.

The three years it took me to complete my degree at Troy State Teachers College (now Troy State University) were painful but liberating and productive. My room was a tiny corner of my aunt's kitchen, with only a small cot and a few shelves as my living space. I had no chair, no desk or table for reading or studying. I prepared school work at my aunt's kitchen table or on her front porch. I had no encouragement and very little support from home. My father grudgingly gave me the money to pay my tuition, which during the 1950-51 academic year was $1.50 a quarter hour. He also gave me about five dollars a week to live on, and for that allowance I was expected to work on weekends in his small country store and to help with such house chores as cutting wood and washing and ironing the family clothes. There were times when he would withhold even that from me, refusing to take me back to Troy in time for Monday morning classes. But I knew that he was the jailor who also held the key to unlock my prison. It was only through him that I could go to college—I knew nothing about scholarships and work study programs—and I knew I had to tolerate his erratic behavior and demands. So I endured and tried not to feel bitter about the cards life had dealt me. I was glad to be pursuing the only option I had. I knew of no other place to go and no one else who could help me. As the months passed, I adjusted to my new life and was graduated in 1953 with a degree in English and history.

During those years at Troy, I experienced a number of firsts: the first time I ever talked on a telephone; the first time I ever tasted such foods as spaghetti or Chow Mein or shrimp or apple pie or asparagus or yeast rolls; the first time I ever had a close friend; and except for my high school class trip to New Orleans, the first time I ever traveled outside Alabama, ate in a restaurant, or stayed in a hotel or motel. Troy was opening a great new world for me, and I had no intention of ever returning to Bullock County, except for short visits. Indeed, I wanted to leave my childhood home far behind. Years later, one of my aunts reminded me of how successful I had been when she said, "Wade Henry, I knowed when you went off to Troy, you'd never come back home again." I did not

The author in 1952 in Troy, Alabama.

intend to sever all ties, but my new home would be always somewhere else—Opp, where I taught for one year in a junior high school; Heidelberg, Germany, where I was stationed with the U. S. Army; Tuscaloosa, where I earned my master's degree at the University of Alabama in 1957; Urbana, where I went for my "northern exposure" and where I received a doctorate in English and history from the University of Illinois; Gainesville, where I taught as a young assistant professor of English at the University of Florida; and for the past thirty years and more, Louisville, where I have taught and chaired the English and humanities programs at Kentucky Southern College and Bellarmine College.

Most of the people I left behind in Bullock County are still there, some living in the communities where they were born and some lying with their kindred and neighbors in church or family cemeteries. Despite some radical changes and improvements, it is still a country I can easily recognize with the same place names and family names. The numerous two-room schoolhouses that served African Americans of my youth have been razed, and the public school facilities are legally integrated and modern. There is still segregation. Most white parents at all income levels send their children to Bullock Memorial School, a private academy, and blacks and whites still attend their own churches.

The people are still intensely religious—even those who don't "belong" to any church—and most claim some sort of connection to one of the numerous Baptist churches, both black and white, that dot the county landscape. As an Episcopal professor at Troy told me one time, "If you take any little backroad in Bullock County and follow it long enough, it will take you to a Baptist church." There are, of course, occa-

The author (far right) with his brothers and cousin.

sional churches of other denominations, especially Methodist, Presbyterian, and Church of Christ, with a sprinkling of pentecostal congregations. There is now even a Catholic church in Union Springs, the county seat, but the local Episcopal church is about as moribund as it was a generation ago.

In my absence a few more dusty country roads have been paved, but they still lead to the same places. The road I took out more than forty years ago is still two-way and now beckons me to return for a special mission—to pursue my most important journey, a Jamesian inward probe to confront and acknowledge the self I thought I had left behind. Indeed, I know now that, for better or worse, this is the place and these are the people that made me what I am. This knowledge has not been a sudden epiphany but a growing awareness that in order to know myself, I must return to where I started. In the words of T. S. Eliot, I must go back to my beginning "and know the place for the first time."

In the mid-1970s I suggested to a friend, Dr. Annie Mae Turner, who has lived her entire life in Bullock County, that we begin interviewing some of the county's oldest inhabitants and thus preserve in their own words lives and patterns of living that were quickly disappearing. "Some of the families we know in this county," I said, "have gone from illiteracy to computers in one generation." She agreed enthusiastically. She focused on people she knew in the northern half of the county, and I took the southern end, the area where I was born and grew up. We did not intend to do a statistical sampling of the population. We chose to interview people we knew intimately, and thus most of our subjects are working-class whites. In fact, most of the people in this collection are related to me by blood or marriage or by such community kinships as school and church. Unfortunately, most of the blacks I knew as a boy had died or moved away by the time I began doing the interviews. Two notable exceptions were Tommie and Verse Manley, with whom I kept in close contact through the years. When I dared to come home without visiting them, I received a verbal thrashing the next time. I also continued to see Luke Mariner when he stopped to "trade" at my father's store.

Our goal for this long-range informal project was, therefore, to talk with people we already knew and have them tell us their life stories, some of which went back into the nineteenth century. The interviews continued for more than fifteen years, the bulk of them having been done before 1980. Dr. Turner tape-recorded her subjects as she had time and opportunity, and I did my share during the three or four trips I made home each year. Before we concluded our work, we had taped some fifty people, most of them born before 1920. As I was preparing the interviews for publication, it soon became apparent that we would not have room for more than fifteen or twenty in a single collection. For this reason, the present book is restricted to nineteen of the people I interviewed from my part of the county. We hope that eventually the entire chorus of Bullock County voices will be heard.

Let me now say a word of caution. These are authentic voices from the Alabama back country of several generations ago, and you must not try to find in them any liberal social or political or religious attitudes—from whites or blacks. Although these people are generous, fairminded, courteous, and loving, they are people who were molded by the laws and customs of an earlier time. They have accommodated themselves easily enough to new social and political realities, but their lives and opinions have been hardly affected. Indeed, many of the older people in these monologues lived their lives pretty much the same as their parents and grandparents. Until the 1950s and 1960s the modern world had simply passed most of them by. Except for the automobile and an occasional radio, most of these people lived pioneer-like, self-sustaining lives, without such conveniences as electricity or running water or telephones. They raised most of their food in gardens, hogpens, and cowpens; and the women made most of their everyday clothes on sewing machines dating back to the nineteenth century. Women wore homemade bonnets that were stylish before the Civil War.

Even when the gadgetry of modern life became available to them, they received it with considerable skepticism. Until she died, one of my aunts kept her wood-burning stove set up in the kitchen next to her electric range—just in case the power might fail or in case she wanted to cook up a batch of good biscuits. An old black man kept water in his backyard well just in case the piped-in water dried up. My aunt never had an indoor toilet, and she never learned to drive a car. In the 1940s electric service was made available to the rural reaches of the county through the Rural Electrification Administration, but well into the 1950s I remember houses that were lighted by kerosene lamps, and most families were still served by outhouse toilets.

The author, 1948.

In these pages, therefore, you will meet real people. I know they are real because I have known them all my life: my mother, two of my aunts, a cousin, a sister-in-law, my high school math teacher, the pastor of my boyhood church. They will speak to you in their own voices and in their own words. They will speak without the interruption of my questions and comments, without the repetitions and false starts and irrelevant blind alleys of normal conversation. Since these people were unaccustomed to one-on-one interviews, I used an informal conversational format to draw from them their life stories. Many of the monologues are composites of several sessions. The taped interviews were

Author Wade Hall visiting the Liberty Church cemetery.

transcribed word for word as spoken, then shaped and arranged in a coherent narrative that allows each person to tell his or her own story in an accurate but effective and dramatic way. The French playwright Jean Anouilh once observed, "Life is very nice but it lacks form. It's the aim of art to give it some." What I've tried to do is provide a form by which each person can best tell his or her life story. The result is, I hope, a medley of voices that are as unique and expressive as fingerprints.

Although no attempt was made to contrive a cross section of people, you will nonetheless meet a variety of Bullock Countians, ranging from the college educated to the illiterate, from poor farmers to a frustrated artist. You will get to know a successful restaurateur who was born into such poverty that she can recall mealtimes when there was nothing to eat. On the other hand, you will hear a woman recounting her privileged girlhood as a member of the country aristocracy. Another woman describes her childhood

home as being so far back in the woods that her first and only boyfriend (and future husband) got lost on his way to their first date. Furthermore, an old woman's plaintive voice begs for help in determining her age so she can "draw the old-age benefits." A childless wife calls her dogs, cows, and cats her babies and pampers them as if they were. A woman profiles her hard life, starting when she was a girl doing a man's work plowing a horse named Maud. There is the inspiring story of a gritty widow whose husband died at forty-three, leaving her alone with two young children to raise. Another woman begins her widowhood at twenty-eight. A woman returns to the highlight of her life when she accompanies her husband to Chicago in vain pursuit of a good job. You will learn to respect and admire the spartan life of a maiden lady who finally died of mouth cancer caused by her one real pleasure in life—dipping snuff. You will suffer with a stoical woman who worked in a cotton mill for almost forty years, with nothing to show for it but a pitifully small retirement check of $85 a month. Finally, you will rejoice with a church lady who mourns the dead only if she believes they died without salvation.

Male members of this country society also get their hours on the stage. You will hear the melancholy story of a folk painter who hated mathematics in school but had to support his family as a bookkeeper. You will laugh with a practical jokester whose real-life stories probably gain something in the telling. You will return with an old man to his youth as he recalls vividly the sardines and soda crackers that were his father's treat when they took a wagonload of cotton to the gin. A honky-tonk operator and moonshiner will swear to you that his life was saved when he was sent to prison where his heart disease was detected and treated. Finally, you will accompany a preacher who is little in size but large in voice as he returns to the mishaps of total immersion in makeshift baptistries. These are some of the men and women who will open up a world that for many of you will be as remote as

Siberia and as dated as your great-grandmother's Easter bonnet. But these lives are no less universal for having been lived in an isolated corner of Alabama. Indeed, all the facets and passions of human life are here presented, from cradle to grave.

Admittedly, in many ways these people are not typical Americans. They lived mainly outside the main currents of American life of the twentieth century; nevertheless, their struggle for survival is American heroism at its best. Most of them never demanded or expected much from life beyond a few clothes, sufficient food, and a house that did not let in too much cold air in winter. The women in particular lived hard lives of unrelenting labor. They married young, sometimes as early as fourteen, and began to have children at fifteen or sixteen. My own mother was sixteen when I was born. To feed and clothe the house full of children they had by the time they were twenty-five, they toiled in the fields alongside their menfolks. Many of these people grew up in grinding poverty on tenant farms, with little hope for a better life than their parents. A few of them were lucky enough to be the sons and daughters of yeoman farmers who owned forty or eighty acres of land which they worked themselves. One woman was fortunate indeed to be the daughter of a village merchant and entrepreneur who enriched himself by "furnishing" (at high interest rates) impoverished farmers the seeds, fertilizer, and other provisions they needed to make a crop. Indeed, everyone was dependent upon a farming economy. Just about everyone did backbreaking farm labor—young and old, men and women, black and white—usually all in the same fields side by side, hoeing and plowing cotton and corn, shaking and stacking peanuts, picking cotton and pulling corn. At home, there was a division of labor according to sex, with everyone assigned permanent chores, the women having to do the lion's share of the work, from cleaning the house to preparing the food.

Most of these people stayed in the communities where they were born, many of them living their entire lives within a radius of a few miles. All of my blood relatives in this book, for example, never lived more than a couple of miles from their birthplace. Indeed, of my parents' five sons, I was the only one to move from the community. My four brothers remained behind to marry wives from other parts of the county and raise their families. Even relatives and neighbors who moved to larger towns and cities to find work maintained a close relationship to the people and places of their youth. As a boy I remember attending numerous family and church reunions where I met former inhabitants and their children. The biggest event of the year at Liberty Baptist Church was Mothers' Day, which was not only a tribute to

The author, right, with Wilbur Hall, Lessie Hall, and Eunice Hall, at Wilbur Hall's cane syrup mill, c. 1960.

mothers but a coming together of separated friends and families from all over Alabama and the Lower South. The big reunion day at Macedonia Baptist Church was July 4, which Hobson Roughton describes vividly in his monologue. Needless to say, our black neighbors had frequent summer and Christmas visitors from big industrial cities like Birmingham, New York, Detroit and Chicago.

The people who stayed in southern Bullock County lived traditional lives that had changed little for generations. They continued to farm and housekeep much in the same ways of their ancestors, plowing with horses and mules, doing most of the other field work by hand, cooking on wood-burning stoves, piecing quilts from scraps and quilting them at community gatherings, making soap from the potash of fireplace ashes, scouring their bare wooden floors with cornshuck brooms, sweeping the house with broomsedge brooms, and cleaning the sandy yards with brushbrooms made from swamp bushes. Many of the women still wore ante-bellum bonnets to keep the sun from darkening their faces when they went outdoors. Most children were born at home until past the middle of the present century. Of my mother's five sons, four of us were born at home in the same bed where she was born. Although these people continued the folkways and traditions of their ancestors, many of them had little knowledge of their forebears or where they came from or how long their families had lived in Bullock County. In fact, most of them are descendants of the original settlers who moved into the virgin land from Virginia, North and South Carolina, and Georgia.

Like many Americans, Bullock Countians speak with an "accent," and like all English-speaking people, they do not pronounce words as they are spelled. I have tried to preserve the voices of all the people I interviewed by recording by vocabulary, their grammar, their syntax, and their idioms. In representing their sounds, I have had to strike a middle course between unreadable phonetic spelling and a completely standard spelling and grammar that would drain much of their color and character. I have, therefore, used selected phonetic spellings to suggest sound and various verbal habits. Occasionally, a person may use a construction that seems to be an editor's error. Preacher John Butler, for example, in describing his desire to publish an affordable book of his sermons, says: "I went to town and bought me a mimeograph machine so I could sell it where people could afford to buy it." In this context "where" does not refer to location. Rather, it means "at a price so that," and the sentence thus means: "I went to town and bought me a mimeograph machine so I could sell the book at a price so that people could afford to buy it." Furthermore, people who had little formal education learned their language and folkways orally and thus retained many of the word forms and grammar and customs of earlier times. The retention of the verb prefix "a-" as in "a-coming and a-going" and the preservation of the excrescent "t" in such words as "once(t)" are two examples of this archaic speech. Such a circumlocution as "step aside," used almost exclusively by women to mean going to the bathroom, reveals a lingering pioneer influence on their language.

I believe that every person has an important story to tell, and the most authentic stories are told by the people who have lived them. In telling their stories they discover truths about themselves, which they share in the telling with all of us. Because these people were not used to being interviewed or thinking about their lives and making statements about them, I had to probe from a number of directions and at different times to get them to open up and talk honestly about themselves. Frequently, a person would respond, "Why, I never thought to ask Grandpa about where he was from or why he came here. I wish I had." Or, "I never really thought about whether I've lived a happy life. I reckon I have though."

In an oral history of a small area, it is expected that informants will allude to the same people, places, events, and customs, thus providing a kind of incremental repetition in which additional information, another point of view, and sometimes contradictory information are given to form a community chorus that is at once harmonious and dissonant. Such is the process by which humans get as close to truth as we are likely to get.

As I have interviewed these people and transcribed their words and shaped them into their likenesses, how much have I learned about them? I have learned that, like many of us, they are victims, trapped by poverty or sex or race and/or by cultural mores and inertia. Unlike a lot of people today, however, they do not assign blame or seek scapegoats. They seem to say, "Well, now that I think about it, life has been unfair to me, but it's really nobody's fault. We all must play the cards we are dealt. We are glad to have been born on any terms into life's great mystery and be a brief part of its immense journey." Despair and suicide are, therefore, almost unknown among such people. They endure, enjoying the few pleasures life affords them. Then they die in anticipation of a fuller, richer life promised in the Bible. Almost one-half of the people in this book are now dead, but for them death held few terrors. Their lives had been hard and exhausting and for them death meant peace and rest at the least— the restful sleep that comes after a long day's work in the cotton field or cotton mill. Moreover, death is cushioned by a religious faith of great promise, such a graphic longing as seen in the words of one of their popular hymns:

> On Jordan's stormy banks I stand,
> And cast a wishful eye
> To Canaan's fair and happy land,
> Where my possessions lie.

The hereafter is a place of complete security and joy:

> No chilling winds, no pois'nous breath,
> Can reach that healthful shore;
> Sickness and sorrow, pain and death,
> Are felt and feared no more.

Finally, what have I learned about myself? After all, regardless of its subject, every book is an author's journey of self-discovery—and all the more if the book touches the people and places of his home. This entire project, from the interviews themselves through the editing and the shaping of them into monologues, has been for me a revelation and a catharsis. I have come better to understand and appreciate and accept the people of my home county, of my home community—my parents and all my relatives and ancestors, my teachers and schoolmates, my neighbors—in short, everyone, black and white, that I grew up among. Furthermore, and without intending any exaggeration, I can better appreciate the worth of every human life, regardless of ambition or achievement. This project has been for me like a search for the pieces of a giant puzzle or a great mosaic—pieces that I have discovered and cut, showing the smooth and sharp edges, the good times and the bad times, the small victories and defeats, the sadness and the joys that are common to us all.

I have, indeed, learned much about the people that I thought I already knew well or well enough. I have seen my mother and father when they were children and newlyweds. I have seen through other eyes and words my father riding his pet goat with a black playmate and thus perhaps developing ideas about race and human worth that were certainly liberated and liberal for his time and place. I have seen my father driving the schoolbus that he never rode to school because he had dropped out before he had learned much more than how to write his name. In a sudden truth, it came to me that, in all the years I was away from home before his death, he had never written me a single letter, perhaps never could have written me a letter, had he wanted to. I realized that, except for the ledger pages in the account book of his small store, I had never seen him read anything—not a book or a newspaper, or a magazine. When he needed something read, my mother read it to him.

Through her own eyes and words as well as those of others who knew her before I did, I have learned to understand and accept my mother's ways, especially her love for my father, despite his unkindnesses to her. I now know why my mother, an only child, always thought of herself as an orphan in the world, a feeling intensified first by her father's death when she was but seventeen and then by her mother's death when she was twenty-six. In addition, I have made more mundane discoveries, including the extent of intermarriage among members of the various families to which I am related. Indeed, my recent genealogical research has revealed that most of my ancestral families—the Halls, the Rollos, the Waters, the Griders, the Allens, the Stewarts, the Gilmores—were friends and neighbors long before they immigrated to the newly opened Creek Indian lands in Alabama from the Carolinas and Georgia in the 1830s and '40s. In fact, I discovered that my mother and father were second cousins.

When I left home for college and started my own emigration from Bullock County, I intended to get as far away as possible. I did not want to know my home place and people any better. They were the reason I was running. They had nothing to teach me. I had nothing in common with them. Or so I thought. Now I know that I am truly my parents' son and the product of the school and church and community that for sixteen years stamped me indelibly and shaped me into the man I was to become. I know now that to understand myself and accept myself, I had to go back to this place and to these people. I had to confront the person I might have become had I, like all my brothers

and most of my schoolmates and neighbors and all the people whose portraits comprise this book, stayed behind and made a life where I was born. Indeed, it was a journey of discovery that would challenge a Henry James.

Although I have kept in close contact with my family through the years, I have never returned to my homeplace to live and have seldom visited for more than a week at a time. Perhaps it is this geographical as well as psychological distance that now allows me the objectivity to see my people and my place on earth for what they really are—and what I am. After all, my immediate response to the question, "Where are you from?," has always been, "I'm from Bullock County, Alabama." Even when estranged from it and living at a distance of thousands of miles, I have always known instinctively that here is my true home. As I have sometimes told friends, with a touch of macabre humor and a lot of truth, "My home is where my family is buried and where I will finally be buried." After all, didn't my Grandmother Waters take out burial insurance on me when I was an infant? The Liberty Church Cemetery is, indeed, the final gathering place for my family and most of my community. As somebody once remarked wisely, "It's that cemetery that has kept the church alive all these years." In this necropolis the population grows every year, even as the county continues to shrink, according to the U.S. Census Bureau. All of my grandparents were buried there even before I left home in 1950. Through the years, my aunts and uncles and other relatives have been added. Then my father died in 1968. When my mother died in 1990, she left my brothers and their families parcels of land. To me, she left her house. She knew what she wanted to happen and how to make it so. She wanted me to come home again, too.

Now, after forty years and more of sojourning in alien places, I am coming home. It won't be the same, of course. But despite the absent family members and neighbors, it will be a good place to live. For most of its citizens, the dramatic social and economic changes that have occurred since 1950 have made it a much better place to call home. When I was a boy, the only black voter we knew of was the undertaker. Now integration has come to Bullock County, and with its large black majority, African Americans hold most of the county offices. The county is still mostly segregated, but there is, nevertheless, a reservoir of good feeling between the races, especially among the middle-aged and the elderly. Indeed, you will find in these monologues little evidence of rage and anger at racial, social, or economic inequalities. Perhaps you will say that because most of my respondents are elderly, I do not have a balanced report on such sentiments. Well, I repeat that, while there are obvious sociological dimensions to this project, it was never my intention to do a scientific survey.

My principal motivation has been to share with others some of the people I have known all my life. Whether they knew it or not, they had something important to say to me—then and now. I believe they have something important to say to you also. I have tried to put on record some of the people G. M. Trevelyan has described in these words:

> The poetry of history lies in the quasi-miraculous fact that once, on this earth, on this familiar spot of ground walked other men and women as actual as we are today, thinking their own thoughts, swayed by their own passions but now gone, vanishing after another, gone as utterly as we ourselves shall be gone like ghosts at cock-crow.

Yes, all of us will soon be gone, but I hope I have helped a few people to leave behind immortal traces of themselves in their inexhaustible voices, in their own "words of life."

Indeed, everyone's life deserves to be saved from the losses of time. Unfortunately, most people get born, live and die, and leave little behind that preserves their unique lives. This collection of voices from a rural Alabama county is but one attempt to show the value of ordinary people—people who never made a lot of money or wielded much power or made any profound discoveries or controlled any events. They are nonetheless fascinating in their ordinariness—as common as a drop of water from the Conecuh River that

Campaign signs, Bullock County, 1990s.

flows through the county and as familiar as the camellia that still grows in my mother's back yard. With all things, they share the miracle of existence, of having come into this world and participated briefly in its miracle and mystery. I hope the few people whose voices speak from these pages will serve to represent in some measure the unknown people who live and die on this earth and return to the oblivion from which they came.

A FEW WORDS ABOUT BULLOCK COUNTY

Located in southeast Alabama, the area now comprising Bullock County belonged to the Creek (or Muskogee) Indians until they ceded their rights under two treaties, the Treaty of Fort Jackson in 1814, which included the western half of the county, and the Cusseta Treaty in 1832, which ceded the eastern half. Soon after the second cession, white settlers from Virginia, the Carolinas, Georgia, and other states began to move into the area. Some of them brought their families, slaves, and livestock and established large cotton plantations on the low prairie lands south of the Chunnenuggee Ridge, which is located just north of the present town of Union Springs. Many of the plantation owners left their farms to be run by resident overseers and built homes on the higher—and presumably healthier—ground of the ridge. Other white settlers included yeoman farmers who worked their small land holdings and white tenant farmers who farmed on shares. By the time of the Civil War, the area was thickly settled and prosperous.

During the war no battles or significant skirmishes were fought in what is now Bullock County. A few detached federal troops camped near Union Springs near the end of the war, and local farms were the objects of a few foraging parties that took chickens, hogs, and an occasional horse or mule. Nonetheless, the area was seriously affected by the war because of the injuries and deaths of many local men who served in the Confederate armies. Furthermore, the protracted war had meant the neglect of farms and homes and the few local roads became almost impassable. It took years for the farm economy to get back to normal.

Soon after the war, many people began demanding a seat of government closer to them than Montgomery, Tuskegee, Troy, and Clayton—the towns that served the area as county seats. Therefore, on December 5, 1866, the Alabama legislature approved an act to create a new county from portions of Macon, Montgomery, Pike, and Barbour counties and named it after Edward C. Bullock, an officer who died in the Confederate service in 1861. Union Springs, the largest and most centrally located town in the new county, was chosen as the seat of government. It had been named decades before for the several nearby springs that form the sources for four streams: the Conecuh River, the Oakfuske River, and the Old Town and Cabahatchee creeks.

The new county soon grew to become one of the most populous and wealthy counties in the state. By 1870 the county had a population of some twenty-five thousand, of which some seventeen thousand were blacks and about seven thousand were whites. By 1880, when its population had reached almost thirty thousand, it was Alabama's tenth most populous county, with seven thousand more people than Jefferson County. While blacks have continued to hold their numerical majority (it was approximately 67 percent in 1980), the county's overall population has steadily declined since 1890 to its present size of some ten thousand. With the loss of population, Bullock County has also lost much of its economic and political influence. In recent decades it has become one of Alabama's—and the nation's—poorest counties in terms of per capita income.

Although there are still farms that grow such cash crops as cotton and peanuts, much of the land is now utilized for growing beef cattle and for timber used in construction materials and paper products. The large grasslands and wooded areas have made the county a sportsman's destination. The National Shooting Dog Championships were run on the Sedgefields Plantation of industrialist Lewis B. Maytag for almost fifty years beginning in 1933, and field trials are still held annually. The county is also the home of the first garden club in the United States, which was organized on Chunnenuggee Ridge in 1847. Prominent people who were natives of the county include Helen Claire, the Broadway and radio actress; Billy Hitchcock, the major league baseball player and manager; Winton Blount, the international builder and philanthropist;

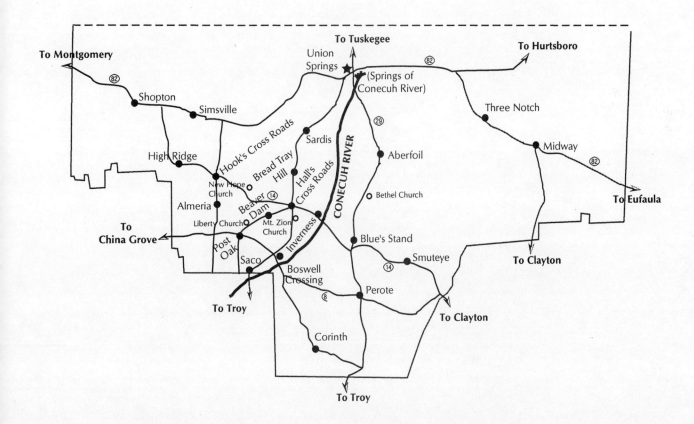

CONECUH COUNTRY (LOWER BULLOCK COUNTY, ALABAMA)

Virginia Foster Durr, the civil rights activist; and, more recently, the ballet dancer Wes Chapman.

The scope of this oral history includes all of Bullock County as well as surrounding counties and towns. The focus, however, is on approximately one-half of the county that lies south of U.S. Highway 82. All nineteen people who tell their life stories for this book are from this half of the county.

Highway 82 enters Bullock County from Montgomery County near Downing, bisecting the county as it runs through Shopton, Hector, Simsville, Bruceville, Union Springs, Three Notch, Midway, and then into Barbour County. Other placenames that are mentioned frequently in these monologues include Almeria, Macedonia, Mount Hilliard, High Ridge, Corinth, Boswell Crossing (or Omega), Sardis, Bread Tray Hill, Liberty, Inverness, Halls Cross Roads, Post Oak, Beaver Dam Creek, Smut Eye, Aberfoil, Scotland, Bethel, Saco (just over the county line in Pike County), Hurtsboro (just over the county line in Russell County), and, of course, the Conecuh River, which has its source near Union Springs and flows generally south through Alabama and upon reaching the Florida border becomes the Escambia River, eventually emptying into Pensacola Bay and the Gulf of Mexico.

CONECUH PEOPLE

VELMA ROTTON DRIGGERS

The Riches of Home

This monologue is based on an interview with Mrs. Velma Rotton Driggers in July of 1977 in the small frame house she shared with her husband Alton. They lived in Inverness, less than a mile from the Conecuh River, which flows sluggishly and swamplike several hundred yards east of what used to be a thriving settlement, with several stores, a post office, three churches—one white and two black—the white county elementary and high school, and a population of more than one hundred. Now only the churches and a handful of people remain. Both Velma and Alton were born on farms a few miles west of Inverness, and they seem somewhat awkward at living even now in "town"—even in this almost deserted village. As a boy I knew them as faithful churchgoers who attended services at Liberty Baptist Church every "preaching Sunday," which was the fourth Sunday of each month.

Velma welcomes me into her "front room," where Alton sits leaning back in a straight chair against the far wall. The room is sparsely furnished but comfortable and immaculately clean. The house was built more than a century before by one of my Grider relatives on my mother's side of the family. Now in their seventies, Velma and Alton are rugged and stoic survivors of a life of hard work and few rewards. In recent years Velma had added some weight to her usual tall, thin frame, but she still appears to have the strength and resolve to do a day's hard work in the cotton field, if necessary. Her strong, almost masculine, face reveals a hard life now softened by peaceful acceptance. Her religious devotion is signaled by a posted sign in the front yard near the mail box: "SEEK YE OUT THE BOOK OF THE LORD AND READ . . . FOR THE DAY OF THE LORD IS TERRIBLE." Alton's usual conversation consists of a few words spread over a couple of hours. Velma has always been the talker in the family, but from time to time she consults Alton for verification of dates and names. They have no children.

Do you mind if Alton stays in the room while we talk? We've been married for about fifty years, and there's nothing I could say that he doesn't already know. We've been together most of our lives, and he can help jog my memory. Yes, today is my birthday. I was born at home on the 18th day of July, 1905, at twelve o'clock noon in the Macedonia community, right direct across from the cemetery, where we'll both be buried one of these days. I arrived before the doctor did, but my daddy and my mother's sister and one of her friends were all there. Mama's sister, Aunt Susy Meredith, was the midwife. Dr. Pitts didn't have far to come from High Ridge, but I couldn't wait for him.

I've spent most of my life right around here. I've moved a lot but it's been mostly in this end of Bullock County. Mr. Wiley Grider built this home where we live now, and he gave the Nigras the lots where they built their two churches, one next door and the other across the road. Yes, I remember exactly when Alton and I got married—December 20, 1929. He was from the Liberty community and was born just before you get to his mama's old house on the Champion Place by that big oak tree. We were both born in the Post Oak Beat, but it was several miles apart in different communities. It was called Post Oak Beat, or Beat 10, because that's where people went to vote.

The voting box was in Mr. Jim Powell's store, and when I was a girl I went many a time to his store. He had one of the few telephones in our part of the county, and when people needed to make an emergency call about an illness or death, Mr. Powell made it for them. Post Oak was a thriving community then, and many families lived in or near there. Grady and Meetsie Sellers lived across the road from Mr. Powell's store, and not far away were the Hosea Sellerses and the Bateses and the Reynolds Sellerses. Mr. Reynolds's mother's people had a big plantation and during the days of slavery had a lot of Nigra slaves. Droves of Nigras still lived all around Post Oak and were mostly sharecroppers, though I believe a few of them owned a little land. Post Oak was the trading center for all these people.

Most of the farmers grew cotton and corn and some velvet beans, in addition to gardens and vegetable patches for their own use. People didn't grow peanuts as a cash crop when I was a girl. I remember when I was about twelve or thirteen my daddy planted some peanuts for us to eat. We used them to make syrup candy and we fed the vines to the hogs. Of course, we didn't have mechanical pickers to pick off the peanuts, so we'd plow them up, take them home and pick them off by hand. Sometimes the farmers would sell some of their corn and velvet beans, but they mostly fed them to their livestock. My oldest brother Estley would try to grow more velvet beans than he needed, and he'd haul em to Boswell Crossing and the McLendons down there would buy em for a dollar a hundred or twenty dollars a ton. Estley was living then just below Almeria schoolhouse, where I got my education, up there on a hill. One year he made twenty tons and hauled most of them to Boswell on a two-horse wagon. I should say a two-mule wagon because he farmed with two mules. At that time he was living on Mrs. Powell's place. She had been a White and inherited that place from her mother and daddy. The place stayed in the Powell family until Mr. Powell died, and then it sold to Mr. Jeff Sorrell, who had started buying up a lot of land for pastures and timber around here.

I come from a large family of seven brothers and four sisters. Course, one of my brothers died when he was small, and I didn't know anything directly about him. I only know what I've heard about him. He burned up. Well, he didn't exactly burn up. He struck a match and swallowed the fire. You know how bad some children are to plunder. Mama thought she had the

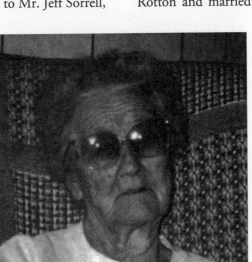

Velma Rotton Driggers.

matches where he couldn't get to them. But he saw where she put them up on the mantelpiece over the fireplace, and when she wasn't looking, he climbed up and got em and struck one and swallowed the flame. That was in the morning part of the day and he died that night. The doctor said it was that fire. He just swallowed the fire and it just burned him up inside. Now, all this is what I've been told. I wasn't there. Mama said as long as he lived he begged for water. He was just burning up. But he didn't live more than a few hours. I believe he was two and a half years old. I expect it's been ninety years. I imagine it has. My oldest sister will be ninety in December and he was older than she was.

Estley was Dean Pritchett's daddy. He's been dead about six years. He was the oldest but the last one of my brothers that died. Then there was Homer, the one that got burned. Then there was Allan, then Frank and Kyle and Randolph and Redge, the youngest. Redge was next to me and he's been dead nine years. It just doesn't seem at all possible. None of my brothers are living now. I have two sisters still living, Mattie Petty and Clyde, Seal Rotton's wife. She was a Rotton and married a Rotton, but they were only fourth or fifth cousins.

Yes, my maiden name was Rotton, and it never sounded funny to me. I was always of the opinion that it was English, but when one of my nephews was in England, he realized that it was more of a German name than English. I was talking one time to a lady who was writing the history of the Barnett family. Some of them used to live in this community, and some of them is buried over there in what they call the Barnett Cemetery. That woman said the Barnett name was French, but I don't know about that. We've all been cut off so long from our old families, it's just hard to find out anything. I think Alton's name is Scotch. One time we ordered a plaque and papers telling where the Driggers name originated and the different ways of spelling it. Some people spell it Driggen. There's a lot of Driggerses around Dothan, I hear. One of them got to be city clerk and then got to be mayor. I know there are Driggerses in Texas too. A few Sundays ago a nephew was visiting here from Mobile, and his wife asked me if we were related to the Driggerses in Mobile. I said, "Are they rich? If they are, we are!" She said she believed that one of them that's in the real estate business is well off. I've run into Driggerses I didn't know in other places. We were down to the doctor's the other day and when they called my name, another lady started to get up. She said, "I thought they called me." I said, "Are you a Driggers too?" She said, "Yeah, I'm a Driggers too. There must be a lot of us."

You know, of course, that all the Rottons and the Rotens and the Roughtons in this county are the same people. I'll tell you when some of them started spelling their name R-o-u-g-h-t-o-n. Hobson Roughton's daddy was the one that did it, and that caused something funny to happen.

Hobson's granddaddy was in the Civil War, but he couldn't get a pension when they started giving them out to Confederate soldiers. He'd send his name in as Jack Roughton—with the new spelling—and he'd get a letter saying there was no such name on their army records. So he finally had to sign his name "Rotton" the old way to ever get a pension. Then when they started giving out these little grave markers for the Confederate soldiers—you know there's a few over there at Liberty Cemetery—Hobson got one for his granddaddy Bruce, but he wouldn't get one for his other one because he'd have to put "Rotton" on it. He refused to do it, and there's not a marker on that grave yet. I think it's a crying shame.

I've never been ashamed of any of my names. They're mine and I'm proud of them because they represent my family. My mama and daddy were both born in Bullock County. Mama's people came from Georgia, but they were originally from South Carolina. Her daddy had eleven sisters and I believe four brothers. They were all farm people. I don't know what else they would have done but farm. Most of my ancestors came to Alabama directly from South Carolina, and some of my people have been back there to check the records but they didn't find out much.

They all came here just hunting for a better place to live, and some of them didn't find it and later kept on going. I know we have people over in Mississippi

and beyond. Papa's oldest brother went to Texas when he was a young man and never came back. They said he left walking. That would have been in the 1880s because my oldest sister was a baby then, and she's nearly ninety now. A few years ago she was visiting her son who was living out that way, and she came in contact with some of our relatives. They've since been back here to see where their daddy was born and raised. My sister had been to the church where he was buried. Now, I don't know how far my uncle walked, but he eventually settled in Cleveland, Texas, which is close to Houston.

I don't believe he left Alabama because he was in trouble, but I do know that a lot of people if they got in trouble would head toward Texas. When they got that far away, they couldn't be found. I once heard of a man—a Mr. Rufus Crowe it was—who killed a Mr. Powell from somewhere around here. Well, he ran away to Texas. That was about 1915. He had a wife and three young children, but he just left them and went out west. He didn't leave his family anything to live on, so people in the community took care of them while he was gone.

After so long a time, he wanted to come back home. So he came back on his own and gave himself up. They had his trial in Union Springs and freed him. After all those years, they proved it was self-defense. If he'd known he could get off on self-defense, he wouldn't have had to go to Texas. But of course he didn't know—probably couldn't know—so he caught the train in Inverness and stayed gone for a long time. When he got back, all his children were grown. After he was freed, he bought a place up yonder where Homer Rotton lives now and settled down and raised another set of children with his wife, who'd stayed true to him while he was in Texas. They had four more children, but none of em live around here now. I remember his oldest son came to the hospital in Troy to see Charley Pritchett the day he died. They all live in South Carolina now, but I think they're kin to the Crowes in Troy because that's where they came from.

When I was a girl none of us strayed far from home. I remember the first time I ever went to town. I was about fourteen years old. A schoolteacher we had at Almeria, Professor Harrison, had a daughter just a couple of years younger than I was. One time she wanted to go with her daddy to a teacher's meeting in Union Springs, but he didn't want to turn her loose on the streets by herself and he asked me to go with her. It was on a Saturday and Mr. Hightower carried us up there on his car. Ruth and I walked the streets and ate chocolate candy all day. It was a wonder we didn't get sick. I looked around a lot, but I'd already been to Troy once on the train and I didn't think too much of Union Springs. We had taken the train for Troy at Boswell Crossing. That was the only kind of transportation we had, except if we wanted to go on a wagon or a buggy. We went down there to see Hobson Roughton's aunt who had TB of the bone and was in the hospital. Mama and Papa went to see her, and I was too small to leave at home.

Whenever we went to Troy, we'd usually spend the day. We took the eleven o'clock Central of Georgia down and the five o'clock train back. The conductor was Mr. John Grider, who was the brother of Mr. Tobe Grider. The old Grider home was up there near Halls Cross Roads where Miss Josephine Pritchett lives now, but all the Griders have been dead for years. The ones that didn't die moved away, and their descendants are living now in places like Opp, Mobile, and Birmingham. The train we took to Troy started out in Columbus, Georgia, and went down to Andalusia. There were two trains every day, and one stayed in Columbus and one stayed in Andalusia at night. When I worked a little while in Andalusia in 1925, I stayed with my brother Allan, who lived right close to the railroad. I could walk over to the depot and catch the morning train, come home and spend the day, and go back that evening. In some ways it was easier to get around then than it is now.

I was living in Andalusia and working in a men's underwear factory. It's a shirt factory now. Two of my brothers, Allan and Randolph, were working down there then. Allan was working in the iron foundry. He used to tell us he was being paid to play in the sand. What he was doing was laying out patterns in the sand. They would first melt that iron ore in huge pots and run the pots on a cable. Then they would lift that pot over to where they had these designs laid out and pour that molten iron in them. One time Allan made my daddy a pair of andirons that weighed seventy-five pounds. I let Mrs. Driggers, Alton's mama, have them until she died. She didn't have any. When she died I got em back and let my sister Clyde have them and then she lent them to Melvin Rotton. I don't know where they are now, but I'd give anything in the world if I could locate them.

I don't remember now what Randolph did in Andalusia. Allan had just married, and I stayed with him and his wife. I was down there for five whole weeks, and it seemed like five long years! I liked it all right but it just wasn't home. I've always been a person who didn't like to stay away from home. That was the only time I ever lived away from home until I got married. But, of course, after Alton and I established our own home, that became my home and I never went back to stay with Mama unless she was sick. Just to go on a visit and stay—I didn't do it. I felt like my home was where Alton was.

Now, we have lived for short periods outside of Bullock County. We started our married life in China Grove, just over in Pike County. We lived over there from January until May of 1930. Then Alton got a job working on the county roads and we moved to Union Springs. Then we lived about three years in Russell County and three months in Montgomery. But now I'll tell you about the biggest move—and the biggest mistake—we ever made.

In 1953 we lived one week in Chicago! It was a

fake all the way around! There was this fellow that came to Union Springs to get mechanics to work on diesel motors. He must have recruited people from all over this part of the country—Bullock County, Pike County, Crenshaw County, Covington County—because we met them when we got to Chicago. But it was all a fake, though we didn't know that until it was too late. Alton and John Ralph Smith went to Montgomery and signed up to work in a certain plant in Chicago. Alton asked that man in particular did he have to go to school—did he have to learn what he was to do out of a book. Alton knew he couldn't learn it out of a book. You know how bad Alton always was with books. Well, the man says, "No, Mr. Driggers, you'll learn by doing." We soon found out that it wasn't so because when we got to Chicago Alton was

Crenshaw County Courthouse, Luverne, Alabama.

told he'd have to take a study course for several weeks before he could have any machinery to work on. Well, Alton flat out knew he couldn't do it. And there was another problem too. Alton was used to Caterpillar motors, and up there they didn't know what one looked like.

So Alton came in after that first day and said he'd

quit his job. He did go out to several places looking for work, but everywhere he'd go he said it was Nigras and that didn't suit him. We'd rented a room for a week and the last day he said, "Well, what are we going to do? I don't have a job and the rent's due again." I said, "I'll tell you what we're going to do. We're going to take what we have left and put it on our bus fare back to Bullock County. That's what we're going to do. We don't want to get stranded up here without any money or a place to stay. Except for people like us, we don't know a soul here. Let's pack our suitcase and go back home."

And we did. We went up there on the bus and we came back on the bus. It was a slow train through Arkansas! When we went up, we left Montgomery at 9:30 one morning and got into Chicago the next morning at six o'clock. All through Tennessee they were working on the roads and we had to detour out of the way and we didn't see much. I was anxious to see Kentucky, but we went through it at night and we came back through it at night. We were in the Louisville bus station at midnight. I couldn't tell anything about Kentucky, but Indiana is really a pretty country. They have such pretty cemeteries where you couldn't even know it was a cemetery if they didn't have a sign telling you what it was. The country was just so level and green, and they had these big fields of corn as far as the eye could see and pretty painted houses and barns.

I think I could have learned to like Chicago if we had gotten work and moved to a better neighborhood. The week we lived there we were in the slums because that's where they sent us. But even there I felt better than I'd felt in years. Before we went up there, I'd had insomnia and couldn't sleep at night. But while we were there I could lay down in the daytime even and sleep two or three hours and sleep all night that night. I liked the climate. Of course, it was cold. It was in late June but it was cold! We lived upstairs on the third floor of this rooming house, and one day Alton was looking out the window and said, "Velma, you know them crazy fools down there is walking around with overcoats on and it almost July!" After dinner that day we went down out on the street, and after a few minutes Alton said, "Them fools was not as crazy as I thought. It's cold out here!" We walked on out to Lake Michigan and watched the boats come in. It was a pretty sight. But people were trying to go in bathing, and it was so cold they couldn't stand the water.

Yes, I do believe I could have learned to like Chicago. When we got there, the bus was underground, and we had to go upstairs to get on the street. Imagine that! And I believe then was the first time I ever rode an escalator. I don't think that the stores in Montgomery had any at that time. It was in a big store and a lady right ahead of me stepped on it and she was as green as I was, and I said to myself, I'm not going to laugh at her because I may do worse than she does. But, you know, I didn't have a bit of trouble! I'd rather ride an escalator than an elevator. We also saw a lot of other sights we'd never seen before—such tall buildings and whites and Nigras riding and eating together. Some of it I liked and some I didn't. There were a lot of places I hoped to see up there, but we just didn't have the time.

Yes, if Alton could have gotten work where we could have lived, I believe I would have enjoyed living in Chicago. We had every intention of staying, but everything about his recruitment was a fake. They were supposed to get him a good job to support us until he learned his new work, but they didn't do anything they claimed. There was two couples there from Greenville in Butler County, but they had gotten enough work to do that they could stay. But they said they didn't like it up there and were coming home just as soon as they could get back. They were almost stranded. They were living together all cramped

Velma Rotton Driggers in her front yard.

up. They were making it, but that was about all. One woman had a baby but managed to get a job, so the other lady kept her baby for her to work. They were all trying to get together enough money to get back home. Well, I tell you I was sure glad when *we* got back home to Alabama and Bullock County. I said, this is where I was born and raised and educated and it's where I hope to live the rest of my life.

Yes sir, Bullock County is a good place to live. I probably didn't learn as much as I should have, but I think I got a good education for that time. I started at Almeria School when I was six years old and I went until I was seventeen. My last year they moved the ninth through twelfth grades to Inverness. Neatha Bonner and I were supposed to go to Inverness for our last year, but she quit and I went there until February and I persuaded Mama to let me quit. I always intended on going back and finishing, but I never did. There was plenty of people I knew at Inverness School, but it just wasn't home. Mr. Peacock, who was principal at Inverness, just begged me to finish and go on to college. He said, "Velma, you're a smart girl and you could make something of yourself." I said, "Mr. Peacock, I just can't go to college. Nobody in my family has ever been, and we can't afford it." He said, "Well, with your grades I know you could get in, and I could help you get a job." But I didn't want to go. I would have had to stay with strangers. That was always my trouble. I just couldn't stay away from home. I didn't like being with strangers.

Wherever my family lived was always home, though we lived on different people's land and moved around a lot. For three years we lived on Mr. Jake Reynolds's property and farmed for him. Then we lived in a big house across from Mount Hilliard Church for two years. When we moved there, I asked Mama to let me transfer to Mount Hilliard School, which was closer than Almeria. Well, I went there about three months, and I knew less when I quit than when I started. The teacher never had any discipline. The children did as they pleased, and I was never used to that. You would try to study and somebody would chunk a spitball at you and hit you up side the head. It was just confusion all the time. One day I left there and took all my books home, and I told Mama the next morning, "Well, I've had enough of that school. I'm going to walk over to Almeria to school." And that's what I did, every day. At that time, there were no buses for anybody, whites or Nigras. Later, I remember Dan McCall, Willie McCall's daddy, would drive us in his Model T car. He'd pick us all up, up and down the road. The older ones would hold the little ones on our lap.

Almeria was a one-room school when I started and it had one teacher. Then they built another room and had two teachers. Then in 1917, I believe it was, they built another room and it was a three-teacher school. There were three rooms and I graduated out of each one of them. When I was in the sixth grade, they combined the sixth and seventh grade and it made twenty-one of us.

At recess we played a lot of different games, but I liked town ball best. I don't know why we called it town ball, but it was practically the same thing as baseball or softball. We used a homemade ball made out of twine. We'd get a walnut and wrap twine around it until it got big enough to make a ball.

I have a lot of memories of Almeria School. One time a big storm came up just after dinner time. They call it a tornado now. Our teacher was scared worse than any of us because it was her responsibility to look after us. She had every one of us get in the southwest corner of the room. Through the windows we could see the wind blowing the trees almost to the ground. We had a big chinaberry tree in the schoolyard and the wind finally blew that tree up. When it fell you could hear us holler for forty miles around! Our teacher shamed us about making all that noise because she felt like we would all be blown away. By the time that storm was over, everybody in the community was at the schoolhouse because they feared that the building had been blown away and us children killed. But the most damage done was to that chinaberry tree. Most of us were glad that tree was gone because the chinaberries would fall on the ground and we'd mess up our feet and shoes when we stepped in them.

I was a good student, but I always had to spend a lot of my time working at home and in the fields. At home I washed dishes, swept the floor and the yard, made the beds, and, when I got old enough, I cooked. Until my older sister got big enough to cook, Mama spent most of her time in the kitchen. Then it came down to me, and after me another one of my sisters took over. We were a big family, but we were peculiar about what we ate. I don't care how many kinds of vegetables Mama had, she would cook some of them all and put them before us. Then it was up to us whether we wanted to eat them. There would always be one or two of us that wouldn't eat something— maybe cabbage or collard greens or squash—but she never made us eat what we didn't want to. I know that's the reason that Alton back there is so curious about what he eats. Mrs. Driggers didn't eat anything she didn't like, and she didn't encourage her children to try anything new.

When her girls got big enough, Mama never knew what it was like to get up and cook breakfast. One of us would do that. We'd usually have butter and biscuits and syrup. Sometimes we'd have hog meat, but we were never big meat eaters. Then when we had to go to the field to work, Mama cooked dinner for us all. It was usually peas and other vegetables and sometimes some fried meat. Then when we came in from the field, one of us girls would cook supper. Daddy wouldn't eat a cold supper, so we'd make up fresh biscuits or cornbread and fry some meat. At our house there had to be three meals a day cooked. If it looked like he might have to eat a cold supper, Papa would get what was left from dinner and dump it in the slopbucket to feed the hogs. So regardless of how hot and tired we were, we always had to cook supper. That was after a long, hard day in the hot sun hoeing or chopping or picking cotton. I didn't like it, but I had it to do. We all did. Nobody had a choice. Farming was all our kind of people could do to make a living, and we all had to do our share. There was no such thing as going out and getting a job to make some money. We had to leave home to do that.

We worked five or six days a week, and on Sunday we rested—except for every first Sunday, when we went to church at Macedonia. The first preacher I remember was a one-legged man named Gilmore. He was the one that baptized me. He had a cork leg because he'd lost his good one in a sawmill accident. He lived over at Louisville in Barbour County and he rode here in a buggy. He'd come on a Saturday evening and leave on Monday morning. He had a niece that lived over at Smut Eye, and sometimes he'd come up there and spend Friday night and come on over to Macedonia on Saturday. We had church on Saturday and Sunday. When we had conference—

what we call a business meeting now—we'd always have that on Saturday night.

I joined the church when I was twelve years old. We always had our revival the first week in August and that's when it was. That'll be sixty years come this August. As far as I know, I've been a member of Macedonia longer than anybody living now. Preacher Gilmore, you remember, had a false leg, and so he had to have someone help him baptize. The year I joined my oldest brother was helping him. We baptized in a pool right across the road in front of the church. The pool was made by seven springs flowing into one. The water was just so blue it looked like it had coloring in it. There was a path going to it from the church. Even though it's been filled up for years, I believe I could still find it. I told Alton that the other day, and he said he didn't believe I could. He said he went through there hunting not long ago and couldn't tell anything about it. I still believe I could find it. Lord knows, I went down there so many times to see new members baptized into the church. We do our baptizing now at East Side Church in Union Springs. There's not enough of us members that want an indoor baptistry at the church, but we have put in bathrooms and central heat.

We used to baptize over at Homer Rotton's pond, in back of his house. I wish you could have seen the last baptismal service we had over there. While the preacher was immersing a bunch of young people and one old woman, a drove of white birds circled over the pond. I said it just reminded me of Christ's baptism when the dove appeared. It was those white birds that follow cows around in the pasture and pick the grains out of their droppings. Alton said when he got there, he saw a drove of wild turkeys flying over. I said, "Well, I didn't see the turkeys, but I did see the white birds." It was the most impressive baptism I ever attended.

I've been active in the church since the day I was baptized. My first job was sweeping the church house.

My daddy told me, "Velma, you belong to the church now, and you need a job. So you can clean it up." Sara May and I would go over to Macedonia and sweep the church every first Saturday afternoon and make sure everything was ready for preaching that night.

When the preacher came, he'd usually stay with our family. He'd come by himself or sometimes one of his boys would come and help him drive his buggy. He was a full-time farmer, so he'd only stay over the weekend. As I said, he'd stay with us because nobody else would invite him. Well, Papa always spoke what he thought, even if it might hurt. After it got so that we were keeping the preacher every time he came, Papa decided he'd had enough, so when time came to call the preacher again, he got up and said, "Let me tell you all one thing now. If you don't think enough of Brother Gilmore to invite him home with you sometime, then don't call him. He gets embarrassed having to go to the same place every time, and I think you all know where that place is. But if I didn't take him in, he'd be left sitting here at the church." You know what? After Papa said what he did, they didn't call him. They decided to call somebody else. You see, everybody liked Preacher Gilmore's preaching, but they just didn't want to take him home.

Another preacher we had at Macedonia also stayed with us when he came. He was Preacher Cook and everybody liked him too, but not enough to invite him to spend the night. One time when he was staying with us, Alton came to visit and Preacher Cook said, "Alton and Velma, I want to marry you all when you decide to get married." I said, "Well, Preacher, you might have a long wait. You might not even be around here." And he wasn't. When we got married, he was preaching somewhere else. Some years later he came and conducted a revival for us and stayed with another family. The last night of the meeting, he said, "Velma, you know this meeting just hasn't been like a revival to me." I said, "What do you mean?" He said, "I just had the idea that you would still be living at

home, and I'd stay with your family again. But since I couldn't stay with you, it just hasn't seemed right."

Talking about company, we knew what company was. Everybody loved to stay with us. One time we had two preachers to spend the night—and Uncle Jim May's family. You don't know what a family he had! There was thirteen children in all! Mama had beds and pallets all over the house. Now, you know preachers like to sleep by themselves, but that night the two preachers had to sleep together because we didn't have enough beds. They were lucky to even get a bed. Everybody had to sleep where they could find a place. Back then people didn't have toast and grits for breakfast, so sister Mattie made sixty biscuits for breakfast the next morning.

On preaching Sunday we never knew how many we'd have for dinner. It was the same way at Alton's mama's house too. Sometimes we'd have half a dozen families to come home with us. We'd fix dinner before we left for church and hope it'd be enough to feed everybody. If we had chicken, we'd have to kill and dress and cook it that morning. People didn't have a refrigerator or ice back then and we couldn't fix food too far ahead. When the preacher stayed overnight, I've gotten up many a Sunday morning and killed and dressed and cooked a chicken for breakfast.

We didn't have electric lights for night services. Our little bit of light came from oil lamps that hung from the ceiling. Nowadays people can't hold revival services in the daytime. It's only at night. We used to have an eleven o'clock service in the morning throughout the week and a seven o'clock service every night. Sometimes we wouldn't get home until nearly midnight. We had a lot of preaching, a lot of singing, a lot of praying, and a lot of shouting. After the service people would stay around and visit with each other. Our revival would last a week, from the first Sunday in August to the second Sunday. Some years we'd have a singing school for two weeks before the meeting started. Professor Harrison taught us to read notes like those in the songbooks we use in church now, but he also taught us to sing the shaped notes, too. He had a little tuning fork he used to pitch the songs.

One year we had a three-day meeting at the little schoolhouse they called Happy Valley. A lot of people lived over in that community and didn't have a way to get to church. That was in 1920. That year sixteen boys joined at Happy Valley and thirty-one people at Macedonia. It was the most we ever had baptized at one time. Two of the boys were on crutches. One boy had been crippled for a long time and the other one had just broken his leg. They sat in a chair and the preacher and deacons took them down into the pool and carried them under the water. They just turned the chair backwards and the boys were baptized.

We always got baptized in ordinary clothes. I've heard that in some of these town churches around here they baptize in robes. I've even heard that some churches baptize in bathing suits. But we still stick to the scriptural commands, and I hope we always will. We'd first sing a song, like "Shall We Gather at the River," and have a prayer. Then each candidate for baptism would walk down into the water where the preacher was, and he would place his hand over their nose and face to keep them from strangling on the water and then baptize them in the name of the Father, the Son, and the Holy Ghost. Sometimes a person would almost panic, but the water was only about waist-high and we never lost anybody. When we rose up from the water, of course we were dripping wet and would go over behind some bushes and put on the dry clothes we'd brought. At the next church service all the new members would be welcomed into the church with the right hand of Christian fellowship. That was at the end of the service, when the preacher would invite them to come to the front and stand while the rest of us sang a hymn, maybe "Trust and Obey," and all the church members walked by and shook their hands and hugged them.

Back then mothers brought all their children and

Mrs. Driggers in front of her house.

babies to church, and they were taught to sit down and behave. If a youngun got a little noisy, he was taken outside and whipped. The only whipping I can ever remember Mama gave me was for carrying on in church. Some other children were running and playing up and down the aisles, and I thought I had to do it too. But she taught me better right then and there. She carried me out and gave me a whipping I'd never forget. From then on, if you see me get up and leave during a service, you can say something is wrong because I don't do it.

At every night service there would be quilt pallets laid out in front of the first row of benches over on one side. The women that were carrying babies would sit over there. They didn't mix with the rest of the congregation. They'd nurse their babies and when they'd go to sleep, they'd put them down on the pallets. I remember a funny thing that happened one time. It was after the service was over and Mama and Papa were getting ready to go home. Mama had left her baby on the pallet and was talking with some friends. When she went over to pick up her baby, there was one left but it wasn't ours. Mama said, "Well, it looks like somebody's got one of our younguns." They were looking around the church, thinking maybe it had crawled under the benches, when a man walked in with our missing baby. He said he'd picked up the wrong one and had got all the way to his wagon before he'd discovered the mistake. One man said he had so many children to look after he had to count them every time they went anywhere. One night after they arrived at church he counted them and found that one was missing. He took one of his mules loose from the wagon and rode back home and found the missing baby asleep in the bed where they'd left it.

I know that some women would dip snuff in church, but I never saw them. Well, wait a minute, I have to take that back. If you've ever seen Pearl Deason in church, you've seen her dipping snuff. Poor old thing got to where she had to quit using snuff just before she died. When she was on her deathbed, they put a little in her mouth so she could taste it. I always said that snuff was Pearl's greatest joy. I guess after her husband left her, she didn't enjoy much else. She died a few years ago in a nursing home, and it didn't look like her in her casket. I'm not criticizing the woman that fixes the hair at the funeral home, but I know Pearl's hair wasn't completely white. It was kind of a dirty gray. But there she was in her coffin with hair white as snow. It looked good but it just didn't seem natural for Pearl, knowing her as I did. That woman normally does a good job fixing the hair, but she didn't get it right that time.

Well, it's getting late and about time to fix supper. Alton always has to have his meals at a fixed time. I don't have much left to say anyway, except that I've had a pretty good life. I learned at home how to get along with people. We didn't have any fussing at our house. We never had any fights. We never had any arguments. We enjoyed each other. When we all got grown, we enjoyed getting together. Alton and I have had a happy married life. We never had any children, and like everybody else, we've had our problems. There's nobody that ever lived that hasn't had problems, but we managed to overcome them. We've had some hard times and we've had some better times. There were times when Alton worked for twelve cents a day and hasn't been paid to this day. But I've always managed to fix breakfast every morning and find something to cook for dinner and supper. We never missed a meal. I knew the Lord was going to provide. We might not have had the things we wanted, but we always had something to eat and wear and a roof over our heads. We always stuck it out when we went through bad times. I always said if I ever left Alton, I'd never come back. It'd be for good. I don't believe in this leaving today and coming back tomorrow. That's not my way of doing business. Now, after almost fifty years, we are still at home together.

POSTSCRIPT: Alton died on May 3, 1989, in the Bullock County Hospital. His funeral was held two days later at Macedonia Baptist Church, with burial in the church cemetery. Six of his nephews served as pallbearers. Velma lived alone at her home in Inverness until her own death on August 23, 1998. Her funeral was held two days later at Macedonia, with burial in the church cemetery next to Alton.

The Birthday Lady

This monologue is based on a visit and interview with Verse Lee Johnson Manley on July 17, 1977. Mrs. Manley lives with her husband Tommie in a four-room, unpainted house at the end of a short unpaved alley less than two blocks from the Bullock County courthouse in an African-American neighborhood. Both Manleys were born on farms about six miles south of Union Springs near Bread Tray Hill, where my father had a country store in the late thirties and early forties and where our family got to know the Johnsons and the Manleys and their extended families. Verse is especially close to my mother, for whom she has done housework occasionally since she was a young woman. Tommie knew my father from the time they were both boys until my father's death in 1968. When I was in the Army in the mid-1950s, Verse insisted that I write her periodically, even though she could not read my letters. She and Tommie are illiterate. She also demanded that I send her a photograph of me in my uniform. For more than twenty years my picture has been proudly displayed in her living room.

Verse's twin passions in life are flowers and kitsch. Her packed-dirt yard is filled with many kinds of bushes and flowering shrubs and annuals. An abandoned antique Ford is sitting on blocks to the left of the house. The tiny porch is covered with potted plants of begonias, geraniums, and ferns; and the interior of the house has more potted plants and is crowded with dozens of knickknacks and ten-cent-store decorations. Everything, from floor to ceiling, is spotlessly clean. Several hound dogs of mixed blood lounge listlessly in the yard and under the house and car. Verse greets me from the front porch.

Baby, get out-a that car and come on in. Come on in this house! This makes three times you been home and ain't even called me. You hadn't came this time, I'd a-busted your head next time I seen you. Don't pay no attention to them dogs. Tommie just crazy 'bout his dogs, but I got my own little baby. Come here, Tiny. Say, "I'm the onliest baby Verse got." Yes sir, you a sweet thing and Mama love you. You sleep in bed with me and Tommie and do any way you want to. You the only youngun us got. You go in the house and jump in the middle of the bed right now, and I ain't gone open my mouth. Tiny is sho' my baby, and she so little I'm 'fraid I'm gone step on her. It would bust my heart if something bad happen to her. I love the little thing so hard.

Yeah, I got my yard full of pretty flowers. This heat so bad and it so dry, all my flowers be dead if I didn't tend to them. I know we supposed to cut down on water, but I slip out every evening and water my flowers with my waterbucket. It look like my azaleas gone all die spite of all I can do. I love to take care of my flowers. Sometime I bring my ice-tea glass out here when I'm tending to my flowers, and I set it down and then can't find it. I has to call my neighbor, "Hey, come over here and help me look for my glass." We had a little shower yesterday, but it didn't do nothing but settle the dust. I can't let nothing happen to my flowers.

That hot rod over there to the side of the house belong to Tommie. I told him he gone have to move it so I could plant me a zinnia bed there, but he said one of these days he gone get it fixed and drive it. It's a old car—so old he got a antique tag on it—but ain't nothing wrong with it but the spring broke. One time in the fall of the year him and me loaded it up with some coal to take out to his store place, and he went to pull off and the spring broke. I don't believe he ever gone get it fixed 'cause it cost more money than he gone want to put out.

Yeah Baby, I got a pretty place here, and I'm sho' proud of it. I been working on it for 'bout twenty years, the whole time we been living here in town. Since me and Tommie married, we always lived in Bullock County. There ain't no other place to live. We lived out near Inverness for a while, then out on the Sardis Road, then we moved here. Them's the onliest places we lived. I like it back here on this dead end. It's so quiet and cool back here with all these big trees, and we not bothered by any devilment. But all in all, I like living in the country best 'cause you got more room. We don't own this house. We rent it from John Lee Carter, a colored man that run a place called the Nite Spot in the Bottom—where colored peoples live mostly—on the by-pass going on to the Big Bear store. We ain't never owned a house. Me and my sister Callie Mae have talked about getting us a little piece of land sometime and building us a little house, but I don't believe we ever will. Callie Mae live in New York, and I don't think she ever move back home.

Anyway, I made this place so pretty I couldn't hardly ever leave it. I got so many flowers I don't know the names of all of them. I got gardenias and sultanas and crepe myrtles and oleanders, and my special flower is my azaleas. I love any kind of red flower. Ever year I plant zinnias and marigolds and all kind of flowers that die down and have to be planted again. I lost a lot of my flowers last winter when it turn so cold. I had the flu and a bad hand and I couldn't see after them. I carried in all my pot flowers to help make my house look pretty, but I couldn't get up at night to keep the fire going in the heater and they all froze. Tommie say, "Versie, don't worry 'bout them flowers. If they die, I get you some more." Still, I hated to lose all my flowers like that 'cause I'd-a-had some flowers out of sight if they hadn't a-died. But peoples been giving me flowers, and my house is running over. I may just leave all this mess of flowers you see here on the porch out here and let them die this winter. I got to be cutting back. I can't take care of them like I used to. And my flowers is not something I got to do, but I just do it 'cause I love it.

Verse Lee Johnson Manley, c. 1966.

Come on in the house, Baby. It been so long since you been here, you done forgot what it look like. If I ain't got a full house, I don't know what one is. I got so much in here you can't stick your finger between my things. Yes, Lord! That's the way I like it. I got my house fixed so I can enjoy it. If somebody come here and they don't like it, they ain't got to stay. Peoples that knows I loves junk and they loves junk wants to see mine. They say, "Verse, you be home today? I wants to see your things." I say, "I be home everday, but it be a good idea if you call first."

Baby, before you sets down, let me show you some of my things. I got dolls and pictures and bird what-nots and dog what-nots. A lady give me a big redbird—like a straight redbird outdoors—but somebody done bumped into it and broke it. It made me mad but I knowed it was a accident. Child, that picture you looking at is two women that had their heads growed together. They was in a show over to the schoolhouse, but I don't care nothing 'bout seeing pitiful things like that and didn't go. One of my neighbors give me that picture. She said she had to take them to the bathroom. They ain't got but one brain between them.

Yeah Baby, I'm attracted to everthing I got. If I see something and want it, I gets nervous to I get it. I ordered that light chandelier from Sears and Roebuck, and I bought that little whiskey bar for twenty-one dollars. You can put whiskey in that little keg and dreen it out in the little glasses. Sometime I buy things and sometime peoples give me things. I'm attracted to them pictures of dogs and horses which a white lady sont me from Eufaula. They was made by hand. Yes sir, I loves everthing you see, or you wouldn't see it in my house. I loves my chenille bedspreads and my embroidered pillow cases. A white lady give me that little radio. She say it won't pick up but one station, but I got it home and plugged it in and it gets ever' station. I ain't told her yet.

Yeah, I been collecting this stuff all my days, and I don't throw nothing away. See my heater? It's cracked all way 'round, and I'm scared to build a fire in it; so I told Tommie we gone put it on the back porch when it gets cold, and I'm gone plant flowers in it next year. I done got it ready. I sont up there to Anderson's Hardware and got me two cans of paint, a can of silver spray and a can of yellow. I sprayed that paint all over the heater and the irons and the skillet and them two kettles and the ash shovel and the poker. I think it's a pretty sight. Me and Tommie talked about making a barbecue pit out of it if I tuck the eyes off and put some wire mesh on top, but since I got it fixed up it's too pretty to put coals in. I think some geraniums and begonias be pretty in it. I tries to keep everthing I got and use it some way, even after it done wore out. Peoples say, "Verse, what you got in your house ain't good as other people's, but the way you arrange it make it look better."

I'm always busy arranging my things. You come back next week and things be different. But it make me so nervous when I wants to do something. When I got that spray paint, I couldn't wait to the next day to paint my heater. I got to bed that night, but my nerves wouldn't let me go to sleep. They got so bad I went to pieces, so I got up and painted it that night. I don't plan nothing for the next day. I don't get tomorrow on my mind. If you say, "Verse, I'm gone come up to your house tomorrow and we gone change the furniture around," well, I ain't sleeping nare bit tonight. I don't get to sleep if I got to think 'bout what I'm gone do in the morning. Baby, I didn't sleep too much last night after Miss Sarah called me that you was coming to see me today. I know you gone stay for supper 'cause I got all the good things to eat what you like—fried fish and fresh butterbeans and corn and salad and egg custard and coconut pie and cornbread and biscuits and Nehi Grape. I got Irish potatoes so pretty you don't know should you eat them or look at them. Tommie be coming in after a while. He looked like he want to go to his place and I told him to go on but get back so he can talk to you. But we not gone wait for him to eat.

Everthing 'bout ready and on the stove. I got a big fresh trout, but I didn't catch it. I had to quit fishing on account my hand won't let me. It just draws up so much I can't hold a pole. Yeah Baby, me and Tommie used to go fishing all the time. Sometime we spend the night on the creek. We been fishing to Eufaula and at Inverness at what we call the Blue Hole. Talk 'bout fish! Man, we used to catch so many fish at the Blue Hole we give everbody fish and then fill up my deepfreeze. Whoooeeeee! Sometime I keep so many fish in the deepfreeze so long they went bad on me and warn't fit to eat. Shoot, I have throwed away fish, fish, fish 'cause it got rotten. But now I has to buy my fish from that fish place in front of the police headquarters. It's not good as the fish I used to catch, but it's better than froze fish. Oh, I wish I could still go down to the creek and catch my own. I loved it! I loved to see that fish sink the cork on my hook! I knowed I had him! Yeah, that's what I liked. That's right, Tiny. Mama sho' did love to see that fish on that hook. That's what Mama loved. But Mama can't fish no more.

Baby, I think it's 'bout time I stop talking and we start eating. I know you ain't had no supper like this for a long time. Come on to the kitchen table and see what I fixed for us. If Tommie ain't in when we finish, we gone have some coffee and talk some more to he come in.

[BREAK]

It don't look like Tommie gone be in for a while, but I be glad to talk with you 'bout what I knows. Baby, I wouldn't take a million dollars to set down here and talk with you, but Tommie the one that knows all 'bout the old times. I ain't been feeling good for a long time, and I don't remember like I use to. I feel so bad sometime I ain't able to do a lick of work 'round the house.

I tries not to worry too much 'cause I know it'll kill you, but I gets nervous and my bad hand just closes up like it is now. I'm all mixed up and I got to think up things to tell you.

I can't be ashamed of something I couldn't help. Baby, I don't know much. Our daddy didn't send us to school, so ain't none of us older chilluns can read and write. We all come up the hard way. My youngest sister did get the chance to learn something, but when us older ones got big enough to work, Papa kept us in the fields. So all I knows is what I been told. I never learned nothing out of a book. I don't know much, 'cept what happened to me after I got up some size. I don't know when I was borned or what is my age, and I needs to know that. I been told I was borned when my mamma and papa was living in the Bethel community over there near where Mr. Houston got his tombstone yard. But they all dead now. My mamma died and then Papa married Miss Beedee. Papa lived a long time and ain't been many years died. I can't hold nothing against Papa. He done the best he could for us.

But Baby, I ain't got no birth certificate, and I got to find out my age so I can draw the old-age benefits. I been up to the court house, and they said all old papers like that been sont to Kansas City. Miss Beedee said all she could keep in her mind was I was borned on September 8. My sister Eddie Vae's boy is smart and he said he's gone help me get my age. He filled out some papers and sont them to Kansas City, but they say they can't find out nothing on me. Then the boy sent my application up to Montgomery, but he said they told him they couldn't find no certificate for any Versie Lee Johnson. I knows there was one of these granny women with Mama when I was borned, but she didn't send in my name. My sister Zella Dean didn't have her age, so she fixed it up and give herself one. She now working in Columbus, Georgia, and got her a driving license and social security and everthing. She say I ought to find somebody to help give me a age. She say if somebody got some more sense than you, they can figure and give you one.

An abandoned African American church in Bullock County.

So Baby, I knows I can put my dependence on you. Now help me figure and see if I can't get me a age and a birthday. One of Eddie Vae's girls sont to Kansas City and got her age. She say she 63 and was borned June 14, 1914. I knows I'm the next one to her. All right, now. Womens back in them times had a baby just about ever' year, so I must-a been borned that next year. What year would that be? All right, 1915. Miss Beedee say I was borned on September 8. So what birthday do that give me? All right, you say I was borned—wait a minute, wait a minute—I was borned—I wants to get this right—I was borned September 8, 1915. I wants to be close as I can. All right, Eddie Vae is already sixty-three this June. So how old I'm gone be when my birthday come in September? I'm gone be sixty-three. Praise the Lord! Now I got my birthday and my age. Baby, bless yo' heart, I think we done hit it dead on the nail. Them peoples up to the courthouse say they can't take old peoples' word about how old chillun is 'cause they didn't have the education to keep up with things like that. But I believe I got it now. I believe they gone take my word for this 'cause I got too much evidence. Now I think they gone give me my age and my certificate. Baby, I sho' feel better just knowing them things.

I'm gone try to get my mind straight and tell you 'bout my other folks. Eddie Vae is next to the oldest one of my sisters. Jessie Mae the oldest. She been living in Detroit a long time. Her husband is from Union Springs and he went up there and worked in a car place where they make Fords, but he retired now. I ain't never been up there to see them, but they come home a lot. Jessie Mae and some of her grandchillun was down here this summer. Next is Eddie Vae. She live out on the Sardis Road and she got six chillun: Louise, Junior, Henry, Bobbie Ann, Annie Pearl, and James. She was borned June 14, 1914. Then I come next, and I was borned September 8, 1915! I know that's right. Me and Tommie ain't had no chillun. I don't know if my nerves coulda stood all that chillun's squalling 'cause I don't like to be 'round all that kind of fuss. When they cry a long time, they make theirself sick and me too. Next come Zella Dean that live in Columbus.

My baby sister is Callie Mae. She the one that live in New York. When they had that black-out up there, I was worried to death 'bout her. I called her up and said, "Sister, is you in the dark?" She say, "Uh huh, Verse, I'm sho' in the dark, but I got me some candles lit up." I say, "Fool, you was borned down here. Don't you know the way back home? You ain't got to move

back here lessen you wants to, but you can come stay with me to they get things kinda straightened out up there and get them lights back on." She say, "Verse, it ain't so bad." I say, "Baby, how you gone cook and eat and clean up in that dark?" She say, "Well, it not supposed to last long, but if it do, I'll let you know when to meet my bus." She didn't seem worried, but if it been me, I'd a-been out there on the street praying to the top of my voice. But it turned out all right. The lights come back on and she didn't have to come home. I don't believe I want to live up there. If I lose my lights here, I can get by. I got my kerosene lamps and my wood stove, and I can cook up all my meat in the deepfreeze. It worried me to think about all that meat up there ruint.

Yeah Baby, I been to New York one time. Me and Miss Beedee went up there on the bus and stayed a week, which is long enough to stay on anybody as high as cooking is these days. I did enjoy that trip and Miss Beedee did too. I liked them sub-trains that run under the ground, but I don't care nothing 'bout them moving steps they call escalators. I get so nervous when I see one of them things on TV I has to turn my head. There's places up there where they was the onliest choice you had. One time my niece got me by the arm and said, "You won't get hurt, Aunt Versie. Just watch me and jump on when I do." I didn't have no trouble at all. I believe I could a-done it by myself, but I didn't have sense enough just to put my foot on. My nerves wouldn't let me do it by myself. I saw some of them women just jumping on with babies in their arms, but it made me nervous just watching them. My sister been up there long enough to catch on to how you do things like that, so it don't bother her. I still won't ride one lessen I have to. Me and my neighbor was up to Montgomery one time, and she wanted me to go up them steps with her. I said, "No Baby, you go on up if you got to. I believe I'll just set down here and hold our packages." So she acted big and jumped on them steps and went all the way to the top. When she come down, she say, "Verse, I was so scared I liked to stayed up there." I said, "Now I reckon you'll stop trying everthing you see." I don't plan to get on nary 'nother one long as I live. I don't care too much 'bout going up in one of them elevators with a door. I don't believe in doing something you don't have to do if it make you nervous.

Yeah, I liked being in New York, but we didn't go outside much. We mostly hung 'round my sister's apartment. She don't get out much neither 'cause her husband do most of the buying. She lived 'bout two stairs up, which was plenty high for me. Her husband fixed transmissions at a Ford place, but they separated now. They was all the time fighting and the welfare separated them. The last time he tried to push her down the stairs, and he did push one of his little girls out on their little porch and she had to be tuck to the hospital. Had either one hit the street, wouldn't a-been nothing to pick up. They got thirteen chillun, but only 'bout five living with her now. The law said they had to stay apart, or they'd take the chillun and put them in a home. The welfare found her another apartment and told her husband he can't come 'round her. They trespassed him away from there.

I just don't know what the matter with that man. I knows his family. He come from a family that had two white girls in it. His mama was married way back yonder close to slavery times and her colored husband got to where he didn't treat her right. He wouldn't get her nothing to eat or buy nothing for their chillun, and she got to be right pitiful. So this white man got to supporting her, and she had two fine pretty white girls by him. The one that was the most white married the prettiest colored man you ever seen, and the other one married a nice colored man too. Yeah Baby, I knowed both them girls and liked them. I never did hear who their daddy was. Maybe my sister's husband got his troubles from being in that mixed-up family. I knows they all had a hard time.

We all had a hard time back in them days, colored

Verse holding the author's younger brother, Jimmy.

peoples and a lot of white peoples too. I have worked hard all my life, but, Baby, I ain't worked too hard. Since I been married, I knowed Tommie gone look after me. I used to wash and iron for Miss Cora and Miss Nannie Ming at Inverness, and I used to help Miss Sarah down there when she got feeble to do her washing and ironing and cooking. I helped her when her youngest boy was borned and she had to be put in a hospital. Then after I got up here to town, I worked for Mr. Jeff Sorrell's baby sister and I worked for Mrs. Dean Waters. I still works for Miss Dean some when she gets in a tight. But Tommie won't let me work too hard 'cause it makes me nervous.

It just don't pay to work too hard. I knows there's lots of lazy peoples in the world, but there's a lots of people that works too hard. They works all the time and they be all the time tired. To save my life, I don't know why they works so much. I say, "Fool, you ain't got to work all the time. Long as you can eat, just work a little and rest some." When I was a girl, I knowed peoples that would just about fall out in the hot sun picking cotton. Shoot, when I got tired and hot, I tuck my sack over to the shade and got me some cool water and rested a while. That cotton gone be there when you come back. It ain't going nowhere. A little rest is better'n any kind of medicine. Baby, if you works yourself to death, that man what owns the cotton field be done hired him somebody else to pick his cotton 'fore you cold in your grave. That's right, Baby. You be done worked your life out and won't be having no enjoyment at all.

Sometime I get so down I tell Tommie to carry me to Miss Sarah's house at the crossroads, and I spend the day with her and help her a little bit 'round the house. It does me good to be there with her and be helping her. But all her chillun and their wives be so busy. Don't say nothing 'bout it 'cause it make me so mad! All this working and working and working and putting up and talking 'bout you just can't hardly make it. All that stuff you saved up won't do you no

good. The Good Lord can take it away anytime He want to—and you too!

Yeah Baby, I lived in Bullock County all my life. I ain't never wanted to move up to the North like a lot of my peoples. That place too cold most of the time and you got to work too hard just to stay alive. Things is lots better down here. You don't have to worry all the time 'bout being killed. You don't have to lock your door ever time you step outside. Peoples up there if they going somewhere can't leave their suitcase on the front porch and go back in the house. They got to take that suitcase in the house with them or somebody be done stole it when they get back. If they take a trip, when they gets back home, they don't have nothing left. You know I ain't gone live in a place like that.

Some of the peoples up there say, "Well, don't the white peoples down there treat you mean? I wouldn't put up with that!" I say, "Me and Tommie been knowing white peoples all our lives, and we ain't never had no trouble with them at all. They is me and Tommie's best friends." All the white peoples I ever worked with been real nice to me. None of them ever said nothing out of the way to me. We don't mind saying "Yes sir" and "No sir" and "no ma'am" and "yes ma'am" 'cause that's the way we was raised to be polite. Some of the colored peoples say, "Well, you don't have to say that no more." I say, "Well, it don't hurt me to say it. They good to me and I'm good to them." Baby, you wouldn't believe how ugly some colored peoples talk to white peoples these days. It make Tommie so mad sometime he say he don't want a nigger at his funeral!

You take Miss Dean. She married to Mr. John Will Waters, head of the road commissioners. She always been real sweet to me. That's 'xactly right! She's all time checking on me and calling to see if I be all right. She that way 'bout me and Tommie both. We be walking up the street and she come up behind us in her car and stop and get out and say, "Verse, Tommie, is something the matter?" Tommie say,

"Nome, Miss Dean. I just got to have me some money." She say, "Well, how much, Tommie?"—just like he worked for her. He say, "I needs twenty dollars." She say, "Would a check be all right?" He say, "Yes ma'am. That be fine." Now you know he gone take all the checks she give him! You see what I'm saying: it's a precious gift.

Sometime I see a flower or some little doo-dad in town that cost 'bout six dollars. I come home and go down to Miss Dean and say, "Miss Dean, I got to have me a little money. I seen something I wants." She say, "Well, all right, Verse. Would a check be all right?" I say, "No ma'am, I don't want no check. I don't want to fool with no check. Ain't you got six dollars in your pocket?" She say, "Verse, you know my check is good." I say, "You know I know your check is good. I just don't want to fool with no little check." She say, "Well, Verse, all I got right now in my pocketbook is a little spending money." I say, "Well, all right. I just wait to you get some 'cause I ain't in a big hurry."

Sometime Miss Dean call up here and Tommie say, "Well, Verse been sick for a day or two and she not feeling too good now." Before you know it, here she come with a sack full of fruit and stuff to eat. She say, "Verse, I'm supposed to go out of town tomorrow. Do you want me to carry you to the doctor 'fore I go?" I say, "Nome, thank you. Tommie can scrape up some money to carry me if I needs to go. I don't feel too bad now. You know I appreciate you, but I'm gone save you for real hard times." Yeah, she so sweet to me. I call down to my sister and say, "Baby, I'm real sick and needing some washing done." She say, "Baby, I ain't got no way to get up there." Shoot, you know she ain't *trying* to get no way up here. I knows I'm stepping on some people's toes talking like this, but it's the truth.

Here Baby, let me pour you another cup of coffee and cut you a piece of this coconut pie. I made it for you 'cause me and Tommie don't like it.

Now, I tries to treat all the peoples right, white and colored. 'Fore my daddy died, he used to call me up and say, "Baby, I'm sick as can be. Can you come out here and help me a little bit?" Well, Tommie never be at home, but I say, "Papa, I be out there soon as I find a way." He knows I'm gone get there if I have to walk. I goes on up town and maybe see somebody that will carry me. If I have to, I goes to the police and say, "My daddy's serious sick out here in the country, and I can't get no way to go. Will some of y'all run me out there?" It looked to me like there'd always be somebody waiting to take me. When I say, "Now, let me pay you," they say, "Naw, I ain't charging you a dime. Anytime you wants to go see 'bout your daddy, you call me and I be glad to carry you." I always say if you get in a tight, you go to the main folks. They gone help you 'cause they *supposed* to help you if you get stranded. Most of the peoples I know that will help us are the white peoples.

It's just like this. If Mr. John Will Waters ain't gone use his truck tomorrow, Tommie can go down yonder and say, "Can I borry your truck for a while?" Mr. John Will say, "Yeah, sho' you can use it, Tommie, but it may be low on gas. Take it by Mr. Singleton's filling station and tell him to fill it up and charge it to me." Now ain't that something? He ain't charging Tommie for the truck or the gas. We ain't gone find colored peoples that treat us like that.

Well now, here's something else, and I know I'm gone be stepping on some more toes. Way back yonder when Tommie was running a big honky-tonk, he joined the NAACP. He stayed with it to he went to the penitentiary and come on back. They told Tommie it was set up to help the old colored peoples, but we found out it didn't do nothing for us. The day they sentenced Tommie he had fifteen dollars in his pocket, and he slipped it to me and say, "Baby, I know that ain't gone help you much, but you take this and do what you can with it." At that time I was doing a little work and making 'bout fifteen dollars a month, so I had a hard time living with Tommie in jail. When he

Verse Manley's grave.

went off, I was owing 'bout sixteen dollars for the telephone bill and I owed one payment from paying off my insurance, and I didn't have nothing hardly to eat in the house.

Yeah Baby, they sont Tommie off for making whiskey. They caught him at his still. He was making for a man over near Three Notch, and he asked this colored girl if he could store his sugar and shorts and whiskey and stuff in her spare room. Well, this girl was going with a white boy, and he got in a fight with a colored boy 'bout that girl. The colored boy didn't like the colored girl going with the white boy and he tried to whup him. Well, all right, the white boy happened to run up on Tommie's still, and he thought it belonged to the colored boy, so he called the still in to the state men and they come out and caught Tommie. They told Tommie, "We are sho' sorry 'bout this, but we had a call and had to come and check it out. But we know you a good man and we gone ask the judge to go light on you." So Tommie

didn't get but a few months time and got home in time for Christmas.

When Tommie got home, he say, "Verse, did the NAACP come and help you out?" I say, "What you talking 'bout? I ain't seen the NAACP." That made Tommie mad and he told them about it. Them peoples was supposed to help us out, and they didn't do nothing. They was supposed to come down here and see what condition I was in. They coulda said, "Well, you can let the telephone go, but we gone see to it the rent is paid and you got something to eat." I didn't need that telephone, and I woulda been glad to give it up. But they didn't come down here, and they didn't call to see 'bout me at all. Yeah, they knowed Tommie was sont off, and I believe they was glad. That's when Tommie left the NAACP.

When Tommie went off, I was working for the chiropractor's wife and went to work that next morning after Tommie left, and they said, "You look so bad, Verse. What's wrong?" I told them I didn't get no sleep the night before. Then I broke down and told about Tommie being sont off. They said, "Well, you ought to let us know. We might could have helped get him off." They couldn't do nothing then, but they sho' help look out after me while Tommie was gone. That man left town and live somewhere up 'round Birmingham. He come back last week to see us in his new car van. It so big he couldn't get it up this little road and had to park it down on the paved street. He come up here and got me and tuck me down and showed me that thing. Whoop-eeeeee! I wish you could see it. It's spanking brand new. We come to find out that man done messed 'round and got him a new young wife and a baby just walking good. And that woman fixing to have another! He say, "Verse, I wish I live close enough to where you could cook me some cornbread like you used to. I sho' wish you'd tell my wife how you make that cornbread. I can eat dry cornbread like you cook and it would be good." Baby, that the kind of folks I knows. If we needs money or any kind of help, they the ones we go to.

I made it all right while Tommie was gone. Yeah Baby, he been caught 'bout thirteen times. I can't keep up with him. But he only been sont off that one time. Who would know how he got off ever time but one? He smart, Baby, he sho' nuff smart. Talking 'bout a lawyer, Tommie is one. He keep everthing in his head, and he got a good mind. I ain't telling you no story. Tommie doing all right now, but his health is real bad. He don't hardly want me out of eyesight. He want me home when he come in. He tries to pacify me and satisfy me and brings me what I want, and I tries to do right by him 'cause I don't want him to get his blood pressure no more out of line.

I been taking care of Tommie so long I can't remember. I don't know how long we been married, but it been a long time ago. We had our ups and downs, that ain't no lie. He old now and don't feel good most of the time, and sometime he hollers at me two hours at night. He say, "Baby, I laid my reel on this table, and there ain't no need for me to go hunting for it 'cause I know you done moved it." I say, "I sho' have moved it, and I don't remember where I put it. The thing for you to do is get in your car and go on back to your business, and if I find it, I find it. Don't holler at me and don't look at me 'cause you know it gonna make me nervous. You shouldn't-a put your things on my things where I decorate 'cause you knows I love my things to be like I fixed them." He come in here and put his reel on this white tablecloth and it dripping grease and he want me to let it stay! Sometime I get a little contrary too and has to tell him what to do 'bout it. But Tommie's a good man. He been good to me. I wouldn't have nobody else. There ain't none but him and if he go, I don't want nary 'nother one.

Tommie got a little place he rent from a white man out Highway 29 going on to Tuskegee, on past Last Chance, right close to where Big Boy used to have his place. He don't have much. He sell beer and got a Rockola and pinball machines. He run it by hisself and open it when he get ready. He don't have no special hours. He been out there tonight. He don't fool too much with gambling no more. His eyes done got too bad. Sometime he go to the Bottom and cuts the game. That mean he keeps things quiet and take a tip for overseeing the gambling. He don't stay out late no more and ought to be coming in any time. That man is still hard to hem up, but when he get here I'm gone corner him for you. He is one smart man. Tommie can tell you all 'bout the Bible and old times, just like he read it, but he only remember what his daddy told him. His daddy so smart he coulda been a schoolteacher. Yeah Baby, Tommie will be tickled to death to tell you how you make whiskey and all 'bout whiskey stills and all kind of old stories. White folks love to hear Tommie talk. Sometime they enjoy him so much, he say, "White folks, I ought to charge you to listen to my stories."

While we waiting for Tommie to come in, just look 'round and if you see anything you wants, just take it. Take anything you want, I don't care how hard I love it. I can't never pay you for helping give me a age and a birthday. I can't wait to tell Tommie what we found out. So you take anything you wants. Here is a old-timey pressing iron that you can use for a doorstop. I have heated it a many a time on the stove and ironed a heap of shirts and britches with it, but I got a 'lectric iron now. Take this bowl of figs home with you. They come off my big fig tree in the back yard. I feel good to give you this bowl of figs. Here's some pears too. I like it when somebody I love be having what I got. Yes sir, I loves a lot of white folks and they loves me, but I tell you there ain't but one white family I really loves, and that the Halls. It seem like we all in one great big family together. It make me feel good for you to have my figs. My insurance man last week say he want some of them figs. I say, "Well, all right, but I ain't gone strain up and pick them and give them to you. You go out and pick you some." He say, "I ain't got time but I send my wife to pick some." I say, "Well, I just change my mind. I'm gone pick em and you gone buy em."

Baby, take this jar of fig preserves too 'cause I wants you to care a little something for me. Something is gone happen one of these days. We don't know that day, and we don't want to know that day. But when it do happen, I want it put in the *Herald* and I want Miss Sarah to call you up to tell you 'cause I wants you to be the man to check me to see if I'm right. If I ain't, I wants you to have me fixed right.

I hear Tommie's car coming up. Now you gone hear some good stories.

POSTSCRIPT: Verse Manley survived her husband by almost ten years and died on June 28, 1993, in the Crown Health Medical Center in Montgomery. During her final years she suffered from a number of complaints, including kidney failure. For several years she was taken by government van to a dialysis center in Troy for treatment. About two years before her death, she asked me to buy her a new carpet to replace one that she said was infested with bugs that "just about eat me up." I immediately made plans for a new carpet, which she showed off to me proudly during my last visit with her. She was survived by three sisters, two sisters-in-law, many nieces, nephews, and friends. She was buried in the New Hope Cemetery next to Tommie. Her obituary did not give her age, but, according to our calculations, she was seventy-seven.

Tavern-Keeper and Moonshiner

Like almost all the people in this book, sixty-two-year-old Tommie Manley has been a lifelong resident of Bullock County, and I have known Mr. Manley and his wife Verse all my life. I can remember when he was working at a nearby sawmill and would stop by my father's little country store in the Sardis-Bread Tray Hill communities and buy a ten-cent can of potted meat, a ten-cent slab of hoop cheese, a nickel box of crackers, and a "bellywasher"—a Pepsi or RC cola or a Nehi, which cost the same five cents as a Coca-Cola but which contained almost twice as much drink. He has known my father, nicknamed Jabo, since they both were boys. I interviewed Tommie and Verse the same evening on July 17, 1977, at the same kitchen table where I talked and ate dinner with Verse. Tommie has been out to his tavern and has just returned to the rented house he shares with Verse and her collections of flowers and knickknacks. His large frame and fierce looks mask a kind and gentle nature. As he tells us, he has worked at many jobs during his lifetime, but moonshining and tavern-keeping are two favorite occupations.

I'm glad you're here. Man, I would enjoy talking with you as much as anything on the face of the earth. I got some knowledge of life, and I remember everything. Verse says I always knows what to say. With the help of the Lord, I'm gone tell my whole story, so you just set down, relax yourself and hear me. Verse will pour you a drink of Nehi grape or orange or whatever you want. I wants to tell you about things like how we made our syrup, how we used to plant rice and how I made whiskey in the woods. I been here in this world a long time and have remembrance of old things. Sometimes I goes down to Halls Cross Roads to the store and set around and talk with Jimmy about the old times when me and his daddy was kids. You take Jimmy, he's so much like the old man. He can set down with one leg under him and look just like Mr. Jabo.

See that woman over there I been living with. Verse sho' looks good to me. Me and her, we don't have no fussing, no fighting, no argument. I try to satisfy her with the house. Anything she say she wants I try to make arrangements to get it for her. That's the onliest way to live. I know I won't find no other woman like Verse. I know I can't go out here and put my dependence in somebody else's hand and expect them to do like Verse. There ain't nary 'nother one like her.

My little house is setting in the same spot here in Union Springs where the midget peoples used to live.

They was little black peoples and wouldn't get as high as this table when they was grown. When I was a young man, we used to come by here, going down to the pasture to shoot dice, and there'd be a houseful of them setting on the front porch. They wouldn't talk to you none. They was so low they wore long things like dresses, and you never would see none of em's little feet. Well, all right, one time I *did* see one of em's feet. After me and Verse was married and moved here to this house, some of them still lived in this settlement in that big house right across the road. The biggest one of the midgets wore her dress so low it covered her little feet. But when she died, we did get to see em. They was round as this plate, like horse feet—with little toes all around. I don't know where in the world they come from. They was already here when I got big enough to come to Union Springs.

Now hear what I say. If peoples knowed what I know about Union Springs, they just wouldn't believe it. When I was a boy, we'd work up to dinner every Saturday and I'd come to town that evening. I have went up and down these streets when there wadn't no pavement or blacktop. It was all sand and dirt. Man, what you talking 'bout? Don't you know I remember when all of Union Springs was just dirt? Where the peoples would be cramming up in them stores trading would be a deep hole in that sand. It was so deep you'd have to reach down and pull the old peoples up in the store. When you bought your groceries and other stuff, you'd just back your wagon up to the store door and they'd load you up, and you'd come on home.

Right where the whiskey store is setting right now there was a watering place for mules where the peoples would park their wagons. There was iron troughs that looked like syrup mill kettles that the mules would drink out of. When the peoples walked 'round from store to store and got together talking, they unhitched their mules and tied them to the wagons and put out feed or hay for them to eat while they's gone. The pigeons would swoop down and eat the corn in that mule feed and waste it on the ground. There'd be so many pigeons in town that peoples would pay you to kill them. You walk out that door right now and you won't hardly find a mule, a pigeon, or a wagon in this town.

But we used to have mules all over the place, and peoples would bring their wild mules to town to be broke. Right there where the recapping place is now was a stable where you could get your mules broke at. If anybody had a mule they couldn't ride, they'd bring him to town and put him in there. On Saturday they had cowboys from Texas that would come and charge you two dollars a head to break your mule. I have seen them cowboys coming down the street whistling and them spurs would be on their boots sticking way out, and they'd be ringing when they walked. Them cowboys would go to the lot at the stable and they'd have lassos, and we'd be outside the fence watching. It'd be like that. One of them cowboys said, "Well, all right. Who wants their mules broke first?" I said, "My name's Tommie Manley. My mule is that one right over yonder." The cowboy would take that rope, throw it over that mule, and it'd fall right over his head. Then he'd go in there and choke that mule down and put one of them cowboy saddles on him and carry him to the gate. That cowboy would jump up in that saddle and say, "Open the gate." That mule'd be bucking just like he gonna kill that man,

and he didn't have no bridle or nothing to hold on to. It was just like the rodeo you see on TV. That cowboy would run his big old spurs in that mule's side and that mule would near 'bout run itself to death. He'd run up and down the street kicking up dust, with that cowboy hanging on. That went on until that mule tired hisself out; then the cowboy'd bring him back to the stable. That mule would be really broke, and anybody could ride him.

I never broke no mules. But you take Verse's brother, Buck, he do it now. Buck will ride any kind of horse or mule, I don't care what it is. If he ain't never had a bridle on him, Buck'll ride him and won't never get throwed. I don't see how Buck can stay on that mule to save my life. There's a white man out here that's got a horse prettier than any horse or mule in this country. It's so fat and pretty it's a scandal! But you get close to it and it'll jump up to the sky, and she ain't never been broke. Buck went out there this summer and said, "Somebody said you wanted that horse broke." The man said, "Yeah, I do but she's so pretty I hate for you to treat her bad like that." And he wouldn't let Buck ride her. Looks to me like he ought to want her broke. I just wish you could see her. She's the prettiest thing you ever looked at.

When I's a young man, we'd walk or either we'd ride a mule to town. Then stay till after night and get on our mules and go back home. I didn't have no saddle, so I'd get me two or three bagging sacks and fold em and throw em 'cross the mule and set on them. Didn't nobody but the big shots have a saddle— maybe the boss man or some rich colored folks, like the Negro that called hisself the foreman at the plantation or the sawmill. Sometime that foreman had a horse and saddle *and* a buggy. Man, I have seen from Union Springs to Sardis when you couldn't hardly get by with a Model T Ford the road was so full of wagons and mules and buggies!

I used to know a little old colored fellow named Shep Shelly. Old Shep was so low till it looked like you could step on him. He had a steer named Joe that had a red head and his body was white. You know a steer is a bull cow, but you cut him—castrate him—and then he's a steer. He can't do his man-business and that tames him so you can ride him or put a yoke on him and plow. Now Old Shep would ride Joe to town. There couldn't a horse or a mule on the road outrun him. Shep could ride that old steer! He'd come along the road and the steer would be a-racking and Shep would be just a-rocking in his saddle, and he wouldn't be no higher than a little baby. Man, he could ride that steer!

A steer is a strong animal. I have logged with a many of them. I have yoked and drove eight that didn't have no lines on them, and I'd snake them big logs out of the woods. Peoples used to work hard! You hear what I say! I would carry along a axe and a hook, and if a log got hung up on a stump or a root, I say, "Whoa," and back up them steers, and prize that log loose. Then I say, "All right boys, get down right here," and they pull and pull, and sometimes I let em rest and catch their breath, and I take my whup and say, "All right boys, git on," to I git that log right where I wants it, and I say, "Whoooaaa, whoooooooooaaaaaaaa. Whooaa now." And them steers stop just where you say. There couldn't be no lines on them steers, but they be trained to obey you. Man, that was some hard work—for me and them steers.

I never rode a steer to town, but I have rode a many a mule. Most of the time I just walked or hitched a ride on somebody's wagon. When we got to town there wadn't much to do, 'cept to just stay around, walking from store to store, talking with the girls and having a good time. Man, them sidewalks be so full of peoples you couldn't hardly move sometimes. When you get ready to walk home, you'd take up with one of the girls. Oh, man! We wouldn't care nothing 'bout walking from Union Springs out to Sardis and on down to the cross roads. That was seven or eight miles—just a fun walk. They used to have

mileposts all up and down the road to tell you how many miles you been gone. Plenty of times we'd walk the railroad tracks on down to Inverness and then walk from Inverness back up to Sardis where we lived. That was just for exercise. On the first day of the month when we got our money, Oh, Lord!, we'd sometimes walk all the way to Montgomery.

But I can't do nothing like that no more. I'm a old man. I was borned December 18, 1914. I'm a heap older than Verse—least I think I am. I have seen things change I wouldn't believe when I's a boy. I was talking to a white fellow the other day. I said, "Just think back to when we was young men. We come up working for five dollars a month, forty cent a day—and glad to get the work. Now you got a boy making no telling how much." But, you know, I believe peoples had more real money behind them back then. What good is plenty of money now? It costs you too much to have money. The government is gonna tax you and other peoples is peeping at you 'bout your money and everbody wants part of it. If you got money now, you owe it to somebody. If you paid your debts, you'd be broke. Back in the old days, if you had ten dollars in your pockets, it belonged to you. But you look at right now. We got utility bills to pay and the expenses of eating and sleeping. We go to town to the A&P and call for a package of pork chops. Three dollars! Just six pieces! When I was a boy, three dollars would buy a whole hog.

I remember the old ways, but I use some of the new ways. In the old days I didn't have lights or a fan or a icebox. One time a man got a new Frigidaire and give me his old one. That thing would growl and act like it was gonna bust, but you put in a jug of water and that thing would keep it so cold and nice. In them days I didn't have a fan running in my house. You just leave the windows and doors open for fresh air. But now you got a 'lectric fan and close up all the doors and have the expense of running it.

Now I tell you the truth, if I could I'd go back to

the old ways. Here's two reasons. Times would be better and health would be better for the peoples. Right now we eat fresh meat the year 'round. Meat's not cured like it used to be. You take that new meat and sometimes it make you sick and cause lots of peoples to have high blood, eating all that green meat from one season to another. Back then we killed our meat and cured it, just like Miss Elma Lee do sometime now. We'd go out and knock that hog in the head with a axe, gut it, and hang it up by its feet in the smokehouse and get some wood chips and build a fire in a tub and put some smoke under that meat. That

Author Wade Hall (left), his brother Jack, Nathan "Bootman" Hall, and a driver hauling firewood in a mule-drawn wagon, c. 1938.

smoke and a little heat would season that meat and make that skin just as yellow and it'd be hard when you go to cut it. You could smell that meat cooking right out into the road. Now, you get some meat out of the freezer and thaw it out and cook it, and you got to keep adding a little salt, but it still don't have the taste it had then. Peoples now will kill something and put it in a freezer, but they won't get to it for a year and by then they won't want to eat it and they'll throw it away. Peoples throw away what used to make a whole meal because they won't eat something that's been froze that long.

I still like cured meat a lot better than froze meat. You can go down to Howard Hall's store and get some cured ham in some thin paper. It's just like the old original ham. You get it home, slice off some pieces and put it in a fryer and pour a little water on there and get some of the salt drawed out of it—oh, man!—it eats just like the old original meat. Yes sir, that old meat eats a heap better than this new meat.

Well, I'll go ahead on, and tell you 'bout my old '46 Ford out there in the yard. Man, I have had that Ford since the last of 1946, but I stopped driving it year before last. A boy told me this morning, he said,

"What would you take for that old model Ford out there?" I told him no, I didn't want to sell it. I put a brand-new motor in it I ordered from Sears, Roebuck in Atlanta. I asked the man, "Do you have a 1946 Flathead V-8?" He said, "Yeah, how many do you want?" I told him just one. So he sent it down to me, and when the man got here I asked him the price of it, and he said it was $257.77, two hundred dollars for the motor and the rest for putting it in. I said, "All right. Go ahead and set it in." And that motor's still in there, and it's still good, but I broke the spring on it, so I parked it to I buy me a new spring. Then I'll have me a new '46. What I'm gonna do then is paint it and put some bucket seats in it and make a beauty out of it. I know a boy that's got one just like it. He put in bucket seats and painted it a gold color. He's got him a radio on it and a tape player and—oh, man!—everbody just want to give him so much money for it. This year he got him a brand-new Cadillac, but he keep that '46 Ford in the front of the Cadillac in his car shed.

It's like a white fellow told me the other day, he said, "I tell you what, Tommie, you ought to get that car fixed up and drive it up to Chicago or New York and work them streets in it. Let the young peoples see you driving that old-model car and everybody'd be surprised. If you ever rolled by peoples with plenty of money, they'd buy it from you for any price so their chillun could see what a old car looked like. They'd say, "This is a car that was made in 1946, way years before I even thought 'bout being borned." Man, I tell you, something else. If you was to come down the street in Union Springs with two mules hitched to a wagon, then you would hear some talking going on. Everbody would be looking at that mule pulling that wagon and you setting on it. A colored man I know was borned and raised here, but he lives in New York. He told me he was gonna buy a old buggy and ship it up there. He said, "Then I'm gonna paint that buggy and buy me a horse and hitch that horse to that buggy and drive on through downtown New York. Man, I'm gone get me some money for that horse and buggy." He say he knows he won't have to bring it back home 'cause when some millionaire sees him up there, he gonna say, "Oh my gracious. How much would you take for this?" He says that's when he gone sell. He ain't done it yet, but he come home ever Christmas and he'll tell me when he does.

Yes sir, peoples keep on wanting to buy that '46 Ford. They had a old car show in town 'bout two months ago, and somebody wanted to buy my Ford then. I told the man about my broke spring, and he said, "It don't matter 'bout that spring being broke. I'll buy it like it is." But I told him I wadn't ready to sell it yet. They had some old Model T's in that show that you couldn't touch for less than eight or nine thousand dollars. I might not get that much for my car, but it'll bring a good price. It's sho' been a good car. I have hauled a many a gallon of whiskey out of the woods in that Ford. I have taken that car and gone right up side my still and set in it and looked at the whiskey run. When I get through running whiskey, I'd measure some out in five-gallon jugs and set it in that car, crank it up and pull on out. I'd carry it on to

somebody I had to buy it. Yes sir, I have hauled a many a gallon of whiskey on that '46 Ford out there.

I done got too old to make whiskey like that, but I have made some good whiskey when I was 'stilling it in the woods. Peoples go to the state store and buys whiskey and all they know is they got whiskey, but how it come they don't know. Up there in Kentucky, the government has got big stills, what they call 'stilling plants. But I made a lot better whiskey than that. Good homemade whiskey is better than storebought whiskey. Some of that state store stuff ain't even 'stilled. It's made out of some chemicals they put together and draw off and sell for whiskey.

Now, I'm gone tell you how to make it right. The first thing you need is a vat that don't leak water—even if it ain't nothing but a barrel or a drum, just as long as it don't leak. You go buy you some rye or shorts or sweet potatoes or corn or anything that will turn sour and make alcohol. I liked to use rye or shorts. Shorts is the bran left over from wheat when you make flour, and it ain't supposed to be used for making whiskey. It's made for cow feed or hog feed. But it does make good whiskey too. Let's say you using rye; so you pour so much rye in that vat. Then you go to the branch and get some water and pour it on the top of that rye. You just let it set there in the sun—maybe cover it over—and wait to it swells and sours. When you stir and see it boiling up, you know it's sour. Then you go and get some sugar. If you running a big operation—what we call a two-side still—you get sixty pound of sugar and pour all of it in that vat. Get you a clean scoop and stir that sugar up in that sour rye real good. When that sugar get in there, it'll make it go to work. Then you full that vat up to near the top with water and leave it alone. You go back there this evening and it's already working. It'll be boiling over and over. That sourness is eating up that sugar and that leaves the alcohol on the top.

Now you ready to cook it and get the steam off it. You put a cap on the top of that cooker, and that steam will go right through that pipe and into another pipe and down into a bucket of water to cool it. When it hit that cold water, that sweat condenses into whiskey. Man, it's strong! You can run a automobile on the first ten or twelve gallons. It'll run your car just like gas. You strike a match around the jug where you catch that first run of whiskey and the whole thing will blow away—and you with it. What you have to do is cut that strong whiskey to where a man can drink it. You take some of your low whiskey—they calls it low wine—and run some of that in it and it cuts the power down. You want your whiskey to hold just enough beads to where when a man swallow it, it won't eat him up. Now you jug it up and you got some good whiskey.

When I was in the federal penitentiary, a man asked me, he said, "Well, Tommie, I heard you was a good 'stiller and you been doing this a long time. Why don't you take a job with the government? They'd be happy to hire you to 'still whiskey for them." I told him, "Naw, I think I rather go on back home when I get out." But he was right. I could make good whiskey for the government. I been making whiskey from the time I was 'bout eighteen to I got to be about fifty. I got caught fourteen times and was sont off two times. Both times I got off easy because I never made the judges mad. The last time I went off Judge Johnson in Montgomery sont me. I didn't give him no trouble at all. He asked me, "Well, say Tommie, why would you make whiskey?" I said, "Well, Judge, it's just a thing I could do to get some quick money out of." He said, "Well, Tommie, didn't you know that you was break-ing the rules and regulations of the federal govern-ment?" I said, "Yes sir, Judge, I did. But I was trying to slip by and not let nobody know I was doing it." He asked me where I bought my sugar at. Now, I didn't want him to know who was furnishing my sugar, so I said, "Well, Judge, I would get some at the hardware store and at different places." He said, "Now, Tommie, the man at the hardware store don't sell sugar." I said,

"Well, you know, they might have didn't. Maybe the man was just buying some to sell to me. He knowed I wasn't scared for him to know I was making whiskey, so he'd special order a couple of tons for me."

Now that tickled them folks to death up there in that courtroom in Montgomery. I said, "But Judge, I know I done wrong, and I'll never do it no more. I just can't do it. I done got too old and I can't handle the weight of that sugar and them shorts and that other stuff." That's the truth. I used to reach and get me a hundred-pound sack of sugar and throw it across my shoulder and tote it 'cross the field and to the woods. I would tote four or five hundred pounds of sugar down to them woods before I'd even fire up my still, and I'd go back and get my jugs. You have to make that whiskey in the deep woods. You don't want nobody to know where you making because you know they gone tell on you. So I'd tote all that rye and shorts and sugar and jugs down to the woods—lessen I had a way to drive my car up to the still—and I'd tote my jugs of whiskey back up to the car. But I ain't got the power to carry all that stuff now.

I made good whiskey. But ain't no still whiskey *bad*. Of course, after you 'still it, you can put it in something that makes it bad. Whiskey is strong, and if you take that strong whiskey and let it set in a metal pan, it'll eat that metal off, and some of it will be in the whiskey. You drink that kind of whiskey, and it'll likely kill you. That's why some peoples holler 'bout homemade whiskey being poison. But I used copper tubs and tubes and caught my whiskey in a glass jug or a wood keg, and wadn't no poison in them. One more thing 'bout whiskey. If you want to flavor it, you put it in a charred wood keg; and it'll be white going in and red coming out. The whiskey sucks the flavor out of that wood.

Bullock County has always been a wet county, so we'd make our whiskey and haul it out to dry counties to sell. I have hauled a many a gallon to Macon County, when it used to be dry. Plenty of times if you see a wet county, you'll find a still there somewhere. Montgomery County is wet, and I saw the other day they was telling on the news on TV they found a big still up there in a used car lot. The man was 'stilling whiskey and selling cars at the same time. When they caught the colored fellow that was making it, they asked him, "Well, say, how long you been making whiskey here?" He said, "I don't know." They said, "Have you been making it ever since the car lot's been here?" He told em, "Yeah, I believe I have."

I know peoples who been making whiskey all their lives and never been caught. This last time I was caught by two young men from Butler and Montgomery county. Turns out they been making pictures of me, my still, my car and everthing from a helicopter. I was already caught and didn't even know it. I seen that helicopter coming across but I didn't pay it no attention. They passed over, went on and found two more stills and went back to Montgomery, put that helicopter up, got in a car and come on back and got me. I was still at the still when they come. They said, "Well, we done been had you caught. Do you want to go by home and change clothes before we take you to Montgomery?" I said, "Well naw, I'll just go on the way I am." So they took me on up and I signed my bond and come on back home until my trial.

They was pretty nice about the whole business. One of em said, "Manley, now look here. I don't know you, but Mr. Justice from over here in Jamback knows you been making whiskey ever since you been big enough." I told him, "Now, that's what you say." He said, "Well, we caught you at it—and you been caught many times before—but I don't want it to go too hard on you. You done got a little age on you. I'm gone tell the judge what a good boy you is. I'll explain to him that you didn't make no trouble for me. You didn't try to run when we come up on you. You go on home now and don't you make no more whiskey. When you get home, you go to the welfare office and order you some food stamps and just be a good boy.

The judge likes it when you plead guilty, so when you get in court, just say guilty and he'll go easy on you."

So when I got in court, I pleaded guilty, and the man told the judge, "This old boy ain't got good health. He an old man and can't get by too good. So I asks you to go light on this man." And he did. Judge Johnson give me just ninety days and no fine. I didn't have to pay a penny—none at all. So I made eighty-one days at the prison camp, and my time was up because I got nine good days off. I come on home and ain't been in trouble since. That federal man come by my house one day after I got home and set down and eat with me and Verse just like you. I liked him. He was a good boy. When he went to leave, he give me this card and says, "Tommie, I want you to get this card made up in metal and keep it to you die. Look me up if you ever need anything." This card say, "Raymond Wrightmeyer, U. S. Treasury Department, Alcohol, Tobacco and Firearms Division." That was the man that caught me and sent me to the pen.

It's hard for them federal men to catch you lessen you been turned up. I always put my still in somebody's woods that I could slip into and out of without them knowing. That's the reason you get caught a lot of times. When the landowner finds out you in there, maybe he go to talking and call in the law. Now, you could ask the man could you make whiskey on his land, but one time out of a hundred he's gonna let you. You know how peoples is. If they can't make a living good and have money, then they don't want you to neither. So you have to hide your still in the thick part of somebody's woods. If you don't, somebody'll see you and they gone talk. Two boys I know passed by one of my stills one time. Now, they had no need at all to say anything about it, but quick as they gets on the street, they tells what they seen. Peoples will sho' do it! They don't want you to get along all right.

It's just like I told Verse the other day. I bought her a picture called "The Lord's Supper" right up there on the wall. I said, "Verse, you take Jesus Christ. He was the greatest man that's ever been on the land. But you look at them old boys on the end of that picture. They fixing to get Him whupped and killed. Judas is down there at one end, and there's Peter standing beside Him with his hand on His shoulder. He got his hand on Jesus's shoulder! That's the onliest man you know of that ever put his hand on Jesus. See, all them boys was close to Him. But anytime peoples get that close to you, they close enough to kill you. And they will! They betrayed that Man and got Him killed. So if peoples will do that to Jesus, you know

A Bullock County lake.

they gonna tell where I'm making whiskey. They can't stand seeing somebody make a living too easy. They'll tell on you. Just look what they done to Jesus. Peter denied Him to His face when the Jews got ready to kill Him. Judas had done already told the Jews who He was. They didn't know Him. Well now, that's the way peoples is about me making whiskey. They gonna tell on me and get me sent to the penitentiary. After they got my still tore up and me sent off, I ain't heard nothing else from them.

Them peoples the cause of that helicopter coming in. Some white fellows up above me found out I had that still and called Montgomery to the Federal Office and told em. Them federal men wouldn't never have found my still if I hadn't been turned up. They wouldn't have knowed where to go to look. Bullock County's got a lot of woods, and look how far I was from home. I was making on this man's place and if he knowed I was making, he didn't care enough to tell nobody. Them federal men never would have found me. They got to have help. They go to a community and talk to somebody who knows something and give them a little tip of money and find out everthing they knows. Them agents don't have to do

nothing. They just got to find somebody that talks. That's the way the world operates. Now you hear me 'cause it's the gospel truth.

It's just like Judas was telling the Jews about Jesus Christ. The Jews was saying, "Now who is this Man?" Judas said, "Well, I can't tell you no more than He is the King of the Jews." You see, Judas knowed that 'cause he was a Jew, too. They said, "Well now, how would we find out which one this fellow is?" Judas said, "All right, you go with me to this house and I'm gonna walk to where He is. That Man you see me hug 'round the neck and kiss on the jaw, that's the Man you looking for." So Judas followed Jesus to the house and the Jews stood back in the dark, so they could see Jesus in the inside light. Judas walked up and hugged Him 'round the neck and kissed Him on the jaw and sopped in the sacrament dish with Him. When the Jews seen him do that, they walked on in. That's when Christ said to all the boys setting 'round the supper table, "The time is at hand." So the Jews walked in and told him and said, "Come on, let's go. You the Man we looking for." Jesus didn't resist. He just got up and walked out with them and on down the road. So Peter he went on behind walking. He was so hurt about what they had done, but he went on behind walking to the temple. They carried Jesus on into the temple, and they put thorned bandages 'round His head and blood was running down His side. Peter heard Him moaning and groaning, and he walked in the door. The Jews said, "Peter, is this the Man you was with the other day?" Peter said, "Naw, I don't know that Man." Peter denied Jesus to His face! Now, when something bad happens to you today, you needn't be too surprised. Peoples just don't like you too much. They tell you they do but they don't. They wisht they had your opportunity. They wisht they had what you got. They wisht they had a way of getting what you got. I knows all that.

No, I don't see nothing bad 'bout making whiskey. It's like the judge told me. He said, "Tommie, there wouldn't be nothing wrong with you making that whiskey, 'cept you making it tax-free. Now, if you was paying taxes on it and we caught you, it wouldn't be bad at all. We couldn't do nothing 'bout it. But you making it tax-free, and what we making you pay for is that tax." Now the Bible says Jesus drunk some wine, and it ain't no telling what else. So, if peoples is gone drink whiskey anyway, I might as well make it like anybody else; and I knows how to make good whiskey a heap better than you can buy at the state store. I have went through a lot, and I done got too old a man to do all the things I used to do. Now, you hear what I say.

Oh man, I have done hard work in my life. Along 'bout 1925 I went over to Columbus, Georgia, and helped build railroad beds for the Central of Georgia Railroad. Two of us would carry that tie—one end on one man's shoulder and the other end on the other man's shoulder—and we'd go down the track toting it to we got to the place where they was building the bed up, and we'd throw that tie down and go get another one. Now they got a machine that can reach down and pull them spikes and old rotten ties out and put a new one in. We used to do all that work from muscle.

I was over there in Columbus working for the railroad during the time it didn't rain in six months. It was six months of dry weather, and all the corn fell down and burned up and the peoples cut and shocked it and took it home and used it for mule feed. And everbody talk 'bout this year being dry! I tell em, "Y'all ain't *seen* no dry weather." When I was over there, the Chattahoochee River was just as dry as this table. You could go down that river walking just like you going down the road. Peoples was just starved for water. They dug any wet place they thought water might rise, but the wells was all dry. When I come home from Columbus, I started hauling water on a wagon all the way from Montgomery to Union Springs. It was so dry in Bullock County we had to dip it out of the Alabama River in Montgomery. There wadn't a drop of water in Union Springs. Don't you know I have made a many a load. We'd leave here at first night and go to Montgomery and fill our barrels full of water, turn around and come back and get in around ten or eleven the next day. Peoples would take that river water and boil it and cook the germs out of it. You'd be issued water 'cause it was so scarce, but you'd be glad to get any kind of water you could.

Man, I used to do all kinds of hard work. Hauling water was easy. Snaking logs out of the woods was hard. There wadn't no such thing as pulp-wooding back in them days, but there was a few sawmills around and about. John Carroll's Lumber Company in Hurtsboro had a sawmill, and one of my brothers worked at the sawmill on Bughall Creek. The McLendons had one at Boswell Crossing, and Mr. Jeff Sorrell's daddy had a big sawmill and planing mill down in Saco. Sawmills in them days was run on steam boilers. The steam would run from the boilers to a engine you had bolted down, and that engine had pulleys that run the saws. The mill didn't have much power, and it was slow work. A man would shave the slabs off, and then cut the block up in lumber. My work was to help get them logs to the sawmill. We didn't have no kind of power to cut them big trees down, just a crosscut saw and man muscle. It was a slow go. In the summer, you'd get so hot you'd have to go set in the shade a while or you'd fall out. But we was glad to make that dollar or dollar and a half a day. I was a logger and drove a four-mule log wagon. We'd go in the woods and have a trench dug out and we'd try to let the wagon wheels fall in that trench. We'd roll them logs on what you call skids, which was made out of logs. We'd trim the skids so they'd fit on the wagon bed and we'd roll them logs up the skids and let em fall over on the wagon. We'd stick some wooden standards down in the holes in the wagon to keep the logs from rolling off. When we got a load, we'd carry it on to the sawmill.

Man, what you talking 'bout! That was some hard work! Sometimes you'd be so tired you couldn't get no further than the porch at night. If you set down on the porch a few minutes, you already gone to sleep. You just be tired to death. But peoples then wadn't sick like they is now. Peoples would work hard and they would sweat. They could handle anything heavy. They was strong because of their muscles. But now a man operates a machine out on the road and don't have to lift nothing heavier than this Nehi bottle. He just mash a button and the machine do all the work. He can set up all night and go to work the next day. He ain't tired. He ain't got nothing to do 'cept go and push buttons. Machines doing all the work.

I never got bad hurt when I was working with logs. I got bruised up a lot, but I have seen peoples almost get killed. Sometimes a log would roll off the wagon and bust a man up, or you'd go to pull the standard out and them logs would work loose and roll down off that wagon and catch a man's arms or legs and break em. I have seen boys running the edger at the sawmill to shave off the slabs, and sometimes they'd let their hands slip and get em tore up. I have seen peoples have their hands cut off on that edger blade. Them pulp wood saws they use right now is dangerous as a pistol. If that thing hits your meat, you cut in two. You can't get out of the way before it done ruint you because that chain is running by gas. If that chain catch your hand, it's off and gone for good. When I was a young man, I worked at Mr. McLendon's sawmill. I have worked for all the McLendons—Mr. Tom, Mr. Bryant, Mr. Clarence. I was working down there at Boswell when Social Security first come out. The Social Security man come down and had everbody get off their job and go up to Union Springs to sign up for a Social Security card.

Yes sir, I have done some hard work in my life, and I ain't even talked 'bout farming yet. I was borned down on the Stuckey Place, right across from where

The Alabama River at Montgomery.

you see Hugh Stuckey living now. It's on that old road that used to go 'round towards Inverness, down and around where Sandy Pritchett live. My mama birthed eighteen children of us, thirteen of us brothers and five sisters. We all farmed for Old Man Joe Stuckey. I started helping out and working in the fields all day when I's 'bout eleven years old. At daylight we was in the field and worked to about 11:30 when the dinner bell would ring. Our sisters would knock off at 10:30 and come to the house and cook dinner for the whole family of peoples. We'd all go back to the field about one.

In the field we'd be raising corn or cotton or sweet potatoes or sugar cane or rice or wheat—anything we could sell or eat. If it wadn't raining outside, I could take you right now to a place where I plowed, and I could show you the old road and the old terraces they put in near Bughall—what they called the rice bottom. That's where we'd sow our rice in the water. We'd break up that land with a two-horse plow, and when it come time to plant, we'd put in the rice, and we didn't care if we covered it up or not. If that rice seed get close to water, it was gonna come up. We had to be careful 'bout where we stepped. There'd be snakes—gracious alive!—in that water. The rain would be standing in that bottom and sometime the mules would get bogged down, and we'd have to dig em out. When it come time to gather that rice, we'd lay it acrosst a pole until it dried. After it dried, we'd pull it off the stems and put it in sacks, and then we'd beat it to get the husks out from around the grain, but it wouldn't be white like it is now. They got a container they runs it through now and it paints that rice white.

After our wheat was dry, we'd thrash it out too and sack it up and take it to Old Man Ross Cogdell's mill down below where Mr. Daniel Driggers used to live. When we needed flour we'd take some wheat over there to have it ground. Along 'bout Christmas, Mama would say, "I got to have a barrel of flour for cooking. Go on down to the mill and get some wheat

ground. We got to have enough to do till after Christmas."

Like everybody else, we had our patches of corn and cotton, and we raised our sugar cane down on Bughall up a little piece from the rice bottom. All the peoples from close around would come help plant that sugar cane. After we broadcast that land, we'd let it rain on it, and we'd come down with a old double-buster hooked to two of the heaviest mules we had, and we'd lay off rows to plant that cane in. We'd have them rows four or five foot apart. We'd bring in our seed cane and drop it in the furrow like you do corn. Then one of us would have a turning plow and cover up that cane. We planted it deep, so it took a long time coming up. But don't worry. It's coming. When we seen that cane breaking up through that heavy sand and dirt, we'd take a garden hoe and skim off the top. Pretty soon you'd see that cane coming up all over the field. It was such a pretty sight. Then we'd go in there and hoe that cane and pull all the grass out of it. After that, we'd come in with the sweeps and side up that cane and break up all the dirt around it. Then we'd take some fertilizer and strow it down right beside the cane and cover that fertilizer up. We plowed it about two more times and hoed it some more, and it'd be so pretty—just like a peanut field you just plowed. Before you know it, that cane done got way up high, higher than me.

Now we 'bout ready to make syrup of that cane. We go in there before the frost kills it back and cut it down and bed some of it and put dirt on it to keep the frost from biting it and have it for seed cane the next year. We'd strip the fodder off the other cane and stack the cane and then pile all that fodder on top to keep the frost off to we ready to make syrup. Then we'd haul that cane on a wagon up to the syrup mill and make syrup. We'd make it up to Christmas, then knock off, and go back after Christmas and finish up. Oh man, growing that cane was hard work. Them cane blades would eat you raw, but peoples got used to it and didn't pay it no mind. We'd put aside some of that green cane and carry it to Union Springs and peddle it on the streets for a dime a stalk. We called ourselves making big money! We'd go home like we's rich 'cause we done sold a wagonload of cane for four or five dollars.

When we got a little age on us, some of us brothers worked for wages and on the first of the month we could go to the store and buy our sugar and coffee, but we raised just about everything else we needed. Coffee come in beans, not like it is now. You would have a coffee grinder on the side of the wall, and you'd pour that coffee in the hopper and turn the handle and grind that coffee up. Then you'd put it in your pan and boil it. It was a lot stronger than coffee is now, and you would pour some cold water in it to make the drugs go to the bottom and settle. When you'd get close to the bottom of your coffee cup, you had to strain out the grounds with your teeth.

We always had hogs for meat, and sometimes we'd trap wild game. I have taken me a hammer and gone around to the sawmill and got me some old pieces of plank and built me a trap to catch partridges. I'd take it out close to the rice field and sprinkle some rice in a trench up to that trap, and them partridges would march right on in. We had to stob that trap down to the ground or them partridges would turn it over and be gone. Sometimes we'd catch two or three dozen at the time. I have caught rabbits the same way. I'd set a trap with a trigger and sprinkle rice on it, and the rabbit would eat off that trigger and the door would fall on him—and we got him! Trapping your meat was cheaper than shooting it or raising it.

Yes sir, the way we come up was the hard way, but we learned to live with what we had. There was a grass that growed wild called pepper grass. It would grow up in a bunch before it went to seed. When it was young and tender, it would eat just like turnip tops or collards or anything you could cut for a spring vegetable. I have seen my mama go along the road banks

and it's be pretty and she'd stop and pull up a whole heap of that pepper grass and fill up a cotton basket. She'd bring it home, cut the roots off it, take the little dead leaves off and take the end tender leaves and cut em up and wash em just like a turnip green out of the garden. She'd put a little piece of meat in the pot and set it on the stove and that's what we had for dinner. Man, did them greens taste good! Now, if you was to tell peoples about eating such stuff, they'd say, "Oh no, I ain't eating none of them weeds." But when I come along in my life at home, we was glad to be eating them wild greens. We didn't have it like we got it now. In them days we got things the hard way. To us pepper grass wasn't weeds. It was something good to eat.

At home we didn't have enough real beds for everbody to sleep on. I have slept on a many a homemade bed we made out of scrap lumber from the sawmill. That bed wouldn't have but two legs that we made out of pieces of two by fours. You'd toenail a plank to the wall of the house and you'd set your two legs out from the wall. You'd build you a frame out from the wall and put slats on the bottom like a regular bed. And—man! what you talking 'bout!—you'd put a mattress on that bed and sheets and quilts and then make it up and it'd look like any other bed. Peoples back then didn't have a cotton mattress or a innerspring mattress, so we'd go to the fields after the frost had killed the crops and look for what you would call crowfoot grass that would grow way up high. We would wring it off, tear it apart and let it get good and dry, then put that grass in a mattress tick, sew it up and put it on the bed. That mattress would be just as high as a innerspring you see on a bed is now. That's the way the peoples would sleep.

White peoples and some of the older colored peoples would have feather mattresses and pillows, but we never had nothing like that. You know, it's always been some peoples that have more than others. Let's say, Miss Tress or Miss Sarah. Verse could go down to Miss Sarah's right now and say, "Well, Babe, I ain't got me no bed," and Miss Sarah would say, "Verse, there's a bed in the back room we not using, and you can have it and everthing on it." That's the way some of the older head white peoples was by the colored peoples. Some of the colored peoples worked 'round the white peoples, washing and ironing, and they would give em old feather mattresses and pillows and quilts; and the colored peoples would use that for what you'd call a company bed when somebody would come and stay all night.

Some peoples made them mattresses out of corn shucks, but we never used shucks for nothing but a scrub broom, like you use to mop the floor. We'd bore holes through a big old wide heavy board and twist shucks and stick em through the holes. We'd spread potash and water on the floor, and the more you scrubbed the tighter them shucks got in them holes and the cleaner you got the floor.

No sir, we didn't have things and go places like they do now. When night come, we went to bed. I didn't wear pants until I was a great big boy, maybe ten or more. I wore long shirts, just like a dress. Peoples thought everbody of the younger race of peoples that was in the children's size was all girls because they had on long shirts. That's a fact. Man, I didn't wear no pants when I was a young boy. That long shirt come down to near about your ankles and had a split in it where you could walk and take long steps and not tear your shirt.

Man, I tell you we'd put on our clean shirts on a Saturday evening or a Sunday morning and go fishing or set around the house or play in the banks of the road up until I was nearly about big enough to be grown. Now a boy of eight or ten or fifteen thinks he's already a man. He's got him a big pistol in his pocket, and he's drunk going down the road whooping and hollering and 'sturbing the peace. Well, when I was a boy that size, I was still in my shirt tail. Until I almost got to be a courting man, I had on a dress.

When I got to be a young man, I learned to shoot dice. I have gambled shooting dice right down that road outside this house in what was a pasture under that big old oak tree that's still there. We would shoot dice for two or three cents and stay up here way over twelve o'clock at night, and then me and brother Johnnie Lee would get out and hit that Sardis road and walk on down to the Stuckey Place. If you called yourself winning the money, it wouldn't be more than two or three dollars. There ain't nothing to shooting dice. You use two dice that's got numbers on them, and you roll them dice out and if they both together stops on six you roll until you make that six, and you win. But if you throw a seven before you roll that six, you lost, but if you throw a seven the first time you roll, you win. I have won a heap more money shooting dice than I have lost.

The first picture show I seen was right up here on the corner of Prairie Street where it is right now. It's that same building and it belonged to Mr. Fred McLendon. It was named for Mr. Fred and Miss Lillian, his wife, and they called it the Lilfred. When they put that picture show up there—man, ooooooweeeeeee!—that building wadn't big enough to hold all the peoples. They had to let some come out before the others could go in and see it. They would start it up on Saturday after dinner and run it till late Saturday night. Some peoples would stay in town to see that picture show and then have to walk eight or ten miles to get home. I done that a many a time. Back in them days, black peoples had to set upstairs in the loft. We'd go up the stairs outside and set in our seats up there, but we seen the same picture shows the white peoples seen.

Most all the peoples in my family was farmers, and we all growed up on Mr. Joe Stuckey's Place, which was three or four miles this side of Halls Cross Roads. We never owned a house or the land we worked on. Man, I remember the good times we used to have down there. Mr. Joe's sister's children from down around Clio and Clayton would come up in the summer and stay with him. All us colored and white children would play together. Mr. Joe had two goats named Blackie and Brownie we used to ride up and down the roads and pastures. The old billies had horns that come way back on their shoulders. We would outrun em and jump on em and ride em all over the place, holding on to their horns just like they was a bridle.

One of them white boys lives in Birmingham now and is a multi-millionaire. Two or three years ago, he come down here to visit his cousin, Hugh Stuckey, and I was in the A&P when they come in together. Hugh seen me and punched the fellow and told him, "That there's Tommie Manley. That's who I was telling you about I's going to find. He's the one that you and him used to ride them goats up and down the woods." The man turned around and looked at me and said, "Good morning. What is your name?" I told him. God knows I didn't know who he was. I hadn't seen him since he's a young boy. He asked me where I lived and I told him Union Springs. He said, "Where did you live before you come to Union Springs?" I told him, "I lived out the Sardis road on the Old Stuckey Place, just above that fellow you there with." He said, "Well, did you ever know a woman by the name of Clara Stephens?" I said, "I sho' did. She used to live down in Blue Spring, Alabama." He said, "Well, did you know any of her children?" I told him I did, and he said, "Who did you know?" I said, "I knowed Dudley and Earl and Elton." He said, "Well, you talking to Elton." I said, "Well, I be doggone."

He shook my hand and said, "Tommie, I'm so glad of seeing you, old boy, I don't know what in the world to do. If Hugh hadn't reminded me, I'd clean forgot you. Do you remember when we used to catch them goats behind the old Stuckey barn and ride em up and down the road?" I said, "You know I remember." He said, "Tommie, you doing all right?" I told

A rural Bullock County road — one of the few yet unpaved.

him yeah, I was doing fine. He said, "I'm just so glad to see you. I'm living in Birmingham, and anytime you there, just inquire for Elton Stephens and somebody gonna show you his house. You can stay with me all night or I'll sleep you in a motel." I sho' was glad to see that man. That big old fat rascal! I never thought I'd see him again in this life.

There ain't many of us old peoples left. Ain't but two of my family living now, me and my sister. She's old enough to be my mama. I'm the baby and here I am 'bout sixty-three. Oh man, ain't no telling how old my sister is. Let's see how many chillun is under her. There's Johnnie Lee, the one that lived down there in the curve of the road near Bread Tray Hill. She older than him. Then there's my brother Mose. She older than him. My brother Jack, too. She older than all these boys. But some of my sisters was older than her. My sister Roberta was older. She used to live down here with my sister Beatrice. But she ain't older than my brother Robert. But she way older than me— like she was my mama. Sometimes I go down to see her and she gets along mighty well. She live down there by Mr. Jim Paulk at Bonnie Plant Farm, and Mr. Jim and them takes care of her just like she was their sister.

My sister Roberta went up North and stayed in Pennsylvania for about five years, but all the others of us stayed right close to where we's borned. We all lived up and down the Sardis Road, and we wouldn't take nothing for it. We liked living 'round here. One time I went up North to New York to raise cauliflower, and one time I went up to Norfolk, Virginia; but I don't care nothing 'bout them places. I love home. I love it here where peoples know who I am. When I walk out my door, I'm just like your brother. If I was going down the road and my car was to break down at the crossroads, I wouldn't be a bit scared to stop by Miss Sarah's house and say, "Miss Sarah, come on and take me home." See, she know me. She'd say, "Well, all right, Tommie, just wait for me to shut the door and I'll carry you." And she'd bring me right on in to Union Springs. But if I was in New York today and my car broke down on the road, well, I wouldn't know nobody. Don't *nobody* know me up there. Ain't nobody gonna fool with me up there. Don't nobody care 'bout me up there. You got car trouble up there, you just somebody out on that highway walking. They probably think you'd kill them if they stopped. No sir, I love it where I'm at. I wants to be here at home where peoples know me.

A girl come out by my place the other night, and

a hose busted on her car coming from Tuskegee. Everbody passed her. Peoples didn't know who she was. Then a boy come along that knowed her car. He stopped and said, "What's the trouble, lady?" She said, "I don't know, 'cept my car done quit on me. It's done run hot or something." That fellow didn't know what was wrong but he said, "I'll tell you what. Just wait till it cools off, then crank it and drive it on down to Tommie's Place to get you some help." Well, she started it and it kept knocking and knocking till she made it to my place, and it got so hot she turned it off. I went out to start the car, but it wouldn't turn over. So I told her, "Your car ain't got no water. More than likely you got a busted hose." So I looked under the hood and sho' nuff the hose had a little stream coming out of a split a couple of inches long. I said, "That's your problem right there. Now you set here till it gets cool and I'll take that hose off and carry you to Mr. Douglas May at the Gulf Place in Union Springs and get you a new hose." Well, he didn't have one that fit, but I took one that was a near-'bout fit and jammed it on and she was able to make it back to Tuskegee that night. The next day she went and got her a hose that fit. Now, you see what I'm telling you? If she'd been where nobody knowed her, she'd been stuck. That's why I love home.

Yes sir, I have loved living here in Bullock County. Peoples have treated me just fine, white and colored. I could depend on the peoples around here. When I got in trouble, I knowed where to go for help. When Mr. Jabo was alive and anything happened to me and I went to him and told him about it, he took care of it. But times has changed. I went to the courthouse the other day to get me a tag for my Ford pickup. In the old times, when I used to need a tag, I went in to see Mr. Kilgore and he took care of me. But since the young race of peoples come, a colored man is head of that tag office. God knows, that fellow ain't qualified for the job. He don't know what to do, and he don't even ask Mr. Kilgore, "Well, say, I do like having this job, but looky here, I don't know much about this work, so when it comes time to do so-and-so, I would thank you to tell me how to do it." But you see this young race of peoples won't do that. They won't ask nothing at all. But I got the old vein of life in me. If I don't know something, I ain't too proud to ask because some peoples knows more than you do.

Just like my '67 Ford out there in the yard. A fellow named Ken fixes on that car all the time. I can fix my '46 car out there by myself. I can mighty near tell what's the matter with that car when I crank it up. But if something gets wrong with that '67, I got to carry it to somebody that's got the late years of operation in them. They can put a machine on that car and tell when a rod's out of whack and they can time it by a machine. Now, I can take my feeler gauge and go out there to my old car, pull the hood up, take the caps off my points and tell you to mash on the starter, and I can see how them points is breaking with that little old feeler gauge. I can't do that with my new car, so I take it to somebody that knows more than I do.

So I went to the courthouse the other day to get my tags, and they had a bunch of these new peoples on the job. It took me a hour or better to get my tags because nobody knowed how to fill out the tag receipts. The man would go down to another table and ask a woman something and she'd say, "You don't have to do but so-and-so." Then he'd have to ask somebody else something. I didn't used to have to wait that long. Used to, you'd go down for a tag, and they'd fill out that tax receipt, you sign your name, you pay your money, and you gone. But you can't do it that way no more.

The colored peoples have got to the place where they act like they want to hate the white peoples so bad. I asked a fellow up town this morning, I said, "Why you black peoples saying what you all say about the white peoples?" He said, "Look what the white peoples do to you." I said, "Well, looks to me like

everthing done to you, you bring it on yourself. Look at me, I'm sixty-something years old. I ain't got a enemy from no white man from one side of Alabama to the other. Why can't y'all live that way? Something is wrong with you, that's what it is. You don't want to do right; then you want the white peoples to let you run over them. I heard what that fellow said over there in that car. He said what makes him hate em is what they done way years back. They ain't done nothing to him or to you. I was living right along there too. It's funny as hell they done something to you they didn't do to me. Carry yourself right among all peoples and you'll be treated right." Now, don't forget this is what a old colored man told you. My daddy told me one time way before he died, "Tommie, if you make your bed hard, you got to lay hard. You can turn it over, but it's just as hard on one side as it is on the other."

Yes sir, you hear what I tell you. If you treat most folks right, they gonna treat you right. Now, sometimes somebody might act a little off from the way you want em to, but don't bother. If he finds out you doing right, he'll come back and maybe beg your pardon. I never will forget the time I walked into Mr. Jabo's store and a white man was in there about drunk. I was a young man along with that man and knowed him all his life. He had a pistol and said, "Hold it right there, goddamnit! You come any further and I'll shoot you down!" Mr. Jabo said, "Hey, there. Just a minute. You damn well know who Tommie is. Now you put that pistol up." I said, "Don't worry. I ain't coming no closer. I done stopped. Now may I pass on?" He said, "Yeah, go on." So I done my business and went on out. A colored boy outside said, "Man, I never would have took that." I said, "Boy, you just a fool. That man inside drinking whiskey. If I ask him about this tomorrow, he don't know about it. Hell, now I ain't hurting, and he ain't hurting. I could've gone on like a fool and maybe the man shoot me dead. He'd be sorry later, but I still be dead. But now I'll see him tomorrow, and I'll say,

'Hey man, I seen you yesterday, and you sho' had you a good drink.' Now, that'll tickle him, and he'll say, 'Tommie, now you know I didn't mean you no harm. We been knowing each other all our lives. You know I beg your pardon.'"

Yes sir, I can go 'round with any of these white peoples. They see me coming and they say, "Hey there, Tommie, how you doing?" Some of these younguns I don't even know, but their daddies done told them 'bout me. I get ready to go fishing and I walk up to a fellow and say, "Look-a-here, what about letting me go fishing in your pond this evening?" He say, "All right, Tommie, go ahead on." I was talking with a white man down at the Gulf Station the other day, and I asked him about his son. He said, "'He's mean as the devil and he don't know how to treat peoples like he should. He gets in arguments and fights. You explain something to him, and he can't see it the same way and he gets mad." I said, "Oh, he's all right with me." He said, "Tommie, he ain't all right with nobody." I said, "Well, I can go along with him when his way of doing ain't my way. So I see him and speak to him and treat him nice and let it go at that, and I don't never have no trouble with him."

Now listen to me. Some peoples is just hard to understand. Everbody's not the same. Say you got a bunch of brothers. Your brothers not like you. They don't do what you do. You can't fall out with your brothers because you do different things and has different ways. One say, "I'm a carpenter." Another say, "I'm a farmer." One man say, "I'm white." Another man say, "I'm black." Another man say, "I'm brown." We just ain't all the same. If you married and I ain't, I can't tell you 'bout married life because I ain't a married man. Peoples is all different. That's why we's so hard to understand.

I try to get along with my own peoples and understand them. In 1955 I joined the NAACP, which was way before integration. I wanted to know the meaning of what that group was, so one night I

asked one of the fellows at a NAACP meeting at the church. I said, "What is the meaning of the NAACP?" Well, he tried to explain it to me. He said it was a group started in one of the Northern states by some Negroes and Jews, but it wadn't for the money. Looked to me like he said it was what they had for a church to help the colored peoples. He said it had been running in the North ever since about 1910 and got to the Southern parts of the United States in 1955. That's when I joined.

I'm a old man now. I do all right but I don't got much health. I can't do the work like I used to do. I can't handle weight. I can't pick up more than twenty-five or thirty pounds no time. I believe it saved my life when I went to the penitentiary. Man, I had a better time in the pen than I did at home. They treat you so nice, and every week I'd go to the doctor and get a check-up. That's where I found out 'bout my high blood pressure. See, I was running 'round and getting tired and couldn't breathe, and I just had to set down a lot and rest. Sometimes I had a bad headache from my blood. What I had was a bad heart and didn't know it. They treated me for all my bad health and give me some medicine and a prescription to go by. I used to think my heart would never heal. But by the help of the Lord, it did get all right. I expect I'd be dead right now if I hadn't been sont to the pen. One day I'd've just fell out in the woods dead. Yes sir, it saved my life. Look at old Red Driggers. When Red went in, he was the poorest old skinny man you ever did see, always looking so bad. Now he's a big fat rascal. He done gained weight, running 'round patting on his belly. Old Red done got in good shape.

My lungs must be strong or they'd be give out by now. I been smoking this Prince Albert since 1924, and I like to roll my own cigarettes. I don't like the taste of ready-rolls. I like the taste of Prince Albert, but I know it puts that nicotine on your lungs. Sometimes I smoke filters now. Them filter cigarettes has cotton that catches the nicotine and it turns yellow to show

how much it saves off your lungs. But I rather be smoking my Prince Albert all the time.

I still got poor circulation or what some peoples calls arthritis. The doctor tells me there ain't no such thing as that because any time when your joints hurt and you can't bend em, that's because the fluid of your body can't circulate to them joints. Your joints becomes dry and crack like a broke stick when you move. If I take the tablets he give me, that will make my fluid circulate to them weak places and make me strong. Used to before I begin taking them tablets, when I would get out of the car and come to the house, and I'd go up the doorsteps and when I got to the last step, I'd get ready to put all my weight on my leg to come on in the house and I would go down on that leg. I had trouble on that porch a many a day. Now when I take them tablets, I don't be weak. When they all gone, I goes to the drugstore and gets me some more.

New Hope Baptist Church in High Ridge. Tommie and Verse are both buried in the cemetery across the road.

I got all them bad ailments to my body that I have to doctor, and I got old age, too. But I'm doing all right. Sometimes all I do is go down to the Gulf Station and set around and look at the peoples, then get up and come on home and go to bed. I know I done got old up in the standard of life. I don't eat much as I used to because I don't have much appetite, and I'm glad of it. I don't due to be fat anyhow. I was weighing over two hundred when I went in the penitentiary, and I come out weighing 161. I weigh 'bout 190 now, but I still feels good. I feels good in my age.

Things just ain't no way like they used to be. If they was, we'd have better living. People talking 'bout, "Man, I wouldn't swap my life now for the old life, uh-uh." Well, I wish all the old times would come back in circulation, but I know the old days ain't never coming back. I was telling Jack Hall the other day that he was as good a carpenter as there is in this country. I said, "Jack, you and your brothers ought to get together and fix up the old house where you was born and bred. I would feel grateful if you boys would do that. Fix it up and give it some paint. I would be so glad to go by there and see where Mr. Jabo and Miss Sarah used to live in the young years of their lives."

Everthing is different now. The young race of peoples don't care nothing 'bout you. Peoples live a fast life. They ain't got time to fool with you. The black peoples is all right—I'm in the race of them—but they don't lose time with each other. One is too quick to laugh at what the other one ain't got and don't know. If I don't know something, I would thank you to tell me. But peoples ain't got time to spend with you now. And you can't tell the young peoples nothing. They'll kill you in a minute—black or white.

I have had a good life. Some parts looked bad to me back then, but it was a better life than it is now. I didn't make much money and I can make more now at my little store, but I had better times. It wadn't no outlaws or rogues then. We never had no misdemeanors because there wadn't no such things as Rockolas and dance halls. Out in the country we'd play baseball and then go home and go to bed. It was a more Christian life. Peoples is so low down and mean now and just wanna do something wrong. The jailhouse up town is full of peoples right now. You wonder to your soul why they done what they done to be there. The sheriff got into trouble because he locked up a woman's son he caught doing something wrong. She said, "I never will vote for you again because you put my boy in jail." Well, that boy deserved to be in jail.

The world just ain't like it used to be. If I was a young child and went down to Miss Sarah's house and done something wrong, she'd whup me, and I'd be scared to tell Mama because she would whup me again when I got home. But now if you hit somebody's child, here come his daddy with a shotgun hunting you, and saying, "What you hit my boy for?" I say, "Well, he done this-and-that wrong, and I whupped him for it." And he say, "Well, don't you ever put your hand on him again or I'll blow your head off." That's the way the world is now. I don't see nothing going on out on the street that concern me now. I go around it and go on ahead because I know I'm gonna get in some trouble if I stop.

I tell you the truth, there ain't but one thing I know I got to do now. I know I got to die. My mama had eighteen chillun, and they all gone but me and one sister. Don't you know that one day I got to go, too. I know that. When you get old and traveled down, you just want to pray and try to serve the Lord. All the power's in His hands.

I'm so glad I been talking to you in my kitchen about what I done in my life. The old days and the old ways are something to think about. When I'm gone you can set down and tell the peoples, "I want y'all to hear 'bout this man. He was a old fellow and I knowed him all my life. I was a little baby when he was a man. These things he told me he had to know, or he wouldn't have been able to tell me." I know you wouldn't take nothing in the world for talking with Tommie. Now I got to go out yonder on the highway and operate my little store. Then I'm gone come home and look at the all-star game on TV this evening.

POSTSCRIPT: Tommie Manley died December 20, 1983, at the age of sixty-nine and was buried in the New Hope Baptist Church Cemetery near High Ridge. According to his obituary in the *Union Springs Herald,* he was survived by his wife Verse and a son, presumably from another relationship.

HOBSON ROUGHTON

Historian and Folk Artist

The interview on which this monologue is based was conducted on July 16, 1977, in the living room of Hobson Roughton's home in the High Ridge community at Hooks Cross Roads. Mr. Roughton and his wife Anne built their small frame house in 1938 and have lived there since. Their only child Carol is married and lives in Anniston. Mrs. Roughton served us lemonade and sat in the room as we talked.

My memories of Hobson are always associated with the annual 4th of July homecoming and all-day singing at Macedonia Baptist Church, which he talks about in detail. With his rather formal manner, his impeccable dress, and proper English, he always stood out in a country crowd. Although, as he tells us proudly, his roots go deep into Bullock County soil, he seemed to me more like a stranger who had come into our community to live. Perhaps that is the way he felt about himself.

I'm an amateur genealogist and I've always been interested in my family tree. My roots in Bullock County go back to 1834, when John Dozier moved to Sardis from South Carolina. He married Amy Youngblood, whose family was also one of the earliest white families to move here when this country was opened up for settlement. My great-grandfather Loveless Roughton was born in South Carolina in 1804 and moved to Alabama in 1837, when he married a daughter of John Dozier and Amy Youngblood. They first lived in the Sardis community, which was then in Macon County, and about 1846 they moved over here to High Ridge. I was able to pinpoint when Loveless Roughton came here because he belonged to the Dry Creek Baptist Church in what is now Saluta County, South Carolina, and he wrote back there for his church letter. He came off without it; and in those days if you moved into a community and were not a church member, you were just about an outcast. I got hold of the minutes of his home church, and they showed where he had written requesting his church letter.

I've also found a record of where John Dozier sold the old Sardis Baptist Church some land in 1842, and the present building was constructed soon after that. The church had been formed a few years before, in 1837.

All my kinfolks—the Doziers, Roughtons, the Youngbloods—were, therefore, pioneer families in Bullock County. In the 1840s my fourth great uncle, William R. Youngblood, built his home just a few yards from where I live now. It is what we call the old homeplace. I lived in that house from 1922 until I married. It's where the Hookes live now. My parents were married there, and that's where they both died. Their caskets rested on the same spot where they took their wedding vows in 1894.

This part of the county was opened for white settlement about 1834. High Ridge was then a part of Pike County until Bullock was formed in 1866. Soon after they moved here, the Youngbloods intermarried with the Beans, another early family that settled around what is now called Beans Cross Roads. Thomas Youngblood, a brother of William, gave the land for Liberty Baptist Church, which was formed in 1837. William and his wife Mary Dorn Youngblood gave Macedonia Baptist Church forty acres of land, but twenty of it was sold off later.

I don't know exactly when my maternal line came from Stuart County, Georgia, to Barbour County; but I know they moved here from Barbour in the latter part of the nineteenth century.

A lot of the men in my family tree have been soldiers. My grandfathers, John Tyler Roughton and Matthew Marion Brooks, fought in the Civil War on the "winning side," the Confederacy. Grandfather Brooks was just a kid and went in along the last of the war and didn't get a scratch. My mother always told me that my Grandmother Brooks, who was a Martin, lost her father and two brothers from Shady Grove in Stuart County, Georgia, in the war. All the men had gone from that community and my grandmother, before she was married, served as the church clerk because there were no men left to take over. I think the Brookses and the Martins had all come originally from South Carolina. I haven't been able to trace them, but I know there were five Brooks brothers that fought in the Revolution. I think James Brooks was the one I'm descended from. Before he came to Alabama, my great-great grandfather John Dozier fought in the War of 1812.

Now we'll get closer to my own time. My daddy married in 1894, and his first child, a daughter, was born in 1895. They had three more girls; then I was born on October 29, 1910. It had been almost ten years since they had had a child, and I could never figure out whether I was a surprise or a disappointment. My oldest sister was Jimmie Lee Roughton, and she never married. She taught school and died in an automobile wreck in 1941 coming back from Florida. The next one was

A newspaper photo of Hobson Roughton.

Dora Mae that married Allen Faulkner. She had nine children and is still living. Eight of her children were with her for the Fourth of July homecoming and singing at Macedonia Church. Another sister was Anna Ree, who married Allen Faulkner's brother, Willie H. Faulkner. They have six children.

My youngest sister Lillian married Seals Hooks, and they have six children, five boys and a girl named Lillian Faye. My niece, Donna Mae Faulkner, is interested in genealogy and has traced the Faulkner family through wills and deeds way back to South Carolina. I don't know whether they are related to the

writer William Faulkner, but I'm sure all the Faulkners are kin if you go back far enough. I've heard that the family was originally German and migrated from Germany to the British Isles.

There's been quite a bit of intermarrying among families on the Ridge, and most of the old families are related in some way. The Hubbards, the Pritchetts, and the Youngbloods and many other families are all kin. In fact, there's distant relationship between my sisters and the Faulkner family they married into and between my sister Lillian and the Hooks family she married into. Many of the black people are related to prominent white families. I know a number of Negroes who are kin to well-to-do whites, but I'm not going to say which ones! It so happens that my wife Anne and I are not related at all. Maybe that's because she's from Bessemer in Jefferson County! From what I can find out, her people were from Birmingham and Huntsville and up into Tennessee.

We met when I was in Bessemer in C. C. C. Camp during the Depression. A friend of hers introduced us, and I still let her come visit us, despite what happened.

One reason for all the intermarrying is that not many new families have moved to the Ridge in the past one hundred years. But there have been a few. Lawrence Maxwell's father, Albert Maxwell, moved in down here in 1921. He was living in Chicago and saw this land advertised for sale and wanted it for his father and mother, so he bought it and moved them and a couple of their girls who hadn't married yet down here. He stayed a while and then went back north. He later went to Kingsport, Tennessee, where he was in the publishing business. He then moved to

Florida, then to Gulf Shores, Alabama, and finally moved back to this community. He is eighty-eight years old and retired. His son Lawrence has lived here a long time and is married to Martha Dean Wilson, a native of the Ridge. There's also a Darling family that has moved in recently, but I don't know a thing about them. And a family with a French name, the Betins, moved in here about five years ago.

So not many people have come in, but quite a few have moved away. We have many names of people in both the Macedonia and Mt. Hilliard church cemeteries that have no descendants living here. I can think of the Cockrofts, who were among the earliest settlers here and helped organize Macedonia Church. Their descendants have all moved to Texas. Up around Mt. Hilliard the McCreus family was very prominent in the early days of this community, but we don't have anybody by that name here now. They all moved to Texas, too. In the 1880s we had a great exodus of people moving out and going to Texas. They thought they could find greener pastures there. I suppose some of them did. Dorn and Strom are two more pioneer names that we don't have here any more. They moved to Texas—or somewhere. I'm sure that the South Carolina Senator, Strom Thurmond, is related to the ones that came here. I know I am, on my Reynolds side.

All this moving out has left the population of Bullock County at a low ebb. The highpoint was around the turn of the century, when most of the land was farmed. A lot of the merchants and professional men in Union Springs had plantations out in the county. Some timber was sold but very little. Then in the 1940s and 1950s cattle and pulpwooding began to crowd out the farmers. Small and medium-sized farms were no longer profitable, and people stopped farming. Everybody was trying to get cows and turn their land into pasture. It's amazing now to see even one field that's plowed. You can ride for miles and miles and never see a sign of agricultural growth at all.

Most farming these days is done on a large scale, and even that's not very profitable around here. The people who were displaced from farming began to get automobiles, and they could still live out in the country but work in a store or small factory in a nearby town. It is very common now for people to commute thirty-five or forty miles to work in Montgomery or Troy and still live in this community.

There used to be a lot of little country stores all over the county. My father kept one most of the time I was growing up. He had some kind of store even before he got married. At one time he ran one out at Mascot, which was a little settlement between Hooks Cross Roads and Inverness. The Howells lived there in a big two-story house, which has long since burned. They had a large general merchandise store, and my dad worked for them for a while. Then he helped run a store over at Thompson's Station.

The store he ran at Almeria was small and when you walked in the door, the odor almost knocked you down—the smells of soda crackers, salt, sugar, coffee, nutmeg and other spices, and salt fish in a large open can. He sold Coca-Colas before they put the corset on the bottle. Back then they were called dopes because they contained a lot of cocaine. In all his stores he sold the goods people needed—sugar, flour in barrels or in twenty-four and forty-eight pound sacks, coffee beans that would be taken home and parched and ground, bulk salt, plow points, sweeps, scrapes, plow lines, mule collars and mule pads. He also carried some dry goods, but for large and more expensive items people had to go to Post Oak, where Mr. Jim Powell had a large general merchandise store. Or they could go over to Mr. Ben Griswold's large store at Mt. Hilliard. He carried a little of everything, too. Once or twice a year farmers might have to go to town to get supplies like seed or guano or to settle up with the bank, but these community stores served their everyday needs. Of course, people raised most of what they ate, so they didn't have to buy a lot. They had pork, lard, bacon, and ham in the smokehouse. They had canned vegetables and meat and sausages and sugar cane syrup. They had chickens and turkeys and guineas in the yard for eggs and meat, and they could always find wild meat in the woods.

Daddy did a good business, but he was not a good businessman. He always let anybody have anything they needed on credit. He'd have had a fortune if everybody had paid him. Almost all his customers were farmers—there was nothing else to do—and sometimes they just wouldn't make enough to pay their accounts off, so Daddy would close a debt—write it off—and then let the man start a new account. He always felt sorry for people worse off than him. Of course, he lost some of his money to sorry white people and sorry Negroes who wouldn't have paid him even if they'd had the money. I think he would have been more successful if he'd lived in a town and become a big-store merchant. He once had an opportunity to open a store in Fairfield, near Birmingham, but he didn't take it. His life—and mine too—might have been different if he had said yes. He loved merchandising but he was just too free-hearted. He didn't know how to say no.

Before my time Daddy also used to haul bales of cotton to Montgomery. The cotton had already been ginned at cotton gins that you could find at every major crossroads in the county. There was even a horsedrawn gin over at the old Hubbard place, and when I was a child, we went and looked at the ruins of it. After their cotton was ginned and baled, farmers who could afford to would hold their cotton until prices went up, and then take it to Montgomery to sell to brokers. They went by wagon and it took two days going and two days coming back. They would form a caravan and camp out on the way there and on the way back. He said they always took a little something to quench their thirst, and they'd have some lively parties going and coming. It was a time of celebration as well as a business trip. In Montgomery they'd sleep

The road marker at the once-thriving Inverness community.

in the hayloft of the livery stables while waiting to sell their cotton.

After the sale the farmers would have a considerable amount of money, and the merchants in Montgomery were always courting them. They wanted to sell them a wagonload of goods to take back home. Daddy used to tell the story about an old farmer who went to an old Jew's store and asked him, "Can you let me have a little sugar, enough to get back on?" The old Jew said, "Go righta in back and helpa yourself. No charge." The storekeeper thought he'd get maybe a few ounces for his coffee while he was camping out on the way home. And he must have thought the old farmer would spend a lot of money on other goods. Well, the farmer stayed and stayed in the backroom and finally came out. It was a sight to see! What he had done was take his pants and drawers off and tied up the legs of his homemade drawers and filled each leg with sugar and then thrown them over his shoulders. He put his pants back on and came out to thank the storekeeper for the sugar. The old Jew looked at the drawers filled with sugar and said in utter disbelief, "You musta live a longa way from here!" I've heard my daddy tell that story many a time and die laughing every time.

Now, Daddy was a big prankster himself when he was a boy, and he loved to tell us stories about the practical jokes he pulled. He and his friends were very mischievous, but they did it all for amusement, without intending to be harmful. Several years ago I wrote down some of the stories he told in a column I wrote for the *Herald* called "Sandspurs and Daisies." One time they made up a prank in which they were going to steal a turkey from Dr. Reynolds, who lived between here and Mt. Hilliard. They always selected a boy who would bear the brunt of the prank. They made it up that they were going to steal the turkey, and they told Dr. Reynolds of their plot. He agreed to play along with them. So one night all the boys gathered at an old vacant house where they said they were going to cook their stolen turkey. My daddy and the boy who was going to be the butt of the joke went up to Dr. Reynolds's house well after dark. Daddy said he made a lot of noise going up to where the turkeys were roosting on a fence. The doctor heard them coming and was waiting with his shotgun, as they had arranged. When Daddy reached up and grabbed an old gobbler, the turkeys started fluttering and jumping and running over tin buckets in the yard. Suddenly, the back door opened and the doctor came running out with his shotgun, which he shot straight up in the air. My daddy fell over like he was shot and started moaning and crying. The other boy jumped over the fence and ran all the way back to the vacant house where the other boys were waiting and hollered out of breath, "They done shot Walt, and he's dying, and I'm going to Texas." Before they could stop him, he took off and the boys had to search all night before they found him at daylight crowded up in a railfence corner crying. He was scared to death because he had been involved in stealing a turkey when my daddy was shot. He was headed for Texas, like a lot of people around here when they got into trouble. He didn't know anything about Texas, except that there he'd be safe from the law.

Lou Hall Driggers and Odessa Driggers at Jabo Hall's country store, c. 1956.

Those were hard times for everybody, and a

A postcard view of Court Square in Montgomery, Alabama, near the turn of the century.

little homemade fun made life bearable. My family probably had it easier than most, and we could hardly get by sometimes. Daddy did a little farming, but the land was so poor he never did make a worthwhile crop. Most of the children in our community attended school at least part of the year, but many of them had to stay home during the planting and growing season and work in the fields. The school term was only eight months long. My daddy never made me stay at home to work. On weekends and during the summers, of course, we all worked around the farm because there was always something to do. As a small child I dropped peas between corn hills and a plow would come along and cover them up. I also remember turning watermelon and sweet potato vines with a stick from one side to the other so that a plow could come through. I've also chopped and hoed cotton. I remember once going to the fields to help bring in a load of velvet beans and having them sting me all over. Now that was miserable! We grew them to

feed to the cows, but I don't know how they ever ate such hard beans. Some people would soak them in water before they fed them to the stock.

I used to do a bit of plowing, but I thought any idiot could get behind a mule and follow him up one row and down another. I began to hate farming with a passion. I remember one time we had an old man who was helping us plow a new ground. A new ground is where the bushes and trees have been cut down and burned and the stumps and roots have been left to rot. It's really tricky to plow. You go a little piece and you strike a root and you break a plow point. Or your plow hits a stump and the plow handles stick in your cheek or stomach. It was painful. Well, this old fellow was out there one day plowing a steer. You know a steer is a bull that has been castrated and is not very cooperative even on the best of land. Finally, the old man hit a stump, broke a plow point and had the breath knocked out of him. I looked over at him, and there he was sitting flat down on the ground disgusted, as he announced to the world, "What, me plow a steer all the days of my life and then die and go to hell? I'll be god-damned if I will!" That's about the way I felt about farming generally. It was too late for the old man to do anything else, but I hoped I could do better.

My father and mother provided our family with sufficient clothes, an adequate shelter, and enough to eat. Throughout most of the spring and summer and fall we would have something fresh to eat from the garden. I remember one mild winter when my mother went out and picked butterbeans for Christmas dinner. We cured our meat and Mama would can sausage in fifty-pound lard cans. We kept our milk in a cooler we dropped down in the well. In the early thirties we got an icebox when ice trucks began to come through our community. Then in 1939 we got electricity and our lives changed dramatically. We could preserve our food and milk, make ice cream, and see at night. Throughout my childhood conditions were gradually improving, but I'd already decided that I didn't want to be a farmer or a storekeeper. There weren't many other career opportunities open to me, but I knew that an education would help to buy me a ticket out of the cotton field and the store house, so I got all we could afford.

I started school at Almeria and finished at Inverness when I was sixteen. Almeria was a three-room school and I spent eight years in those rooms. My most influential teacher at Almeria was Charles R. Harrison, who taught me all I know about plain old English grammar and all I know about plain old arithmetic. At Almeria we had chapel daily and Mr. Harrison would read the Bible, but he was so slow I thought he'd never get the children of Israel out of the wilderness! He was a Bible scholar and would read and explain in detail each verse. The Israelites wandered forty years in the wilderness before they could reach the Promised Land, and I thought it was going to take Professor Harrison that long to tell us about it. He was

from Greenville and came to the county in the 1890s and taught first at Mt. Hilliard and then in 1920 came to Almeria, where he was a teacher and principal. He was a widower and raised his son and daughter by himself. He had his own house but it was a custom that single teachers live with families in the community. One of the teachers, Miss Annie Jenkins, boarded with us for a while.

I enrolled at Inverness School in 1924 and had some wonderful teachers there: Miss Myra Cade, Miss Louvinia Chance, Miss Ethel Ellis, and Mr. Marcus Lawson. I had finished when Mr. John Floyd Hamilton became principal in the fall of 1927; but since I couldn't go to college then, I went back and took some more subjects. I had flunked plane geometry under Mr. Hightower and took it again under Mrs. Estelle Campbell and made an *A*. She knew how to teach math. I also took English under Mrs. Campbell for one year, but she wasn't such a good English teacher, and that was my best subject. I was always fond of Mr. Hamilton, and after I was grown and married we became good friends. My wife and I spent Sunday afternoon with him two weeks before he died.

I wasn't an athlete in school, but I did like dramatics. Back then the faculty would put on an all-school play at the end of the school year, and I was in several of them. People in the community would really turn out for them. There was a picture show by then in Union Springs, but that was a little far for most people to go out at night, even if they had a car. I'm still interested in dramatics and recently the Happy Valley Recreation Club staged a womanless wedding at Almeria, and I played the drunken minister who performed the ceremony.

Although I wasn't much involved with sports in high school, like everyone else in grammar school I played a lot of different games, like townball. It was different from softball or baseball because you were put out between bases by being hit with the ball. You could also be put out after you batted if someone on the opposing team caught your ball in the air or on first bounce. All the batters had to be put out before you could change sides. The balls were homemade and softer than balls today. We would start out with a small rubber ball and wrap unraveled socks around it until it became the size of a baseball. I remember one time somebody took tongues out of old shoes and sewed them around the ball to make it look like a baseball. If that ball hit you, you felt it. We also made our crude-looking bats, which were usually little more than flat boards with one end shaped for a handle. Paddle-cat was another game we played. It was played with four people, two on a side—a pitcher, a batter, a hind catcher, and a fielder. There were two bases and the object was to hit the runner between bases.

Another game we played that you never hear of anymore was called stealing sticks. You draw a line and have a pile of sticks on either side. Then you choose an equal number of players for both sides, and the object is to cross that line and grab a stick without being caught. If you were caught you were put in your opponents' stickpile, and to be released, a player from your side had to slip through the line and grab you by the hand and get you back across the line before he was touched. The game was won when one side had stolen all the sticks from the other side. It may sound like a very simple game, but it was a lot of fun to play.

There were many other games that we country children played without benefit of store-bought toys. We boys had jumping and running contests. For jumping we'd go in the woods and cut us down two little saplings and trim off the branches and set them up in the ground and put us a reed across them and raise it as we jumped higher and higher. Another game we enjoyed was skin-the-cat, which was played with a limb which had been stripped of its bark and placed between posts several feet above the ground. You would jump up and catch the limb and raise your body supported by your hands and bring your feet up and take them in between your hands and the limb.

Then you'd flip over, turn loose, and hit the ground on your feet—or so you hoped. It was something like playing on the parallel bars in a gym today. We also played see-saw with a piece of plank across a block of wood, and sometimes we'd make what we called a flying jinny. That was a tree trunk with a piece of board fastened to it that would spin around on the trunk. It was arranged so that as you ran around the trunk it would lift you off your feet and take you spinning round and round.

Serenade was a community game that was played not only by young people but people of all ages. It was a sort of practical joke that people played on each other. The players would gather all the noisemakers they could find—pans and tubs and spoons, plow parts, bells, hunter's horns, anything you could make a noise with. Then the players would meet at the first house they planned to serenade and everybody would beat and rattle and blow their noisemakers loud enough to wake the devil. When they had aroused all the people in the first house, they would move on to the next one and then the next far on into the night. One time my father found out that he was the target for a serenade and decided to play a trick on the serenaders. He tied a plow line across the front of the house inside the gate; and when the serenaders rushed through the gate, they were knocked down by the tight rope.

Christmas and the Fourth of July were the two holidays that children looked forward to. We'd get a few gifts from Santa Claus at Christmas, plus fire-crackers and candy, fruit, nuts, and other drugstore treats we didn't see any other time of the year. But the biggest community event for all ages was the Fourth of July Singing at Macedonia Baptist Church just down the road from here. It was already an institution when I was a boy, having started a few years after the War Between the States. I remember hearing old people telling about the beginning of the tradition, and I've tried to reconstruct the early years of the event. Times were very hard for our defeated ancestors and many changes were taking place in their way of life. People in this community felt the need for some wholesome diversion to take their minds off their troubles. They decided upon an all-day singing with dinner on the ground. On July 4, 1870, people from many miles around drove to Macedonia Church in their wagons, buggies, on horseback, and on foot bringing boxes and trunks of food for the first all-day singing. They also brought their books of Sacred Harp songs, a type of singing that is done without musical instruments. The singers sing just four notes, then go back and sing the words.

At noon on that first singing the people left the church house and went outside to open their boxes of food brought from home—just everything you could imagine—from fried chicken and squirrel to bowls of garden vegetables and delicious desserts of sweet potato pie, cobblers, and egg custards. A very special feature was also started that first day, barbecue pork and Brunswick Stew that were prepared on the grounds. The barbecue was cooked in pits dug in the ground, starting before daylight in the morning. The stew was a kind of hash made from pork, chicken, wild game, as well as such vegetables as corn, tomatoes, and butterbeans. When they finished eating dinner, they went back inside the church for an afternoon of singing. The first gathering was so successful, the church decided to make the singing an annual affair.

Social life was so limited in those days, and news of the singing spread so rapidly, that large numbers of people began to gather each year. Women would spend days preparing food to bring in their baskets and trunks. Soon the annual affair became also something of a fashion parade. Every lass, no matter how poor, had to have a new outfit, usually homemade. The boys and men, too, strutted in their new clothes. Many a romance sprang up as boys and girls got to know each other, sipping lemonade and strolling down the shady paths to the nearby spring or singing

harmony in the old church house. Of course, not everyone was inside the church all the time. A lot of people milled around outside all day, visiting, courting, and eating ice cream. For youngsters, it was like Christmas in the summertime. Lemonade was made by the barrel and ice cream was made in five-gallon freezers turned by the Negro help who sang their own songs as they worked. The lemonade was served in glasses and the ice cream in saucers which were dipped in water after each serving. This, of course, was the time before ice cream cones, paper cups, and all the to-do about sanitation. As late as the thirties and the forties it was unusual for most people to have ice, so someone would buy large blocks of ice and put them in pits in the ground covered with sawdust. Then they would chip off pieces as needed to freeze the ice cream or to cool soft drinks.

Some of the wealthier families brought their Negro nurses to look after the babies. They spread pallets in the shade and visited while the youngsters they were tending crawled about or slept. In those early days some families were driven by their Negro drivers, who stayed with the animals, feeding and watering them throughout the day.

For almost a century it was considered an all-day affair, with people coming early and staying late. The sun rose on many a family as they jostled for miles along dusty roads in wagons and buggies—and later, cars—to attend the big singing. Some people didn't see each other except on this occasion each year, and they parted reluctantly. The setting sun caught many families still on the road, the children drowsing or sleeping after a long day of play and food, the older people reminiscing about the songs they sang and the people they saw during this special day that came but once a year.

Well into the 1960s and even down to the present, people still gather to sing the old-fashioned music and eat barbecue and good homecooked food. But the numbers are down from what they were when I was a boy. A lot of old people still consider the singing almost a religious obligation, but other forms of amusement and fast cars take many of the young people to other places on the holiday. There have been other changes too. In addition to the Sacred Harp singing, people sing the seven shaped-note music to the accompaniment of a piano. People have become so softened by electric fans and air conditioning, they won't brave the heat to walk about the churchyard, eating and visiting, and they certainly wouldn't stay inside a steamy church to hear old-timey singing all day long. So now the church is air-conditioned and has all the comforts of a modern home. Most people who come stay for the morning sing and noon dinner and then go home. They no longer mill about and go down to the old spring. Some of us now bring lawn chairs and park them in the shade outside and don't even go inside to hear the singing. For us, it's mostly a homecoming time when we can renew friendships.

Well, maybe it's for the best. Maybe the fewer people who come to the singing now are coming for the right reasons. In the old days a lot of people came to do mischief and because they didn't have anything else to do. Our baptismal pool was next to the spring that was across the road from the church building and down in the woods. The growth down there was so dense that you could go a few yards in there and nobody could see or hear you. When I was a youngster, I remember there was a peg-leg man who came to the singing every year. He never went inside the church. He'd go across the road, deep into the woods. Everybody said he was a big-time gambler. I don't know anything for sure about him, but I do know for a fact that there was a lot of drinking and gambling that went on out in those woods. A lot of young boys got their first taste of whiskey out there. From the beginning, the singing attracted people who had no intention of listening to the singing. It was just an excuse to get together.

I'll have to confess that I was one of that number. I seldom went inside. I don't care much for the Sacred Harp, high-pitched music. I prefer trained voices. So I mostly stayed outside and clerked at the concession stand, which the church rented out each year to the highest bidder. My daddy won the franchise almost every year, and we sold ice cream, lemonade, chewing gum, and bottled drinks. I suppose that's the reason I don't remember much about the actual singing or the singers. The only singer I can call to mind right now is Charley May's wife Hattie, who sang high soprano. But I recognize that the singing has served an important religious as well as social function for this community for well over one hundred years. It's an important part of our tradition.

Macedonia, the home of the singing, is my home church. But I've always been kind of a half-breed. My daddy was a Methodist, and my mother was a Baptist, and neither one of them would ever change. In those days most country churches had services once a month, so their services didn't conflict, and we attended both. When I was sixteen, I joined at Macedonia and was baptized. My wife is a Methodist, and when our daughter chose the Methodists, I went over with her so we'd all be together at Mt. Hilliard Methodist Church. Anne has always said she couldn't join my church because she'd have to be immersed, and she was afraid of that much water. So my family now goes to Mt. Hilliard, but it's at a low point. Only a few families have kept it alive. Both Macedonia and Mt. Hilliard have gone up and down. One time Mt. Hilliard had a very active Sunday School, and we didn't have one at Macedonia, so a lot of Baptists went over to Mt. Hilliard. The two churches are just a few miles apart and have always cooperated, arranging their services and protracted meetings so as not to conflict. In fact, we've had so much intermarriage that we've had to learn to get along together. The Baptists and Methodists have always gotten along very well around here, but a few years ago, back in the 1950s, the Church of Christ came into the Almeria community and caused a lot of dissension. They are like the Catholics. They believe if you're not a member of their church you're lost and condemned to hell. I hear there's been a Holiness Church started out on Rabbit Road between here and Beans Cross Roads, but I've not been there and I don't intend to. The Methodists and the Baptists are sufficient for me and my family.

I hate to see churches fight each other and steal each other's members because the churches are an important influence and have been centers of community life. Most of the older churches still survive, though a few have had to close for lack of members. One such church is not far from here, the Old Union Baptist Church, a Primitive Baptist church that goes back to 1835. Our county historical society helped to get it placed on the Alabama Register of Landmarks and Heritage a couple of years ago. At one time in the 1890s it had a membership of more than seventy, but it dwindled and finally stopped having regular services in the 1920s. Like most churches in the South before the Civil War, it had a number of slave members and special pews where the Negro members sat. After they got their freedom, blacks began forming their own churches, and they quickly became centers of black community life. During the civil rights movements of the 1950s and 1960s, blacks held meetings in their churches. In the early 1950s they secretly organized a chapter of the NAACP at a black Baptist church over near Midway.

I've always gotten along fine with Negroes. I've had many Negro friends through the years. I used to be a very liberal person, but when forced integration came along, I became a strong segregationist. I'll be very frank. I don't want anything or anyone crammed down my throat. I want to select my own friends. When I was a boy I would slip off and play with the black children on our farm. They taught me one of my favorite childhood pastimes, how to take a stiff wire and roll an iron ring along the road. The rings came from wagon axles. The wire was straight except at the bottom where you folded it and put it under the wheel to control it while it was rolling along. It may not seem like a very exciting game to children these days, but we got a lot of enjoyment out of rolling those rings up and down the roads. It required a lot of skill to push the ring along and keep it going without falling over. It took special skill to run it through a sandbed.

I learned a lot from my black playmates. I'm sure I liked to play with them because they were so agreeable. It had been inborn into them to take orders from the white man, so even as children they respected you. I never did mistreat them. They always went along the way I wanted to go and play the way I wanted to play. We had a lot of good fun together. Even today there are some Negroes I'd rather associate with than whites. Before forced integration, if a Negro wanted to come to my church and worship, I'd say yes, come. Today, I'd be suspicious of their motives because they might want to stir up trouble and not worship. I don't think integration has been very good for either race. Our educational standards are lower now. People have become lazy. The government is handing out too much for nothing. They are feeding kids at school for free and teaching them that they don't have to work because the government will take care of them. Yes sir, my attitudes have changed a lot since forced integration.

I have lived in Bullock County all my life, and I suppose I'll die here. Anne and I still live in the house we built and moved into in 1938, almost forty years ago. Our daughter Carol has married and left home. She married James Beverly Hodge in a big church wedding at Mt. Hilliard. We were so sad to be losing her, but we knew she was a grown woman, and it was time for her to make a life of her own. Just before the wedding, however, we thought she might change her mind. She cried all day long the day before the wedding. Anne said, "Carol, now if you don't want to go through with it, there's still time to reconsider." Carol said, "No, Mother, I know I want to get married, but I've just realized that I'll have to leave my home and my parents." Even the wedding itself was tearful, not only for Anne and me but for the bride and groom. Both of them cried so much throughout the service we couldn't hear a word they said.

I'm retired now and spend my time in a lot of activities. I have a great deal of trouble hearing and depend solely on my hearing aid, which I started wearing in my thirties. I've tried not to let my hearing be a handicap, and I don't intend to let it be now. I don't spend my time rocking on the front porch and watching the world go by. I'm active in a retirees club that meets at noon every two weeks down at the Almeria clubhouse, the same building I used to go to school in. We have a community club that meets at night. We play games like bingo, and some of the ladies knit. Our members include friends we've known all our lives—Mrs. Hosea Sellers, the Jim Roughtons, Mrs. Ford Windham, Annie Mae Brooks, Lorene Brooks, the Jim Caylors, Albert Maxwell—he's eighty-eight now—Clarence and Gladys Riles, Mrs. Sally Davis—about seventeen of us in all.

My retirement has also given me time to indulge my long-held passion for history. Several years ago I helped Mrs. Walter Cogdell and others organize the Bullock County Historical Society, and I've been active in helping to record community and church histories and stories. My research has taken me to the county records and newspaper files in the courthouse. I've learned a lot about the people who lived in this county before us, both the saints and the sinners. One of the most fascinating stories I've learned about concerns a family that used to live over near Farriorville, which is now called Post Oak, back in the 1850s.

An old man named Frizzle, a prominent slave owner and a deacon at Liberty Church, had a widowed daughter and her children living with him. At that time there lived in Farriorville a blacksmith and carriage maker named Herman Comisky, an immigrant from Poland. He was shrewd and resourceful—and as it turned out, a fugitive from justice, a fact which Mr. Frizzle apparently found out about. When he discovered that Comisky was paying court to his daughter, he objected strenuously. When he learned that they planned to get married, he made plans to go to Troy, which was then the county seat of that part of what is now Bullock County, and ask the grand jury to indict the Pole for his crimes. On the day he was to leave for Troy, he became ill after eating breakfast and died soon thereafter, along with two or three of his grandchildren. It was soon determined that Comisky had learned of Mr. Frizzle's plans and had bought a large amount of arsenic. He then persuaded Anika, a young mulatto girl who assisted the old black cook Nancy in the Frizzle family kitchen, to mix the poison with the meal in the meal barrel. Unknown to her, the cook had used the poisoned meal in preparing Mr. Frizzle's breakfast. Both slaves were arrested and convicted of the crime, but only one was to be executed. Back then, when slaves were executed for a crime, the state would pay half their value to the owner. Since the older woman was valued at around five hundred dollars and the younger Anika was worth more than a thousand dollars because she was of child-bearing age, the decision was made to hang Nancy, though everyone knew that the mulatto was the guilty one.

In those days the sheriff was required to execute death sentences. He could not delegate that unpleasant duty to anyone else and was not even allowed to resign to avoid the responsibility. The reluctant sheriff, M. M. Nall, had to carry out the law and hang the innocent Nancy. It changed his life. He vowed he would never again serve as sheriff, even if everybody in Pike County voted for him. Mr. Nall was later ordained to the Baptist ministry, and the rest of his life was lived in penance for the gruesome and immoral act that he had to carry out. The main culprit, Herman Comisky, was given life imprisonment and sent to the state prison in Wetumpka, from which he tried several times to escape. One day while cutting up wood in the prison yard, Comisky took the broad axe he was using and split open the warden's head. For this murder he was tried, convicted, and hanged inside the prison walls. And justice was at last done. What an incredible story! And to think it happened less than half a dozen miles from where I'm sitting now.

Here's another story that took place here in my own community. It's a story I remember hearing often when I was a boy. Many years ago the Macedonia community had two cemeteries, one next to the church house, which was known as the church cemetery, and the other one, separated by trees and dense undergrowth, which was the community cemetery. Both cemeteries had fences around them, as was customary, to keep animals from trampling the graves of the dead. These burial grounds had served the community since the area was settled. In those days there were few stone markers and it was common for a relative to build a small house over a loved one's grave. The community cemetery had one of these grave houses near the gate entrance next to a seldom-traveled sandy road. The little house had wood shingles for a roof, walls of lattice woodwork, and a door. As I heard it, the story had two participants, a white man and a black man.

One dark night the white man was walking past the cemetery when a terrible thunderstorm developed suddenly, with keen flashes of lightning, followed by peals of rolling thunder. The man quickened his steps to find shelter before the rain began. There was no shelter to be seen. Not even the church house was close enough. Then the desperate man saw something. The constant flashes of lightning brought his attention to the little house in the cemetery. Without pausing to consider his fear, the man jumped over the iron fence of the cemetery and rushed to the grave house, and opened the door just as the rain began to come down in torrents. He had barely escaped being soaked as he stood peering through the latticed walls, listening to the rain drops pelting the roof just above his head.

As the great flashes of lightning continued to light up the night, the man could see for long distances, his view blurred only by sheets of water coming from the low clouds. As the man looked down the narrow road he had just left, hoping for a let-up in the rain, he suddenly saw another traveler bent over in the storm, plodding along. Wanting some company as he waited out the storm in his lonely refuge, the white man waited till the stranger was even with his shelter; then he shouted above the thunder, "Friend, come on in here where it's dry!" As soon as he heard this unexpected voice coming from the cemetery, the black man froze in his tracks and horrible thoughts ran through his mind: "It's a haint doing that talking in there, I know it!" He also knew as quick as a flash of lightning that he would not be accepting the invitation. There was but one way out. In a flash he dashed into the woods with break-neck speed, and the dense, wet trees and underbrush swallowed him. So fast had the black man moved that he had completely disappeared by the time the white man's invitation was out of his mouth, and the white man wondered if, indeed, he had seen a ghost. Nevertheless, he waited bravely and patiently until the rain had become a trickle before he ventured forth again to complete his night journey.

Now, this is not the end of the story. When I was a youngster, I heard the story many times. I would also see a big black man come from time to time into my father's store, and my attention was always drawn to his huge mouth with no front teeth. One day after the old man left the store, I asked, "Papa, why doesn't George have any front teeth?" With a mischievous twinkle in his eyes, my father said matter-of-factly, "Well, son, I heard that George got scared one dark, rainy night and ran into a tree and knocked all his teeth out." Years later, after I became a young man, I thought about the story and about my father's remarks about George's missing teeth, and I put the two together. I concluded that George was the black man who had heard the ghostly voice coming from the cemetery on that stormy night. And I have often wondered if it was not Papa himself who was in that grave house and issued the friendly invitation. Even as a young man, Papa had a reputation for his pranks and practical jokes.

Soon I will be as much a part of the past as Papa and old George. Maybe, if I'm lucky, people will tell tales about me and my life—if there's anything to tell. If I'd been able to realize my dream of being an artist, maybe my life would have been more exciting and eventful. Yes, art has always been my first love, ever since I was a boy. I never got to go many places when I was a child, but once I visited several of my great aunts in Tuskegee, and one of them gave me a paint set. I think it changed my life. From then on I wanted to be an artist. Before I started school and learned to read and write, I had crayons that I would draw and color with. One time I left my box of crayons out in the sun and rain and they melted. I cried my eyeballs out because I thought I'd never get any more.

At one time I wanted to be a cartoonist, but the art field is so competitive I knew I'd have to leave the country and go to the city to find any kind of work in the art field. I was never able to study art formally, but it has always been my first love. I've done some drawings throughout my life, but I was fifty years old before I picked up a brush and started painting oils on canvas. No, I was never fortunate enough to live with my first love. I've even had to make my living working with figures, the vocation next to farming that I hated most. I'm a self-taught bookkeeper. When I got a job with the state many years ago, I was supposed to have a degree in accounting, but I managed to pass the examination on what I had taught myself. I learned the florist business the same way I learned accounting. I just watched florists and copied what they did. For about ten years I had a little florist shop that gave me a lot of pleasure because it let me express myself artistically. I can't now cry over what might have been. I've been able to do some of the things I wanted to do, and I've been able to avoid some of the things I hated.

A painting by Hobson Roughton.

So what have I learned in my lifetime? Nothing ever remains the same. You have to be ready for constant changes. Not all change is good, but some are. Now it's easier to get an education that will allow you to do what you want to do. I wanted a career in art so badly, but when I finished high school in 1927, my folks were not able to help me go to college or art school. There was no government aid like today. I never got a second chance. The Depression got my education and my second chance. So I've had to make the most of what I've had. Like everyone else, I've been a victim of circumstances—and these circumstances were no one's fault. I've learned to do the best I can with what I have—and therewith to be content. I know I've wasted a lot of talent. I didn't get to do a lot of the things I aspired to do when I was young. Maybe I had set my star too high. . . .

That's about all I have to say about myself. We have a lot of better storytellers around here than I am. I wish you could have met Mr. Ford Windham. He could tell the funniest stories about himself that I've ever heard. His family was always moving from one location to another. His daddy would move to a place, develop a store, and sell out at a big profit. One time his family was on the move again, and he and his brother were driving the cows to their new home when the cows got tired and stopped in the middle of the road. The boys got the notion of putting a stick crosswise under each cow's tail to irritate them and make them move on. You see, when you do that the cow will clamp down with her tail and that will hold the stick in place. Well, they got sticks inserted under each cow's tail and drove them on down the road until they got to a schoolhouse on top of a hill. The children were out for recess, and when they saw the herd of cows marching along with sticks under their tails they thought the circus had come to town and wanted to leave school and go to the circus.

Mr. Windham was famous for his pranks. Another story he told on himself had to do with an uncle who kept all his valuables locked inside a trunk and wouldn't let anybody look in it. Ford and his brother decided to fix it so that he couldn't get inside either. They got some chicken manure—when Ford told it to other men, he used a four-letter word—and packed that lock so full no one could get a key inside the lock. The uncle had to break the lock to get his trunk open. He was mad as a hornet. He had his suspicions but never could prove who did it. Ford was a born story-teller and would have all of us rolling on the ground when he told his stories.

But, fortunately, not all our good storytellers are dead. There are a few left. One of them is Jim Rotton, who lives less than a mile from here out on Rabbit Road. I'll arrange for him to tell you his stories—even if I have to play a trick on him. Have a glass a lemonade and we'll plan how to get Jim over here.

POSTSCRIPT: Hobson Roughton died in November of 1986, leaving his widow, a daughter, and two grandchildren—plus a small artistic legacy of several dozen oil paintings that are now valued by collectors of folk art. Funeral services were held at Mt. Hilliard United Methodist Church, with burial in the Macedonia Baptist Church Cemetery. In his obituary in the *Union Springs Herald* he was called "a devoted family man, a willing community leader and worker, a dedicated church member, a witty storyteller and writer, a talented artist, an authentic historian, and a loyal friend."

Storyteller

At the end of his own interview, Hobson Roughton promised to invite Jim Rotton to dinner, where I would have a chance to hear him tell some of the stories that for years had made him one of the county's best known storytellers. Four days later, on July 20, 1977, Mr. and Mrs. Rotton joined me at Hobson and Anne Roughton's for an evening of talking and eating. Hobson warned that a tape recorder might inhibit Mr. Rotton and suggested that we hide it while we were talking and listening to his stories; then later we would reveal the trick we had played on him. Reluctantly, I agreed. Before we ate, we sat in the Roughton's living room with Mr. Rotton at center stage, telling us of people and incidents in stories that he had evidently honed in repeated tellings to significant exaggeration and in near perfection.

Jim Rotton is a self-motivated storyteller who needs little prompting to launch into a sequence of hilarious yarns. Occasionally, Hobson would suggest that Jim "tell Wade the one about Old-So-and-So" or "about the time you did such-and-such," and Jim would be off and running with the confidence of a master artist. It soon became apparent that I was in the presence of a natural-born storyteller in the grand tradition of the oral humorists of the Old Southwest, of which Alabama was a part.

He lived in the Macedonia community and I had grown up in the adjoining Liberty community, but we were of different generations and attended different churches, and, therefore, I had never heard him tell his stories—though I certainly was aware of his reputation. As we sat under his spell, it seemed as if one of Mark Twain's yarnspinners—say, Simon Wheeler or Jim Baker—had been reincarnated.

You know old Wilber Sikes. He's *curious*. He's the one that wipes his hands every time he touches something. But he won't use nobody's towel but his own. He won't even dry on the towel at home that his folks dry on. He's got him a certain one. He won't drink water from a dipper after anybody. Now why is that? It's because he's *clean* and he's *nice*. He thinks it's not only his folks but everybody's nasty but him.

Anyhow, way back in the thirties I was staying over there with my brother-in-law, Jackson Earles, and driving the schoolbus for him. I was also pretending to cut hair, and Wilber was one of my main customers. You might have knowed his boys, Dinzel and Dalton. Well, I never charged but a dime for a haircut, but none of em would ever pay me. I didn't charge but a nickel to shave. Well, Wilber had never shaved hisself—*said* he hadn't. He always depended on somebody else. You'd see him off with his beard out half a inch. He'd get first one, then another, to shave him—Sam Vance and different ones. Old Fletcher Sikes would shave him now and then. You remember him. So school was out and I was plowing over there for my brother-in-law. We'd just come in for dinner. Travis Holmes run that little old store over there at Stills Cross Roads. Well, we was waiting for dinner out on the front porch and looked up and could see Wilber a-coming way down the road. We knowed who it was because he always walked around

with his coat on his shoulder. Even if it's August or July, he's gone carry that coat on his shoulder no matter where he goes.

I looked up and seen him coming towards us. It was a pretty good piece from the house down to the road. He turned up the road to the house, and I said, "Well, I reckon the old devil wants a haircut or something." I'd just been worried with him and worried with him. My brother-in-law had a old dull straight razor all gapped up, and when I went over there to stay with him, I said just use mine. So he had his laying up on the old fireboard. We was all setting out on the porch. My sister had dinner about done, I know, and I knowed she had two kettles of water on the stove—one iron kettle and one aluminum kettle. I knowed that and didn't even have to go in the kitchen because she always kept em boiling when she was cooking. So Wilber was walking on up. I said to my brother-in-law, "Can I use your razor?" He sorta laughed and said, "Yeah, but you know it won't cut. You ain't gone use it on Wilber?" I said, "Yeah." He laughed and said, "Well, *good.*" The old man, Jackson's daddy, was living then, and he was setting on the old bench and he said, "Naw, don't you do that. You might hurt him."

We was all laughing and Wilber was coming on up to the porch. He stopped and propped his foot up on the steps and said, "How y'all today?" We told him we's doing pretty good. He was standing there, one foot on the ground, one on the steps and holding on to the porch post. He said, "I'm kindly in a hurry. Travis Holmes is going to Troy this evening, and I want to get over there and catch him and go with him. He's gonna leave 'bout one o'clock." Then he said, "Jimbo"—he always called me Jimbo—"what about shaving me?" I said, "Well, I reckon so, Wilber. Come on in. I'll go get some water." He come on in to what they called the front room then. Wilber always had a thin beard, but that day it was about a quarter inch long.

I went on through the hall to the back porch and got me a pan of cold water out of the waterbucket and took it back to where Wilber was setting. I put it down and reached up and got that dull razor and a bowl and went to lathering his face. Wilber pulled back a little and said, "Hey Jimbo, ain't you got no hot water?" I said, "Hell, naw." And I kept on daubing him—even got some in his mouth. I got through and reached up there and got Jackson's old dull razor, and I went at it. Wilber begin to say,

Jim Rotton.

"Ohhh. Ohhhhhh. Ohhhhhhhhhhhh." He wouldn't move but just kept drawing up. I kept on a-shaving and a-raking him off. When I put down my razor, he said, "You through?" I said, "Yeah." He said, "Well Jimbo, you won't never shave this old boy no more." I said, "Well, I'm glad to hear that. You owe me and owe me and won't never pay me. So now I done got my fun out of you." He never come back to get another shave from me. That wound him up. He went on to Troy with Travis that evening and bought him a safety razor, and there ain't been no man that's ever put a razor on his face since. He told me, "Jimbo, you learnt me a lesson. It was a hard way, but you

learnt me a lesson." He never come back for a shave. But he ain't never paid me neither.

I don't reckon you knowed Old Lump Boswell. Every time I think about him it tickles me. I's thinking about Old Lump going to see his woman just today. It used to be a double-pen house opposite of Macedonia Church, out there to the right in a grove. It was a pretty place after you got there, and that's where Old Lump lived. I don't think he ever did marry. It was after World War I. The reason I remember it, I hadn't never seen hosses around here with big feet up until then. After he come back out of the war, he bought him a long-bodied, pretty hoss with nice, big feet. She was as pretty as a picture when he got her, but after he'd kept her for a while, you could hang your hat up on her rib bones.

Anyway, through that old road where we live now, there was just room enough for a wagon. There was bushes growed up to the road and a big swamp just below it. On this side of the creek on the main run, there was a low place in the road, and it always stayed about a foot deep in water unless it was a mighty dry year. It had a little old foot bridge below it made out of some wide planks set up on some stobs. You could walk it on down to the main creek. It was so thick down there the sun couldn't get in. It was near about dark as pitch even in daytime.

Well, Lump's old woman lived over there across that creek, and he'd go over to see her twice a week at night. It was back over there near where I live now. That evening my daddy had gone over to see my sister. After he left, which was about sundown, I got to thinking about Old Lump and his woman. So I told my brother Carl, "Let's go drag Old Lump off into that mudhole tonight." He said, "How you going to do it?" I said, "Easy enough. His hoss ain't a bit taller than our mule. She's longer but not any taller, I don't believe. We'll go on down there and take a plowline with us and mark off where to put it in the dark. I'll set there on the mule and you tie a rope around that poplar tree below the road and that old willow tree just above the road." A plowline, you know, would reach over good across that road.

Well, we went on down there and I turned my mule around and headed him back towards the house. I taken that rope and chunked it to Carl and he tied it to that old willow up high enough to catch Old Lump around his belly parts and drag him off his hoss. Then I throwed Carl the other end and he measured it up on that poplar and guessed at it being about right. He taken his knife and put a notch in them trees so we could find where to put that rope when it got pitch dark. We didn't want to catch him till he was coming home. Then we taken the rope down and come on home. Mama begin to suspicion something and said, "What y'all up to?" Finally, I had to tell her. She said, "You better not do that. That's wrong. Old Lump don't bother nobody." I said, "Mama, we ain't gone hurt the old rascal. We just want to have a little fun." We kept on and directly Mama said, "I expect your daddy'll whup you." I said, "Well, I'm willing to take a chance this one time."

We went on and eat supper. It wudn't no need being in a hurry. We knowed he wouldn't be coming along till way late, ten or eleven o'clock. Well, we had two bad dogs at that time. One was a old July hound. He had long hair and he'd bite anybody. He hated Negroes worst than anything. Then we had a old half bulldog. Either one of them would bite, but the old hound was the worst. So that night while we was eating supper, the old dogs run out from under the house just a-barking. I went out and peeped and it was Old Lump going by on his way to see his woman.

There was still enough daylight so I could see good. We knowed we had a long time to wait, so we drug around the house after we finished supper.

We didn't have no flashlight. I don't reckon I'd even seen a flashlight then—didn't even know what one was. We had some fat lightwood splinters to see by, and I taken my daddy's old twelve-gauge shotgun. I wudn't gone shoot the old fellow, but I wanted to scare him good. The old-timey black-powder shells they used back then would go off like a cannon—a lot louder than we got now. We went on down there to the creek, and the dogs followed us but we run em back. We lit our splinters and put up the rope and set down to wait. I was setting there and setting there, and Carl he's propped up against a old tree next to that little old bridge. Soon he commenced to nodding and like to fell off over in that mudhole hisself. Way after a while, I heard a hoss hit that little branch that run into the creek. The road run into the branch and followed it to the main run. It stayed about two or three inches deep all the time, so I could hear that old hoss coming towards us. Then I happened to think it might be my daddy, and I didn't want to drag him down in that mudhole. So I taken my knife out of my pocket and felt for that rope. If I'd thought it was my daddy, I was just gone cut that rope and let it fall and there wouldn't be no more to it. He couldn't of seen us nohow. But I could soon tell that hoss coming towards us had big feet, so I knowed it wadn't my daddy 'cause he was on a mule.

When they got down to the creek, that old hoss stopped and I could hear him slurping up some water. Directly, Old Lump said, "Come on. Hurry up here." I shut my knife up and put it back in my pocket. I knowed for sure it was him. They come on up and I could tell the old hoss smelt us, so he stopped. He might even have seen us. Lump hit the hoss with his reins and said, "Come on. Hurry up here," again. Right after that they hit the slough and they kept a-coming on fast. I begin to think he might be laying down on his saddle and he wudn't gone get drug off. About that time I heard a awful scuffle—'course, I couldn't see good 'cause it was dark as smut—but it seemed to me like she jumped twelve feet in the air, and when her or him one hit the ground, that muddy water fell all over me and liked to knocked me down. Old Lump jumped up, reaching out for his hoss. I had the old gun there in my hand, and I just throwed it up in the air and pulled the trigger and Old Lump hollered, "Whoooo-ooooo-ppppppppppp!" and run out of that swamp up the road towards our house. We could hear his old hoss crashing on down through the branch. In a few minutes I heard our dogs a-barking up there at the house and I told Carl, I said, "Old Lump done lost his hoss and now the dogs is after him." When things quieted down, we lit our splinters and me and Carl taken our rope down and come on home. We slipped in the house and went to bed without saying a word.

A few weeks later I was telling Otto about the prank we pulled, and he said Old Lump was crossing the creek now down yonder close to Mr. Al Roughton's. "Let's go down there and drag him off again," Otto said. But we never did get around to doing it, and Lump never found out who done it to him that night. I was scared to say much about it on account of I was afraid my daddy would whup me. Old Lump might have thought it was a haint that done it. All I know is Lump never went through that way to see his woman again.

We played a lot of pranks on people, but we never intended to hurt nobody. We even pulled some tricks around churches—not many, but some. One time me and my brother-in-law Frank Kinard throwed a hor-nets' nest in a Negro church. I was down there this side of Needmore way down in Pike County spending a day or two with my sister and Frank. There was a little branch head that come up pretty close to his house, and there was just enough room for a garden between the house and the branch. I noticed a hornet's

nest big as my head up on a little old bush out there on the edge of the branch. It was summertime and the Negroes was running a protracted meeting about a mile up this way at their church. Old Frank he couldn't talk plain, but he said, "Aftah dahk, let's us get that thang, take it up to that chuch, and I thow it ovah in there." Well, you know I was right up for it. My daddy wadn't down there and I *had* to go in with him. His mama tried to get him not to, but we went on ahead anyhow.

We went on down there to where the hornets' nest was. There was a heap of em flying around outside the hole, so we lit a splinter and held it up there, and the ones that didn't drop went back inside the nest. When they was all gone, I crammed a stick in that hole so they couldn't get out. We left the nest on that limb, and Frank cut it off and toted it on up to the church. While we's walking along we could hear them hornets roaring inside that nest, mad as the devil. When we got to the church, it was already dark, and there was mules and wagons all over the place. There was a little bit of light inside the church where they had these little side lamps up on the walls and one hanging down in front of the preacher. The light was shining on him pretty good, and he was up there making the biggest racket, preaching and sweating. It was mostly dark all around the church, but there was people coming in and out all the time, so I stayed out in the dark twenty or thirty foot from the windows. All the windows was open and we could hear the preacher doing some cold preaching, and all the people was shouting and getting happy. While this was going on, Frank slunk up there to the window next to the preacher and pulled that plug out of the hornets' nest and eased it over that window sill, and we both got on back in the woods a piece.

I don't think anybody ever did see or hear him. Every little bit I'd step out and take a look, and I could see them hornets flying around between me and them kerosene lamps. In a little time them Negroes begin to stir around, and before we knowed it, they commenced to come out of the doors and windows, hollering and running all over one another and the old preacher too. That was in rocky country, and there was rocks all over the ground, so after we left we could hear wagons bumping all over them rocky roads for about a mile. I reckon the hornets got to the mules too, 'cause they come flying up and down the road. When we heard one coming, we'd just step off to the side in the bushes and let it pass.

That was on a Friday night, and the next day, Saturday morning, all of them Negroes would go to town, to Troy, in their little old one-hoss wagons. There was this one old Negro I knowed—Frank did too—Charley Ramsey, and he come by there the next morning going to town. Me and Frank was setting on the front porch. Old Charley had this flour sack tied around his head, and Frank said, "Charley, what the hell the mattah with you?" Charley said, "Well, I tell you, Mr. Frank, there was some hornets got loose in our church last night, and they liked to stung us Negroes to death!" After he drove on, we had us a good laugh. Them Negroes never did find out how them hornets got inside their church. I reckon they thought the devil put em in there.

I know you knowed Seals Caylor. Did you know Lawrence Maxwell and Holloway Bickerstaff? I thought you did. Well, Holloway used to live down here in that big house that Johnson's got now. He was right well fixed and sent off one of his boys to college. One morning Seals went up there to see Holloway about something, and Holloway's wife told him that he'd just walked over to where Lawrence was planting corn. He had a old Negro man, Charley Ellis, laying off corn rows for him. Well, Seals walked out to the field where they was all working. Lawrence had just bought him a new planter, a corn dropper, and it was broke down. The wheels would lock up or something was wrong with it, and Holloway and Lawrence was trying to work on it. Old Charley was already a few

rows ahead of them, and Seals said, "You reckon Charley could fix that?" Holloway said, "Oh, hell no. That old Negro don't know nothing." But Seals walked over to where Charley was, and asked him if he thought he could fix it. Charley said, "Yes sir, I think I can do it." So Charley walked over to where Holloway and Lawrence was working on the planter, and Holloway said, "Charley, see if you can fix this damn son-of-a-bitch!" Seals said Charley squatted down and done a little something to it and the planter started working again. Charley went on back to his plowing, and Holloway throwed his hat down on the cornbed and hollered, "Oh hotdamn! I done sent the wrong damn man to college!"

My cousin, Abe Rotton, is sorta timid, shy. He's Lige's brother. One time I spent the night with his wife. I ain't never been more miserable in my life, and I know she was too. She's real timid, like him. If you was to go up to her house this evening and pick her and Abe up to carry them somewhere, she won't set up there in the front seat next to another man. She'll make Abe set next to him and she'll set next to the door, or she'll set in the back seat by herself. She's scared of everybody. I reckon she's afraid they'll *attack* her. And the poor old critter is like myself. She ain't much to look at. I don't know what kind of courting they done, but I think he finally asked her could she cook his hoecakes. That must have been how he proposed. They married in the fall of '26.

Anyhow, my brother Carl and him was going to see two sisters that lived just this side of Banks, down below Ebenezer. They was working over here at the sawmill and every Saturday they'd go down there to see them girls. They struck up with them at Macedonia at the Fourth of July singing, and they was carried away with them. Both of them boys wanted to marry, you know, in the worst way, and neither one had ever been with nobody. They was ashamed to get at it. Anyhow, Carl he run after them girls all day down at the church. In them days I used to think everybody in the world was at the church on the Fourth. It was so crowded you couldn't find nobody if they got away from you. Even the roads was full of folks walking. So Carl he followed them girls around all day. Abe he would run up on em every now and then, but he wouldn't run after em like Carl. He'd just let em go. Them girls come to Jackson Earles' with their brother on a one-hoss wagon the day before the singing. After they got to know them, Carl and Abe made up to take them back over to my brother-in-law's that evening. Everybody just about stayed to the singing to nearly night. Well, Carl had one of them old Model T's you had to crank with your hand. I was standing off to the side watching them. Abe was walking 'round the car smiling, looking at the girls, wanting to get up close to em but didn't know how. The girls went on and got in the back seat. Carl looked at the oldest girl and said, "Hey, why don't you come up here and set with me?" She finally got out and come on around and set down there with Carl, and Abe got in the back seat over to one side. Carl got out and cranked up and off they went. He told my daddy, "I'll be back in a little bit." Daddy had a big old box Mama packed our dinner in, and Carl had carried it to the church in his car. Daddy waited and waited for Carl to come back and get that box, but Daddy finally had to tote that box home. Carl and them didn't get in to about midnight. They was courting *heavy*.

Old man Bill Lacey he went home with us that evening and spent the night. You remember him. We had a big supper when we got home, and Mr. Lacey had eat so much all day long he needed to get up during the night to go to the toilet—which was the woods. He was sleeping in our little old shed room by hisself, and he was hemmed up in there. He started scratching the walls, looking for the door or a window to get out. It was late at night and we was all asleep. Me and my brother was sleeping in the next room, and there was people on pallets all over the house. I could hear Old Man Lacey crashing around and

Jim and his dog.

calling out, "Jimmy, Jimmy. Open the door. I got to get out of here." I could hear him plain, but I was asleep and just couldn't wake up. Then I heard my daddy say, "Jim, get up from there and let that old fellow out." I don't know what was the matter with me, but I just couldn't move. The old man finally got out of his room into one of the big rooms, and then he stumbled over a pallet and fell down. When he begin to get up, he reached up on the bed where I was sleeping and pulled at one of my legs, and I jumped up and said, "Yes, sir." I reckon he thought we tripped him, and he said, "Quit now. Let me alone. I got to get out in a hurry." I led him to the outside door and off he run to the woods. He'd been in that room bumping around so long, I didn't know where in the world it was safe to step. But I couldn't see no damage he done—leastwise not any that I stepped in.

That was the first time Carl and Abe ever went courting. After that, they'd go down every Saturday to Banks, and they even got to spending the night and coming back home late Sunday. They'd take them girls to all the big singings they used to have down there—places like Zebulon and Enon. The girls' house was built on a little hillside, and the back of the house was so high off the ground, they used it for a wagon shelter. They put Carl and Abe back there to sleep when they'd spend the night. Well, one night way before day, Carl woke up and had to get out of there to do some business. I wadn't down there, but I know the moon was shining because it was up here. He didn't want to have to wake up the old man and the old lady and tell them what he needed to do. So he woke up Abe and he let him down through a window with his arms as far as he could and then let him drop on down to the ground. Carl went on out to the woods and done what he had to do. He said it was near about daylight by then, and the chickens was beginning to crow for day. So Carl come back to get in, but Abe had done gone to sleep again. He found some old chicken coops and stacked them on top of one another, and got on top and tried to reach the window, but it wadn't high enough. He finally found a old fishing pole and hit the window with it and woke up Abe. So Abe reached down and near about had him up to the window, when Carl said, "Abe, turn me loose quick. I got to go again." Abe dropped him and he hit the ground and run back to the woods. This time he got back and roused Abe and got through the window. But by then it was already turning day and the old lady was up cooking breakfast. Carl told me he didn't know what it was that tore up his bowels, but it must've been something he eat.

One time Carl went down to see his girl and wouldn't let Abe go with him, and it kindly made Abe mad because he wanted to court too. Abe asked me to carry him down to his daddy's house in Pike County on a Wednesday. I was right up for going. I'd done laid by my crops and I wadn't doing nothing special. So I went down there with him to my uncle's. We thought we'd stay till Sunday, when they was having

a big singing at Hopewell Church. I carried me some Sunday clothes to wear. On Saturday Abe got up and said, "Jim, you know I don't care much about staying down here for that singing. I'm 'bout ready to go back to Bullock County. You 'bout ready?" I was beginning to get homesick, so I said, "Yeah. I'm ready. I don't care nothing 'bout staying down here."

Well, I didn't know he had it in his mind to come by Banks and see his girl. But just before we got to Troy, he said, "You wouldn't want to go by Banks and let me see my girl, would you?" I said, "Yeah, I'll go by there." At that time I don't believe I'd ever been to Banks. I'd heard Carl say you turned there at Number 29 before you get to Banks. It might have been a gravel road there then, but it wadn't no blacktop. Then he said to turn between two little houses and head toward Culpepper's Store. So that's what I was doing. Abe said, "Where you going?" I said, "I'm going to see y'all's girls." He said, "Naw, this ain't the way." I said, "This is the way Carl said to go." He said, "Naw, it's not." Well, I figured he ought to know because he'd been down there a dozen times or more. So I backed up and went on past another little swamp, and then we thought we'd better stop and change our rags and eat our little grub. We had stopped at one of them little stores this side of Troy and got us some salmon and some canned goods and two Nehis. After we eat we went over close to the swamp where we could hide and changed our clothes. When I got my pants on and went to buckle my belt, I didn't have one. I asked Abe to let me borrow his belt because his pants fit him like a carpet. He give me his belt and I put it on. When we got back to the car, Abe looked at his pants and said, "Jim, this won't do. Bessie will think I ain't got no belt." So I had to go back to the swamp and strip and put on my old overalls again.

Abe was putting on his belt when we seen a wagon coming down across the old dirt road from across the swamp. It come on up and it turned out to be Bessie's brother Ed. I said, "Where are you going? Are you headed to Banks?" He said, "Naw, I'm going home. I been over to the gristmill." Him and Abe got in a argument over which way it was to where he lived. I said, "Abe, it seems to me like he ought to know where he lives." Abe said, "Well, let's go on, but I don't think it's the right way." We set there and give Ed time to get home, but it didn't take long because it was only 'bout a mile away.

When we got there, Ed had done put up his mule and wagon, and they was all in the house setting there at the foot of the bed. Of course, I wadn't wanting to court myself. I don't know where Carl and his girl was, and nobody ever told us. We went on in the front room, and their daddy was setting on a box by the fireplace. He was a great big old man. Me and Abe set down on a trunk, and some of the girls was setting over there next to the bedstead. I didn't say nothing, and Abe he didn't, neither. The old man he done all the talking. Every once in a while, Abe would say, "Yes sir. Yes sir. That's right." He'd nod his little head and smile.

Their daddy said they had some watermelons there in the back room on the bed. Amos was a little yearling boy, and he went and got one of them watermelons, and one of the girls got up and got another one, and they taken em on out to the front porch and cut em. Abe and me dug in to them pretty well. Every once in a while Bessie would say, "Abe, you better have some more. You go on and have some more." He eat all he could and said, "I done had a plenty." That's all I heard them say to one another till we's about to leave. Then Abe said, "Well, I might see you next Sunday." She said, "All right." Now that's all that passed between them. After we left and got up on the hill, Abe looked over at me and said, "My girl talked pretty good, didn't she?" I said, "Hell, Abe, I never heard y'all say nothing."

Abe and Bessie got married late that fall, but we didn't know nothing about it. By that time Abe had done left from up here and was staying down there with his daddy down below Troy. That was my Uncle Walter. You know Allen Rotton. Well, he wanted me to go down that way with him. He used to work for a man named Smith way down there around Andalusia, but he'd moved to somewhere below Troy on the old Henderson Road. Allen called hisself courting one of the Smith girls, and he said there was another one I could go see. So we went on down there, and Papa and them went with us to see Uncle Walter. We went on through Troy to Uncle Walter's, and some of em said, "Abe and Bessie is getting married today." We put Papa and them off and went on back to where the Smiths lived. Allen had a pretty fine voice and sung some old songs, and I set there with one of the girls but didn't say much. She was a pretty girl, but I never did see her again. We stayed there pretty late and then went on back to Uncle Walter's. Abe and Bessie was there, but they'd done already gone to bed. They was sleeping in the front room across the hall. I never will forget it. There was some old paper curtains over the windows, and one of the window panes was broke out. Me and Lige was sleeping together, and I asked him, "Is that window pane still broke out?" He said, "Yeah. It's still out." I said, "That's just what we want. We'll just slip around the house and see what's going on."

Me and Lige eased on out of the room we's in and on out the back. He said, "I got some lightwood splinters cut up under the porch." So we got a handful of them and we had some matches and we slipped on around to the window in the front room. We lit that splinter real good and stuck it through that broke-out pane. It lit up the room, and Abe he come a-hollering and a-flying out of there. He hollered for his daddy and said, "Pa, make Lige and Jim stay away from over here." Uncle Walter hollered at Lige, and we knowed we'd better get on back to bed. We didn't bother them no more that night, but we would have if Uncle Walter hadn't made us stop.

That was the first night Abe spent with Bessie.

Now I'll tell you about the night I spent with her. After they got married, Abe moved near his daddy below Troy in a little bungalow, they called it. I was working over here at the sawmill at the time. I was young and wanting to ramble. Carl hadn't married yet, and was working down there cutting logs at the sawmill in front of Abe's house. Well, they was all up here one Sunday and got after me to go down there and help stack lumber for five dollars a day. The fellow they had stacking lumber had done quit. They piled it high as this loft and it was hot work and I didn't want to do it. But I told em I'd go down and try it for a week. So I was stacking lumber and staying with Carl at Abe's house, and one day an old man from another sawmill come by and wanted me to do some logging. I went to work for him and about the second night I come in, Carl and Abe was gone. I didn't see their car or nothing. Bessie said they knocked off about dinnertime and went on up to Banks to see about renting a place to farm. They said they'd be back about dark. Bessie was there by herself. Well, they never did come back all night. We found out later they got up there and broke down. The cotter key fell out of the drive shaft. That was one miserable night for Bessie because I knowed she was expecting me to attack her or something. Finally, I said, "I believe I'll go on to bed." I went to bed but I don't think she ever did. She set up and played with them two kittens they had. I never did say nothing much to her. The reason I was so timid was I knowed she was. Now if Abe had been there I might have said something to her ever now and then. But with nobody there but me, I was scared if I said anything she might think I was trying to have a affair with her. We didn't even talk when she fixed supper for me.

One time we tried to play a trick on Abe and Bessie, but it kind of backfired on us. It was during the '30s and they was living there on the old Reynolds place. It was a big swaybacked house with a big fireplace. At that time me and Morris Holmes and some of the Earles boys—a big bunch of us—serenaded around in the community. Well, we was determined to serenade Abe and Bessie, and we had plenty of firecrackers. So we slipped up there on Saturday night, and we hope Morris and he clomb up that old rock chimney, and he lit a whole box of them little bitty firecrackers and dropped them down the chimney in the fireplace. We could hear them firecrackers just a-popping off, but we couldn't hear nobody moving in the house. We knowed then we wasted our firecrackers on a empty house. Then we was scared to leave, afraid one of them would pop out on the floor and set the house afire. So we had to stay there a long time, peeping in at the window from time to time to see when the fire was out. Come to find out, Abe and them was over to his mother-in-law's that night.

I had my fun with Abe and Bessie, but they had a hard, sad life. They had two children, both dead now. The oldest one was a boy and he died of pneumonia when he was about eight or nine. Their girl was named Lois. She was a smart girl, a good girl. She finished up high school over at Inverness and was going to that Christian college in Montgomery when she got drowned. Abe and Bessie lives up in there now near Union Springs by theirselves. And they's still timid.

Well, I done told you about everybody but me, and there ain't much to say about me. My daddy was Jack Rotton, and my mama was a Phillips from down here at Boswell Crossing. Papa was borned just up the road between here and Mt. Hilliard, but I never learned just which house was the old homeplace. I was borned right down the road here, near where I'm living now. There's a house there, but it's not the same one. The house I was borned in has been tore down. Still, I live about fifty foot from where I came into this world in 1907. That makes me sixty-nine this year. Papa bought this place one year and I was borned on it that next fall. I was raised right here on Rabbit

Road, in a house that Uncle Pete used to live in, in a bunch of old oak trees. I'll tell you who named that road. It was Allen Dykes. When Carl Green went in office as road commissioner, Allen was running one of them road graders. Roscoe Hall operated the other one. Allen didn't want to come way over here to work the roads. He wanted to do all his work down in yonder near where he lives, and he thought he could talk Carl out of the notion of doing anything around here. So he said to Carl, "Ain't no use to grade that road. Ain't nothing gone travel it—even if it was blacktopped—unless it's a damned rabbit." So everybody went to calling it Rabbit Road.

Well, I'm just about talked out, and I'm hungry. Let's eat.

POSTSCRIPT: Actually, Jim Rotton ended his monologue by saying, "Well, I'm just about talked out, and I'm hungry. You can turn that damn recording machine off and let's eat. I knowed what y'all was up to from the start, but I thought I'd go along with it." Mr. Rotton had a good laugh on us over our failed attempt to trick him; then we all ate a hearty supper. He still lives with his wife in their small frame house on Rabbit Road near Macedonia Baptist Church. His fenced yard is occupied by his wife's flowers and shrubs and by a noisy, mixed-breed watchdog, which he has yoked to keep from jumping over the fence.

INTERLUDE: SCHOOL DAYS

*O*ver the years, many of the whites interviewed — or their children — attended the Inverness Consolidated School. Segregation, of course, meant that African Americans attended separate schools, if they were able to attend at all. Of the children captured here in "School Days" photos, all were students at Inverness. They are: (starting at the top left) Wade Hall, '40; Dean Driggers, '45; Jill Hixon, '47; Elizabeth Hall, '42; Juanita Hatfield and Wilma Bristow, '46; Donald Hall, '52; James Hall, '43; Jack Hall, '45; and Jean Brooks, '48.

At right is the program for the commencement ceremony for 1950, the year the author graduated. The school closed in the seventies.

GRADUATION EXERCISES
INVERNESS HIGH SCHOOL
Friday Evening, May 26, 1950
8:00 o'clock

Processional—"Marche Militaire" _____ Schubert
Accompanist, Miss May Belle Rumph

Invocation _____ Dr. Claude M. Haygood

Salutatory _____ Virginia Sellers

Piano Solo—"Rustle of Spring" _____ Bennie Hixon

Introduction of Speaker_____J. F. Hamilton

Baccalaureate Address_____Dr. C. M. Haygood

Piano Duet—"The Dance of the Firefly"_____Lineke
Misses May Belle and Frances Rumph

Presentation of Diplomas_____J. F. Hamilton

Valedictory _____ Wade Henry Hall, Jr.

Benediction _____ Dr. Claude M. Haygood

Recessional

ESTELLE COPE CAMPBELL

Teacher

Remarkably spry and mentally alert at 87, Estelle Cope Campbell talked with me on July 5, 1975, about her life and fifty-year teaching career. We are sitting in the Victorian living room of her modest frame house at Inverness, less than a mile from the swamp-like Conecuh River and one-half mile from the now abandoned Inverness Consolidated School, where she taught math and other subjects to several generations of country children, including my mother and all four of my brothers. She is handsomely dressed as if she were going to church or leaving for an all-day trip to Troy or Montgomery. She is expecting me, but she is the kind of woman, who even at such a great age, is always groomed for company.

As you may remember, I'm not one for idle chatter when there's work to be done—a theorem to be learned, a play to be rehearsed, a child to be disciplined—therefore, I'll get right to the business at hand. And I'll begin where I should, at the beginning. I was born in 1888 and have been a widow for almost sixty years. My husband was nine years older than I, but he was only thirty-seven when he died, leaving me with an unborn child—a daughter it turned out to be—to support and raise. I did what I had to do. I did my duty. For fifty years I taught school, first the elementary grades and later high school math. I think I've done some good in all those years. I've lived in this house in Inverness for forty years, and I'll probably die here—not four miles from where I was born over on a country road.

My father, George Cope, was born on the land where he later built his own house. His father had come from the Carolinas and homesteaded the land long before the War Between the States, soon after this part of Alabama was opened for settlement. He surveyed a tract of land for himself and then some for his neighbors. My father bought some of that property his father had homesteaded. In those days, of course, this was all virgin territory. Even when I was a girl large tracts of trees covered much of the county. I remember walking through thick woods from my father's to my grandfather's house. Then the land was cleared for row crops like cotton, corn, and peanuts.

But I do believe the woods have taken over Bullock County again since the decline in farming. It's beginning to look more like it was when I was a girl.

My mother, Eliza Bates, was born just a few miles up the road on the throughway to Montgomery, just before you get to Hooks Cross Roads. Her father and maybe her mother were also natives of this county. They would have been the first generation to have been born here after the Indians cleared out. My father just missed the wars of his time—the Civil War and the Spanish-American War—but Grandfather Bates was a Confederate soldier and fought till he was captured and put in prison. After the war closed, he was some time in getting home because he had developed an illness and stopped off at his relatives in Carolina until he got well. It was a big surprise to his family when he came home. I remember my mother telling the story. It was six or eight months after the war, and no one knew for sure whether he was alive or dead. It was on a Sunday and my grandmother was at church when he arrived. And nothing on the place recognized him—not even his own children—nothing but his old dog. Of course, he'd been away four and one-half years and had changed a lot.

Grandfather Bates fought for almost the duration of the war, but I don't believe he owned any slaves. I don't recall anyone saying that he did. But I do know that Grandfather Cope had slaves. Right down the road here a short piece is a Negro who is descended from his slaves. He recognizes me every time I walk to the store. "Good morning, Miss Estelle," he calls out to me from his front porch. And I tip my hat and walk on. A good many of Grandfather Cope's slaves remained on his plantation and sharecropped for him after they were freed. They held on to their former loyalties because they had been treated well when they were slaves. At our house when I was growing up, we did most of our own work, but we did have some Negro help. One member of the household from the family servant times was Aunt Jane. She was Aunt Jane Cope and got her name from my grandfather. She helped my mother around the house, cooking and cleaning. She also did our family washing down at the spring in the pasture behind our house.

Cope is an English name. One of my ancestors was Sir John Cope of England. I believe Bates is also an English name. My people have been in this country so long we've lost our early connections and contacts.

Estelle Cope Campbell, 1956.

Campbell, my married name, is, of course, Scottish. A lot of Scots settled in this county, and we still have many Scottish names around here. The McCalls live in the Macedonia community. The McFarlands live in Ft. Davis. The McGradys are from Bethel. The McLendons come from Boswell Crossing. The McMillans are from Midway, the McNairs from here in Inverness, the McWhorters from Perote. There used to be a colored McGowan family that lived over near Liberty Church.

But I think most of us around here are of English descent. The white church here in Inverness is Baptist. We've never had a Presbyterian church here. My parents were members at Indian Creek Baptist Church, but when the Inverness church was formed in 1900, they moved their letters here. When I was growing up at the old homeplace, it was a good distance to Indian Creek, and I usually went to the Presbyterian church at Bethel. I joined the Inverness church soon after it was established and have been a member ever since. I was about fourteen when I was baptized into the church. I joined during the protracted meeting when the preacher was Tommy Thomas, a distant relative of ours. My grandmother Bates lived in the house next to the church. It's still standing. So many youngsters were joining the church during the revival that she thought it was just a big case of excitement. So I stood back a long time. Finally, she caught on that she'd said too much. I joined one night and was baptized at the end of the meeting over there in Jenkins's Pond. It's now called Mr. Hamilton's Pond since he moved here to head the school and bought that property.

We used to have a large membership when Inverness was a larger community, but a lot of people have had to move away to find work to do. Church membership in Inverness now counts fewer than one hundred, unless I count both races. I haven't tried that. We have two colored churches in Inverness that have larger memberships than ours. An old man named Grider gave them the land where they built their churches. They're right next to me, across the street from each other. They've never given me any trouble, and I've never given them any. They go to their churches and I go to mine.

Oh yes, I remember my girlhood very well. Until I was seventeen I lived on my father's farm and helped with the farm work. I also helped with the house work, and I helped with the community work. I am from a family of workers. We are all believers in taking part in whatever we think is good for us and for the community. It was a hard life. But we had our entertainments, especially at school. My favorite game was townball, which is sort of like softball because you hit the ball with a bat and run the bases. I was pretty good and took pride in beating my brother J. T. and other boys who were younger.

There were ten of us in our family—five girls and five boys. One died when it was about a month old of some kind of lung sickness. There are only three of us left now. The other night I was thinking about it when I should have been asleep. I was going over in my mind how they've all dropped out but us three. My brother George lives in Tennessee, and my sister Minnie Cope Cade, who is five years younger than I, lives in Atlanta now with her daughter. I talked with her just last night over the telephone, and we had a nice conversation. She called to ask why I haven't written lately. I told her I've been too busy entertaining company. She married Jim Frank Cade, but she's outlived him and her son.

Indeed, I remember all my brothers and sisters, the living and the dead. Lonza Cope, the oldest, lived to be an old man here in Inverness. He died at seventy-five almost blind. The next one was sister Anna, who married John Hoffman and moved to Dale County. She was fifty when she died and left a family of ten or eleven Hoffmans. Next came James, who also lived here and died at seventy-five. Both Lonza and James were farmers and raised cattle. James moved to Clayton after his wife got sick and when he was about blind. Our eyes, you know, give out eventually, if we stay here long enough. My eyes are holding out rather well, and I can still drive my car.

Then came sister Minnie, who called me the other night from Atlanta. Next came my sister Ethel Cope Smith, who lived to be sixty-five. Then I came. Woe be unto me! Well, I can't complain. I've not had

a bad life. Then came brother J. T., who passed away about nine years ago. He did a little farming but spent most of his life as a merchant and postmaster in Inverness. He kept his post office in a corner of his store. His widow still lives up at my father's old place. Then there was my sister Ruth. Then the boy William who died at one month. Last was George Ernest, who visited me last week from Leoma, Tennessee. He never farmed. He sold cookware from door to door. When he went back home last week, he sent me the nicest utensil I've ever had. I'd like to show it to you. For years he called me every Sunday morning before church, but now he's reduced it a bit and calls me every other Sunday. Minnie calls me regularly too. It's like a triangle, with corners in Alabama, Georgia, and Tennessee. Neither one has given any thought of coming back to Bullock County. Minnie is happy with her daughter in Atlanta. Ernest married a Tennessee woman and has made a home there. He sold his son their homeplace and he and his wife live in a trailer close by. I imagine they'll both be buried close to where they live. Soon we'll all be gone, and before long I'll rest by the side of my husband in Headland.

But oh, I have some fine memories when I look back over my life—memories of home, of family, of friends, of church, of school, of the hundreds of students I've taught. I began my education in a one-teacher, one-room school at Bethel. There weren't enough pupils to have grades, so I went at my own speed. I started off with the *Blue Back Speller* and progressed to McGuffey's readers. I stayed at Bethel until I got to be an advanced student, and my parents sent me to live a year with my Methodist preacher uncle in Ramer in Montgomery County. At Ramer they had the higher grades, and I stood up fairly well with the ninth-graders. It was the first time I left home to go to school. At Christmas time I took and passed the state examination for third grade teachers. When I left Ramer I came home and went before the county superintendent and took the test for the second grade.

I got that grade, too. I was climbing higher and higher! I was seventeen and had a little ambition even then. The next school year I taught all the grades in a one-room school in Pike County, and I learned a lot. After summer school at the University of Alabama, I took the test for the first grade. Thanks to somebody's kindness, I got that certificate too.

When I was nineteen I went to Newton, a Baptist boarding academy below Ozark. On that first grade teacher's certificate, I entered the senior class, and there I met my future husband. Before we married about two years later, I came home and taught in communities like Smut Eye, places where we don't even have schools or communities now.

Then I married, and my husband and I taught one year in Houston County, not far from his home in Headland. Then we moved to Walker County, where Mr. Campbell had been elected principal of a mountain missions school at Eldridge. It was supported by the Baptist Home Mission Board, but it has since been disbanded and its work taken over by the public schools. There I taught math and enjoyed my work very much. We left Eldridge to go to Florence Normal School, but my husband's illness forced us to leave there. So we came to Bullock County and I taught one year while he regained his strength. We thought he was well enough to return to the mission school, but he passed away before the school term opened. That was in September of 1916—almost sixty years ago. We buried him in Headland, where he's waited for me all these years.

The mission school insisted that I stay on and teach, but I couldn't. I was too far away from my people, and my daughter Emily was to be born six months later. I never remarried, and I've never regretted it. After Emily grew up, she married the son of Dr. George Guthrie, our doctor in Inverness, and they've lived most of their married life in Birmingham. He died a few years back and was buried here. Emily visits me often and was here to help me entertain my

Mrs. Campbell at the time of her interview.

company from Tennessee.

After I buried my husband, I came back to Bullock County and spent five years as principal of the little school at Bethel. When that school was moved here to Inverness, I came too and have taught here ever since. I lived with my parents till my mother died and my brother J. T. and his family moved in with Papa. Then I moved to this house, and I've lived here since about 1935. During the summers I managed to finish my full degree from the University of Alabama in Tuscaloosa. It was a difficult task. I had to teach every year to make a living for myself and my daughter. I couldn't beg from people, not even from my own family. I was healthy and intelligent and I knew I could make it on my own. And I did. My degree is in mathematics, and I even finished half of my master's work. Then I stopped and decided I'd take it easy the rest of the way.

I've had a rich life as a teacher, not in salary but in other compensations. I've taught all the elementary grades, and in high school I've taught mainly math. At Bethel I coached the boys' basketball team. We didn't have an indoor gym, so we played outside. My boys got to be pretty good, dodging bumps and stones and tree roots and putting the ball through the basket. I've learned—and I've tried to teach my students—that you can do very well with whatever you have. You don't have to have first-rate facilities and equipment to do first-rate teaching and learning. Of course, I've had students who came from very poor homes, but I believe most of the children I've taught had enough to eat and shoes and clothes to wear. I do remember one little boy who just wouldn't wear shoes in school, even on the coldest days. But I know he had them to wear. Maybe some of the youngsters who didn't have sufficient clothing didn't come to school. I know there were many who didn't have all that nature needed.

I've had problems in school. No one can teach for fifty years and not have some. As a rule, however, my children were respectful and obedient and tried to learn what I tried to teach. I suppose I was a strict disciplinarian. One of my old students told me just the other day that I used to pull his ears. Indeed I did, but only in kindly correction. I never tried to pull anybody's ears off! It was simply my way of saying, "Get to work." I believe all my students accepted my corrections beautifully. Maybe I had to be a little mean at times, but they knew my heart was never mean. One thing that contributed to discipline and good behavior in my classroom was that I did nearly all my teaching standing up. That way I could see all my children, and I could nip any disorder in the bud. If I had hidden behind the books on my desk, I wouldn't have been able to maintain order so well. And I knew that misconduct by just one student would ruin everybody's opportunity.

In addition to teaching at Inverness, I directed the senior class play every year. It was an extra-curricular job I always enjoyed. Each year I tried to select a play with the exact number of characters we had in the senior class. That meant that usually we had a play with eight or ten or twelve characters. If we needed extra actors, I could always dip into the junior class. Of course, I had to use plays that were simple and humorous—plays with titles like "A Date with Judy" and "Bottoms Up."

I seldom had any trouble with my actors. They learned their lines and followed my directions. I do remember two exceptions. One time a character didn't show up for school the day of the play, and his friends told me he wouldn't be there that night either. He had decided, they said, to spite the school and the principal. As soon as I heard this, I said, "Never mind. I'll take care of him later. Right now, bring me Morris Boswell." Morris was a junior, but he was smart as a whip, and I knew he could do the part at the last minute. When he came to my room, I read through

the play with him and sent him off into the field behind the school to memorize his part. Believe it or not, he went on stage that very night and starred! He did it! He did it without any practice and was perfect. One other time a girl stayed out the last day, and I took her part that night. I'd been through the play so many times I knew her role anyway. I won't tell you what I did when those absent characters showed up in class the next week, but you can be assured they never forgot it.

Yes, I can say that, all in all, I've had a full life and a wonderful career as a teacher, sending young people out into the world and seeing them become successful men and women. Just yesterday I had a visit from a boy I taught over forty years ago. You can't imagine how much I enjoyed seeing him. He told me all about his work and his twelve grandchildren. When he got up to leave, he shook my hand and said, "Miss Estelle, you're the best teacher I ever had." You bet, I wanted to hug his neck. When you've spent your life trying so hard to be a good teacher, you appreciate it when someone says, "Well, you did succeed on me." That's all the reward I ever needed.

POSTSCRIPT: Before I left, Mrs. Campbell insisted that I have a glass of iced tea on her front porch and take a few minutes to admire her potted plants and yard flowers. I saw her a few more times on my visits home before she died. As one of the last ties to Inverness School, her death closed a chapter of local history. Her home was sold to another widow, her friend Julia Thomas Cope Scroggins, who served as lunchroom supervisor at Inverness School for many years.

Local Historian

When I telephoned her, Julia Thomas Cope said she'd be delighted to share with me her life and knowledge of local history. She asked me to come to her mother's home, about a quarter of a mile from hers, just off Highway 14, halfway between Inverness and Blues Old Stand. It's July 20, 1977, and it's hot and humid as we sit down to talk on her mother's screened-in porch. Mrs. Cope is well known as an active church woman as well as a rapid-fire talker with strong opinions on most subjects. She is also a well-read, well-experienced oral newspaper of local life and history.

Let's sit out here on the porch while we talk. This is Mama's house, but I come up here twice a day to see about her since Daddy died. These screens will keep out the flies and gnats and dogs, and it'll be cooler out here. Mama doesn't have air conditioning. She's cold-natured. It was the first of June before she pulled her sweater off.

The pediatrician's wife in Union Springs came down here the other day, and we were talking about those potato logs that they make down at the Piggly Wiggly in the delicatessen. They are just delicious. She's a Yankee, you know, and says she likes everything down here but the hot weather. I said, "I'll tell you it's not like this all the time. Some of us have air conditioning, and I heard on the news that it got up to 101 degrees somewhere up north yesterday." When I told her that, she started laughing. She should have lived here long as I have; then she'd know what it's like to get hot.

I've been living in this country a long time. I was born in Covington County in 1909, the daughter of Grover Thomas and Artie Lee Maddox Thomas. Mama was born in 1888 and raised in Bullock County over here close to Indian Creek, four miles from Indian Creek and four miles from Aberfoil. Daddy was born right close to Smut Eye. You get to Blue's Stand and then take the first road to your right and you keep going maybe two miles, and you'll see a big old white two-story house on a hill. My daddy was born in that house made of lumber and boards planed by hand. He left Bullock County to go where he thought there were more opportunities and to get a start on his own. That's why he went down to Covington County and farmed a while. Then he decided he wanted to get into the railroad business, which he believed was the coming thing, and so we lived for a while in Linwood in Pike County, where my sister Gladys was born.

I believe we settled back here in Bullock County about 1915, when Daddy was still working for the Central of Georgia Railroad. He was a section foreman and had a gang of Negro hands that helped him keep up his section of railroad tracks and right-of-ways between Union Springs and Saco. The railroad furnished us a house just below the depot in Inverness. Later, they cut out all the sections and the agents and had what you call caretakers, and they tore the section house down.

While Daddy was still with the railroad, he bought this land we're living on now and rented it out. When the boll weevil came about 1925, he just about lost everything he'd ever made. He was running a four-mule farm, which was a big spread in those days. He was working for the railroad and farming at the same time. He thought he was going to get rich—till the boll weevil came along and spoiled it all. Mama said, "Grover, don't you keep on planting that old cotton." So Daddy kind of drifted out of cotton and started planting peanuts as his cash crop. He worked for the railroad for twenty-five years; then he worked for a number of years for the county helping to keep up the dirt roads and the right-of-ways, and he was ready to retire. We were fortunate because our daddy worked for the railroad. It was considered a top job. He always had work and got a check. A lot of people had it real hard, especially during the Depression, but we always had real money. We children could buy all the Co-Colas we wanted for a nickel a piece or a whole sackful of candy.

That's when we lived in Inverness in the railroad section house and had it real good. Inverness was a thriving little place back then. We had four trains running every day. There was a nine o'clock train that went up every morning and a ten o'clock train that came down. In those days the Central of Georgia went all the way down to Andalusia. Our house sat back in a big pasture, and we had a walkway up to the big gate by the railroad tracks. Gladys and I would climb up

Julia Thomas Cope.

on the gate post and we'd sit there to watch for Daddy Moore's train. He was an engineer. He was a friend of our grandfather and was real fond of Daddy, and he just loved us to death. He'd watch for us on the gate post and when he'd pass he'd throw us some candy or an apple or orange. So when we knew it was his run, we'd beat it up there and get on that post. One time he came to see us and he asked me, "What is your grandpapa's name?" I said, "His name is Papa." I was real small and didn't know any name but Papa. Mama liked to have taken a hole out of me she pinched me so hard when I said that. She was embarrassed that I didn't know my granddaddy's name.

At that time we had just about everything we needed right here in Inverness. We had a post office and a cotton gin, our schoolhouse and churches and four stores—Mr. Boyd's store and Mr. McNair's store, which joined together with a little walkway; Mr. Bates' store; and Mr. Alex Smith's meat market. You could buy most everything you needed in those stores: food supplies, household utensils, pots and pans, candles, clothes, shoes, plow harnesses—just about anything you wanted, though I think you'd have to go to Union Springs or Troy to buy big items like wagons or buggies or you could order them from the Sears and Roebuck catalogue and have them delivered by train. A little earlier there had been a commissary store for the Sellers plantation. Most of the farmers on the Sellers land around Inverness were sharecroppers, and the commissary was set up for them to buy on credit, but anybody else could trade there too.

I've heard that the big house next to where Coy Kinard now lives was once a hotel, and teachers and drummers would board there. The drummers would come to Inverness by train and rent a horse and buggy and make their calls on merchants in places like Perote, Post Oak, and Boswell. The drummers would take orders and have them shipped to the Inverness depot, and the merchants would pick them up there. Even when I was a girl, a lot of that business was still going on.

It was sort of like the Watkins Liniment man who would go around making up orders and then ship the merchandise a week or two later. Inverness was a distribution point for a lot of these nearby farming communities because we had a depot. There was also one down at Linwood, where Mr. Joe Sorrell was the agent.

When people in this part of the county needed to go to a larger town, they usually went to Troy. That habit probably goes back to the time before the Civil War, when we were a part of Pike County, and people around here had to go to the courthouse at Troy to do their legal business. You know, of course, that the Baptist churches in this end of the county used to belong to the Salem-Troy Association. When Bullock County was carved out of Macon, Barbour, Montgomery, and Pike counties right after the war, people had to start going to Union Springs to do their legal transactions.

Even after we got our own hospital in Union Springs, people here preferred to be sent to Montgomery or Troy. They said, "Well, when Mama was sick, she was taken to Edge's Hospital in Troy, and that's where I want to go." Of course, we had our own doctor in Inverness. Dr. George Guthrie and his brother Emmett both made doctors, and Dr. George practiced in Inverness and Dr. Emmett in Simsville. Their brother John was a farmer and a cattleman, and along toward the end of his life he became a road commissioner.

Dr. George Guthrie had the first car in Inverness, and Mr. Boyd had the second, and along about 1919 Daddy bought us the third, a Model T Ford. I remember a funny thing that happened with that old car. We'd been to Mama's old homeplace over in Indian Creek. It was Mama and Daddy and Gladys and one of Mama's friends, Kate Ming, and me, and we were coming back late at night. We got over here just this side of Aberfoil under that big huge oak tree that's still standing there now, and we gave out of gas. Daddy left us sitting by the side of the road and went up to Mr. Beverley's big old white house up on the left and borrowed his mule and his kerosene can. The closest filling station was in Smut Eye. There we sat on that dirt road with no traffic at all, and Daddy got on that mule and rode him all the way back down to Smut Eye to wake up the storekeeper to fill up that can with gas.

One car did come by about three o'clock in the morning, and we were just four women huddled up together frightened to death because we couldn't lock ourselves in that car. There we were all night long waiting for Daddy to ride to Smut Eye and get that gallon of gas, and then he rode back on the mule and poured the gas in the car and took the mule and can back to Mr. Beverley and then walked back down the road to where we were and we all got in and putt-putt-putted on home. It was about seven o'clock in the morning when we finally got there, and it was time for Gladys and me to go to school and for Daddy to go to work. It was lucky for us that Daddy knew everybody and could get gas that late at night.

Of course, my people have been living around Inverness a long, long time. It used to be named Thomasville after my family. I've heard my daddy say that my great-great grandfather came from South Carolina in a covered wagon and settled here. All his

Court Square in Troy, c. 1950.

children were born right close by, and he gave the right-of-way for the railroad. Two of my daddy's daddy's brothers fought in the old Confederate war. One of them was named Ira B. Thomas. They said he'd been fighting a long time and went to his commanding officer one day and told him he wanted to come home. The officer said, "Well, just wait until after the next battle is over, and you can have your furlough and go home." Ira Thomas said, "Then I'll never make it." The officer said, "Oh, Thomas, you've been through battles before, and you know you'll come through this one, too." But he didn't. He was so badly wounded they put him on the hospital train for Atlanta but he died before he got there, and they buried him in the Confederate cemetery when they arrived. We've never seen the grave, but my son Oscar Thomas lives in Georgia now and he wants to visit it.

There was a good history of Inverness that ran in the *Union Springs Herald* a number of years ago, and it told a number of interesting facts about this place. This area was settled on both sides of the Conecuh River by soldiers who obtained land grants. The white men moved in with their Negro slaves from Georgia and the Carolinas and the other older states. As I said, my family was among the first settlers, and they named the settlement after William Thomas. He built his home on the east side of the river near Cypress Pond, which was named for the great big cypress trees growing there. His property extended all the way to what is now Halls Cross Roads. Other pioneer families were the Townsends, the Jenkins, the Browns, and the Gilmores.

The Bethel community, about four miles east of Thomasville, was settled by some Scotch people a little earlier. They named it Scotland in honor of their native country. Many of those early families have descendants still living around here. The land was rich in both communities, and farming became the main occupation as more slaves were brought in to clear and work the land. The produce was taken by wagon over

An abandoned country house.

trails and rough roads to such river towns as Eufaula and Montgomery, and it would take three or four days to make the round trip. I've heard Daddy tell that as late as his time they carried bales of cotton to Eufaula and camped out at night.

There was some rivalry between Scotland and Thomasville, but Thomasville won out when the railroad was laid through here. It was called the Girard and Mobile Railroad and ran from Union Springs to Thomasville and later extended on to Troy. Thomasville's name had to be changed when it was discovered there was already a town by that name in north Alabama; so Mr. John Graham, one of the local Scotch settlers, suggested that our town be named for the home of his ancestors in Scotland, and so they renamed it Inverness. In those early days there were lots of saloons in town, but they were closed after it was incorporated. People began moving into the town—the Blues, the Adams, the Varners, the Philips. The Lockwoods moved in with their daughters, who were graduates of Tuskegee Women's College and conducted a private school for several years. The Grider family, who were moneylenders and builders, moved in about the time the town was incorporated and built a number of houses. Daddy said the Griders were kin to the Thomases.

There have always been a lot of churches in this part of the county. The Baptist church at Mt. Zion, about four miles from here over on Highway 223, was built by the Thomasville community, and the people at Scotland built the Presbyterian church at Bethel. The Inverness Baptist Church wasn't organized until 1900, when it began in the Sellers schoolhouse with J. H. Cogdell as the elder. Daddy's oldest brother, Uncle Tommy, was its first pastor. He was a graduate of the seminary in Louisville, Kentucky, and had served as a foreign missionary to China. In those days they didn't take very good care of the missionaries and he became ill and had to come home. When he recovered he became pastor at Louisville, Alabama, and at Indian Creek, and then he came over to preach at our church when it was constituted. There had been a Methodist church in this settlement and Baptist churches all around, but never a Baptist church here. The slaves, of course, had belonged to their masters' churches until they were freed, and then they formed their own churches.

About the time the Inverness church was organized, this community was a thriving little place. Mr. Cogdell owned a cotton gin and built a sawmill on what came to be known as Moccasin Flat. There was even a drugstore run by W. H. Sellers. But a terrible fire in 1906 almost wiped out the entire town when most of the stores and the gin were burned to the ground. Within about two years, however, the stores were rebuilt and a new gin and a grist mill were in operation. The old schoolhouse was torn down in 1914 and a new school was built by Mr. Hitchcock and Mr. McNair and the Reverend Rocket. From time to time, rooms were added to the original building, and in 1924 the school was accredited with Mr. Peacock as principal.

Now we're in the period that I remember very well first-hand. A brick high school was built in 1929 and the old wooden building became the elementary school. The first principal of the new combined school was Mr. J. F. Hamilton. All the little schools from places like Mt. Hilliard, Bethel, Boswell, and Jenkins Cross Roads were closed and the children were brought to the new Inverness Consolidated School. Now, I want to give credit to Mr. Hamilton. When he was principal, we had a good school. The children that finished at Inverness left there knowing a lot. We had good teachers. We had good discipline. The students knew that if they didn't toe the mark Mr. Hamilton would attend to them. Of course, I went to school at Inverness before Mr. Hamilton came over here from Chambers County. I wasn't quite six years old when we moved from Linwood in Pike County up here. It was in January and Mrs. Addis Boyd was the first grade teacher. We had just moved in when Mrs. Boyd came down to see Mama and said they were doing a little operetta and needed a little fairy. Even though I wouldn't be six until August, she asked Mama if she cared to let me come to school and be in the play. After a few days she asked Mama to buy me a first grade reader, and I learned to read before school was out in April. Then I started to school officially in September.

I was in school with the Hitchcock boys, though they were a little ahead of me. Davis Hitchcock became an all-star baseball player. One time he and Dewitt Brabham went to sleep in school and woke up with the teacher whipping them with a switch. After school all us school children walked down the sidewalk singing, "Listen, let me tell you the truth: Davis and Dewitt got a whipping in school." We thought it was funny because they were almost grown boys.

One year we had a bad storm that blew the roof and the posts on the schoolhouse porch down, and all of us little girls and boys were so frightened we didn't know what in the world to do. We were afraid we might all get carried away, but Magdalen Deason stood against the door and kept the wind from blowing it open. She was a really large girl and strong. Another time when it looked like a storm was coming up, I was walking to school from where we lived near the depot, wearing my raincoat and carrying my umbrella. Cecil McNair was walking along with me. It started to rain and the wind began to blow, and when I opened up my umbrella it picked me up right off my feet and I was sailing around hanging onto my umbrella. Cecil caught hold of me and pulled me down, but I had to drop my umbrella and it blew away.

I went to Inverness School for twelve years. I started at one end of the school building and came out the other. It was a hard school. I studied Latin taught by Mr. Hightower and physics and geometry taught by Mr. John Reagan. We had fun too. We had good ball teams, boys and girls. The girls would put on their bloomers and get out there and play Josie and Union Springs and other schools. Now don't you know we were a sight for sore eyes, playing in our black bloomers! We had a yell that went: "Go get a surrey; go get a hack; take old Perote way, way back." The Union Springs teams would fight like dogs and scratch like cats because they didn't want a little country school like Inverness to beat them, but we'd win nearly every time. The Boswell boys were good basketball players and so were Mr. John Henry Hall's boys. One time they even played Troy Normal School, which is now Troy State University. We didn't have a gym, of course, so we had to play outside on the hard ground. One time the boys' and the girls' teams were going to Josie to play, and the bus got bogged down up to the axle in the mud going up Davis Hill just before Perote. We had to get out and walk up the hill in all that mud, but after we unloaded the bus we were able to get through and to Josie in time to win both games.

We also had a number of activities in school. We had two literary societies, the Heflin and the Brandon, and they would give programs in chapel. Brandon was named after an Alabama governor and Heflin after a senator from Alabama. Fred Hall was so good at memory work, and everyone enjoyed it so much

when he gave a recitation. I think he could have been good on the stage if he'd just been able to cultivate his talent. We also had what we called field days before the little schools around here were consolidated at Inverness. That was when children from schools at Boswell and Perote and other places would come to Inverness and we'd have contests like jumping matches and sack races and speech recitations. After we got consolidated, we'd have competitions with larger schools at Midway and Union Springs.

At the end of school each year we'd have plays and operettas. I remember one operetta when all of us girls were dressed like flowers and we'd sing songs and do little dances and finally, one of the flowers was chosen to get the Prince. Avis Hall was the little daisy and out of the whole bunch of flowers she was chosen to be kissed by the Prince. The cos-tumes were made out of crepe paper because it was cheap and stretchy. You could flute or ruffle it and you could sew it on the machine. But it wouldn't last more than one time. If you wanted something more permanent or if you needed a lot of ruffles, you would take an old worn-out bedsheet and sew ruffles on top of each other until you got as many as you wanted. It was sleeveless and didn't require any hemming. I don't remem-

Dean Driggers at Inverness School, c. 1949.

ber the name of it, but one time I had to do a little song about my kitten and a boy had to sing about his dog. We had a live dog and cat on stage, and Mama curled my hair up in long rings, and the dog was playing with my curls all the time I was singing about my cat. I don't know how good we were, but we managed to get through it all right. Most of these musical entertainments were near the end of school,

The eighth grade class at Inverness in 1947. Author Wade Hall is on the far right of the back row.

but we also had little plays around Christmas. One year we did a play about Old Scrooge and Tiny Tim, and, of course, we had pageants about the birth of Jesus.

I finished at Inverness in 1927 and went to Montgomery. After I got married my husband and I lived there a pretty good while, but we finally moved back here to be with Mama and Daddy. While my husband was in service during the war, we lived in North Carolina, Kentucky, and Tennessee. I've worked in the lunchroom at Inverness School for a long time. When they opened it, I was living in Montgomery and Mr. Hamilton got Alice Kinard and Emily Bonner to run it. Lunches cost a dime then, and some students had to get government assistance to pay that. After we moved back here, Emily quit and Mr. Hamilton wanted to know if I'd help Alice because we

were such good friends. So I did. Then when Alice died, I took it over. I've seen a lot of changes since I've been in that lunchroom. Of course, at the beginning it was all white, but now it's almost all black, about eight whites out of 250 students. There have been a lot of changes in the lunchroom facilities too. When I started, we had a wood-burning stove to cook on. Now we have electric stoves and ovens and four deep freezes.

I get along beautifully with all the black people at the school. I have four black women that work under me. My assistant is a black woman. It's a job to make out the menus and do all the buying and keep all the records. I have to keep track of all the purchased food and all the commodities that come in. It costs close to seventy-two cents now to make one lunch, though most of the students get theirs free. It's been hard work but I have enjoyed my years in the lunchroom, seeing the students start out in the first grade and go on to graduate and then go out into the world and make something of themselves.

I have two grown sons and one husband named Oscar. And yes, Oscar is still living, though some people think he's dead because back last winter he was real sick. One Sunday morning the telephone rang and a lady from church said, kind of hesitantly, "Ah, how are you all this morning?" I said, "We are all right. How are you?" She went ahead and talked a bit and then asked me if we were coming to church. I said we were. Then she asked if Oscar was coming too. I said, "Of course, Oscar is coming too. He always comes with me to church." Then she said, 'Well, Julia, I'm so glad to hear that because I'll just have to tell you we heard in Union Springs that Oscar was dead. I thought it was something I'd missed somehow." I said, "No, Oscar has been sick, but he's certainly not dead." She said, "Now, Julia, don't you go and tell Oscar. Don't you tell him what I said." I promised I wouldn't and said we'd both be in church alive in a few minutes.

POSTSCRIPT: Following her husband's death several years after my conversation with her, Julia Thomas Cope married the Reverend Stafford Scroggins, a local Baptist minister who has since died. The Inverness School which she attended and for which she later served as lunchroom supervisor has been razed and the students moved to Bullock County High School in Union Springs. She is now retired and lives alone in Inverness in the house which once belonged to Mrs. Estelle Cope Campbell.

INTERLUDE: CHILDREN

*C*hildren in rural Alabama in the first half of the century had a rich life, if not in material things. These photos are of the author's family, but are typical of the period. Clockwise, from top left, cousins piled on a Model T; Jack Hall and a black playmate remembered only as "Preacher"; Wade and Jack Hall with their tricycle; T.C. Brooks and Wade Hall at the edge of a cotton field, 1937; Jimmy Hall in the chicken yard; Sarah Waters Hall and Wade, c. 1936. Finally, the numerous small graves in Bullock County cemeteries testify that many children did not live to maturity. At left, the 1937 funeral of one of the author's first cousins, a Driggers. Louise Hall's two brothers, Kizzie and Ned, are the pallbearers holding up the right side of the tiny casket.

BEANSIE HALL HALL

Housewife and Surrogate Mother

Beansie is my beloved aunt, my father's sister—the relative I always felt closest to when I was growing up. Like all the members of my father's family, however, she has very little formal education. I have never seen her write a word—not even her own name—or read anything—not a book or a magazine or a newspaper. She has lived in a completely non-literary world. The few literacy skills she acquired in the few months of schooling she had as a girl she has apparently forgotten.

She married a distant cousin, Caswell Hall, called "Fraze," on the eve of World War II; and they lived in a succession of primitive rented houses until the early 1970s, when they managed to buy a couple of acres of land on an unmarked, unpaved road off County Highway 111 in southern Bullock County, and placed a used mobile home on it. It is the first time they have ever owned any real estate. They have no children. The conversations on which this monologue is based were taped between the late 1970s and the early 1980s in their mobile home. She makes frequent references to other members of her family, including her older sister, Elma Lee, and her younger brother, called "Jabo," my late father. Her name is pronounced "Bee-ann-see."

Me and Fraze done eat, but I got plenty. I'm over seventy years old and I ain't starved yet. These biscuits is cold, so I'll make up some more and fry you a egg. I got plenty of grits and sausage left over that I can warm up. I'm still trying to get used to this little trailer kitchen, so you set down and get out of my way. I'll fix your some breakfast and tell you all I can remember about me and Fraze.

Look out the window and see if Whiskers is in the road. Lord have mercy, I'm worried to death about my babies. There's some that run by here and just kill all my babies. They don't slow down, and my poor babies just get run over. I have to chain Whiskers ever night to keep him out of the road. Or he'd be dead, too. No sir, I don't like living this close to the road, but hit's the only place we could get a little pasture and a cowpen, a chicken yard, and a garden. But won't nothing grow in that hard ground in the front yard. That scuppernong vine looks like it's about to give up. I'm rooting me a camellia in this glass of water, but I got no confidence it'll grow in that hard dirt, even if it does root. When it rains, the water just dreens off. We got a well but the water's got too much lime and iron in it, and we can't use it. We have to haul our water from over to Elma Lee's.

I used to want a trailer, but after I got to going to Lou's, I didn't want one. No, it's not that it's too little. It's just not a house. And when we moved here, we couldn't keep all our cows. When we sold em, I squalled like a baby. I wanted to sell to somebody who'd take em off where I'd never see em again. But we sold to a man down the road, and, Lord!, he didn't tend to em and feed em, and they perished to death. Before they died, their bones was sticking up to their skin. I don't know why people is so mean to the poor animals.

I'm getting used to the trailer now, but I still don't like it. When we moved over here from Tress's old place, Fraze went to work that Monday morning and I squalled and squalled. I'd get out and walk and walk, and I'd go back over to Tress's house, and I'd set there and squall some more. But I knowed we couldn't move back. I says to Fraze, "I can't hardly stand it, but I know we got to stay. We got our money in this land and trailer, and we can't go back."

Our trailer is tied down good, but I'm scared when a bad cloud comes up. I don't like to be in here when the wind's a-blowing. I've heered too many stories about people being blowed away and killed in their trailers. So when it starts up a storm, I run up to Bennie's and Bessie's and stay till it clears off again. Last year when that bad storm nearly blowed down Josie's old place, Fraze run in and said, "We'd better get out of here." I says, "Fraze, you know we can't run ever time it comes up a cloud." So we was up to Bennie's when the storm got that big chinaberry tree in their front yard. It wadn't solid. It just hit in streaks. If it'd hit solid, there wouldn't a-been a thing left in this world. We was worried about Elma Lee, afraid she might a-been on the road when the storm hit. But when Fraze went over to her house to see about her, she was all right.

You want some coffee while you wait for the biscuits to cook? I got some huckleberry pie in the safe I made yesterday. Cora Gause give me the berries. Elma Lee's got too feeble to go huckleberrying any more. But the pore critter still walks the roads. I'm scared she'll lose her mind and wander off in the woods and we'll never find her.

Taste these grits to see if they's salty enough. Where I learnt to cook was at Maggie's. When I's a girl, her and my brother Kinch was a-living across the field from our old homeplace. She showed me how to make up biscuits and cut up chicken and cook peas. After a while, she let me cook for her, so I'd have dinner ready when they all come in from the field. Elma Lee and Maw done all the cooking at home. I thought I's big to be a-cooking for ten or twelve.

Beansie Hall Hall and the author.

I still love to eat, but I don't have the appetite I used to have. I like my chicken and hog meat, but don't give me any of this deer meat peoples is eating these days. Do you hear about Jeanette? Before daylight one morning, she was a-setting up in a tree waiting for a deer to come by so's she could shoot it. It turned real cold that night and come a big frost. I know the tree was slick and she just slipped down that tree and hit the ground and broke her back. I says, "Jeanette, damn the deers. You leave them alone, and you won't get a broke back. They ain't been a-bothering you." She says, "Beansie, deer meat is good if you grind it up with some hog meat. It

makes a good sausage." I says, "Well, hit may be good to some people, but hit ain't good to me." Fraze says he thinks he et some horse meat in the Army! It wouldn't surprise me none. I've heered that people will eat worms and snakes and grasshoppers and sich. Lord have mercy, what is this world a-coming to? I reckon some people would eat bears and bobcats and beavers. I just hope they don't ask me to dinner.

We do have plenty of sich animals in the woods now. There used to be a bear just below here down at the old bridge, and the swamps is full of beavers. Beaver Dam over there near Liberty Church is full of beaver dens. They's bobcats all over the place. Fraze killed one over in Josie's yard between the kitchen and the house. He went over there to see about her cows and when that thing run out Fraze killed him. Lillie taken a picture of Fraze and the bobcat.

Now I *will* eat a turkey. I got a turkey hen setting on twenty eggs out in the bushes behind the chicken house right now. Hit takes four weeks for turkey eggs to hatch, and hit takes three weeks for chicken eggs. No, I can't say I mind eating a animal I raised, if it's a hog or a chicken or a turkey. I've even et guineas. But I won't eat cow meat—not from any cow I raised up. I loves my baby calves, and I looks after my cows. In the summertime I get up at four o'clock and get to the cowpen by sun-up. I'm not going to let my cows stand penned up after daylight. I just got one baby calf now, but I got other babies. I got four baby kittens left. Something got two of em when they's little, and Fraze killed one with his truck. Hit got cut all to pieces when it curled up and went to sleep under the hood of his truck. The

The Hall sisters (from left): Elma Lee, Beansie, and Lou (Driggers) holding her grandchild.

fan blades tore the pore little thing up when Fraze went to crank it up. Lord, they was fur all over the yard. I hollered and hollered and made Fraze find all the pieces and bury the pore little thing. Fraze says, "I think I'll make me some cat sausage." I says, "If you do, I'll make me some Fraze sausage."

But Whiskers is my best baby now. It come from Columbus and belonged to a boy that lived close to Adolph and hung hisself. His daddy was going to have his little dog put to sleep, and Adolph says, "No, I promised I'd get Beansie a little dog, and I'm going to take it to her." Lord, he's a mess! When Baby gets out, he'll come to the door and scratch and scratch and whine and whine till I let him back in. He loves me a lot, and I loves him. But sometimes he makes me so blamed mad I could kill him. 'Course I never would. He follows me wherever I go—up to Bennie's, over to Josie's old house, out to the garden, down to the cowpen. That day it snowed Baby had a time out there a-slipping and a-sliding. Lord, I thought I'd lost him one time. Jack sent word that somebody had run over my dog in front of his house, so me and Fraze went over to get him. But when we went to pick him up to bring home and bury the pore little thing, he walled his eyes up at us; and I knowed he was hurt real bad but not dead. We brought him on home, locked him up in the chicken house and he got well in a week. I loves my baby. I buy cow liver for him. He won't eat dog food. Poor old Whiskers has got so old his hair's turned gray. Look out there again and see if he's in the road.

I oncet had a little old feist dog named Brownie. Lady was her mammy, but she got to killing chickens, and I let a boy have her. He raised the puppies and give me one. When we got Brownie, she wadn't big as my fist. They wanted me to have her tail cut off, but I said hit was put on there for a purpose and I's going to let it stay. She was a pretty baby, Brownie was. One time she was in heat and a fit hit her, and she taken off behind the house a-running. I taken off behind her, but I couldn't keep up. I looked and looked for her, but I never did find her till the next spring, when we's walking through a back field and found her bones in a gully. I knowed it was her before I got up close.

I've loved all my babies. I had Pollie a long time. He was full blood, but I don't know what kind. One night Pollie didn't come up, and I called and called him. The next morning I went out looking for him down in the branch next to the road. Somebody come by and says, "Beansie, where's your little dog?" I says, "I don't know where he is. Somebody may have killed him or he may be run off." He says, "Well, I'll tell you where he is. He's down there at Beaver Dam dead." I got Fraze to take me over, and there the little critter was. I believe somebody killed him first and throwed him out on the road. I don't think he got hit by a car. It's been a long time since Pollie died, but I still miss him. I don't know why I named him Pollie. I knowed that wasn't no name for a boy dog, but I just got started calling him that.

I just got me a new baby calf. His mammy found him in the pasture and I was going to let him stay out there till he could walk, but the buzzards nearly got him. If I'd left him a minute longer, he would a-been et up. He's under the shed in the cowpen. I do love my pretty thing.

And I got doll babies too. When I's a girl my brother Toodle bought me a doll that was made out of chalk. He made like Santa Claus brung it to me, and I loved it so much. One morning they's all up there in front of the old homeplace a-picking cotton, and me and Jabo was playing out in the yard. Granny Rollo was in the house by herself, and all of a sudden, I heered something drop and break on the floor, and she says, "Well, I reckon the little bitch'll kill me." Now, they said Granny never did cuss much, and I knowed something was bad wrong. I flew in the house, seen my doll all broke to pieces on the floor, and I jumped on her and got her by the coattail and pulled her down on the floor. In them days women used to wear big old long skirts a yard wide. I commenced to crying for my doll and 'cause I knowed I hadn't ought to a-pulled Granny down on the floor. I had wrapped my baby up in a piece of quilt and put it in one of them long drawers in the sideboard. I know she pulled the drawer out and started to unwrap the doll to see what it was and it fell to the floor. I felt sorry for myself, and I felt sorry for Granny 'cause I knowed the old critter didn't know my baby was in that quilt.

I never did have another doll baby until Robert Turner brung me one from Columbus after I's married. I kept that baby till one of Jabo's boys got mad with me one time and tore it up. The next doll baby was give to me by Jabo's oldest son, and I still got her. She's the prettiest thing. She's got pretty white hair and a long lace dress. I keep her standing up in my chifforobe.

I was nearly the baby in my own family. I was borned the last day of April in 1908, at the old homeplace up near the old claypit, just a few miles from where I live now. There was five boys and four of us girls—Simon, Toodle, Elma Lee, Jennie, Kinch, Lou, Nathan, then me and Jabo, the youngest. All of us was healthy, but for Simon. He had the diphtheria, and what killed him was the doctors wouldn't let them give the poor little thing no water. He just burnt up with fever and it killed him. Now, that's what I been told. I didn't know Simon. He was dead before I's born.

But I do remember Jennie. She died not long after she married Tom Boyd Norris. I don't remember much about how she died. In them days they wouldn't let younguns go around sich. Lord, now younguns know sich things before they get the pippin off em good. Their mothers talk about it in front of em, and they ought not to do it. Elma Lee won't talk much about Jennie, but I've heerd Lou say she was having fits when her baby was being borned. She killed the baby when she's having them fits. It hadn't been borned yet but it was getting close time. The doctor got there and got the baby but hit was dead already. They said Jennie never had fits before. That was the first time she'd ever been that-a-way, and it killed her and her baby. When Jennie died, people didn't go to the doctors like they do now. When a woman finds out she's that-a-way now, she puts on her hat and goes to see the doctor two or three times a week. Long back then, they had these granny women that would come and help take care of things. Younguns won't allowed to be around sich as that till the baby got maybe a month old.

Me and Jabo was the babies of the family, and we never had to work much as the others. We went to school for a while over at Almeria Schoolhouse, and we played games. We played at school and at home and each other's houses. One time me and Jabo made us a playhouse out of old tree branches and played house with Joe Ed and Annie Ruth Gause. We wrung us some broomstraw to make the walls of the house. We stripped oak leaves from the branches and made a leaf dress for me and Annie Ruth and a leaf blouse for Joe Ed and Jabo. We'd make like we'd cooking. We played like we's married—Joe Ed was my old man and Jabo was Annie Ruth's. Lord a-mercy! Younguns these days would think that was fogy.

A game we played at school was called stealing

sticks. We'd draw us a line, and some of us would get on one side and some on the other. We'd lay the same number of sticks on each side on the ground. When one side got all the sticks, that was the end of the game. Sometimes we played hiding and dropping the handkerchief and sugar lump and stealing the penny. When we played hiding, one of us would close our eyes at home base and count to a certain number while the rest of us would hide. Then we'd try to get back home without him tagging us. When we played dropping the handkerchief, we'd get in a big ring and one of us would walk behind the others and drop the handkerchief behind somebody and that person would have to tag the other person before he could run around the ring. When we played stealing the penny, we'd have a big crowd setting around and somebody would put a penny in his hand and then put his hand over everybody else's hand and drop it in one hand, and the person that had it dropped in his hand had to catch him before he could get back to his place or he'd be "It."

Fraze Hall, 1986.

When I got a little older, a crowd of us young people would go to one another's houses on Saturday night and play games and make syrup candy. The way you make syrup candy is to take some syrup and cook it until it gets thick like candy, then cool it and pull it until it gets white and put it down on the table and cut it with a knife. Sometimes we'd not pull it but put parched peanuts in it and roll it out in little balls. Sometimes we'd have a candy drawing. We'd all chunk in and buy so many lemon and peppermint sticks and mix it all together in a box with a hole in the top. Then each one would stick his hand through the

hole without looking and keep on drawing out as long as he kept on getting the same flavor. When you drawed one that didn't match, you had to stop. One time I almost drawed the whole box before I had to stop! When we had candy drawings, we'd have big crowds, we would!

'Course the boys, when they got big enough to hold a gun, would go hunting; and all of us would go fishing. They used to be a heap of fishponds around here. I never was one to go fishing much—I never had the patience—but I've been over to Tress's old pond a many a time. If you go over there right now, you can still see part of the dam, but it's all growed up with bushes and trees and briars. We'd get fish bait from the worms on the Catalpa trees or we'd catch crickets or we'd grow our own worms. We always had a fish bait bed off the back porch where we'd throw out the dishwater. We'd put a few boards on top of the ground and keep it wet and the worms would grow there aplenty. I never could bait my own hook, but I've caught a few fish when somebody else would bait it. If we caught enough fish, we'd have a big fish fry and hush puppies and have a big crowd eat with us.

Lord a-mercy! Younguns these days can't sit still long enough to fish. They got to be on the move and drink and go nekked. Why, the other day I seen Jimmy feeding his little baby girl a can of beer! I'd a-blistered his tail if he'd been one of mine. I say, "Jimmy, how do you think she's a-going to turn out, a-drinking beer before she can walk?" He laughed and says, "Hush, Beansie, she likes it." I tell you, this young race of people, they just do anything they've a mind to. They ought to be ashamed. And they don't wear nothing these days. You might as well say they go around nekked. I have seen grown girls up there in town, with a little piece up here and a little piece down there, and it didn't hide much. They might as well take it all off and go buck-nekked!

And younguns know everthing before they can talk. They know where they come from before they's dry. Let me tell you what: I've seen a woman a-having a baby over television. I've seen horses a-having a colt, cows a-having a calf, and all sich as that. I know what I'm a-talking about. I've seen it with my own eyes! It's not right for little younguns to see sich as that. They'll know it time enough.

It's sort of like when we stayed over there at Tress's old house. I had a cat that was about ready to find kittens, and I didn't want my little niece to know it. So I put the cat out in the old smokehouse, and she had her kittens out there where nobody could see her. Well, one day Sharon was poking around and found the cat and the kittens.

She says, "Beansie, where did you get them kittens?" I says, "Sharon, I didn't even know they's out here. I reckon their mama scratched a hole in the ground and found em." She says, "No, she didn't neither. They come out of her belly. Mama told me." I says, "My God!" Younguns is just too little to know things like that.

Lord, I been talking on and on and the biscuits is about cold. I don't have no cow butter. My cow got in some bitterweeds and the butter tastes nasty. Here's some margarine, if you can eat it. I got plenty of grits on the stove and a piece of fried ham left over from yesterday. They'll just be to throw out.

When my mind gets on younguns these days, I forget what I'm a-doing. It makes me glad I never had none of my own. All this nekkedness and women a-having babies on television is causing em all to go wild. They don't marry. They just shack up with one another. That's the style these days. And when they get tired of each other, they switch and get them

another one. And you got all these babies that don't know who their daddies is. Lord a-mercy, I don't know what this world is a-coming to! Hit may all be signs of the end of time.

People don't come see each other and visit like they used to. I don't even see my own kinfolks much any more. Naw, they don't come around much. I used to see a lot of Kinch's people and Lou's that moved off, but I don't see em much now unless it's at a funeral. I couldn't get off to go to the family reunion this year over in Georgia. Elma Lee says when she was over there to see some of Lou's younguns, they told her she couldn't come in their house unless she took her shoes off. I says, "Elma Lee, shoot fire, if it'd been me, I'd a-said, 'You kiss my foot and go to hell,' and turned around and come on back home." You know, they got this white shag on the floor, and they ought to knowed blamed well they couldn't keep it clean. I ain't been over there to visit and I don't intend to. I don't like that part of the country anyways. But I can tell you what's wrong with a lot of people these days. One thinks he's better than the others. I tell em of it too. If they's too good to come around me, they can stay away.

Me and Fraze has been married for forty-two years. We was married on the seventeenth day of June in 1939. The other day I says, "Fraze, I wish I could call back them forty-two years." 'Course, I didn't mean it. Hit's not been bad. I was a Hall a-marrying a Hall, but we's not close kin. He's about five years younger than me, and we've knowed each other all our lives. We played together when we's little, we did; and when it come time to marry, we knowed each other real good and just figured we ought to do it. His mama and papa was born somewheres around here, and he was, too, but I couldn't tell you where. He was in Michigan and South Carolina when he's in the Army. We was married by then, and I went to see him on the bus one time when he's up in Charleston, but I was glad to get back home. I didn't like them people way up there. He didn't go overseas when he was in the Army, but he got his leg hurt when he's jumping over a ditch and it still bothers him some. He gets a little pension check from the government. Since we's been married, Fraze has farmed, run a store, and worked on the road for the state. Like a lot of em around here, he's made a little whiskey in the woods. But he don't do nothing much now.

We look after the things around the house, and we look after pore old Elma Lee as much as we can. When we need to go anywheres, Fraze drives his truck. But he won't drive it to town or to Troy or Montgomery or Columbus 'cause he never got a license.

I've worked hard since I married. I didn't know what work was when I's a girl. As I said a while ago, the others worked in the fields, but I didn't hit a lick. I mostly stayed at home and played. Lord a-mercy, I learnt what work was after I married Fraze. The hardest work was farming. I hope in the fields, chopping cotton, hoeing cotton, picking cotton. I never did plow. That was a man's job. I never was much of a hand with a hoe, but I done my best. Cotton was the hardest crop to work. It had to be planted, then chopped, then sided with a plow, then hoed, then the middle busted with a plow, and then laid by. We'd always plant sometime around in April, about the time we heerd the first whippoorwill. 'Course, after it made, it had to be picked two or three times. Now that was the hardest work of all—pulling that heavy cottonsack down them long rows! I wore cotton gloves with the finger-ends cut off to keep my fingers from getting stuck by the cotton burrs, but they's still bleeding by the end of the day. I was a pretty fast cottonpicker. The most I ever picked was two hundred pounds in one day, but that cotton was thick and I picked from daylight to dark, with just a little time off for dinner. Let me tell you something: I was tired when I come in that night! If I'd been hired out, I'd a-made close to two dollars that day, and that was big

money. Some years we'd be a-picking when there's frost on the ground, but by then the cotton had been picked over so much we couldn't get more than forty or fifty pounds a piece in a whole day.

To have a good stand of cotton, we'd sometimes have to replant it with a hoe where there were skips. We most always had to replant some of the corn where it didn't come up, and the crows would be bad to eat the corn after it did come up. It was nearly about as hard to work as cotton. When we gathered the corn, we pulled it off the stalk by hand. Hit wadn't bad work, 'cept when we had velvet beans planted in the corn rows so it would grow up the stalks. That velvet bean fuzz would get on your skin and you'd itch to death before you could get to the house and wash it off.

Fraze always planted a few acres of peanuts, but there wadn't a whole lot to do to them. They didn't need a lot of hoeing, and he'd weed em and plow em and lay em by. But shaking them was hard and nasty work. You'd get dirt and sweat all over you from head to foot. After the men plowed up the peanuts, we'd shake the dirt off and throw them in piles. Then we'd use pitchforks to stack them on frames to dry. The men always did that work. I always looked forward to when the peanuts was getting mature along in August. We'd pull up some bunches, pick off the green peanuts and boil them in salty water. I could make a meal off of boiled peanuts. I still can. 'Course, when the peanuts dried out, we'd pick some off and parch them in the oven or in a baker in the fireplace. I did love parched peanuts. I still do.

Not long after we got married, me and Fraze lived up there at Bread Tray Hill in that little storehouse that Mr. John Henry Hall run later on. We lived in a room at the back and had the store in the front. We sold general merchandise like flour and kerosene and sugar and coffee and lard—whatever people wanted. When Fraze was in the Army, I lived in Jabo's old storehouse over at Tress's place, but I didn't try to run a store by myself. After Fraze come home, we moved over to Mr. Cleb Tillery's house, just down the road from where this trailer is now. That was when we worked Toodle's land. Long as we could farm we had plenty of corn and peanut hay for cow feed. I never had to worry about cow feed. Then as long as Fraze was working on a regular job, we could buy cow feed. But feed's so high now. We have to pay ten dollars for a sack of ground-up feed. That's why we had to get shed of most of our cows when we moved to this trailer.

Hit sure was hard for me to move here from Tress's old house. I loved that old place, and if it'd been left up to me, we'd still be there. 'Course, the old house needed some work done on it, but it was a good house. I didn't even get scared of the haints over there! Sometimes when Fraze'd be gone, I'd hear the awfulest fusses up there in the loft, and one evening by myself I heerd trace chains a-rattling. Hit was a terrible racket! I got scared and run out of doors, but I soon went back in, for I knowed that whatever it was wouldn't hurt me. I knowed everbody that ever lived and died in that house, and I knowed I never done nothing wrong to them. So they couldn't mean me no harm. I believe it was a warning some way or other, but I never found out what kind it was. I never have *seen* a haint, but I know they *can* be seen. I heerd Elma Lee say the day Jennie died, that morning early before day she was going out to the smokehouse to get a rasher of meat to cook for breakfast when something covered in white got behind her and followed her all the way there and back. Jennie died that night. Elma Lee says it was Jennie's haint already walking around before it had to leave to go to the grave.

Pore old Elma Lee's mind's not right. She talks more and more about Jennie and Maw and Nathan and Jabo and other dead people. She goes out hunting for them. She come in here the other day crazy as a betsy-bug and says, "Hit looks like Nathan would come on home. I don't know what's the matter with him. Where is he at?" I says, "Elma Lee, Nathan's not here." She says, "Well, where did he go? He stays gone all the time." I says, "Elma Lee, you might as well stop looking for him. He ain't going to come back." You know, her and Nathan lived together all their lives until he died. Night before last, she liked to scared me to death. She jumped up and said, "I want to go stay with Maw. I'll never leave her." I says, "Elma Lee, you can't find Maw. Hit's dark outside and you'll get lost." If Fraze hadn't a-been here, I don't know what I would have done with her. But we managed to hold her until she settled down. And she talks about going huckleberrying all the time, even when there's ice on the ground. The other day she says, "Where's Wade Henry? He'll go a-berrying with me." She wants to go to town tomorrow to a shoe sale somebody told her about. She's already got four pair of shoes now she never wears, but she wants another pair. Pore old critter. She's a pity to look at. Her tongue is all swoll up from that cancer. The other day she run into some bob-wire and cut her leg real bad. Don't none of em come around her any more. I have to see about her by myself, and it's about to worry me to death.

She spends ever night with us in the trailer now, but Fraze has to carry her home early in the morning. The other evening we went over to get her and she wadn't ready. So I says, "Come on, get ready, Elma Lee. We got to get home before dark." And she says, "Shoot fire, Beansie, I'll come when I get good and ready." I don't know how much longer I can manage her. She needs to have somebody clean out her well. I know there's something live down there. It may be a fish or a frog or it could be a little alligator. But she won't have nobody to go down there to see. It's getting so I'm scared to use the water myself.

And she still tries to keep all her cows. She's got thirteen head now, and her little old red-faced heifer found a calf last Sunday night. I found the heifer and her calf in the pasture on Monday morning and put them in the pen. You know if you don't milk a cow with her first calf, you can't ever milk her. So I went back over there yesterday, and Lord, both the cow and calf was out. I just knowed the calf was run over. But there was the calf laying there by the side of the road. So I drove them back to the cowpen and says, "Elma Lee, you hain't got no kind of cowpen to keep your cows in. Buy you some planks and get somebody to make you a good fence. All that wire is rotten and tore down. I don't see how them cows stay in at all." Know what she said? She says, "They's my damn cows. If they die, they die mine." I says, "Elma Lee, them pore cows is hungry. There ain't nothing in that pasture for them to eat. You ought to buy them some cow feed." But I can't tell her nothing. She was fussing this morning about the little bit of milk she gets. I says, "Well, the devil, Elma Lee, them cows can't make milk if they ain't got nothing to eat." Lord a-mercy, I feel sorry for the pore old cows. I wish she'd sell em but she won't. But I feel sorrier for pore old Elma Lee. I don't know what's to become of her. Like I told Fraze the other day, what would become of Elma Lee if something happened to us?

You want something else to eat? Did you have enough? Come back and eat dinner with us. I already got my butterbeans and peas shelled, and the okra is in the icebox. I can kill a chicken and make some gravy. Wait a minute before you go. I got some pillowslips I been had embroidered for you and meaning to give you for a long time. Go on and take em and use em. If you leave them here, they'll just stay folded in my dresser drawer. I'll go on out with you and see about my babies. I know they's hungry. I can hear em calling me.

POSTSCRIPT, August 1989:

Fraze: "Y'all get on out. Ain't nobody here but me and my sister Verna Mae out behind the trailer. She's snapping beans for my supper. Since Beansie's been gone, if she didn't come over and cook for me once in a while, I reckon I'd starve to death."

Beansie Hall died of a stroke on July 1, 1985. She lived long enough to see after her sister Elma Lee, who died two years earlier from cancer of the mouth developed from a lifelong habit of dipping snuff. They are both buried in the Liberty Church Cemetery near their parents and most of their brothers and sisters. Elma Lee had lived with her parents until they died, then with her brother Nathan—nicknamed Bootman because he loved to wear boots—until his death in 1964. Now she rests beside him. Beansie's tombstone gives her birth and death dates and the birth date of her surviving husband.

ELMA LEE HALL

An Independent Woman

A college professor visiting the United States from England during our Bicentennial year met my maiden aunt, Elma Lee Hall, during a trip to Alabama. When he returned home he wrote an account of his year abroad and his impressions of Americans and sent me a copy. I was startled to read that he had singled out my aunt as the strongest, most representative American he had met coast-to-coast during the entire year. Perhaps I shouldn't have been surprised. After all, her fierce self-reliance and her primitive—almost frontier—lifestyle are as American as the Fourth of July. But I had known her all my life and took her for granted. She had always been a constant, sustaining presence during my boyhood.

Elma Lee loved all her brothers' and sisters' many children as if they were her own—not in a soft, sentimental way, but as a tough, disciplined, caring aunt. Her dinner table was always set with good country food, and her food safe was always loaded with cold biscuits that, filled with fresh butter, hungry little boys cherished as much as ice cream. But she gave me more than food. My parents were never able to find any successful treatment for the chronic asthma I had as a boy. One day, as I was suffering from a severe attack, Elma Lee said to my father, "Jabo, go to town to Bob Owen's Drugstore this minute and get this boy some asthma medicine. He'll know what to give you." That simple, direct command changed my life. My father came back with an over-the-counter medicine that opened up a new world for me. For the first time, I was able to get instant relief from attacks that hitherto had forced me to struggle for hours to breathe. Elma Lee never had any money or influence to help me get established in life, but she gave me much more—her many acts of genuine kindness. All my grandparents were dead by the time I was ten, and Elma Lee by default served me as an elder relative.

The bulk of this monologue is based on conversations taped in the late 1970s in the small four-room frame house in which she lived alone after the death of her brother Nathan in 1964. The final section was taped during a visit to the Liberty Church Cemetery in August of 1981, about a year before her mental condition began to deteriorate.

Y'all get out and come on in. I'm fixing dinner and you can eat what little I got. My yard's as dry as a flour barrel. We ain't had no rain for the longest. My well's about to go dry. But this hot weather don't bother me. I been living in it all my life. I ain't been doing much of nothing, 'cept trying to keep my yards clean. My brush broom's about wore out, but there's plenty more elder bushes down in the branches. Turn off that TV in the front room and come on back to the kitchen. I do enjoy my stories like "As the World Turns" and "The Secret Storm," and sometimes I stay up to 11 o'clock at night a-watching. Nathan liked to watch them stories too before he died.

The wind's been a-blowing and hit looks like a black cloud's a-coming up. We might have some bad weather, but hit don't scare me. I been through a lot of storms and I ain't been blowed away yet. My chickens already know rain's a-coming. They's gone under the house to keep dry. A few sprinkles is already a-falling. My tin roof makes it sound like it's a-coming in, but I ain't got no leaks. If I'd been expecting you, I'd a-fixed something more to eat. But I got biscuits and peas and sausage and chicken and some froze hash I can heat up. There's some late apples here on the cooktable. They's sweet and good.

Yes sir, I raise my own chickens and I got a right smart of em. I don't like store-bought chickens. They tastes like old cankered meat to me. I get five or six eggs a day, and that's more than I need. But if my blamed dog keeps on, he'll eat up all my chickens. He's got the devil in him. I used to set my hens and hatch em off, but I mostly buy my biddies now. Fraze run over this chicken I'm a-cooking with his truck this morning when he brung me home. I spend the night over at Beansie's trailer, but I come home early as I can ever day. I don't like to stay in that trailer more than I have to. Cora Gause brung me this mess of peas. They been a-cooking more than two hours and are nearly 'bout done. I put three eyes of grease in my peas. Yes sir, I use a lot of hog lard. I buy it in twenty-five-pound buckets. I used to make my own lard when I could kill my own hogs, but I can't get nobody to help me make lard and sausage. They's too damn lazy if you ask me. I had me a hog last winter, but I couldn't get a blamed soul to help me kill him. So I took him to Brundidge and had him killed and cut up. He dressed out to three hundred pounds. If I'm a-living another year, I'll have me another hog. I like to season what I eat with my own meat. Then I *know* where it comes from! And I cook my peas till they's done. I have seen people eat peas when they rattle in your plate! No sir, I don't like them old green English peas. They's not fittin' to eat I don't care how you fix em.

I make biscuits every day, yes sirree, and I use a lot of lard in them. I used to make up biscuits three times ever day, but now I'm by myself I cut back to oncet a day. When I could get it, I used Robin Hood and Sellers Best and Blue Seal flour, but now I use White Lily. I used to buy it in hundred-pound sacks, but now I'm down to twenty-five-pound sacks. When I's a girl Papa would buy it by the barrel. It come in a real barrel and weighed about a hundred pounds. When they started putting it up in sacks, we still called a hundred pounds a barrel of flour. We used to use a lot of flour. There was eleven of us in the family and we had company to eat with us most ever day.

Last night something got after my chickens. I went out to see about them and burnt up my biscuits! I think hit was foxes but I didn't see em. Hit's this damn stove that burnt up my biscuits. Hit's the aggravatingest stove I ever cooked on! You can see I still got my old wood stove set up, and I can use it any time I want to. Hit still cooks better'n this new thing. I told Nathan I didn't want no 'lectric stove, but he went up to Mr. Jackson at the Western Auto Store and bought it anyhow. I told him it was sorry enough to make a preacher cuss. Sometimes I feel like tearing it up and throwing it out. One time I burnt up my peas and my boiler too. I throwed out the peas and went back to my garden and picked and shelled me some more, and I built me a fire in my old stove and cooked my peas the way I wanted to. The heat never bothered me—not even during the Dog Days of August. I have stood the heat a long time, and I reckon I can stand it a little bit longer. Yes sir, on this new stove you can burn things up if you turn your back, and I'm a-scared my grease will catch on fire. Now, a wood stove stops putting out heat when you stop putting stovewood in it, but this 'lectric stove just keeps on heating up. I

Elma Lee Hall, huckleberrying, 1975.

wisht I had all the meat I burned up and the peas I scorched when I'd be outside a-sweeping my yard.

This here is Granny Rollo's biscuit plate. Her mammy raised her younguns on it, and Granny raised hers on it, and Maw raised us on it; and I've helped raise a heap of my nieces and nephews on it. I used to make a extra baker of biscuits ever day so's I'd have some left over to butter cold when Jabo's and Lou's boys come over. Everbody wants me to give it to them, but I told em they won't get it. I don't know what I'll do with it, but hit's mine and I'll do what I blame well please. I'll *break* it if I want to.

This chicken'll be done in a few minutes, and I'll make some milk gravy. Everything else is 'bout ready. Y'all can set on that side of the table on that old bench. Hit's so old nobody knows where it come from.

I wisht I could raise everthing I eat, but I can't do what I used to. I still keep my cows and hogs. I feed my hogs corn and table scraps and milk I put in my slopbucket at the back steps. My cows eat grass in the pasture and I feed em some bought feed. I enjoy keeping my hogs and my cows or I wouldn't do it. I never have done much I didn't want to. I'm milking two cows now. Like I said to Beansie the other day, "If I'm still a-living I'm still a-milking." I milk em twicet a day, of a morning and of a night. I told a woman down the road I'd give her some if she'd help me milk. She said it was too damn hot. I told her hit wadn't a damn bit hotter for her than it was for me. Hit's not too hot for her to drink the milk, but she's not going to drink any I milk. She's just lazy. Somebody told me her old man quit her 'cause she was too sorry to cook. I know she's got a enlarged heart and bad feet, but if she didn't eat so much she wouldn't look like a bale of cotton. I got me a old Negro woman named Old Sarah that helps me some. I pay her in milk. That's all she wants. I like to milk but I can't hold out like I did.

I been a-milking since I used to go to the cowpen with Grandpa Ben Rollo. Before I learnt how, he let me pretend to milk. I remember one old cow that never seemed to get enough to eat. So one day he said, "I'm going to take her enough this time to give her a bait." So he filled a handle-basket full of corn. Grandmaw saw us headed towards the cowpen and hollered. "Ben, if you give all that corn to that old cow, it'll kill her." He hollered back, "Well, if hit does, I reckon she'll die with a full belly." And she did. She et so much she swoll up and died. When I got back to the house, Granny says, "Well, Elma Lee, where's the milk?" I says, "I didn't get none. The cow died."

Yes sir, I been a-milking all my life. And I been a-churning all my life. I still skim my milk and put the cream in my churn. I feed the skimmed milk, what I call blue-john, to the dogs and cats and hogs. I got a churn full of milk and cream souring now. Yes sir, I like my own milk and butter better'n that old store-bought stuff. When I eat my own butter I know what I'm a-eating. That old bought butter is nasty as the devil. Store milk is nasty, too. Separated milk is nasty as a hog. One time I seen Hollaway Bickerstaff separate his milk, and that separator got so full of flies it'd clog up. I scald my milk things and keep em clean. The milk in this churn is about to clabber and I'll churn it before I go to bed tonight. Hit takes a long time for the butter to come. I have churned and churned and the butter wouldn't come, and I'd get so mad I wanted to kick the churn out the door. I never did, but I felt like it.

I don't buy much at the store, but I buy more'n I used to. I buy flour and coffee and sugar and things like I always bought. Sometimes I buy steak but I don't like to eat it. I'd rather eat hog meat any time.

We had a damn sight better to eat when I's a girl than we have now. We had most anything we wanted and we growed it ourselves. We always had us a big garden and fertilized it with guano and chicken manure. I buy drinks at the store. But I can't drink Co-Colas. They's too strong. You want a Nehi Orange or Grape with your dinner? I got a RC too.

Well, we's about ready to eat. Y'all go ahead. I can't eat much since I lost most of my teeth. I have to gum most everything I eat now. Here, let me give you some of these here hot biscuits. Butter you as many as you want, and here's some milk gravy too. You want some scuppernong jelly? I got plenty of butter. I made some butter rolls last Sunday, thinking somebody might come. But nobody did, and I had to throw them out to the chickens. If I had some now, I know you'd like em. This is how I make em. I take some dough and roll it out. I don't put baking powder in that dough or it'll go to pieces. So I roll it out and put in some sugar and lots of butter and roll it up, and then I pour some sweet milk over it all and bake it until it turns brown. Last week, I made a biscuit pudding, but nobody was here to eat it with me. With Nathan no longer here, I've lost my appetite. Food just tastes better if you eat it with somebody. Biscuit pudding is easy to make. You just put together some eggs and sugar and biscuits and butter and a little sweet milk and cook it in the oven a few minutes.

Here, take this pulley bone and have some more peas. It'll be throw out if you don't eat it.

I wisht you all had been here when I fixed some huckleberry pie. I don't go a-huckleberrying much any more. Won't nobody go with me. I ain't a-scared to go myself, but Beansie and them says I might get hurt and can't get back home. I says, "Shoot fire, Beansie, I been knowing them woods all my life, and I ain't gone step in no hole." Me and Cora Gause went oncet this year in that pasture in front of Miss L's old place. We found a sight of berries! I don't believe anybody had been in there and picked em. The bushes was so full we could just strip em in our buckets. I don't care if Beansie never goes with me again. She's always quarreling. "Don't go in that thicket," she hollers, "they's snakes in there!" I says, "Shoot, Beansie, if you don't bother them snakes, them snakes won't bother you." Leastways, I never had trouble with em. All I need is a stick to knock em out of my way. I ain't a-scared of a snake.

Now, I like Cora. She goes berrying with me and helps me around the house some. Her and Cleo got a nice house down next to Beaver Dam. Cleo moved it there ready-made from the Sims Place. It ain't no big fine house but hit's good enough for anybody to live in. Cleo makes good money a-working on the road with the state. Cora and Cleo's always been good to help people out.

Yes sirree, I always got plenty to eat, but I just don't like to eat much no more. Dr. Barnes in Montgomery told me what to eat and I told him I'd eat what I damned well pleased. He said I need to eat more and gain some weight, but I can't do it. I keep falling off from what I was. I got me a set of false teeth but I can't wear em. They don't feel right in my mouth. This patty sausage I bought at the store ain't got no taste. I bought me a string of sausage and hung it behind my wood stove to dry out, but hit wasn't no good either.

I'm skin and bones now, but I can thank Old Marster I ain't had much sickness in my life. Our doctor used to be Dr. George Guthrie at Inverness but I never needed him. I'm all right now, 'cept for my mouth and a cataract on one of my eyes. About eight years ago my mouth started getting sore, so the doctors in Union Springs sent me to Montgomery to Dr. Barnes. He wanted to help me get up on the table, and I says, "Shoot, I don't need no help," and I got up on it by myself. He checked me over and I says, "Now, I don't want no lie." So he says, "Well, Miss Elma Lee, you got cancer, and I'll have to operate." I says, "Go ahead. I'm not a-scared." So he cut out part of my tongue. Then he come and set on my bed and says, "I

Elma Lee and Beansie Hall, 1948.

think I got it all, but I can't be sure. You're gonna have to give up snuff." I looked him straight in the eyes and says, "I been a-dipping snuff nearly all my life, and I don't intend to stop now." And I didn't neither. I been going back ever few months but he ain't found nothing growing back yet. I don't want to have to stay up there again. I was in Jackson's Hospital for three weeks, and I didn't like it. Here at home I sleep on my feather bed, and I can sink right down in it. I can't sleep on them cotton beds. They's too hard. I told Dr. Barnes his hospital beds was as hard as a rock. No sir, I didn't like it up there at all. I couldn't get out and stir around.

Oh yes, I been away from home before. I went to Florida once and to Columbus a few times. When I's a girl I spent the night sometimes with Debelle and Mary Hall. But I never been to Birmingham. I don't like to go far enough away so's I couldn't walk home by night, if I had to. Yes sirree, I like to walk. I used to

Elma Lee Hall, 1982.

walk a lot at night and people said the devil would catch me. I says, "Well, if he does, he'll turn me loose when day comes." I got paths all through the woods around here. You can't get me lost in any of these woods. I know em as good as the back of my hands. I walk the roads too and I seen it when they was all dirt and clay. It makes no difference to me. I hear a car coming I just step out of the road in the ditch and keep on walking where I want to go. I always get there soon enough.

I ain't afraid of nobody, white or black. I'm not a-scared of staying at home by myself. We always had Negroes living around us, and we always got along. You remember old Uncle Tom Boswell and his wife Eaf? He said he's been born in slavery times. Now, Eaf was a real good cook and, boy, could she play the organ! There was a old washerwoman that lived right

up the road here a piece. She was called Old Fudder and she washed for a lot of white people. I have seen her walking up and down the road many a time. She would pick up the dirty wash early in the morning at daylight, tie it in a sheet, and walk back home with it on top of her head. She could wash it, hang it out to dry, iron it, and get it back the same day. But hit commonly took two days to get it all done. White people didn't wash for other white people. That was Negro work. Old Fudder would make twenty-five cents or fifty cents for a big washing, but that was good money for anybody back then. A old Negro woman over near Beans Cross Roads used to wash and clean for white people too, but I heerd she knowed how to make more money off the white men and not work so hard. I heerd she done right well and built her a nice house over there. They said Nathan used to go see her, but he never mentioned it to me, and I never asked him.

I don't have much company these days. People run up and down the road like a fart in a whirlwind, but don't many of em pull in here. Most of my brothers' and sisters' younguns moved away, and them that lives close by don't visit much. I don't care. I don't need to see them. They don't come about me and I don't go about them. If they's above me, I'm above them. Oh, of course, they come when they want something, but that's about the onliest time they do. When them younguns was all a-growing up, people used to say, "Elma Lee, why don't you take care of them younguns for a while so's Kinch and Maggie or Jabo and Sarah or Lou and Charley can get off to theirselves?" I says, "Shoot, that's not my job. They had the fun getting them. Now let them have the fun taking care of them!" I meant it, too. I didn't bring em into this world. Their mammies and daddies done it. Now, I always shared what little I had. They's all eat many a biscuit at this table setting on that bench. I've give them money when they needed it and I had it. But no sirree, I don't tend to other people's younguns. That's their job.

A sight of people have died around here. They's not many left of my age. Dink Brooks is dead and I miss her. But I don't miss her as much as I miss Corine Arrington. I miss Corine worse than anybody. Dink didn't stir around much. She just set on her front porch and watched people come along the road. When we'd be out walking together, she'd poke along, and I'd say, "Make haste, Dink. Make haste." But Corine was good to visit. She'd set with me and help me shell peas. I do miss her. And I do miss my brothers and sisters. All of us are dead now but me and Beansie, and I reckon I'll be the next one. I had four sisters and five brothers. This is the way we come: Toodle, then me, then Kinch, then Jennie. She was about nineteen years old and was married when she died of convulsions. After Jennie was Lou, then Nathan, which everbody called Bootman. The last two was Beansie and Jabo. Jabo's real name was Henry Wade, but it got turned around to Wade Henry. He was named for Uncle Henry Hall, who come here from South Carolina. Beansie nicknamed Jabo after one of our old mules. I forget what year I's borned, but Pap's sister, Aunt Bob, told me hit was the same year and a month before Rube Gause. He was borned the 8th day of December and I's borned the 8th day of November. I's borned just a little piece across the road over there on a hill. You can just about see the place from my front porch. The house burned down a long time ago and the road to the place has growed up. You couldn't even get a wagon over it now. There used to be a big magnolia tree over there in the front yard. One time Jabo said he's gone cut it down, and I says, "Cut it down, damn you, and I'll cut you down!" It was just pure meanness. That tree lasted longer than

the house, and it lasted longer than Jabo. Uncle Johnny Rollo named me. He was Maw's half-brother and named me after a girl he saw when he's working on the railroad way over in Georgia.

Yes sir, we had good times when I's a girl. What we done for fun? Everthing that was mean is what we done for fun. Well, we had plenty of watermelons at home, but we must go to Tom Outlaw's patch and steal his seed watermelons. They's the biggest and the best. Sometimes we wouldn't even cut em open, but we'd bust em on the ground and eat the heart out and throw the rest away. Oh, we had the devil in us. Or we'd sew up somebody's pants so he couldn't put his foot through. That was meanness, but hit was our fun. Sometimes I'd get the devil in me and run off to Grandpa's house when Maw was down at the spring. We didn't have a well then, so she had to tote water from the spring. Yes sir, I done everthing but the right thing. I was mean but Papa never hit me a lick in his life. And Grandpaw wouldn't let Maw whup me long as he's living. But when she did light into me, hit was something!

We played games too. The girls played whatever the boys played—marbles and ball and sich like. We made our balls out of old socks. Our bat was a hickory tree limb. Ever Saturday we had a baseball game over at Boswell Crossing. The McLendons owned a sight of land over there, and we used one of their pastures that was level. At them games the boys played, and the girls just watched their fellows play.

No sir, I never had a fellow when I's a girl. I never needed nary'n. But I'd go with the rest of em by the wagonload to the dances. Most every Friday night me and Kinch went to a square dance at Almeria. Some of em done round dances but I never tried that. Sometimes Jennie and Lou and Jabo and Beansie would go with us. We'd hitch up the wagon and before we got loaded they'd be twelve or fourteen to go. We danced until it got real late and get home at one or two o'clock in the morning. One time Mildred Cook and Doc

Elma Lee Hall's niece ("Toodle's" daughter), Nell Hall Hubbard, with her husband and daughter, Janice.

Rotton dared Jabo and Beansie at a dance and Jabo and Beansie won. Mildred and Doc couldn't keep up. I remember one time me and Kinch went to town in the buggy, and I bought a pair of shoes at McAndrews. That night we went to the dance at Almeria Schoolhouse and I danced my new soles out. The next time I went to town I took them back and said them was sorry soles or they wouldn't have wore out in one night. I got a new pair for nothing. 'Course we traded a lot at McAndrews, and they wanted to keep our

business. It's where me and Kinch bought clothes and shoes for all the family. Him and me done the trading.

We always had a good time at Almeria. There was three Negroes that played for us. They was Charles and Sam Foreman and Ole Peg Floyd, and they played the guitar and the fiddle and the jew's-harp. One night Kinch says, "Let's dance to we make Old Floyd give out." I says, "Shoot, he'll be playing when we're give out." That Negro could work in the field all day and play his guitar and harp all night. We never could make him give out.

Sometimes we'd go to dances at Logton, down near Linwood, in Pike County. Hit was a long way to go but we went when we felt like it. One time we went down there on Christmas night and it cold as the devil. The mud come up to the axle on the wagons and froze to the wheels. Hit was all the mules could do to get us back home the next morning. We'd use our mules one week and the next week we'd use Uncle Buddy Hall's so we wouldn't strain em too much. Down at Logton they had five Negroes that played the fiddle, the guitar, the mandolin, and the banjo. Yes sir, them Negroes could flat-out play! Negroes can naturally play better'n whites anyway. We didn't pay them a certain amount, but when all the dancers got there we'd take up a collection and give them a nickel or dime apiece. They was always pleased with what they took in.

I didn't go to school long, and I didn't learn much but meanness when I went. Where I went was the Mascot School right about where Wavey Brooks lives now, near where the old claypit is, and not far from Q. P. Deason's place. One of my teachers was Miss Eason, who married Turner Bates. We also had Miss Laura Turnipseed from Troy and Miss Mattie Lou Williams from Hatchechubbe. Now she was the devil! She was mean to us and we was mean to her. We done all the low-down things we could think of to aggravate her. One morning John Will Deason and Kinch and Mary and me set out early for school walking through the woods, and we started to turn over ever log we could find looking for a snake. We got us a little one about eight inches long. We got to school before the others and wadded our snake up under the school bell.

When Miss Mattie Lou picked up that bell to ring, the snake fell out. She jumped up and hollered and says, "I'm gone wear out whoever put that snake under that bell!" But she never wore out nobody. She never knew who to hit. But I'm telling you she was careful when she picked up her bell after that. We didn't try that trick again, but we done other meanness. I thought I'd learnt enough when Miss Jessie Pitts went to teaching, and I quit. She didn't know no more than me.

I learnt a lot more at home. I learnt how to cook and wash and scrub floors and make soap and milk and churn. I never learnt to spin and weave, but I remember Granny Rollo working her spinning wheel and weaving her cloth. I chopped cotton and hoed corn in the fields, but I never done much field work. I never learnt to plow because I warn't cut out to plow. That's a man's job. Soon as I's big enough, I learnt how to cook, and I stayed home with Granny and cooked, and Maw worked in the fields. She said she rather chop cotton than make biscuits and cook over a hot stove. So Granny bossed me, and I done most of the cooking.

For dinner I might cook a chicken, and we'd have vegetables like cabbages and snap beans and turnips and peas and roast'n'ears—but not all at one time. I'd make plenty of cornbread and biscuits. I been making biscuits ever since I had to stand in a chair to reach the biscuit tray. I'd make up to a hundred and fifty biscuits at the time, and I'd bake em in two pans that helt seventy-five biscuits a piece. For supper we'd have what we had leftover from dinner, and I'd make a fresh baker of biscuits. I always cooked biscuits three times a day. Paw and the others would've pitched a fit if they had to eat cold biscuits.

I never used yeast, but I know Granny did. No, I don't know where she got it; but if you'll tell me where she got it, we'll both know. For breakfast we'd have biscuits and syrup and sausage or ham and coffee. I never did like to eat eggs but some em did. We had chickens whenever we took a notion, three or four times a week in the summer. We mostly ate hog meat. That's what we all liked best.

We most always killed hogs before Christmas on a cold day. It was safer to do it before Christmas and before most of the cold weather was gone. We got us three or four Negroes to help, and we paid em with a rump piece or some backbone or spareribs or liver. Once in a while we give em a hogshead to make hash. They liked to get the guts, too, but Granny Rollo kept some to eat herself. She liked em mealed and fried. Papa would hit the hogs in the head to kill em or he'd take a gun and shoot em in the head. I could hear em squealing, but it didn't bother me. It was just something we did. I reckon I could've killed em myself if I'd had to.

When he's dead, the men would put the hog in a barrel and pour a washpot full of boiling water on him. That'd loosen the hair and they'd scrape it off

Granny Rollo's biscuit plate.

with butcher knives. Then they'd hang him up by the hind legs and cut him open and gut him; and when he's clean, they'd take him down and put him on a big table and cut him into pieces. The women would cut him up in sections and drop the fat pieces in the pot and boil the fat out. We called that drying out the grease. Then we strained the cracklins out and eat em with salt. Us younguns always like to eat cracklins. Maw always made some cracklin bread, but it was so rich it would make you sick if you ate too much. I have made many a piece. It's just like making cornbread, only you add cracklins to your dough. You just take about a quart of cornmeal and a cup of cracklins and mix them together with a little buttermilk and soda and salt—just enough to make a stiff dough. Then you make it in little pones and cook them in a iron spider in the oven until they's brown and crusty. It's real greasy and you have to be careful not to eat too much.

'Course when I was a girl we didn't have a icebox and the fresh meat would be ruint in a few days if we didn't eat it up or cure it. If it turned too warm all the meat would go bad. Many a time we lost nearly a whole hog. So we'd eat the ribs and backbone and the fresh meat, and we'd give away some. But most of the meat we packed in the salt box in the smokehouse. We'd salt down the hams and shoulders about nine days to cure them, then rub cornmeal and red pepper on em and hang em up and smoke em over hickory coals. The smoke filled the smokehouse and went out through the cracks. It smelt good but I couldn't go near the smokehouse when the meat was smoking or I'd start coughing. It took several days to dry out and be cured.

If we had good luck and our meat didn't ruin, it would last us until we got ready to kill hogs again the next year. Ever year we killed from five to ten hogs and we had us a smokehouse full of good meat all year long. We'd fry it three times a day and boil it to season peas and butterbeans and other vegetables when we

had em. 'Cept for chicken, it was about the onliest meat we ever had. I used to love to eat, but nothing tastes good as it used to. I eat by myself most of the time. Looks like everbody else is dead and gone, and there's nobody left to eat with.

Well, hit looks like the storm has slacked up and the sun's a-coming out. I don't think hit's too wet if you want to drive over to the graveyard. I ain't been over there in a long time, and I want to see about Nathan's grave.

[LATER: AT THE LIBERTY BAPTIST CHURCH CEMETERY, ABOUT A MILE AWAY]

We warn't what you call church people. I never even joined the church. I never felt I needed to. I always thought I's as good as the members. We did go to 'tracted meetings when they was held all around—at Post Oak and Inverness and Boswell Crossing and Macedonia. I didn't belong as a member, but we always thought of Liberty as our home church. We come to preaching here when we went anywhere regular, and it's where we bury. I always did like Preacher Vickery. Now, he knowed how to preach! I didn't like it when they tore that old wood church down and built this little brick house. Hit was over a hundred years old, and Maw went to school in that old church.

Grandpa Rollo is buried here close by in the graveyard. Most of my kinfolks is buried here, and it's where I'll be buried one of these days. Hit's a pretty place, but I'd like it better if it was cleaned off. I don't like all this grass. People is just too lazy these days to have a real graveyard cleaning. We used to cut up all the weeds and grass and burn it just like we's hoeing cotton or peanuts. Now they bring them old mowers over here and cut it off. Shoot, used to we'd bring our dinner and work all day long. They have put up a good fence to keep the wild animals off the graves. See them graves over yonder outside the fence? They belong to the Negroes. I believe they been burying there long as we been burying over here. But I don't know nothing 'bout their business. They's on their side, and we's on our side.

Yes sir, I knowed most all these people when they's alive. I know where they used to live all up and down this road. And I know where they's buried now. Here's Grady Sellers. He died forty years before Meetsie did, but now they's buried side by side. There's the Gauses—Jesse and Joe Ed and Ethel and Rube. I's borned a month before Rube, and he's been dead a long time. I'm still a-living. Moray Gause died when he's seventeen. They said he went in a-bathing so much he got a piece of trash on his brain and it killed him. He was Ethel and Jesse Gause's boy. They had a pack of younguns.

Right here's where the Boswells bury. Seales Boswell drunk poison and died. Look over that-away and you can see where their house used to set on the hill above Beaver Dam. I drunk many a gourd of water from his well and eat crabapples from the tree that used to be by the side of the road in front of his house. They say he killed hisself when he's caught messing around with his boy's wife—or trying to. Now, I can't say for sure, but I know people do strange things in this world.

Over yonder is the Griders' graves. They's borned in a old house that used to stand a little piece down this dirt road. A old Negro man named Will McGowan who used to cut hair lived there after they all left. When he died the place sold to Jeff Sorrell, and he tore the house down and made a pasture and planted pine trees. See them big cedar trees over there a-shading Tress's grave? I remember when she planted them. Old-timey people said you'll die when a cedar grows big enough to cover your grave.

The Corleys are buried over there by the japonica bushes. They used to live down this road below the Griders. Jennie. Will. Jim. Ben.

Sal. John. There must've been forty-nine of em! Sal Corley could sing! I heerd her sing many a time here at Liberty, but she won't sing here no more. Jennie used to be scared to death of cars, and she died in a car wreck. Yes sir, they's all here now, a-gathered up. I don't know of any of the old people still a-living.

Let's walk over here to where we bury. I can't stay out here too long. My head hurts so much. My bonnet and scarf keeps the wind out, but I still get the awfulest pains in my head. Right here's all my people.

Outside Liberty Baptist Church, 1944.

Nathan. Aunt Net Waters. Papa. Maw. Jennie. Simon. Nathan. They's all here. Papa died when he's helping push off the schoolbus. Jabo was a-driving the bus, but hit wouldn't start and they had to push it off ever morning. Papa had a heart attack while he was a-pushing the bus. I was helping push too, and when Papa fell, he fell on me and died with his head in my lap. When the doctor got there, he was already dead. The doctor said he was purple between his shoulders from pushing that bus.

Papa's name was John Henry Hall, but everbody called him Jack. Maw died of high blood. She died holding my hand. Simon is buried here. He was my oldest brother and six years old when the typhoid fever took him. I warn't there when Jabo died, but I got to him right after. Lindbergh, Lou's boy, come after me, and I got to see him before the undertaker got him.

Lou was in the hospital when she died. She breathed her last breath with my hand under her head. Just before she died, she says, "Elma Lee, I want a dip of snuff." When I went to raise her up to put the snuff in her mouth, she was already getting stiff as a board. I couldn't even bend her hand. I run to the door and hollered, "I need some help in here!" The nurses and five doctors run in, but she was already gone. I believe she had a stroke.

Here's the graves of two of Lou's and Charley Dell's babies that died before they was named. That's why they's buried without names on their stones. Bettie Gean was about five years old when she died. What killed her was that diphtheria shot. Dr. Emmett Guthrie said they had no business a-giving that shot to her. Her bronchial tubes was just as clear as anybody's, but that shot stopped em up and she choked to death. I was there when the little critter died. She was still warm when they put her in her little casket. I don't believe she was full dead.

Both of Lou's boys is dead now. Buddy was a-working under his car when it fell on him. Lindbergh

died of a heart attack just before he was forty on Valentine's Day. That was Papa's birthday too.

Sister Jennie died in 1921 a-giving birth. Hit was not more'n a year after her and Tom Boyd Norris was married. The youngun died too, and they buried it one day and her the next. Maw said she warn't going to let em bury that baby with her, so I don't know where it's buried. After they's married, her and Tom Boyd lived a little piece up the road from us. She was taken sick one night. All that day I kept a-seeing her come out her door and go back in, and I says to Maw, "There's something the matter with Jennie. She's come out that door a dozen times." Our supper was on the stove when we got out and walked up to see about Jennie. Our supper burned up. When we got in the front door, she was a-having one convulsion right after another. When she died I was up on the bed a-trying to feed her. And over there is Nathan's grave. I'll be buried next to him.

These old graves is where Grandpa and Granny Rollo is buried. They both lived with us at the old homeplace until they died. He went away and was in the Confederate army. Both my grandpas fought in the old Civil War, but I don't know where it was they went. And no, I don't know where they all come from when they moved here. They used to say Grandpa Rollo come here from Texas and Grandpa Henry Hall come here from old Carolina. But I never thought to ask anybody about it.

Grandpa Hall died before I could remember him. But I was a-standing on the back of Grandpa Rollo's chair early one morning when the clock was striking seven when he looked up at the clock and says to Maw, "Mollie, I hain't got but twenty-four hours to live. When that clock strikes seven times tomorrow morning, I'll be dead." The next morning I was a-standing on the rockers on the back of his chair a-combing his hair when he died. The clock struck seven times. Hit was the fourteenth day of October, and he hadn't laid down on the bed since March of that year. If he'd a-laid down, he'd a-stifled. He had the heart dropsy. He swoll up and the water run out of him clear as the water in the well bucket. His stomach was poked out so far you could set a saucer on it. His legs swoll up big as logs. Ever morning he begged us to whup his legs to make em go down. Hit was a pitiful thing to see. He'd say, "I'd do it if hit was you." I didn't want to, but ever morning I whupped his legs with holly branches until the blood and water run out together. The doctor said there was nothing he could do. Maw slept in her bonnet ever night at his feet on the floor.

Yes sir, I recollect it all. I knowed em when they's alive, and I remember em now they's dead. Nearly all my brothers died of heart attacks. Kinch and Jabo and Toodle. And Nathan. I lived with him all his life. I was a grown girl when he's born over at the old homeplace, and I helped to raise him, and sometimes I'd whup him when he wouldn't mind me.

We lived together 'cause we wanted to. We took care of Maw and Papa until they died. We never had arguments or fights. I done what I wanted, and he done what he wanted. He used to do a little cotton and peanut and corn farming. I kept the house and done some of the work in the fields. After he got older, he got a job cutting right-of-ways and driving a dump truck on the county roads. He didn't have to go to the Army, and he never went many places around here, 'cept to the woods to hunt.

On payday the first Saturday of the month he'd drive his dump truck to town to buy what we needed and to see the picture show. He loved them shooting pictures. I went to the picture show with him one time, but I didn't like it, and I ain't been back. We always rented our land until he bought twenty acres and the house I'm a-living in from Toodle's boy about thirty years ago.

Nathan didn't believe in banks. When he died, he had six hundred dollars in his pocket. We always looked out for one another. If I had money and he

didn't have none, I give him some. If he had money and I didn't, he give me some. As long as one of us had money, both of us had money.

Since Nathan died and I had my operation, I spend the night over at Beansie and Fraze's trailer about two miles over on the old Boswell road. But I'm not crazy about it. I want to sleep in my own bed. I walk over there late in the evening after I've seen about my cows and chickens and done all my night things. Sometimes Fraze will come over and pick me up in his truck. If he's late in coming, I start out a-walking and meet him. Early the next morning sometimes I walk back before the dew is dried off the grass. I have to get back home early to see about my things. I ain't a-scared of staying by myself at night. I can take care of myself. Ain't nobody ever broke in on me. If they did, it'd be their last time. Somebody did break in one day when I's not at home, a-looking for money. But they didn't know where to look.

I ain't lived many places. When I's a girl we lived for a while on the Carlyle Place, then the Waters Place. We stayed a year at Jake Reynolds's; then we moved to the Sims Place. That was where we was a-living when Maw died. After that, Nathan bought our place from Clarence Hall, Toodle's boy.

I liked everwhere we lived. Nobody never bothered me, and I never bothered nobody. Right now, 'cept for spending the night in Beansie's trailer, things suit me all right just the way they are. I like to watch my stories on television. I got plenty to eat. I'm on the old-age pension, they call it. I just got a Negro to clean the wiggletails and trash out of my well, and I can drink the water again. My cows ain't gone dry. They's giving more milk and butter than I can use. I got chickens, four cats and a dog. I did have four Collie dogs, but somebody run over the last one of em. Folks drive by here like they's going to the doctor.

I got everthing I want. I don't need nothing else. I don't pay attention to things I don't like. I live now pretty much the way I've always lived. I feel like if

Maw would walk in my front door this evening, she'd be right at home. I never done anything I didn't want to, and I don't intend to start now. I can set on my front porch and see just about everything I want to see.

But hit's getting late. My head's starting to hurt, and we ought to get back. I got my night things to do, and then I got to go back over to Beansie's trailer.

POSTSCRIPT: Elma Lee Hall died of cancer on March 13, 1983, in Bullock County Hospital. Funeral services were held at Liberty Baptist Church, with burial in the church cemetery across the road. She was survived by one sister, Mrs. Beansie Hall, and a large number of nieces and nephews. She was eighty-eight.

LUKE MARINER

Sardines, Soda Water, and Catfish in the Well

Luke Mariner lives with his second wife, Mattie Lou, in a small frame house on Bread Tray Hill in a curve of Highway 223, about six miles south of Union Springs. In front of his house is a brightly colored carving of Uncle Sam holding the family mailbox. Mr. Mariner speaks rapidly, frequently slurring his words. His wife occasionally makes low comments as she goes in and out of the screen door which opens into the front of the house. As Mr. Mariner talks, his voice is sometimes drowned by trucks speeding down the highway hauling huge loads of logs to the railroad depot in Union Springs. He has been acquainted with my family all my life and frequently "traded" at one of the small country stores my father used to operate between Union Springs and Halls Cross Roads. As he tells us, he had known my father when they were both boys and played together. My father hired him to barbecue a pig for an outdoor dinner to celebrate my discharge from the Army at my homecoming in 1956. My interview with him took place in the shade of his front porch in the late afternoon of July 12, 1985.

Y'all get out and come right up on the porch. Yes suh, I got plenty of time to talk 'bout anything you want. Just set there in the shade where it's cool. Mattie Lou can jog my mind when I forgets something. I been down to the cross roads and just got home 'bout thirty minutes ago. That grass is 'bout to eat up my yard, but it's too hot to do anything but set here and fan and kill flies and talk. I'll try to talk over them trucks that come by ever few minutes. I can't hardly sleep at night when they run by.

To start with, I was borned in Bullock County down here on Mr. Joe Stuckey's Place on Bug Hall, right there where it jined Mr. Luther Jenkins. I come into this world on May 17, 1908, and I ain't done much but farm a little bit and make a little whiskey when I needed to and stay out of trouble. There was six of us, four brothers and one sister. I can count them out to you. My sister Lottie married Jim D. Martin and died two or three years ago. Ain't but two of us living, me and my brother Lennon, the one they call Luck, and he in New York. My oldest brother was Hollis. He married Jennie Boswell, and they lived over there on the old Hough Place up above Will McGowan's on that old dirt road that went by Liberty Church graveyard.

Will used to cut hair, you know, on his front porch—mostly white folks' hair. He'd be out in the field plowing and somebody come up and want a haircut and have twenty-five cent, so he take them mules to the lot and go in the house and get his clippers and stuff and come on out on the porch. Oooooooo-weeeeeee! His wife had so many pretty flowers on that porch in old cans and slopjars. Will would bring a straight chair out of the house and set the man in it and stand back there with his scissors and cut that man's hair so good you thought it was cut by somebody in town. Yes suh. But now all them flowers and the house gone and all them people dead. Hollis and Jennie both buried 'round in there too.

Then I come to a brother name Embra, but we call him Emory. He work up there 'round Peachburg, and he come to be a preacher, a pretty good preacher everbody said. I don't know if he was a Baptist or a Methodist, but he was a Baptist when he jined the church over here at Sardis. Another one of my brothers was Elmore. He went to World War I and when he come back he married and stayed down yonder below Brantley. Next was a brother name of Sanford. That was his real name, but everbody nickname him Curdee. He work up there with Mr. Paulk at the plant farm at Sardis, and one day he went out to the field and just fell up 'gainst a truck and 'fore they got him to town, he was dead as a doornail. I 'spect he had a heart attack or something like that. Then I had two half-brothers name Doss and R. C. Let me count em out again: Lottie and Luck and Hollis and Emory and Elmore and Curdee and me. That make seven, so I got five brothers. There was a big bunch of us, but we all dead now, 'cept me and Luck up there in New York. Doss and R. C. dead, too.

My mama was a good lady, name of Anna Cope from down at Inverness. If you ever heard of Barley Cope, well that was her brother. I don't know where my daddy come from, 'cause when I was big enough to know him he had done married Mama and I was a little bitty boy. But I think all them folks was from 'round here in Bullock County, and I don't know where they come from 'fore that. I 'spect they all been here since the days of slavery.

When I got up some size, my daddy was farming on Mr. Stuckey's place. He didn't work on halves. He rented some land. We raised everthing—cotton, goobers, peas, peaches. Cotton was what we sold for money. The rest was to eat. We all helped Daddy in the field, Mama and everbody else. I started out when I got big enough to tote water. Me and my sister toted water out to the field in a bucket with a dipper, and they drunk it and throwed it on their face to cool off. When we got up some big-

Luke Mariner, 1985.

ger, Lottie hoed and I tried to plow, but my main work was to cut bushes off the stumps in the newground. Sometime I had to pick velvet beans! Ooooooooo-weeeeeee! They like to eat me up! They was not for us to eat but to feed to the cows and hogs and stock.

Most everthing we eat we raised—peas and corn and greens and chickens and hogs and taters. We had a big tater hill and eat taters all year long. Ever fall we put in a tater hill. You first got to dig a hole in the ground and get some cornstalks and pine straw. Put a whole lot of that pine straw in that hole. Bring in a wagonload of taters now and dump them in. Just stack them taters all 'round that pine straw; then you turn 'round and put some more straw over them taters and cover them up. Then here come the cornstalks. You cover all of it with them cornstalks, and next thing is here come the dirt. You cover it all so it look like a little hill. Now you leave the top open so you can dig down in that hill to the taters, but you put a piece of tin or something like that on the top to keep the rain from getting in.

You get all that done and, man oh man, you gone have taters any time you want em, July or January. Yes suh, all you got to do is reach in there and pull em out. When you can't reach no more taters up there on top, just go 'round to the side and dig a hole in there 'cause they still be taters in that hill. No suh, you ain't never gone be hungry. Man, we just love taters—anytime.

We love possum too, and Mama put taters 'round that possum when she set it on the table. We set down to eat, and I say, "Mama, I wants the tail!" Everbody laugh, but that tail was good. Ever part was good if it was cooked right and Mama knowed how to fix it. She boiled that possum to it was done and then she put some red pepper and butter all over him and stick him in the oven and let him cook slow—just let the fire burn down low. Man oh man, that was the best meat I ever eat! It was better than hog meat—oh yeah, way better. Cook him slow and you can't eat nothing better. Now, you got to take his hair off. You can't let his hair touch that meat, so Daddy skin him first and gut him. Then Mama took him and wash him with baking soda—just wash him out two or three times with that baking soda, and that kills the wild taste. No suh, you do it like that and you can't get nothing better to eat.

We don't even have to fatten up Mr. Possum. He feed hisself in the woods, and then we catch him. My brother Luck sho' love to hunt for possum. We go out at night and come back 'fore it gets light 'cause you ain't gone find no possum when it gets daylight, no suh. Luck sometime get so many possums when we go hunting I get tired toting em. If we get close to the house, I take em on home and come on back and we catch some more. We didn't have no gun. We just catch em with our dog. That dog run the possum up the tree—tree him—and then Luck go up the tree and shake him out. Mr. Possum fall out and still be alive when he hit the ground, and that dog right on him, holding him down. Luck take a axe handle and break that possum's neck. He put that handle behind that possum's neck and bend it back over and it pop just like a stick and 'fore you know it, that possum dead.

I sho' like to go hunting with Luck, but I don't care 'bout toting all them possums. Rabbits, too. Man, we catch more rabbits than you can count. We hunt them rabbits with long sticks with taps on the end, and I carry a croker sack to put em in. We go to the field and start a little fire in that dry grass and weeds, and them rabbits run out and we knock em down with that stick. We get a sack full and take em on home and skin em and gut em and drop em in some boiling water and take em out and scrape all them little hairs off and cut em in pieces and you ready to fry it. You roll them pieces in some flour and salt and pepper and heat up a lot of grease in the skillet and drop that rabbit in and put a top on it and let it cook to it's brown. Oooooooooo-eeeeeeeeee! You just 'bout want to eat his bones it smell so good! Now you take some flour and stir it in that rabbit grease and pour in a little sweet milk and you brown it and you got the best gravy in the world! Then you get one of them big taters that Mama got cooked up in the warmer, and you set down with that fried rabbit and gravy and

some biscuits and buttermilk, man you feel so good you think 'bout running 'round in the field like a rabbit!

Yes suh, what meat we didn't catch in the woods, we growed at home. Mama had chickens in the yard and Daddy put up five or six shoats about the first of November when it start getting cool and fatten em on corn. When you take that hog out of the pen, he be so fat he can't hardly stand on his legs. When he get ready to kill, he be dripping with grease. That be sometime in December, 'round Christmas, when the sap is down. So you get the smokehouse ready and the salt-box cleaned out and lots of salt ready to pour in there on the meat. You go knock that fat shoat in the head with a axe and put him in some boiling water to get all that hair off and hang him up by his hind legs and cut him open and clean him out. Then you take him down and cut him up and take the pieces to the smoke house and hang him up under some hickory coals to smoke him and in a day or two you got some good ham and shoulders to eat. Then you put some of that fresh meat in the salt-box and cover it up with salt to cure it and keep them worms out. Man, you got meat any time you want it!

Folks come down there and help Daddy kill them hogs and he give them a good mess of chitlins. Way back yonder I used to love chitlins, but I ain't eat none in a long time, and I tell you why. One time I got more in my chitlins than chitlins. Somebody give me a mess already cooked, and, man, they looked good. I bit my teeth in them chitlins and I felt something funny, and I had to run to the door to spit em out. Whoever fried them chitlins cooked everthing that was in there! I mean everthing! You supposed to split them guts open and clean em out, but they had all that mess still in there—all that corn that hog been eating and all that in them wrinkles. I said that was enough chitlins for me, and I ain't never touched none since then, no suh.

Now, I do love to eat barbecue, and I have

barbecued many a hog. Me and Big Stiff used to go all 'round here barbecuing hogs for folks. He help me get that hog killed and cleaned and spread out. I build me a fire in a pile of hickory wood and let it die down to the coals, and I turn 'round and dig a hole in the ground and stretch out that pig over that pit and put them coals in the bottom. I keep it wet with some barbecue sauce I make out of vinegar and a little ketchup and sugar and let it cook slow all day. Oooooooooo-eeeeeeee! When that meat get done, it's something to eat. I have barbecued a heap of hogs for people all up and down this road and all back in yonder—for Mr. J. W. Driggers and Mr. Jabo Hall—all the way up to town and down around Saco and Mr. Jeff Sorrell and over there to Thompson. Mr. Mann Driggers have a big to-do down to Saco and he come up here and say, "Well, Luke, we want you to barbecue a pig for us." So me and Big Stiff go down there and kill that hog and dress him and start that barbecue going 'round daylight. I never charged much, maybe two dollars on up to ten dollars, but way back yonder you could buy a wagon for fifteen dollars. That was the kind of money you could put in your jumper pocket. I got old and got to where I couldn't run 'round like I used to, so I had the peoples bring me their meat to my house. I dug me a pit back here in my back yard and lined it up with brick and I went on barbecuing right here at home.

Well, I was talking 'bout what I liked to do when I was coming up. What we liked to do besides hunting was play fireball. I don't 'spect y'all know much 'bout fireballs, so I'm gone tell you what it was. You go down and get you some old rags and roll em up in a tight ball and get you some kerosene and soak em and take em out and stick a match to em and throw em up at the night. Everbody have his own fireball, so you might have a dozen or two out there the same night. It was so pretty, them fireballs shooting up in the sky. We throw them balls to one another and keep them going up there all the time. You throw them with bare hands, yes suh, hands just bare as a barefoot. You grab it quick and yonder it go and it don't burn you. If you don't catch that fireball when it come at you, you reach down and pick it up. We played fireball many a time out on a big old level place like that field next to where Mr. Lee Hall lived. If any grass or bushes catch fire, we stomp it out. We never started no big fires. Oh man, it was pretty. People come from Union Springs and Sardis and everwhere to watch us play fireball. You get up on a hill like up here at Bread Tray and people down here look up and see all them lights going up and falling down in the dark. It was just like the stars coming down.

Something else we done was have a candy draw. That's when you go up to the store and buy three different boxes of candy, a peppermint box, a lemon box, and a blue-striped box. Then you put so many sticks of this kind of candy and so many sticks of the other kind of candy in a little cigar box and you cut a little hole in the top and you shake it all up and you pay a nickel to play. You stick your hand in and pull out a stick of candy and you keep on pulling to you pull out a different kind. Then you drop out and somebody else plays. Yes suh, when you pull that first one out, you got to keep on pulling that same color out.

Now when we was living over there close to Bug Hall, peoples used to give suppers. There'd be all kind of cakes and custards and everthing good to eat and everthing be free. People come and stay all night long and sleep on pallets on the floor. Sometime we make our own ball and a bat out of a poplar limb and play baseball, but that be in the daytime.

I learnt to pick cotton when I's just a little boy. Mama got me a flour sack and sewed me a strop on it so it'd fit on my shoulder. That cotton got open along in August and September, and Daddy say, "All right now Luke, you big enough to pick some cotton. You pick that cotton good and I take you to town to the gin." So I took my sack to the field with the rest of em and started picking, and after a while, Daddy look over at my row and say, "Luke, you ain't getting all that cotton. You got to reach way back in yonder in that boll and get all of it. Don't leave nothing in there, or we won't gin a whole bale. And pick that trash out of that cotton. They ain't gone buy it if it got trash in it." No suh, I never will forget picking cotton in my little flour sack. I don't know how much I could pick in a day back then, but when I get a sack full, I turn it in to Daddy and he empty it in the cotton basket, and when that cotton basket full, he empty it in the wagon. I know after I got up some size, I could pick two hundred pounds and more a day. I sho' could. I pick with both hands. I straddle that stalk and pick cotton with both hands and put it in that long sack right in behind of me. Man, I pick cotton like a woman shelling peas I was so fast.

Back when I was picking in my flour sack, ever once in a while Daddy'd look over and say, "Well now Luke, you pick hard and I take you to the gin with me, and I get y'all some sardines and soda water when we get to town." Man, we sho' picked hard. We pick that cotton like rabbits out there in that hot field 'cause we want to go to town. When we get a bale picked, we put the high body on the wagon and load that cotton and stomp it down to we get it all in. Next morning we leave way 'fore day and head to town, and the road be full of wagons going to the gin. Daddy drive the mules and us chillun set up high on the load of cotton we pick with our own hands, and we get to town 'fore daylight while it still be cool. It don't take us long to get to Mason's Store right this side of town. Mr. Mason's gin be already working, and we get in line and wait our turn. My half-brother R. C. work at the gin and he be done got that wood burning and that boiler popping off that steam. He fire up that furnace that run the gin. R. C. get that steam up high and that gin be running just fine. Peoples cut firewood for Mr. Mason after they laid-by in August and bring it up there and sell it for seventy-five cent a cord. They bring in that wood, green or dry, and stack it up out there and that stack I 'spect go from here way down that road yonder. They might already owe Mr. Mason something he put on the book, or they might take it up in flour and coffee and stuff like that. That wood them folks bring in R. C. burn to make the steam to run that gin. It warn't no motor or gas back then—didn't use nothing but that steam R. C. made from that wood. Then the power company come, and everbody stopped chopping wood for the gin.

We jump off the wagon when it come our turn to gin, and we peep 'round where R. C. fire up that boiler. We watch them gin that cotton, suck it up out of the wagons, and put a belt on them bales that done been ginned, and then weigh it and let it down. Then we mostly stay in the wagon, and Daddy go in the store to do his business, and he say, "Now y'all boys stay here and watch the

Waiting to unload at the cotton gin.

mules and I bring you something back to eat." We stay out there in the wagon, and in a few minutes here come Daddy out of the store with stuff like sausage or sardines and a short pone of bread. That bread warn't cut in pieces and we had to dig in there with our fingers and pull some out. He maybe bring us some sweet soda water, like lime water, and we open them bottles with our teeth 'fore you can turn 'round. Pepsi-Colas hadn't come in here then. Nothing in here but Co-Colas, and we never did drink them 'cause they come in little bitty short bottles and cost as much as the big bottles. Sometime we pick up bottles longside the road and sell em back for three cent. Sometime Daddy come out of the store with a big hunk of cheese and some soda crackers. Oh man, I could eat cheese and soda crackers all day long if I had a belly-washer to drink with it. Sometime he would bring us a great big George Washington Pie that cost a nickel, like a Moon Pie. You get one of them things and a Ne-Hi Grape, and you think you already died and gone to heaven.

After we eat and pick up our cotton bale, we head on down to Mr. Tucker's warehouse, right there where the Eat and Sleep is now. Daddy gone sell his cotton so he can straighten up with Mr. Stuckey and the bank and the stores where he been furnished. I tell you them was sho' some good times when we got to go with Daddy to town to the cotton gin. Sometime he might let us go with him when we didn't have a load of cotton, but we didn't get that soda water and sardines on them trips.

One time when I was in town in my boy days, I got to go to the picture show. I just went one time and got scared and come on out. What scared me was seeing all them things up there on the wall and watching them folks shoot at each other. Back in them days, colored peoples had to set way upstairs at the picture show, and we clumb up some high steps on the outside to get in there. I got scared 'cause I was up so high and 'cause I thought them people on that

screen was real. My oldest brother took me, and I ain't telling you no lie, I was scared all day and all night, yes suh. So I wait outside for him to come out, and we got on home and I ain't been back no more, no suh. I told em I rather set at home and parch goobers—just stay home and parch goobers, yes suh, and maybe play Jack-in-the-Bushes. I been up all night long playing that game. You put something in your hand, say some goobers, and say, "How many goobers did Jack put in the bushes?" If he say ten and you got fourteen, he have to give you four. But if he say fourteen, you got to give him what you got in your hand. Folks used to walk to each other's house and eat supper and put Jack in the bushes all night.

One more thing I want to tell you 'bout. When we live on the Stuckey Place across from Bug Hall from the Biggerstaff Place, we raised goats. I had a goat and I was crazy 'bout him. Daddy sold Mr. Tudy Hall a goat for Mr. Clarence, his boy, and Mr. Jabo's daddy bought one for him. We was all 'bout the same age, and we would get on our goats and ride em all up and down the road and in there under that bluff. That was when Mr. Jabo's daddy, Mr. Jack, lived over there on the hill next to a old colored man named Pat Waller that had a boy name Morris. Mr. Hall live in a house up there close to where Mr. Wavey Brooks' house is now. Well, Mr. Hall was a fine man, and he made the best syrup I ever sopped in my plate. Ever year 'bout the time they go to making syrup here come Mr. H. T. Brooks over there to get some of that good beer—you know, the sour skimmings they take off the syrup kettles. Me and Mr. Jabo, we'd slip off and get us some of that beer and put it in a bottle and go to the woods and make like we was grown men. It made us feel pretty good, yes suh, me and Mr. Jabo. We sho' had us a good time together when we was boys.

No suh, I didn't go to school much when I was a boy. I went for a little while up here to the Goodman School right there by Mr. Hobson Creswell's. I had

An Alabama tenant house.

one teacher name Montecue and one name Owens, but I quit 'cause I didn't like dodging them switches. Mr. Owens say, "All right boy, I'm gone get you tomorrow. I'm gone whup you to you can't set down." Well, you know that next day I play sick. I say, "Mama, I don't feel like going to school." She say, "Boy, you sound like you sick. Go out there in that field and dig up some of that fever grass and some roots and I make you some medicine." So I take that medicine and never did go back to school.

Oh yeah, I been going to church off and on all my life. Mama took all us chillun to Old Sardis Church up here, and that's where all my folks is buried at today—Mama, Daddy, and all of em. I got sprinkled in the Methodist Church, Old Zion Church, close to where we was living. Then when I got up grown, I jined the Baptist church and was baptized under the water up there in Mr. Hugh Stuckey's pond. I 'spect I was a great big man when I got sho' nuff baptized.

I been knowing Mattie Lou all her life, and we was married on March 1, 1950. We been married thirty-five years and move to this house in 1956. We

don't have no chillun together, but I had three girls by Mozelle Townsend. One of them died but Alminia and Algertha living up there in New York with their mama. I don't know why she left here and went up there, 'cept she had some aunties living 'round New York. A lot of my folks went up that way, but I ain't never been and don't want to go. I stay right here in Bullock County, but I been all 'round Florida ever which way, on down there all over Miami. I ain't seen some of my kinfolks that went up north in I don't know when. One of em worked at a powder plant up there in Birmingham and got a whole lot of powder up his nose. He can't hear nothing and can't even talk on the telephone. You got to get right up to him, with all that powder in his head. I been all 'round in this part of the country, and I heard of a lot of places I never been. I ain't never heard of one good as right here in Bullock County. I like it right here ever time. Yes suh, ever time.

Things not like they was when I was a boy, and I like some of them changes. I like the power that come in and the telephone and lights and the frigidaire and all like that. Mama used to hang her milk on a rope and put it down in the well to keep it cool. That water way down there is pretty cold. Well, that milk didn't get very cold—not like ice—but it keep from getting clabbered. Yes suh, I knows how to dig a well. I dug that one out here in the yard. All you need is a spade and a scoop and a hole digger. That old hole digger over yonder leaning up 'gainst the tree is one I used on my well. 'Fore they put them water pipes in through here 'bout five years ago, they say, "Luke, you better jine up for that water," and so I jined—paid them twenty dollars. But nobody else 'round here would jine but me. They say, "Man, what do I need that pipe water for? I got plenty of water in my well. I don't need no more." I say, "Well, I gone jine up 'cause sometime that well might go dry or get wiggletails in it or something be dead in it." Not long ago, some of them same folks say they believe they want that pipe water now, so a few of them been added on.

Oh yes suh, I still got my well out there and it still got water in it. It stand in a low place and ain't but fifteen foot deep. I keep it cleaned out and I got me a catfish running 'round in it. I just got one, and I seen him swimming in there this morning. He still little, 'bout from my middle finger down halfway to my elbow. I'd go out there and show him to you, but it getting too dark down there to see him. But you come by here in the morning 'bout sunrise and if the light is right, you see him in there shaking that water. Ever morning I walk out to the well and there he is swimming 'round and 'round wagging his tail just like he own that well. Ever day I throw him down a biscuit, and he growing real fast. I don't know 'bout getting him a playmate. When he get big enough, I 'spect I pull him out of there and throw him in the skillet.

I love to eat em, but I never did like to fish. 'bout ten years ago I bought me some hooks and lines and got me a pole and tried to do a little fishing, but I don't like to set there and wait for Mr. Fish to come. Anytime I got to set there and wait for him and don't know if he come or not, well, I can't do it. I put my hook in that water and wait a while and nothing happen and then move on down the creek and wait and nothing happen and then move on again, and first thing I know I be back at the house with no fish. No suh, I ain't got time for Mr. Fish to come to my hook. He down there in that creek swimming 'round and 'round, dodging my hook, and ain't nothing I can do 'bout it—so I come on home.

What I like to do is seine. Way back yonder, we got us some croker sacks and sewed em together and made em 'bout eight foot long and four foot wide. Then we put poles on both ends and wired some trace chains on the bottom to hold it down in the water and carried that seine to the creek. We muddied up that water to make them fish come up from the roots and holes where they hiding to get some air. When them

fish come up, we be there waiting for them with our seine. We drag it on the bottom and then pull them poles together and bring it up on the bank and we have a sack full of fish. One time we got two big old catfish 'bout as big as your leg tangled up in that seine, and when we pulled them mamas up, I'm telling you it scared us boys to death 'cause we didn't know what it was. Ooooooooo-weeeeeeeee! We drop that seine and make tracks fast as we could out of that creek and up that bank. When we come back, them fish done flipped back in that water and gone.

What I like 'bout it is with that seine you catch a big mess of fish in no time. We get our sack full and take em on home. Then we skin em and gut em and dip em in cornmeal and salt and pepper. Mama had a great big old pot—not a wash pot but a dinner pot—and she put in plenty of hog lard and heat it to it get real hot, and then throw that fish in there and just step back. They be done when they come to the top. Then she took a big old dipper that got holes in it and she reach in there and strain em out. The grease drip back down in the pot, and she put it in a fruit jar and save it for the next time. She didn't know nothing 'bout hush puppies back then, but she make up cornbread pones and cook em to they brown. Man oh man, that old-time cooking can't be beat. Folks was healthy back then. They knowed where their food come from. All this stuff you buy now at the store is high pumped up, and you don't know what you eating.

I ain't never tried to work myself to death, but I work hard on my little farms and sometime I made a little whiskey on the side. I had a farm on the Pitts Place under the bluff down there, and I growed corn, taters, peas, and cotton. I helped Mr. Mann Driggers, farming and working 'round his place. I don't do nothing now, 'cept for a little work 'round the house. See out there where I been mowing my grass. That place is where I makes mens, Uncle Sam mens that holds up mail boxes. I got three I'm working on now standing up 'gainst the house. I cut em out and dress em down and now I got to paint em. I got me a can of white paint and a can of red paint and a can of blue paint in town at the hardware store, and I'm gone put down some stripes on my Uncle Sams. Then I paint his hat on and fix it to he look like he got on a pair of boots. His hands reach out and hold that cross board what you put your mail box on. Booster Jackson up here on the ridge learned me how to make em. I made I don't know how many, but I give em all away. I ain't sold but one to a white man up here in town. I got plans drawed out to make crawfish and chickens and dogs and all like that.

I been handy with my knife since I was a little boy, and I used to make baskets, cotton baskets. But I done got too old now, and all them old baskets I made done been used up. I ain't got a one left. I made a heap of them baskets for Mr. Mann. There ain't nothing to it if you know how. You just cut down a white oak tree and saw it up in logs 'bout the size of housewood. Then you split them logs in four or five pieces and put them pieces in a vise and take your knife and peel off them splints right there between your legs. Now you soak them splints in water, and you can twist them any which way when you start to make your basket. It was my daddy that learned me how to make baskets. He make em so big and strong they can hold a hundred and fifty pounds of cotton. They be so heavy it take two men to tote em.

Well, I won't be making no more cotton baskets and not many more Uncle Sams. I ain't got much time left in this life. I been a happy man, yes suh. I ain't never had trouble with nobody, white or colored. I feel like my daddy and mama trained us all to do right. Ain't never been in a fight. Ain't never had no trouble with nobody. Like the Bible say, I try to live by the Golden Rule and treat folks the way I wants them to treat me. Yes suh, I kept out of trouble. I ain't never been in jail. I ain't never even been to the courthouse 'cept to get my hunting license and my car tag.

I'm just so glad y'all stopped by. It sho' been a long time since I seen you. I wish I had a Uncle Sam ready to give you. Next time you come I'm gone have one put back for you, and it won't cost you a nickel.

POSTSCRIPT: Luke Mariner died Monday night, January 14, 1991, at the age of 82 at the Bullock County Nursing Home in Union Springs, in the same nursing home in which my mother was living when she died some eight months earlier. Funeral services were held five days later at the Old Sardis Baptist Church on Highway 223 in the community where he lived all his life. Burial was in the church cemetery. He was survived by two daughters in New York and two sisters-in-law and one brother-in-law, all of Union Springs. His wife had predeceased him.

From Cotton Field to Cotton Mill

Martha Hall Driggers is in her mid-seventies and retired from her job as a cotton mill worker. It is March 18, 1992, and we are talking in the living room of her small concrete block home on State Highway 223, ten miles south of Union Springs and one mile south of Halls Cross Roads. During our conversation her ailing husband George sits dozing in a reclining chair, occasionally contributing such bits of information as names and dates. The living room is modestly furnished with several easy chairs and small tables, two sofas—one covered in brown ersatz leather and one with a cloth cover draped over it, a television set, and a large wood-burning heater jutting out into the room. Several small pictures and framed family photographs hang on the walls. A reproduction Victorian lighting fixture hangs incongruously from the ceiling. Mrs. Driggers is thin and agile and lively despite her age and years of hard work on the farm and in a cotton mill factory. She is distantly related to my family, and her brother Caswell (she calls him Buddy) married my father's sister Beansie.

Knock them cats out of your way and come on in. George is setting in here, but he won't bother us. You take that chair right over there and I'll talk to you as long as my voice don't go bad. Me and George both has a bad cough and my throat gets dry. I don't know whether it's a cold or allergy or this here pollen that's in the air. I take these little old tablets from the doctor, and they helps some. I just don't want you to make my picture with me looking like something the cat drug up and the kittens refused. I ain't combed my hair today and my eyes is a-watering. If you make my picture with me looking like this, I'm gone wear you out!

Well, to begin with, I was borned on August 8, 1917, somewheres here in Bullock County, but I don't know where. I just don't know where'bouts Mama and Papa was a-living then. It must a-been somewheres close by, but I ain't never heard any of them say where it was. Buddy and Verna Mae might know if I ask them. I'll ask Buddy when he calls me directly. He calls me ever hour or two since Beansie died, so he's bound to call before I'm finished giving you my life history.

I know I was borned at home, but I don't remember if Mama said she had a doctor or not. Her name was Mary Ethel Hall. She was a Gause and her daddy was Joe Gause. There was four of them: Aunt Debelle Driggers, Uncle Jesse Gause, and Uncle Rube Gause. Best I can remember, they was all borned right around here. I know Papa was borned in Bullock County, too, but I don't know much about him or the Halls. There's a lot of them Gauses. I got some old pictures of the Gauses, and Mama used to call one of them Uncle Jule. Some of them lived in Texas. They moved there before I was borned, and I don't know if any of them is still a-living. I wisht I'd a-talked to Grandpa about sich as that, but we never thought about things like that when we was a-growing up. So I don't know a thing about where my folks lived before they come to Bullock County—somewheres over the water I reckon.

I first remember living up above what they call Stills Cross Roads when Cooter was little. His name is Wade but we all call him Cooter. He was borned in 1922. I don't know whose place we was a-living on then, but it could a-belonged to a man named Arnold Teal. There's a Teal buried over here at Liberty Church Cemetery, but I don't know if it's the same one.

There was a lot of Sikeses that lived there close to us, Wilber Sikes's mama and papa and a lot of others. Debelle and Dan'l Driggers lived close too. I remember the night Cooter was borned. It was April and I think we had a little fire because it was dark and a little bit chilly. I was setting in Papa's lap by the fire, and it must a-been after Dr. Ayres left. I had been a-sleeping and woke up after it was all over with. I wasn't even five then and Lord no, they wouldn't a-let me watch.

Back then they never mentioned to younguns where babies come from.

The place we lived in at Stills Cross Roads was a long wood house with a big front porch. We had a great big kitchen and dining room together and two or three bedrooms. We didn't have living rooms back then. Except for the kitchen, ever room had one or two beds in it. We had benches around the dinner table, and I remember eating many a time on them benches. I know Papa must a-made them because they didn't look store-bought.

Cooter was the youngest, so I already had a brother and a sister. Verna Mae was the oldest. She was borned in 1910 and married Jesse Driggers. Buddy was next and he was borned in 1914. His real name is Caswell, but we call him Buddy. A lot of people call him Fraze. He married Beansie Hall.

Martha Hall Driggers, 1974.

There goes the telephone, and I bet it'd Buddy. — "Hello. I'm a-giving my life history, and I don't know where I was borned. Oh, I was? Well, where was Verna Mae borned? Say she was? All right. No, J. W. ain't come by with the mail yet. Yeah, I know it looks like we might have some bad weather, and if I's you I wouldn't stay in that trailer. All right. Bye." —

Buddy says I was borned over there close to the clay pit near Uncle Jesse's old house in Annie Ruth Gause's house right there where there used to be a lot of old canes. He says Verna Mae was borned up there in a house that's no longer there across from where Royce and Ann Rotton lives. It was close to where Mr. Q. P. Deason used to live.

As I was saying, I don't remember anything until we moved to Stills Cross Roads. Papa worked at a sawmill, which I think was owned by a Mr. Teal. I believe it was. Papa snaked logs with cows—well, steers. You know they used to do that long time ago. What I mean is they was bull cows that was worked on—cut—and made into steers. When they was cut it made them strong and easy to handle. They didn't belong to Papa, but I remember seeing him drive them steers up at night and pen them in the lot and water and feed them and then drive them back to the woods early the next morning. That's one of the first things I can remember, Papa driving that team of steers down to the woods.

While he was snaking logs for Mr. Teal, Papa didn't do much farming. He didn't have time to, and he was wore out when he got home ever evening. But we always had little patches of vegetables and a garden and growed what everbody else did—you know, peas, butterbeans, cabbage, collards, onions, turnips. Except for the time we lived in Phenix City, I don't remember a year when I ain't had a garden. If I didn't have a big one, I had a little one. But I may not have nary'un this year because me and George neither one ain't hardly able to work in one now. And the bugs is so bad to eat up everthing!

When I was a girl, we moved around a lot, about ever year or two. For several years we lived on a place over near where Mattie Clyde Brooks has got her store, but a few years ago somebody burnt down the house we lived in then. We growed cotton, corn, velvet beans. I couldn't handle them velvet beans, so Papa and Buddy picked them. They stang me too much. That fuzz would get on my skin and clothes and I'd itch and scratch and itch and scratch. But I worked in the fields a lot, chopping and hoeing and picking cotton. Picking cotton was real hard work. You had to pull the cotton out of them sharp-pointed burrs and drop it in a long sack that you drug behind you down the row. You just try that for a day in the hot sun and you'll be dog-tired before night! I never did learn to plow. The men done the plowing. I never seen her do it, but George's mama said she could plow. We always worked somebody else's land. Papa never owned any land that I know of. George's mama give him this fifty-seven acres we live on now. She heired it from her daddy, and she give all her younguns a place.

I reckon the houses that we lived in looked about like everbody else's. They wasn't fine but good enough to live in. We always kept the house and yard clean. One thing I remember is helping Mama sweep the yards when I was little. We kept the yards clear of grass and weeds and swept out the leaves and trash and chicken manure and sich. We kept our yard like we kept the cemetery. I remember we'd go over to Liberty

at least oncet a year in the late summer and cut up all the grass and rake it up and carry it out. People would come from all around and bring dinner and stay all day long until we got the whole graveyard cleaned off. There'd be a big crowd and some would be hoeing and some raking and some carrying it off to the woods. We'd start up next to the gate at the road and work our way to the back fence next to the colored cemetery. Now, don't ask me why we cut all that grass off the graves. I just don't know. It's just something we always done. A few years ago they got to letting the grass come up and started cutting it with mowers. I think it looks all right, but I've always liked a pretty clean cemetery like they got down at Sandfield in Pike County.

I been going to Liberty Church most of my life, but I joined at Macedonia in 1932. Papa was farming for Miss Ticey Reynolds and we lived in a big old house right close to the church. It was during a revival and several of us joined at the same time. We was all baptized in a pond that was back of our house.

I went to school at Almeria and then to Inverness, depending on where we lived. In 1925 we moved to Phenix City and I went to school there, but I can't remember anything about it at all. We didn't stay there but a year, and Papa moved us back home. He moved there to work in the cotton mill, and I don't think he liked living over there. I was so little I don't remember whether I liked it or not. I went up to the tenth grade at Inverness and then I dropped out because I had to walk too far to catch the schoolbus. We was living down in the swamps near the Conecuh River at what they called the Old

Birds Eye View of Phoenix, Ala.
Paul E. Trouche, publisher, Charleston, S. C. —

An old postcard shows Phenix City, Alabama, as seen from the Chattahoochee River.

Tank Place. There was a tank there where the trains stopped and got water. It was way back behind Mt. Zion Church back of the Cogdells. There was a old wagon road that went by the Cogdell house down to the swamp. Well, when the weather got bad, we just couldn't get to where the bus picked us up and I got so far behind I quit.

No, I didn't quit to get married. I stayed at home and helped Mama around the house. She always done the cooking, but I milked and helped sweep the yards and washed and ironed—things like that. Mama would never let me iron the starched clothes. We used a flour paste to stiffen pieces like shirt collars and fronts and cuffs and bonnets and pillowcases, and when they got dry we'd sprinkle and roll them up till they got damp again and then we'd iron them dry. Mama thought I couldn't iron them right because I was too young. So one day when we was living up here in the curve of the road where Uncle Jack and them used to live, Mama was cooking and I slipped a starched piece out and ironed it. I took pains with it and done a real good job. I done it so good that I had to iron all the starched pieces after that. I said, "Oh oh, I wisht I hadn't done it." But I reckon I felt growed-up when I could iron starched clothes like a woman.

Papa's real name was William Woodard Hall, but everbody called him Boss. He died in 1953. Him and Mama broke up housekeeping after he had a stroke, and they got to living around with us children. All of us was living in town then except for Buddy and Beansie. Papa died in the Mill Village at Cooter and Joyce's house. Mama lived to 1973 at Jesse and Verna Mae's. She was staying around with all of us, but that's where she called home.

I think I hear J.W. with the mail. He's Verna Mae's boy and is our mail rider now. He makes good money at it.

[PAUSE]

J.W. says he heard on the radio there was some

bad weather heading this way and they done got a tornado watch out. I'm not scared of the wind in this house, but I don't want to be in Buddy's trailer when it gets bad. As I was saying, Mama and Papa are both dead now. All of us children are still living and we are mostly retired. Buddy farmed and then worked a while with the state on the roads. Verna Mae worked some in the cotton mill and Jesse worked in the post office until he opened up a little store in Union Springs up there on the hill from the old depot. After Jesse died, she sold her house and moved over here with J. W. on the old Boswell Road near Buddy. It's not more than a mile or two from here. Cooter done a little farming and worked in the mill; then he got to be a policeman until he got sick and had to retire.

Me and George got married in 1935. He is from right around here, just like me. I had a few fellows when I was going to school, but I don't remember any of them. George didn't want to leave his mama, so after we married we moved in with her. A few years later, we moved to Phenix City for George to work in the mill, and we stayed there a year or two. George's oldest sister Eula Mae and her husband Harvey worked in the mill and got him the job. Harvey was like a foreman. George didn't have to take any kind of test. I believe we moved there about in 1940 because George had to sign up for the draft about that time. He went up to Ft. McClellan to be examined for the army, but they turned him down on account of his bad back. They called it lumbago. He's had a bad back all his life.

Back then, a lot of people from Bullock County went to Phenix City and Columbus to work in the mill. They mostly lived in Phenix City, but the mills was right across the bridge in Columbus. They had a bigger mill than we had in Union Springs. When we lived up there in Phenix City, we stayed in an apartment house with a lot of other mill workers. Some of the workers that had been there a long time lived in company houses on Broad Street. I never worked in the Columbus mill, but the very day we moved back here, I got a card to go to work. I went in the mill many a time because they would let you take in dinner to the workers.

While we was gone, Verna Mae and Jesse moved in with George's mama, and they moved out when we come back. George done some farming for a year; then we both started working at the Cowikee Mill in Union Springs. Verna Mae and Jesse was working up there, and we knowed a bunch of people that worked there—like Raymond Head, George Thomas Head— well, a lot of them Heads. They was my cousins, Papa's sister's children. Bennie Driggers, Joe Ed Gause, Lessie Hall, and a heap of others from out here in the country worked up there a long time. It was about the time the war started, and we didn't have no trouble getting a job. We just went up there and they hired us. After George worked up there a few years, he quit and opened up his little store that was out here in the front yard. Before we was married, George also used to do what he called "branch work." He was arrested at his still down on the branch when he was nineteen years old, and they tuck him to Montgomery. He spent one night in jail, but they didn't send him off. I think that just about cured him from making whiskey out in the woods.

Oh Lord, it's that telephone again. I like having a telephone, but it rings too regular. I know it's Buddy again. — "Hello. Yeah, J.W.'s been by. No, I'm still a-giving my life history. Yeah, it's getting dark here. J. W. said we was under a tornado watch. If we get some bad wind, you better leave that trailer. He did? All right. Bye." —

Buddy says J. W. just drove up. Since Beansie died, Buddy won't even try to cook. I don't reckon he'd learn to fix something to eat if he's a-starving. I used to carry him something ever oncet in a while. He will fix a sandwich. Sometimes Verna Mae goes over to his trailer and cooks up something, and ever now and then J. W. takes dinner and they eat together.

Lord no, George can't cook neither. He can fry a egg, but that's about all. Now, Cooter can cook. When he first got sick on disability and Joyce was still a-working, he'd have supper done when she got home ever evening from the shirt factory in Hurtsboro.

So as I was saying, George didn't work long at the mill, but I stayed there for thirty-seven years. I didn't make good money when I started, but it was still more than I could a-made anywheres else. George was making forty and a half cent a hour in Columbus, and I expect we made less than that in Union Springs. Of course, when I retired several years ago, I was a-making a pretty good wage. We both started working on the third shift, and that meant we went on at ten at night and worked until six the next morning. We had a old car and picked up a load of workers and carried them to the mill—Fanny Norris, L. A. Driggers, Beatrice Driggers. I reckon we could a-took our lunches, but there was a old man that went around the mill selling hot dogs and hamburgers, so we bought from him and eat at our machines. I eat so many hot dogs I ain't never wanted to see a weenie since. Later on, they put in a lunchroom where we could set and eat, and we tuck our dinner. They had some old sandwiches and stuff in machines, but I never could eat it. I don't believe we had any rest periods at first, but they must have give us time to eat and go to the bathroom.

Before I retired, I was working on the first shift, which run from six in the morning to two in the evening. We had a ten-minute break at eight o'clock; then at ten we had twenty minutes to eat in, and at twelve we had another ten-minute break to get water and go to the bathroom. I worked on all three shifts, but I like the first shift the best. We never had any say-so about when we worked. They'd generally hire you on the third, and if they had any room, they'd move you up. I didn't like the third shift because I got to where I couldn't sleep I was so nervous. I'd come home and go to bed early in the morning, but I just couldn't sleep. I never could sleep in the daytime. I'd doze a little bit, then start to toss and turn and I'd get up and then couldn't go back to sleep. I'd pull the shades down and make like it was dark, but I still couldn't sleep. In the summertime it was too hot to try to sleep in the daytime anyway, and I didn't have a fan to cool off with. Finally, I told them at the mill I was a-going to have to quit. I reckon they must a-liked the way I worked and wanted to keep me on because they raised me to the second shift.

I started off as what they called a winder. They would spin big wads of cotton into threads and wind it on a big bobbin. I then tuck that bobbin and run the thread off onto big spools. That's what the mill sold, them big spools of thread. It was made into cloth somewheres else. We didn't do it at our plant. After a while, we got new machines that made bigger spools of thread, and that's what I was running when I retired. The mill shut down not long after that, but the building is still standing up there in town.

No, I didn't mind the work. It wasn't all that hard. It was just so steady, and I had to stand all the time. I couldn't set down. I had to go up and down the aisle by my machine and take off the spools when they filled up—we called it doffing—and put on empty ones to catch the thread. Sometimes they would run the machines so fast I couldn't keep up and had to shut down my machine to catch up. The boss didn't like that, but it couldn't be helped. Yes, I think they treated me all right. Our manager was Mr. Watson—I never knowed his first name—and he lived right across the street from the mill. He looked mean and everbody was scared of him, but I don't believe he was mean as he looked.

When I first worked at Cowikee, there was a lot of lint in the air, and I had some trouble breathing; but then the government made them put in a filter up near the ceiling and that cut down on the lint. Eula Mae got breast cancer, but I don't think it had anything to do with the mill. Now, you could get hurt in the machinery. I don't remember anybody that got bad hurt, though I had a accident just before I retired. I went to doff one of them full spools and it was about lunchtime and I was in a hurry. I was fixing to throw the spool on top of the shelf behind me when I hit my elbow on the shelf. It didn't knock me out right then, but after I got to the other end of my machine, I begin to get sick. I seen a black woman coming over to go with me to eat our lunch, and I says, "Whoooooo, Mattie, I'm so sick." She grabbed me and hollered to another worker to stay with me while she went to get the bossman, and that's the last I remember. I just plain fell out. When I come to, I was laying there in the middle of the aisle with Mattie holding me in her lap. They called the ambulance and carried me to the hospital. Dr. Emfinger looked at me and said I'd hit a nerve in my elbow and it just went all over me. He wanted to give me some medicine, but I says, "No, I'm all right now. That's all I did was hit my elbow on that shelf." When we got back down to the mill, Laura Hall—poor old thing that works in the office—she run up and just hugged me and says, "Oh Marthy, I'm so glad to see you back. You looked so bad when they tuck you out of here."

I stayed at the mill the rest of my shift, but the bossman wouldn't let me go back to my machine. He wouldn't let me do nothing for a long time. He said I might have another spell. I says, "I'm not sick. I can work. All I did was hit my elbow on that shelf." So he put me to doing some light work, and I went back on my spooler the next day. They was only supposed to pay you for the hours you worked, but I got my full pay for that whole day because I stayed at the mill until the end of my shift. It was just like I was a-working the whole day.

Yeah, Mattie worked at a machine right over from me. By that time, we had some black people working there. But when we started, it wasn't nothing but whites. We all got along good together, blacks and whites. They was good workers. To tell the truth, the black men was really better to us than the white men. If we went to the lunchroom and it was full, the black men would give us their chairs and set on the floor. The white men never did do that, the lazy scoundrels! Well, one or two of the white men might give us their chairs, but that was all. I reckon they figured they was tired as we was and wanted to rest too.

I never knowed any mill workers that got bad hurt on the job, but I do remember the time four workers on the next shift after mine got killed coming to work. We had just got off our shift, and I was riding with L. A. Driggers that night, and we come along the road where the accident just happened. It was a little after ten because we worked until ten and come straight on. Them pore people was coming in to work the ten o'clock shift. When we got up close, I could tell something terrible had happened, and I wanted to stop to see who it was. But L. A. was so scared she wouldn't stop and the police just let us on by. But I could see them pore people laying out there on the highway. It looked so bad, just like little children spread out on the road. We didn't find out who it was that got killed until the next day. We heard that a big truck that belonged to Bryant Junior McLendon's transfer lines sideswiped the truck the workers was on and sheared off one side and killed the four people setting on a bench on that side. One of them that got killed was Mamie, Homer Driggers' wife. There was a young boy that got killed but I don't remember his name. I knowed them all. They were coming in to take our places at the mill, and they never made it.

Naw, I never belonged to a union. They might have started one in Columbus after we left, but I know we never had one in Union Springs. Some people come there one time to try to start one, but the mill owners wouldn't let them inside the gate. They locked the gate ever time the shift changed, and they said for us not to talk to them outside, and we didn't. I don't know much about the union. I don't know if it would a-been a good thing. Some said it was good and some

said it wasn't. But by the time they tried to come in, we was already getting pretty good wages. They also was also giving us insurance and retirement from the company, though it didn't amount to much.

George didn't work long enough to get any retirement from the company. He draws a little Social Security check, and me and him both has Medicare and a Blue Cross supplement policy. I get a pretty good check ever month from Social Security, a heap more than I get from my retirement. I worked up there at the mill for thirty-seven years and I only get forty dollars a month from the Cowikee retirement. Then I get another retirement from Avondale, which bought the mill from Cowikee before I left. It amounts to a hundred and thirty-seven dollars ever three months. So in all my retirement is about eighty-five dollars a month. But no, I don't regret that I worked at the mill. I liked the work. It was the best we could get around here. But I do think they ought to a-had a better retirement plan. Don't you think so?

Now, me and George don't do much of nothing, except piddle around the house a little. We do spend some time with our children and grandchildren. We have two children, Bessie Mae and Joe Martin. She was borned in 1936 and married Tommy Meredith. He works with the state and they live over at Stills Cross Roads. She has three children and works at the Health Department in Troy. Joe Martin works for the state out of Seale, and he lives in Salem, Alabama, between Opelika and Phenix City. He drove them big pieces of road equipment until he got hurt. It was the year we had that big ice storm. They sent him out early one morning, him and another man, and they was cutting trees off the road so people could get through, and a black man come zipping down the road a-flying and run over him and knocked him about fifty foot. It broke his leg all to pieces. The state tried to get rid of him—you know they try to do that now—and Joe Martin was out of work for over a year. But his doctor said they couldn't fire him because he got hurt on the job and deserved to be kept on. Joe Martin goes to work ever day now, but his leg still hurts him bad. He married Sylvia Green—we call her Tina—from up here in town, and they got two adopted children. Bessie Mae brings her children to see us pretty regular, but Joe Martin and Tina lives too far off to come ever week. They come when they can. But we do enjoy our grandchildren! That are a sight!

I reckon I been lucky and had pretty good health most of my life. I was grown and married and had two grown younguns before I had appendicitis—what the doctor said was chronic appendicitis. I tried to keep on working, but it kept bothering me and bothering me. Finally, the doctor said a operation would be the only way to help it. So I says, "Well, let's get em out." They tuck me on down to Edge's old hospital in Troy, and they operated. That was the only time I was ever in a hospital, and I ain't had no trouble since. You know that Dewey Hall died of appendicitis because they didn't know what it was and waited too long. He was the brother of Louise Hall that married Joe Ed Gause. His appendix ruptured and he died. Mattie Clyde Brooks's husband's brother died of the same thing. He was just a little boy.

I know you heard Cleo Gause died. Well, after Cora died, he seemed like he didn't know what to do. They found him in the kitchen on the floor. Didn't know how long he'd been dead. It was a heart attack.

My throat is getting hoarse and I've done told you all I can remember. You got my life history now, sich as it is. We ought to check outside and see if the bad weather is gone by.

POSTSCRIPT: We walked outside to see that, indeed, the bad weather had passed over without doing any damage. I took some pictures of Martha in front of her house, then drove back to my mother's home at Halls Cross Road nearby. Since George's death about a year later in March of 1993, she has lived alone.

INTERLUDE: COMMUNITY LIFE

In rural Bullock County, social life centered around the church and the school. The photos here were taken at a 1949 program at the Inverness Consolidated School. At right, teacher Morris Hale, Dozier English, Wade Hall, Howell Sellers, and James Wilson, performing a skit on a highly decorated stage. Below, a line-up of Inverness teachers, including, at far right, Principal John F. Hamilton, and, fourth from right, Mrs. Estelle Cope Campbell.

EUNICE DRIGGERS HALL

A Good Life of Hard Work

Most of the old families in Bullock County have lived as neighbors since the area was opened to white settlement during the several decades before the Civil War. Indeed, many of them had known each other in Georgia and the Carolinas, whence most of them came to Alabama. These families have intermarried over the century and a half of their close association. It is, therefore, likely that most of the families represented in these interviews are related to one another, though the kinships are often distant. As she tells us, for example, Eunice Hall's mother was a Hall who married a Driggers. Eunice, in turn, was a Driggers who married a Hall. Only an expert genealogist could unravel such tangled bloodlines. Mrs. Hall's kinship with my family is, therefore, obvious but vague. Nevertheless, she and her family have been close friends with my family all my life; and she and another widow, Nell Driggers, accompanied my mother on a visit to my home in Louisville, Kentucky, where this interview took place on June 25, 1979.

My mother was Bessie Hall, and she married Johnny Driggers. I don't know when that was, but I was born February 12, 1913, so it must have been sometime before that. Mama was nineteen when I was born. Mama's papa was Ben Hall. Her mama's name was something like Narcissus, but they called her Nurse. Papa's people were Tom Driggers and Ella Nichols Driggers. I think they were all born in Bullock County, but I don't know for sure; and I don't know where my people came from before they were here. I never thought to ask them. All I know is they've been here a long time.

I have one brother, Eugene, who is ten years younger than me. I was born on the old Adams Place under the hill back of the John Bates Place. We stayed there for about a year and then moved over to the place where I live now in a little house. It's not the same house I live in now. It was Mama's daddy's land, which she inherited and I later inherited from her. Then about a year later Papa bought the Jim Bates Place, and we moved over there on the Inverness Road. That's the house I grew up in. It was a big wood frame house and had a long porch all the way across the front. It was L-shaped and had a tin roof. In the main part of the house we had two bedrooms on the right of the hall, and the first room on the left was what we called the front room—like a living room today, except we had a bed in it too. If it was cold, we'd sit in it when company came because it had a

fireplace. Most of the time we'd sit on the front porch. Behind the front room was another bedroom and then the back porch leading into the kitchen and dining room. My husband Roscoe's mama's and daddy's kitchen was built off from the house with a board walkway connecting it with the main house. But our kitchen was built inside our house. Their house was about a mile below the cross roads, out where Wilbur and Lessie Hall lived. The kitchen's been torn down but the main house is still there. I imagine people used to build kitchens away from the house because the cookstoves burned wood, and it would heat up the whole house too much in the summertime. There was also the danger that a fire could get started and burn down everything.

We didn't have a lot of outbuildings, except for a smokehouse where we cured and kept our meat. Oh yes, we had two cribs. One of them was for our corn and hay, and on its right was a mule stall and on the left was the wagon shed. In front of that crib we had a lot where the mules could get out and walk around. In the other crib we put our peas and potatoes. I almost forgot. We had a toilet outside, a one-holer. I never used an inside bathroom until after I was married, except when I was at school. Well, come to think of it, the toilets at school were outdoors too.

Around our house we had a dirt yard. We never allowed grass to grow in it. Anything in the yard like grass or weeds or leaves or limbs would have been an embarrassment to us. We kept it swept clean with brush brooms made out of gallberry limbs. We'd go down to the woods and cut some limbs and lay them out to dry, then shake the leaves off and tie the limbs together to make a tight broom. Dog fennel also made good brush brooms in the fall when they died down. They had a busy top and swept the ground clean, but they didn't last long as the gallberry brooms. Both kinds of brooms kept the yard clean, and we liked pretty clean yards. Our chickens, turkeys, and guineas had the run of the yard and left their droppings that we had to sweep up. We didn't like to get any of that mess on our feet or shoes and track it in the house! I especially liked the guineas. They would get up in the trees and pot-rack, pot-rack, pot-rack all night long.

We got our water from the well out by the side of the house. It was deep—about forty or fifty feet—and had some of the best water any-where around here. We'd sometimes have wiggletails in the water. I was told they hatched from mosquito eggs laid in the water. When they

Eunice Driggers Hall.

stayed in the water so long, they'd turn into mosqui-toes, at least that's what we were told. That's why we didn't leave water standing in old buckets and tires. But no, we were never bothered too much with wiggletails or mosquitoes.

Papa farmed about eighty acres, and we raised corn, cotton, peanuts, and cows. Me and Eugene helped in the fields, but Papa also had some colored help. The family of black people we had living on our place had two boys, and they worked in the field too.

Another Negro family used to work for us. They were Lee Walker and Lee, Jr., and J. L. One time Lee Walker got drunk and fell in a pond and drowned. They all used to get drunk whenever they could. Little Doc was Lee's brother, and one night we heard a noise under the porch, and we went out and there was Little Doc drunk as a dog. They're all dead now and buried in a little cemetery Jabo Hall gave them up close to the cross roads.

I did whatever I had to do in the field. I chopped cotton. I dropped corn. I have dropped corn when it was so cold my hands would nearly freeze. Back then people planted corn in March. The seasons were different, and if you didn't plant early, you couldn't make a good crop. I also plowed. I'd rather run a plow any day than hoe. I could plow a mule or a horse. It didn't matter to me. I believe I'd rather plow a horse—one time we had one named Maud—but it seemed like the old mules could hold out longer. Men mostly did the plowing and women did the hoe work. But I just liked to walk behind the plow. It was easier work than hoeing. When you hoe you have to pull that hoe back and forth, back and forth, until your back and wrists just give out. When you plow, all you got to do is follow the mule, turn him around at the end of the row, and get him started back in the next row. It seemed to me that women always had to do the hardest work.

We owned our land, and sometimes we'd have people working on halves with us. I remember one time Ethel and Rube Gause worked on halves, and they lived where I'm living now. What we meant by working on halves is that the landowner got half of the crop and the tenant got half. We would divide the cost of the guano and the seed, and the landowner provided a place for the workers to live. The tenants did all the work and gathered the crop. It was mostly white families that worked on halves with us. For a while Dan'l and Debelle Driggers worked on halves with us. For our own selves, we ran a two-horse farm. That meant we worked two horses or mules. We also had a two-horse wagon, which we'd hitch the horses or mules up to with the wagon tongue between them, and we'd go everywhere in that wagon—to the Crossing, to the store, even to church.

Farm work was long and hard work. We always got up early, before sunup. Mama got up first and started breakfast. While she was cooking, I'd make the beds and sweep up the house a little. Papa would go out to the crib and feed the mules and him and Eugene would get them ready for plowing. I'd do the morning milking; then we'd eat breakfast—usually fried meat and buttered biscuits, and homemade sugarcane syrup—and we'd be out in the fields before eight o'clock. Mama might help some in the field, but she'd mostly stay home and fix dinner and she'd ring the dinner bell at 11:30. We'd come in and have a big dinner of peas and corn and potatoes and cornbread and sometimes fried or boiled pork. We'd go back to the field about one and work until close to sundown and get back to the house in time to do the night work before dark. What we ate for supper was usually left over from dinner, with maybe some hot baked biscuits.

Papa always took his cotton to Boswell Crossing to be ginned and sold. The McLendons had a gin down there and a planing mill and a store. The Crossing was a thriving place at that time. Jerry Head also had a store. You could buy anything you wanted down there—groceries, fertilizer, plow points. We didn't buy many groceries because we grew most of our food. But when Papa sold his cotton, he always bought some cheese to bring home. It was too expensive to buy at other times. We'd have a feast when Papa sold his cotton—cheese and crackers and salt fish. Papa loved salt fish. He'd owe some money to the McLendons because they had furnished him. I mean they had given him credit when the crops were making. But after he'd straightened up with them, he'd have a little cash left over, and we'd buy a few things to eat and wear that we couldn't afford at other times.

We didn't have a lot of clothes but enough for everyday and Sunday wear. Women didn't wear anything but dresses back then. I never wore shorts. A lot of times I wore dresses that Mama made out of feed sacks. She was a good seamstress. She had a pedal machine, a Singer, and she could make most anything—my dresses, shirts for Papa and Eugene, and even bonnets for herself. I never did wear a bonnet much, but mostly my sun hat when I was in the fields. For a long time, Papa and Eugene wore overalls; then Papa got to where he wouldn't wear anything but pants and a shirt.

I never went to Union Springs very much when I was a girl. Papa would always go in the

Mechanical peanut pickers were a later innovation than the type of tenant farming practiced by many of the families in this book.

late fall after he'd ginned his cotton and pay his taxes. In the very early days he'd go by wagon or on horseback. I remember when he bought his first car, a Model T. Of course, he didn't know how to drive it when he bought it, but got in with the Negro man that worked with him, got it out in the road in front of the Ford Place in town, and learned to drive on the way home. He never told us how many horses and wagons he ran off the road.

Sometimes I'd go to town with Papa on his car. But the main thing I remember is going with him to square dances every Friday night before I was old enough to have a boyfriend. Somebody would give a dance just about every Friday night. Papa enjoyed dances. I mean he enjoyed going to dances. He didn't do any dancing himself, but he'd stay right there until it was time to go home. We'd have somebody to play a fiddle and guitar and a jew's-harp—maybe Wade Rotton, Jim McInnis and an old Negro named Pennington. They'd play the same tunes over and over, and we danced on and on. Grady Sellers and Reynolds Sellers would do the calling, and we'd dance way past midnight. We mostly danced in the front room, where we'd take the beds down and move over the furniture to the sides. We didn't have any rugs on the floor, but we'd sprinkle meal on it so we could slide along. When we stopped, they'd sweep up the meal with the dirt in it, and the floor would be so smooth it looked like it was sandpapered.

Sometimes we'd get tired of square dancing and try some other dances. Believe it or not, I could even do the Charleston! Sometimes we'd have the dances at our house, and sometimes it would be at other places. I remember one time Papa carried me over to Kinch Hall's in his pickup truck. Well, we didn't have any headlights, and Buford Lott didn't have any on his car either. So when the dance was over and we both started to leave, we hit each other smack in front. It didn't hurt anybody, but it gave us all a jolt. Then we all went home.

Another thing I liked to do when I was a girl was go horseback riding. We'd generally ride down the road a piece and then come back, but I remember one time we went all the way around by Macedonia over to Beans Cross Roads. It's been a long time, but I remember how much I used to enjoy horseback riding. We also enjoyed playing any kind of game—dominoes, Old Maid, drop the handkerchief and all kinds of ball games. I played on the girls' basketball team for the last four years of high school at Inverness. We played a lot of schools, but what I remember most was the tournament we played in at Lanett, Alabama. Mr. DeWitt Brabham, Mr. Hamilton, our principal, and Mrs. Campbell, our math teacher and coach, carried us in their cars and we stayed the whole weekend, and we won the tournament. I played forward and I thought I was a pretty good player. At that time, the forwards played around the basket where we made our goals, and the guards defended our basket from the other team. The centers played in the middle of the court. Being a forward, of course, I made a lot of goals. I must have been pretty good to be on the team for four years.

I never went to school a day anywhere but Inverness. I started in the old building, but in 1930 my class was one of the first to graduate in the new building. Our principal the whole time I was there was Mr. John Floyd Hamilton. He was a fine man and knew how to keep order. We knew he meant business. I think we had a better school in those days than we have now. I believe we were more serious and learned more than children do these days. I know we behaved better! I was able to get a lot more education than Papa or Mama. They didn't have the chance I had. Papa couldn't write much, but he could write his name. Mama could write a little more—not good, but some. We never had books or newspapers or magazines in the house—except for the almanac, the family Bible, and the Sears and Roebuck catalogue.

At school we didn't have a lunchroom, and I

didn't bother to take my lunch. I just got in the habit of waiting until I got home to eat. When I got there, I'd make for the kitchen and fill up on biscuits and butter and cold meat. Some of the other children took their lunches and had biscuits and meat. And I'll never forget some of them bringing butter rolls, the kind that Elma Lee Hall used to make. They sure were good. It never bothered me to see other children eating their lunches in front of me. I got used to it. I'd rather wait till I got home than fool with taking my lunch.

At home we always had plenty to eat—fried chicken and fried pork, peas and butterbeans, and cakes. I especially liked chocolate cakes and pecan cakes. Mama made tea cakes for the children. Roscoe's mama was one of the best I know to make tea cakes. They were easy to make out of what she had on hand—flour, sugar, sweet milk, lard, and spices. I don't know why we called them tea cakes because we never had tea with them. I loved iced tea with dinner, but I've never liked hot tea. We also drank a lot of sweet milk and buttermilk. My favorite bottle drinks were R. C. Cola and Pepsi-Cola. Coca-Colas were real small back then, and they cost a nickel, the same as the big drinks. Sometimes we couldn't drink our cow milk because the cows would get into bitterweeds in the pasture and the milk would be real bitter. There wasn't a thing we could do but wait until the bitterweeds got too old for the cows to eat. Back then we didn't have bush hogs to cut them down with, and there were too many for us to cut by hand. We couldn't even use the butter, and we fed most of the milk to the chickens and pigs until the bitterness left it. I said we had plenty of fried chicken to eat. Well, we didn't have fried chicken every day—just once in a while or when the preacher took dinner with us.

Mama and Papa were both members at Mt. Zion, but when that church died down, they started going to Liberty. They never moved their letters from Mt. Zion and are buried there in the cemetery now. At

Liberty we had church once a month on the fourth Sunday. Before Papa bought his Model T, we usually went to church on the wagon. But the night I joined the church we walked from where I live now through what we called the Big Pasture. Our cat followed us all the way over there and stayed under the church steps until we came out. Verna Mae and I joined that night. I was about sixteen. We were baptized in our regular dresses at Mill Creek, which was on the other side of Liberty on the road to Post Oak. When I went down in the creek to be baptized, I bogged up to my ankles in mud! It nearly scared me to death. We had a pond and I liked to fish in it, but I've always been afraid of water. I never did learn to swim. Even when I go wading in water, it seems like it just takes my breath away. I like to be close to water but not in it. I knew when I got to be baptized I'd have to go all the way under, and that was the only part I didn't like. It was at the end of our protracted meeting, and Preacher Carter baptized us. He was from down in there somewhere around Troy, and he preached our revival.

I didn't get to go many places when I was a girl. Sometimes I'd go to Union Springs and spend the weekend with my granddaddy, Tom Driggers. He lived near town over off Highway 29. Then sometimes I'd go stay a while with my cousin Annie Belle Driggers at the Mill Village in town. She didn't work at the cotton mill but her brother Jesse did. The mill was up there above the railroad and the mill houses were down below the mill. The Cowikee Company owned the mill and the houses and rented them to the mill workers who lived in town. A lot of people out in the country would ride in every day to work at the mill. Some of them still do. People from Corinth go by my house every morning between five and five-thirty and come back about two-thirty every evening. Country people liked to work in the mill because they thought it was easier than working in the fields, and it brought in cash too.

I never worked in the mill, but I went in there one

time to see about a job. The cotton lint and dust bothered my nose so bad they wouldn't even talk about giving me work. I'm glad now they didn't because I don't think I could have stood all that lint and dust. As soon as I went inside the mill, I felt like the lint was smothering me, and I began to pick at my nose, pulling out dust and cotton. Martha Driggers right up the road from me has worked in the mill for more than twenty years and will retire in August.

I remember an awful thing that happened to some mill workers from the country in the late 1940s. That was when four people on their work to work at the mill early in the morning before day got killed. They were riding on a pickup truck with a tin body and wooden seats along the two sides, and a big McClendon freight truck sideswiped them and killed all four of the ones on the right side—Buford Meredith, Mamie Driggers, Virginia Hall Deason, and a young boy named William Rotton. I believe I heard that McClendon settled with each family out of court for about fifteen hundred dollars each. It was a terrible accident and just tore up a lot of families.

I finished high school in 1930 and married Roscoe Hall in 1932 when I was nineteen. I'd been knowing Roscoe all my life. His folks lived out across the field from us in the house where Wilbur Hall now lives. They had a path going from his house to our house through the woods and field. His people thought a lot of my people, and my people thought a lot of his people. We grew up right close to each other, and finally, before I finished high school, he got to coming to see me. We wouldn't go any place much but mainly sat around the house and played records on my crank Victrola. On Sundays in the fall we might go hunt chinquapins and chestnuts in the woods up on the Jenkins Place. After a while, he'd get his daddy's car and we'd go driving.

Right after we were married, Roscoe and I lived for about a year in a little wood frame house just before you get to Mt. Zion Church on the right. I really don't know how we did it, but we lived on five dollars a month that we borrowed from somebody—the bank, the McLendons, or maybe his daddy. Of course, it was during the Depression and a twenty-four-pound sack of flour only cost thirty-five cents then. We already had fourteen dollars, which I got when I sold some turkeys just before we married. I don't believe Roscoe had any money at all. We just made out on what we had. Our families gave us a cotton mattress and a feather mattress and some small things. We bought a bedstead from Mr. Felix Hixon, and we got a couple of straight chairs from somebody. Then Papa bought me a rocking chair.

I started out doing my washing and ironing at Mama's, but the following Christmas Papa gave me a pair of sad irons so I could iron my clothes at home. They were the kind you had to heat on the cookstove or in front of the fireplace. And oh yes, we got a wood-burning stove from somebody. For a kitchen cabinet we had an apple box tacked up on the wall with a curtain over it. The McLendons at the Crossing let us have our seeds and fertilizer and what all we needed to make a crop, and that first year we planted cotton and corn. Now that I think of it, it must have been the McLendons that furnished us the five dollars a month we lived on. It was a one-horse farm, and there was always lots of work to do. I did all my house work and helped Roscoe out in the field whenever I could.

Mama died in 1933. We never did know what she died of. Dr. George Guthrie at Inverness was our doctor, and if he ever told us, I don't remember it. But knowing what I know now, I kind of feel like it was cancer of the liver or the stomach. Her stomach collected fluid, and Dr. Guthrie would draw that fluid out in a foot tub with a needle. Her stomach would then go down for a while, but she continued to lose her appetite and finally got down to nothing. Mama died real young, somewhere in her forties. I didn't have her but part of the year after I married. She died in June after I married in November.

Papa never did remarry. He stayed in the same big old house until he died in 1960. Mama's sister Jenny lived with Mama and Papa, and after Mama died she raised Eugene. He was a little boy and she was a mama to him. Eugene is married now and lives in a nice brick house across the road below the old home place as you start down the hill to Inverness.

My first baby was born in 1937, but I lost him. I don't know what the problem was. I guess I just wasn't right. Now, I don't know if this had anything at all to do with it or not, but we had a crazy Negro woman that lived down below us. She had spells and we were all afraid of her. One day she walked over to the house and I looked up and she was coming in on me—in the back, up on the porch—and it nearly scared me to death. As I say, I don't know if that had anything to do with the baby being deformed or not, but it was born soon after. And it died.

The next house we lived in was across the branch on a dirt road over there where Mr. Chris Grider used to live. It was a bigger house, with a hall and a kitchen

The author with Nellie Ruth Hall, Eunice Hall's daughter.

and dining room built on like an L. Our first house had three little rooms, two bedrooms and a kitchen. We were living in the Grider house when Howard was born on April 5, 1939. Then Randolph was born November 17, 1942, and Nellie Ruth, the last one, was born June 24, 1944. I always helped Roscoe in the field, and as the children got old enough, they helped too. When they were in school, I worked in the field plowing or hoeing until they got home; then I went to the house to do my work there and they took over in the field. We still farmed after Roscoe got a job working with the county running a road patrol. His job was to grade the holes and bumps out of the dirt roads and build up the shoulders. Later, he got a better job working on the state roads. He'd have to get up at three or four o'clock in the morning to get to work on time. One winter his old car got to where it wouldn't crank, and I'd have to get up in the cold and help him push it off to get it started.

We had some hard times and some sad times. I almost died the first year I was married. I'm lucky to still be here. Papa killed hogs that November and he came over here to get us to help him. I had a fever blister on my lip, and during the night when we got back home, it begin to puff up. It swelled up so much it was turning wrong side out. The next day they took me to Dr. Guthrie down at Inverness. He looked at my lip and said, "Mrs. Hall, you have blood poisoning." I knew then that it was from the blood getting into my sore lip from that hog we helped Papa kill and cut up. Dr. Guthrie lanced my lip from the inside and drained it and said if I hadn't got to him when I did, it would have been too late. I was lucky because people back then died from such things.

When I was a girl, I was never sick very much. I had infected tonsils and measles when I was small, but to this day I've never had the mumps. I slept with Papa when he had them, but I didn't catch them. That was when I was real small and slept in the same bed with Papa and Mama. Now since I've gotten older, I've had a lot of sickness and several operations. In 1956 I had a malignant mole taken off my right arm and a goiter cut out of my neck. The mole had worried me for some time. It would get a little red edge around it, and it would peel off the top and be white-like. It would itch and then all of a sudden a sting would go through it but then be gone in just a minute. At that time Roscoe's mama had a lot of things wrong with her—bladder, kidneys, nerves— and I was carrying her to see Dr. Edge in Troy. So one day when I was down there with her, I showed Dr. Edge my mole, and he says, "Yes, it's got infected." He painted it with some Mercurochrome, and I went about my business. But it didn't seem to get any better, and several months after that, when I was down in Troy with Mrs. Hall, I showed the mole to Dr. Edge again, and again he says, "Oh, it's just infected," and didn't do anything about it. I want to be fair to Dr. Edge. I didn't go to see him about my mole. I just showed it to him when I was there in his office with Roscoe's mama.

Well, later when I had to go see my own doctor, Dr. Colley, about the goiter in my neck, I showed it to him. It was black—been black all my life—and it'd been there ever since I could remember, about the same size. He examined it and says, "Mrs. Hall, this thing's got to come off your arm." So when I went back the next Friday for the operation on the goiter, he cut off the mole too. I was in the hospital in Troy for several days and was ready to come home. Wilbur and Roscoe were there to pick me up. I was sitting on the side of the bed, dressed and ready to leave, when Dr. Colley comes in and says, "Mrs. Hall, let me talk with you a little bit." He sat down on the bed beside me and says, "I've got to go in again and cut deeper because we just got word back that the mole was malignant. We'll have to take some skin off your leg and graft that on your arm." Well, I sat there on the bed ready to come home and cried. Then Dr. Colley put his arm around me and said not to worry because they were going to take good care of me.

There I was, ready to come home. My neck had healed up. I was all dressed. But I had to stay another eighteen days. No, I don't blame Dr. Edge for not knowing the mole was malignant. I wasn't going to him. He wasn't my doctor. And he was a good doctor for a lot of people in his time. A lot of people around Bullock County used to think he was God Almighty Himself. He did a lot of good and waited on a lot of poor people for nothing. No, I don't hold anything against Dr. Edge. But if Dr. Colley hadn't caught that cancer in time, I wouldn't be here today. I've also had some back trouble and went to chiropractors for a long time, but I finally wound up having to have an operation for a ruptured disc. My back's not given me any trouble since my operation.

Roscoe didn't have a lot of illness until he begin having heart trouble. He died on March 19, 1976, of a massive heart attack. It was his third one. He was sixty-six. We'd been married for forty-four years, and I still miss him a lot. We had a good life together, as good as I could hope for. Of course, Roscoe had his ways. For a long time he'd drink too much, but before he died, he quit. It didn't seem to bother the children too much, but it's always a problem for the family when a man drinks.

Now I live by myself but my three children live nearby and come when I need them. I'm proud of them. They all finished high school. All three of them went to Inverness School—never went a day any-where else, just like me. They even had some of the same teachers I had—Mr. Hamilton, Mrs. Waller, and Mrs. Campbell. They all have good jobs. Howard runs a grocery store in Union Springs. Randolph works with Dixie Electric Cooperative in the Water Department. And Nellie works at the Dollar Store as assistant manager. They're all married and I have a number of grandchildren that I'm proud of. I go on trips with some of the other widows in the community. I still work some. I've helped Howard out in his store, and sometimes I work at the Dollar Store when they need somebody extra. I always have work to do at home in my yard and garden. Every year I have a big garden with a little bit of everything. I keep busy. I've had a pretty good life. I remember times that if I knew then what I know now, I'd have done things different. But, all in all, I'm pleased with my family and my life. I can't complain.

POSTSCRIPT: In 1998 Eunice Hall was still living by herself in her home on Highway 223, about ten miles south of Union Springs. She spends time with her children and grandchildren and takes occasional bus trips with other local widows.

A Survivor

Nell May Driggers is related to my family by marriage. Her niece, Lenita May, married my brother Donald. When Nell married J. D. Driggers, she moved into the Liberty community from her native Macedonia, some four miles distant. As her self-profile reveals, she is a hardworking, single mother who has not only survived but triumphed over tough odds. The conversation on which this monologue is based took place on June 25, 1979, when she, Eunice Hall, and my mother were visiting me in Louisville, Kentucky.

Yes, I've done just about anything I had to in order to survive—from selling moonshine whiskey to working in a baby furniture factory. I never had a choice. My husband died of a heart attack when he was forty-three and left me with two young children to raise. It's been a hard but worthwhile and rewarding life.

My name is Nell May Driggers, and I was born October 18, 1922, in Bullock County, right down below Macedonia Church. We could see the church from our house. The church is still there. They've remodeled it, but they didn't tear it down like they did the old church at Liberty. My parents were Charley and Hattie Head May. My mother was forty years old when I was born and my father was fifty. My younger sister and I always thought our parents were so old, and I guess they were. They were both born around in Bullock County. Mama was from down below Boswell. They are both dead now.

I don't remember any of my grandparents because they were all long dead when I came along. Mama's papa got killed in his cotton gin out close to where we used to live. Mama said one of the belts came off the pulley, and he didn't stop the gin when he tried to put it back on, and it snatched him into the gin and killed him. As far as I know, all my grandparents were born in Bullock County, but I don't know where my people came from before they settled here. I do know that Papa's people came from the same place where Velma Driggers said her mother came from because my father and her mother were brother and sister. It may have been South Carolina.

I was born at home, but I believe Mama had Dr. Ayres with her. All my older brothers and sisters were born with the help of a midwife. The house I was born in was L-shaped and had eight rooms and a big front porch that opened into the two bedrooms at the front of the house. There was a long open hallway that led into several bedrooms and a dining room and the kitchen off the back porch. There was so many of us that me and my baby sister had to sleep in the same bedroom with my mother and father. After we moved to another house when I was about thirteen, we started sleeping in a bedroom by ourselves. By that time, several of the older children had married off and left home.

Mama had what I call two sets of children. She had four children and waited eight years and had another five. One of my living sisters is around thirteen years older than me. She was in the first set. There were five of us girls and four boys. The girls were Annie and Buenna Mae, Mattie Lou, and me, and Catherine. The boys were Clarence and Johnny and Buster and Clyde. Annie, Clarence, and Buster are all dead. The rest of us are still living.

Papa was a farmer and a carpenter. He farmed from spring to fall, and after the crops were gathered, he'd go off and build houses. He also had a shop

NELL MAY DRIGGERS 147

where he fixed wagon wheels and spokes and sharpened plow points for other people. In the late fall he'd go to the woods with some other men with his axe and crosscut saw and cut wood for people to burn in their fireplaces in the wintertime. He'd rack up the wood and sell it for a few dollars a cord.

I went through the sixth grade at Almeria School; then I had to catch a bus to Inverness, where I finished high school in 1942. Almeria was a two-teacher grammar school when I went there. Mrs. Lulu Griswell taught the first three grades and Mr. Hightower, a big old fat man, had the other three. They didn't have a science teacher or an English teacher. Mrs. Griswell and Mr. Hightower taught it all. We didn't have a lunchroom at Almeria, and I'd take my lunch of fried meat and biscuits and maybe a sweet potato. At home we had lightbread my sister baked, but I preferred biscuits and still do. I can remember my sister making up the bread and putting it on the window sill in the sun to rise. We younger children had to watch it to keep anything from getting in it.

Nell May Driggers.

During my first year at Inverness in the seventh grade, we lost two classmates out of a class of twenty. A girl named Mildred Watson died Christmas Eve with pneumonia. When we went back to school after Christmas, we were all sad because we missed her so much. That following summer Moray Gause died. They said he had an abscessed wisdom tooth and it got poison in it. Back then a lot of people died of things like that.

I was lucky I didn't have much sickness as a girl. Our doctor was Dr. Emmett Guthrie, and he lived over on Highway 82 going towards Montgomery near Bruceville. When one of us got sick, Papa would put us on his wagon and carry us over to Dr. Guthrie's office, which was a little house in his sideyard. If one of us was too sick to be carried, somebody would ride a horse over to get Dr. Guthrie, and he would come to our house in his Model T.

When I was a little girl, we didn't go many places except church and to visit people in the community. The only time I ever went to town was when the schools had the May Day celebration in Union Springs. The schools at Perote and Almeria and Inverness and other places would go to town for May Day, when we'd plait the May Pole. There would be streamers of crepe paper hanging down the pole, and we would take the ends and go in and out and around the May Pole, threading it in different colors. Those were the only times I can remember going to town when I was real young. When we needed new shoes, Papa would measure out our feet on a piece of pasteboard, and he would go get shoes to match the lines he drew. There were nine of us children, and he couldn't carry all of us to town.

All of our entertainment was in the community. One of the biggest days of the year was the Fourth of July singing at Macedonia Church. They had a stand there where you could buy ice cream. We'd have maybe fifteen cents or a quarter a piece to spend all day, but we could get a big cone for a nickel. For a nickel we could also buy us a big glass of lemonade. Oh my, that was something for us children to eat ice cream and drink lemonade while our parents were inside the church house singing. My mother and father were what they called fa-so-la singers. She sang treble, which was real high, and he sang bass, which was low, and they would sing all day long. That kind of singing was also called Sacred Harp, which meant that they would sing the notes first and then go back and sing the words. It was pretty singing, I thought, but nobody much sings it anymore except for Dixon Hickman, my first cousin.

After I got married, we'd go to the picture show once in a while on Friday or Saturday night at the Lilfred Theater in Union Springs. We didn't have much money, but it only cost a quarter for grown people and ten cents for children. We just couldn't wait for the weekend to come! That's about all we did for recreation, except visit our parents. We never had a vacation. We didn't know what one was. We did have a lot of barbecues back then when we'd kill three or four pigs at the time. It was nothing to go out and kill a hog and then invite half the community. We were always having company. Some would come without warning right at dinnertime, but we'd always have enough for everybody to eat. Now, if you come to my house at dinnertime, I doubt if I'd have anything cooked!

I married J. D. Driggers in 1943. His daddy and mother were Dan'l and Debelle Driggers that lived over near Mt. Zion Church. I met him at Mothers Day at Liberty, which is where they went to church. J.D.'s uncle lived catty-cornered across the road from us, and he'd visit them and started coming over to our house. That's when I started dating him. We went around together for two years before we married. He didn't have a car but somehow he'd get over to his Uncle Rube's house and then walk over to ours. Sometimes his sister Mary Winnie—she was younger than J. D. but was already married to Bruce Buford— would bring him over. After a while, his daddy got an old car that he would come over on. He was in service in Atlantic City, New Jersey, in 1943 when we married. I went up there to get married; then I came back home and he went overseas. When he got out of

service in 1946, we lived several months with his mama and daddy; then we rented a two-room apartment in Inverness from a Mrs. Green. J. D. worked for the R.E.A. for a while. After that, he worked as a laborer for the county on the road.

Then we started making our living by making whiskey. It always bothered me, but we did it. J. D. built his still in a number of different places in the woods, wherever there was a good spring of water. You have to have fresh water to make good whiskey. J. D. made the still himself. He made the vats out of galvanized tin, but the condenser the whiskey was run through was made out of copper because it made the whiskey taste better. He knew what he was doing. I have seen him put the stills together with a soldering iron. He did it fast and he did it right. He started making whiskey before our daughter was born in 1949 and made it through the fifties.

Nobody in my family ever made whiskey, but there was one family in our community that did. They were the only family that had anything nice—a nice car and clothes and other things the rest of us didn't have. I used to go to their house, and they'd have the prettiest cakes and so many good things to eat. They were generous and shared what they had with my daddy's children. That was the only family in the Macedonia community that I knew of that made whiskey, but in J. D.'s community it was common that people made whiskey for a living—or at least to supplement their farm income. It was just a different custom.

When J. D. was running whiskey, we sold it mostly to people in nearby dry counties where you couldn't buy whiskey legally. Bullock was a wet county. Macon was a dry county, and we could sell our whiskey up there any time we had it and get a good price. He'd haul it up to Macon in jugs or kegs in a car or pickup, and sometimes I'd go with him. I was always scared on those runs because every time I saw a car coming, I'd think, "Oh Lord, that may be the

Law. We're gonna get caught." We always knew the bootlegger we were carrying the whiskey to, but we couldn't take it to his house. We'd put it off at a certain place—like the side of a field road in the woods—and then we'd go to his house and he'd pay us. Sometimes people would come to our house and pick it up. Many a time when J. D. would be gone, I have taken a bootlegger to a place where J. D. told me the whiskey would be, and the man would load his whiskey, pay me the money, and get gone. It always left me a little weak-kneed, and I was glad when he got out of sight. We sold it pretty cheap. It was according to the bulk.

Almeria Schoolhouse.

The more a man bought the cheaper it would be, maybe eight or ten dollars a gallon. Then the bootlegger would retail it for, say, a dollar a Co-Cola bottle full. He could make a lot of money off each gallon he sold that way.

We also retailed some whiskey in Bullock County. We'd moonshine it and then bootleg it at the little store we ran for a long time—a Co-Cola bottle full for a dollar. A few whites would buy it, but the most we sold to blacks who made good money from pulpwooding and sawmilling. They got paid every Friday and on Friday nights and Saturdays we could sell a lot of Co-Cola bottles full of whiskey.

Yes, all the time we were in the whiskey business it kept me scared. I was always afraid we'd sell to somebody we weren't supposed to. I knew, too, that some people in the community were looking down their nose at us, and that bothered me, and I worried about what our children would think when they knew. But we did it because we felt we had to. At that time it was about the only way country people could make any money. We thought it was the only way we

could survive, the only way to get us and our children what we needed to live on. Now, I think we could have made out some other way because we eventually did. As years went by, things began to get better for us country people. They opened factories in town where women could get jobs and earn a little money to help their families out.

J. D. did get caught one time. He should have known better, but he sold some whiskey to a Federal man. He didn't get caught making it. He just slipped up and sold it to the wrong man. A Federal man came in disguise looking for whiskey to buy, and J. D. took his money and told him where to go to pick his whiskey up. He went to the woods and got it, then came back and picked up J. D. and several others and took them to Montgomery. J. D. got out on probation because he'd never been in trouble before, but he never did make or sell any whiskey any more. It scared him that he might have to do time if he was ever caught again. We worried what effect that would have on our children. Our daughter was getting old enough to wonder what her daddy was doing in the woods and what he was selling at the store. So J. D. said, "If I ever had to go to the penitentiary, it would embarrass my children. So I'm not going to fool around with whiskey any more." And he never did. We started making out some other way. Maybe if we'd thought about it right to begin with, we'd never have had to do it in the first place.

My two children are Nelda Faye, born December 10, 1949, and Danny, born January 15, 1954. Nelda is now a registered nurse and works in a urologist's office in Macon, Georgia. Danny works for Georgia Power Company in Milledgeville. He was named after his daddy, Joseph Daniel, so he's a junior. Grandma Driggers—Miss Debelle—nicknamed him Danny because there were so many juniors around here. She said, "I'm just not gonna call him Junior any more. Gonna call him Danny." And he's been Danny ever since. One time I called over to the plant where he works and asked for Danny Driggers, and the lady said, "I'm sorry, ma'am, we don't have a Danny Driggers working here." Then I heard somebody in the background say, "Oh, I bet she's talking about Joe." I said, "Yes, I'm talking about Joe." But he'll always be Danny to me.

We were making it all right until J. D. died; then I had to take whatever job I could to support my family. Finally, I got a good job. Now, I'm a nurse at the Bullock County Hospital and Nursing Home. I got my training in Eufaula at the Chauncey Sparks Trade School back in 1967 and 1968. I was in my forties then. I just got tired of working in cafes and on assembly lines and in factories for such low wages, and I decided I could get to be a nurse. I worked for several years at the Welch Factory in Union Springs. They made baby buggies and baby beds and other things for babies. It was long and hard work. Nursing is hard work too, but it's a different kind of hard work. It's always interesting and I enjoy it. At the Welch plant I operated a cutting machine on a cutting table, and I did the same thing hour after hour after hour. I left

that job and helped run the Coffee Pot Cafe and Service Station on Highway 82 out from Union Springs on the road to Eufaula.

One day I was talking with Lyra Richardson, who had worked with me at the Welch Company and quit after she found out she had breast cancer. When she had her operation and recovered, she decided she'd go to nursing school. So she said to me, "Why don't you, Nell? You can do it too." I said, "Well, I'm certainly not satisfied where I am or with anything I've done. I don't have anything to lose. I think I'll try it."

I first signed up at the state trade school in Montgomery and went there for three months, but I dropped out because it was too far to drive back and forth by myself. One day I saw John Smith in Union Springs and he told me the state had a bus going every day from Union Springs to the trade school in Eufaula, which was closer. That made it where I could go three or four miles to Smut Eye on my car and then catch that bus.

We had to pay fifteen dollars a month to go to school, but we didn't pay anything for the rides. I bounced on that old bus twice a day, five days a week for a whole year, but it was worth it. It was about forty miles to the school, so we had to leave pretty early to get there for class at eight o'clock. Then we'd get back to where I left my car at Smut Eye about three o'clock, which would give me just enough time to get to Union Springs to my job as a nurse's aide in the nursing home from four to eleven. It was the only way I could go to school and keep my children in school too. Nelda was in college then and Danny was in high school, so it was a very hard year. But I made it, and it's been a blessing to me that I did.

J. D. wasn't but forty-three when he died of a massive coronary in 1961. At first I didn't know what I would do. I didn't know what I could do. I drew a little money from Social Security and a little from the Veteran's Administration, but it wasn't enough to keep us up. I had no choice. I had to work somewhere.

Through all those hard times, however, I had a lot of good help from Eunice Hall's brother Eugene and his wife, L.A. They helped take care of my children while I worked. Even now, Nelda and Danny love Eugene and L.A. like a daddy and mama. They always tell that when Danny comes home he's got to see Eugene before he sees me. My other relatives helped take care of my children some too, but financially I raised them by myself. I'm proud I could do that.

That year I was in school and working full time I didn't get much sleep. I also had to do all my own cooking and cleaning and washing and ironing. I didn't even have the weekends free to catch up in because I'd work at the nursing home on Saturday and Sunday, sometimes on a double shift. It was a very hard year. At times I'd think I couldn't make it, and I have to give Nelda a lot of credit for keeping me going. She was taking a fashion course in school in Atlanta. When I'd get worn out and disgusted and say, "Well, I'm gonna quit," she'd say, "Mother, if you quit, I quit." So I'd smile at her and say, "Well, I guess that settles it. I can't quit."

I can't imagine now how my life would be if I'd dropped out. I'm thankful I held on and finished my nursing course. I'm thankful I held on and kept my family together. I've worked hard to give my children a better life than J. D. or I had. When J. D. died, we were living in a little house on seven acres of land in the curve just below Inverness School that J. D. had bought from Jeff Sorrell. About two years later, I bought three acres of land from Eugene across from Mr. Hamilton's old house just down from the schoolhouse. I was able to build a nice brick house so that Nelda and Danny would have a better place to grow up in than J. D. or I had. It was a big risk, I know, but I guess I've been taking risks all my life. I've always been a pretty independent woman that took chances. It was the only way I could get ahead. It's how I've survived.

POSTSCRIPT: In 1995 Nell Driggers was still living alone in her comfortable brick home on the outskirts of Inverness and working as a nurse in the Bullock County Nursing Home in Union Springs.

Baseball was by far the most popular organized sport in Bullock County in the first half of the century. At left, Charles and Bruce East in uniform for Corinth about 1943. Teams for men were sponsored by communities and sometimes by textile mills but had died out by the close of the 1950s. Below, a Bullock County Little League All-Stars team from the mid-1950s. The author could put names with only a few of these players. From left, second on the first row, Donald Hall; second on second row, Randolph Hall; fifth on third row, Sonny Hall; and sixth on third row, Jimmy Coston.

FRANCES MCLENDON WHITE

As Sturdy as the Oak

Frances McLendon White was born into a family of country aristocrats in the southern Bullock County trading center officially named Omega but commonly called Boswell Crossing (or simply the Crossing) after a family that lived near an early ford or crossing of the Conecuh River. Her father, Clarence McLendon, owned large tracts of land which he rented or farmed with sharecroppers. As a merchant and informal banker, he also "furnished" local farmers with seed, fertilizer, farm equipment, and money that they needed each year to make their crops of corn, cotton, and peanuts. The daughter of perhaps the wealthiest family in the area, Frances lived a privileged, pampered life. Her rose-colored memories of the past and her present Pollyanna optimism are legacies of that life.

She and my mother grew up in the same community, but the discrepancy between their social and economic status quickly became apparent during our interview. She and my mother are now good friends, but during their girlhoods they lived in very different worlds. During the interview, she would often turn to my mother, who had accompanied me to her house, to seek verification regarding the way things used to be. My mother would nod an affirmation, even when Frances spoke of experiences that were totally foreign to the daughter of a yeoman farmer. "Sarah," she might say, "remember the wonderful parties we used to have in so-and-so's ballroom in Union Springs?" My mother, of course, had never been invited into the homes of such wealthy families. Indeed, her father—my grandfather—had been one of those subsistence farmers who were "furnished" each year by her father with the wherewithal to make their yearly crops.

Our conversation took place in the parlor of her large frame house at 204 South Prairie Street in Union Springs, where she has lived since moving from Omega in 1941. Her husband died in 1970, and since her sister's death several months ago, she has lived alone. A maid comes every morning to cook and clean. Mrs. White married at 56 and was widowed at 59.

Honey, I don't know very much. After all I've been through with my sister's illness, I don't have any marbles left. It takes a lot away from you to lose a sister you've lived with all your life and to live alone for the first time. But I'm recovering. I'm getting back on my feet. Dr. Cawthorn said to me the other day, "Frances, you're just in the prime of life." I certainly hope he's right because I want to live until at least the year 2000.

Make yourselves comfortable while we talk. Cindy has fixed us some iced tea and sandwiches. Don't eat too much because I want to carry you all to dinner at the country club. They have a new cook over there, and the food has improved so much. I see you all admiring the things in my living room. Yes, I love to have outstanding objects in my home. Those little pictures you're looking at now on the wall came from an art gallery in Rome, Italy. My sister Laurie brought them to me from one of her trips. I said if she thinks that much of me, then I won't put them in cheap frames. I had the Framery in Montgomery fix them up for me, and it set me back almost two hundred dollars. I don't cut corners when I want something beautiful.

A lot of this Victorian furniture was made by my cousin Carleton, Father's brother's son that used to have a furniture store in Montgomery. I just love the work that he did. He was a master craftsman. You know he didn't have but one child. She married a doctor and moved to Atlanta. After she developed cancer, Carleton decided to move over there to be with her what time she had left. He's still there, and I don't think he'll ever come back to Alabama. Oh honey, he made such beautiful furniture. When they restored Ford's Theater in Washington, they asked him to make the reproduction chairs that Lincoln and his party were sitting in when he was shot. Carleton received a special invitation to attend the opening. That sofa you're sitting on is a sample of his work, and it makes me sick to think I've let the moths eat on it. I know they have to have something to eat, but they didn't have to eat my beautiful sofa.

I've always loved to surround myself with beautiful furniture and art. Just before you came, I was reading this notice about a replica of the Statue of Liberty that's made out of metal taken from the actual statue. When the letter came this morning, I went crazy over it. It's high, honey, but I want to order it. It costs four installments of $37.50 each. That's about $150. I got to go slow for a while. My accountant says he's scared to death I'm going to have to pay inheritance taxes on my sister. She had such a big estate. I'm having to be careful until I see where I stand. Of course, I got plenty of my own. I don't need a penny she had. But it makes me feel so good to know that she loved me so much she left me everything, just everything.

Laurie and I loved each other so much. Here's

another letter that came this morning. It's a living memorial certificate that says, "I hereby certify that a tree will be planted in living memorial as requested by your funeral director through an agreement with the U. S. Forestry Service and the Batesville Casket Company. When a life ends, a new life begins." I think that's such a beautiful sentiment. Oh, I so much hope it's an oak tree they plant in one of our national forests in Laurie's memory. It would be so appropriate because our family motto back in Scotland was "As Sturdy as the Oak." And here's another lovely sentiment I received a few days ago in memory of my beloved sister. Six stores in Union Springs went in together and sent me this wonderful leather book called "Lift Up Thine Eyes." It has such beautiful, consoling poetry in it, and I do love good poetry. I'll bet you didn't know it, but I've won a national poetry contest, and next month I'm going to Reno, Nevada, to get my certificate. Oh, I'm so scared and I'm not going to say a word, not a word. Listen, honey. They say if you *don't* say something, people will *think* you're a fool, but if you *do* say something, they will *know* you're a fool. So I'm going to keep quiet while I'm out there.

Frances McLendon White.

Oh, I'm dying to have this little statue. It says here in the advertisement that it's plated with copper taken from the real Statue of Liberty in New York City. They're selling these replicas to make money to repair Miss Liberty. I really think I ought to help, don't you? Wouldn't it be something to have one of these? I've got to have it. Yes, I'm going to get one. Oh, I'm extravagant, so extravagant! They say it's a limited number available, and I know everybody will want to have one. I'd better order one today.

I'm so excited about that statue I don't know if I can settle down and talk about myself. To begin with,

a lady shouldn't tell her age, but I will tell you that I was born at home in Omega, Alabama, in southern Bullock County on November 10, 1911. That was before Dr. Ayres moved to Omega, so Mother had Dr. Thomas from Perote with her. Perote had three doctors at that time. Can you believe it? It was such a wonderful addition to our community when Dr. Ayres moved to Omega. He was a capable doctor and a leader in religious work. He had his office in an upstairs room in my Grandfather Head's store. In those days we didn't know anything about going to the drugstore to buy medicine because he kept shelves of medicine in his office and mixed it himself.

My family has lived in Omega for generations, long before the War Between the States. Before that, we go back to South Carolina and then to Scotland. I have a family tree that Carleton's brother, the one that became a lawyer, gathered up and wrote down. It's in this drawer. I'm having trouble seeing because I sat down on my glasses the other day and cracked them. But I think I can make out some of the information about the McLendon family. Originally, there were three brothers that lived in Scotland. After their parents died, two of the brothers came to America and landed in Charleston and settled in Edgefield, South Carolina. The brother that remained in Scotland was a bachelor and when he died the family property went to the state and was sold for taxes. The McLendon cabin in South Carolina was burned by the Indians, and their Bible and all their records were destroyed. One of those two brothers in South Carolina was my great-great grandfather, who was the father of William Frederick McLendon, who was born in 1813. In 1838 he moved to what is now Bullock County and married

Sarah Williamson of Sardis. He was a big plantation owner, and they say he owned so many slaves he did not know some of them when he saw them. We used to hear stories about one of the slaves that came straight from Africa. When he would get upset and homesick, he would go down in the swamps close to the Conecuh River and hide out for a week or ten days, but he would always slip back at night to get something to eat. My great-grandfather was a good businessman and with the profits he made from raising cotton, he would buy more slaves so he could grow more cotton and buy more slaves and land. All his children had their own personal servants. When one of the servants did something wrong, the overseer went to their owner, but his children always took the blame so their slave would not be whipped.

My great-grandmother McLendon had seven children, including Maston Frederick, who was my grandfather. He was born in 1848. But a sad thing happened soon after their youngest, John Madison, was born in 1852. My great-grandfather and another man started to Montgomery one day on a buggy. They had put an open bridle on a horse that had always been used to blinders; and when he looked back and saw the buggy top, it frightened him, and he ran away. My great-grandfather tried to jump out of the buggy, but he fell and got caught between the wheels and was killed. His widow later married Rube Lawrence of Briar Hill in Pike County. The children did not approve of the marriage, so the eldest, Louise Catherine, put them all on a wagon and took them to Texas. She became a good businesswoman and managed to raise all her brothers and sisters. They all stayed in Texas, except for one, my grandfather, Maston Frederick, who rode back to Alabama twice on horseback. On his first trip back, he met Laura Bethany Head of China Grove and fell in love with her. He promised her, "I'm coming back to marry you." And so he did, on February 18, 1875. While he was still in Texas in the Brazos River country, he took

a pair of pants and tied the legs up and filled them with wild pecans and brought them with him to Alabama. He distributed them in Bullock and Pike counties, and to this day some of those trees are still bearing pecans.

My Grandfather and Grandmother McLendon later moved to Omega, where Grandfather died in 1887. I didn't know him, of course, but I do remember my grandmother, who lived until 1939. Their oldest child was my father, Clarence Augustus, who was born in 1875. He married Molly Bates from Goshen in Pike County. There were six of us: Beulah, the oldest, Willie Clare, Frederick, Lillian, Frances—that's me—and Laurie, the baby. Grandmother Bates used to tell us that when Beulah was born my parents were very young and looked even younger. At Beulah's birth there were in the room Grandmother Bates, Father, and the physician, who looked at Father, then looked at Grandmother and said, "Get that little boy out of here!" Grandmother replied firmly, "That little boy is the father of this baby that's about to be born." Five of us are still living. Our chain had not been broken until May 22 of this year, just two months ago, when I lost Laurie. She was seventy-one.

We don't know much about our other ancestors, but I do know that Grandfather Head had owned a plantation in China Grove. Whenever the United States got into a war, he would always be one of the first to join up. When the war with Mexico broke out, he went to help free Texas. When the Civil War came, he organized a company at China Grove and became its captain. During the war he was captured and made a prisoner at Mobile. While he was away, the Yankees came through his plantation. The family thought they could trust an old slave to take all their horses to the swamp and hide them. But when the Yankees arrived, he told them where the horses were hidden, and they stole all of them except one that was very old. Their eldest son Walter was only thirteen, but he jumped on the old horse and raced after the stolen ones. He couldn't catch them, and I don't know what he could have done if he had.

By the time my father started raising his family, the South had recovered quite a lot from the war. Our community at Omega was prosperous, and a lot of people were living in and around this little town. In addition to our family, I can remember the Stuckeys, the Sellerses, the Englishes, the Copes, the Newberrys, the Burtons, the Stricklins, the Bushes, the Daniels, the Spencers and others I can't name. These were just the white families. We had maybe twelve or fifteen Negro families that lived in or close to Omega. They lived all around us, and we thought nothing of it. Many of them lived in my father's houses, which had three or four comfortable rooms. Father always told them they could live around us as long as they behaved themselves, but if they didn't they'd have to go. Most of the Negroes worked on my father's farms as tenants. Sometimes they worked on halves, and sometimes they were furnished. By furnished, I mean that Father would provide them whatever they needed through the year from his pocket and his store, and they would pay him back when they sold their cash crops, mostly cotton. Remember that despite the boll weevil, cotton was still king back in the 1920s and 1930s when I was growing up and a young woman.

Father meant a lot to his black tenants. They even came to him to get their teeth pulled. He had several tooth-pulling tools, but no novocaine or any kind of painkiller. It was terrible, but they suffered it out. I don't see how my father was able to pull teeth because he was such a tenderhearted little man. But there was no one else to do it, so he did. He even pulled white people's teeth if they couldn't get to town to see a real dentist. He provided just about everything the black and white farmers around Omega needed. The farmers didn't know what it meant to come up to Union Springs and buy a sack of flour. They could get all they needed at Omega.

Father was good to all the Negroes who worked

for him, and they loved him dearly. We never had any trouble with any of our black tenants. When he passed away, his body was brought up to Union Springs to Oak Hill Cemetery for burial, and the Omega Negroes came up to the cemetery by the truckloads. They were all allowed to come inside for the graveside service. They loved him so much because they knew they could come to his store, and he would say, "Go on in there and get anything you want. If you can pay me what you owe me at the end of the year, I want you to, but if you don't have it, don't worry about it." Honey, my father was a good man and everybody knew it.

Father was also a good provider for his family. He built us a fourteen-room house with lumber he had brought up from Bartow, Florida. He provided us with all the servants we needed to get everything done around the house. Mother had muscular dystrophy and was a semi-invalid for most of her later years. The maids took care of her. They bathed and dressed her and did everything she needed done. Father always kept a colored boy at the house to pick her up when she fell. The boy also had certain other chores to do, like bringing in the wood and coal and making all the fires in the stoves and fireplaces before the family got up every morning. For many years Tempie was our cook, and a wonderful cook she was. With a houseful of children, an invalid mother, and constant visitors who would sometimes spend a week or more with us, I don't know how we would have managed without our servants.

Yes honey, Omega was a marvelous place to grow up. We had such a happy family life. Father might have a little grape or scuppernong wine occasionally, but he would never allow hard liquor in his house. The only exception was at Christmas, when he let us all have a little spiked eggnog—just a little tiny spike. Father's only bad habit—and we didn't think it was so bad at the time—was that he smoked cigars, and he smoked them all the time, *all* the time.

Judson College, Marion, Alabama, founded 1838, c. 1915.

Christmas was our main celebration. It was always a big affair, a big affair for both blacks and whites. First, we would go to the woods and get a huge cedar tree—big enough for at least a dozen people to stand around—and set it up in our entrance hall next to the winding staircase. Then we'd put candles in little tin holders which we'd attach to the Christmas tree. How very beautiful it was when the candles were all lighted and blazing in dozens of little flames. I'm utterly surprised that we didn't set the house on fire each year. We also decorated the tree with tinsel and colored ropes and balls and put up holly and green vines all over the house. Santa Claus always brought us too many presents, too many. I got all kinds of toys, from bicycles to dolls and doll buggies and books. I remember so well one year when I got a doll buggy and piled it full of my dolls and toys and other presents and pushed it up the road to show my grandfather and grandmother.

Oh yes, it was such a marvelous, joyful time of the year. At night we'd set off firecrackers and Roman candles and those wonderful little sparklers. It was a great time for everyone. Our black tenants would buy Santa Claus at our store on Christmas Eve, and the next morning the little black children would have their clothes and toys and fruits and nuts just like us.

Throughout the year, we enjoyed going to church, and we white children sometimes even attended Negro services, which we thoroughly enjoyed. At Mount Olive Church there was always a back bench reserved for us on Sunday nights. We went with a serious purpose, and we were welcomed. You see, honey, we were among friends who loved us. Every time we went to Mount Olive, we had a one dollar bill rolled up to drop in the collection plate. One of our great thrills was to attend the colored baptizings, which they always held in one of our ponds after their summer revivals. We enjoyed hearing the shouts of victory as the new church members were gently submerged into the water. Oh, that was so long ago. But recently I was happy to be able to have a part in remodeling their church. It is such an important part of my past that I wanted to help preserve it.

Of course, we had our own church in Omega, our own Baptist church with the most outstanding ministers obtainable—such as the Reverend Tommie Emfinger, the father of our beloved Dr. Emfinger; the brilliant Dr. W. R. Richards of Hurtsboro; and Dr. Tom Foster of Midway. We always had the very best ministers because my father paid most of their salary. We had a tiny membership, but when we called a new minister Father would say to him, "Now, don't worry. I'll make sure you get paid." Our Aunt Essie was the church organist and Laurie and I spent a lot of time pumping the organ for her. Oh my, I can still hear that wonderful old organ, and I can hear my father singing his favorite hymn, "Lord, Plant My Feet on Higher Ground." It was one of the songs we sang at his funeral.

Just like the black church, we had a revival every summer. Because we were the only family who had running water and electric lights, the visiting preachers always had to stay with us. Sometimes there would be three or four of them. That annoyed us children because we had to entertain them on the front porch and were not allowed to leave the house and play while they were there. Sometimes the preachers realized we didn't like being prisoners, and they'd suggest that we all walk out to our pool and they'd watch us swim. That was what we wanted to hear! We'd also walk around the yard with them and pick plums and scuppernongs. Then they'd go back to the house to their rooms and take a little nap before dinner or preaching. We children enjoyed going to church, but we just didn't like being tied down too much.

We had plenty of other things to do in addition to going to church. We never had a picture show in Omega or an opera house like they did in Union Springs, but we did have traveling carnivals and shows that came through and pitched their tents out in one of Father's pastures. They had little monkeys and sideshows and games. Everybody would try to see those shows, and I believe that the Negroes were allowed to come at certain times. Back then, the races didn't mix like they do now.

Yes, there was always something for us children to do in Omega. We played all kinds of ball games. I've mentioned the pool where the ministers would watch us swim. Well, that was the first swimming pool in Bullock County. My father built it because we always had an abundance of water from our seven overflowing wells. They were called artesian wells. Father had the pool dug into the ground and a wooden bottom put in. It was a marvel to behold and many of our friends from Union Springs would come out to go swimming in our pool. Another thing we loved to do was visit with our friends and spend several days or several weeks. Sometimes I'd have house parties that would last a week. We'd love to put on barbecues and all of Union Springs would come out as well as our cousins from Montgomery and Troy.

Traveling was easy in those days, in some ways more convenient than it is now. We had cars, of course, but the roads were usually rough and unpaved and always washed out after a heavy rain. But the trains were wonderful and dependable. In Omega we

had two trains that came through in the morning and two in the afternoon. If we wanted to go to Troy, we could go down in the morning at nine o'clock and come back in the afternoon at five. It was just so easy to get to Montgomery or Birmingham or Mobile or any place you wanted to go. People would come from miles around to catch our trains. I was talking just yesterday with two Rotton women about those days. I said, "I remember you all used to come to Omega to catch the train when you were in college in Troy. I can remember the beautiful clothes you wore." They are twins named Eva and Elois and they live now in Ft. Davis, but they grew up in the country out from Omega. They went to Troy Normal, what's called Troy University now.

We had such wonderful institutions at Omega, certainly our church but also an excellent elementary school with fine teachers. My sister Beulah was one of the teachers, and I remember also Miss Mittie Wilson and Miss Emmie Anderson, Frank Anderson's aunt in Union Springs. Mr. Jay Lawrence, who later became school superintendent for the whole county, was our principal. We had good teachers for the same reason we had good ministers. My father would say, "I'll see that you get paid." And he did. The school was about a half mile out from Omega. There was a clump of trees near the school where we built us a playhouse with boxes for furniture. We kept an old rag doll in the playhouse with her stuffing coming out. It was our favorite place to play at recess.

I went to Omega School through the sixth grade, which was as high as it went. Then I came to school in Union Springs. Father rented a house for us to use while we were in school up here. He was determined that none of his children would have to go to school at Inverness. He thought Union Springs was a better school, and he never wanted anything but the best for us—the best school, the best church, the best friends, the best of everything. Beulah stayed with us and we had a cook to take care of our needs. I never went a day to Inverness School and graduated from Union Springs High School, but Laurie and Marjorie got tired of staying away from Father and Mother and went home to finish at Inverness. My brother Fred, who later owned the picture show, the Lilfred Theater, lived with us until he got married.

Our cooks in Omega and Union Springs fixed us such marvelous meals, with much of the food coming from Father's smokehouse and gardens. Every year he had three gardens going and planted them so that when one ran out, another one would begin producing. He grew peas, snapbeans, butterbeans, tomatoes, eggplant—just about everything. Dinner was our big meal at noontime, when the table would be covered with delicious dishes of meats and vegetables and breads, especially when we had company. Then we always had big platters of fried chicken, though Laurie and I were always afraid when we had ministers that they would eat it all up and not leave us a drumstick! I've never yet seen a preacher that didn't love chicken. Mother was careful about what she allowed us to drink, but we all loved iced tea. She didn't like for us to drink Coca-Cola between meals, and she made us nectar out of blackberries and put ice in and served it to us as an afternoon drink on the porch. You see, our parents always wanted us to be healthy and have the best of everything.

Father worked hard to provide us with what we wanted. He was a jack of all trades in Omega. He was postmaster, railroad depot manager, and owned a cotton gin and planing mill as well as a great big store and numerous tenant farms. In his store he sold everything from straight pins and flour to fertilizer and caskets. He had a special room in back where he kept the caskets on display. Oh yes honey, he could take his customers and tenants from the cradle to the grave. My grandfather Bates also had a large store in Omega, and he sold a general line of merchandise like Father. The upstairs of his store was used as a Masonic Lodge. We were strictly forbidden ever to enter it.

When we asked Father, "What do you do up there?," he laughed and said, "Ride the goat."

We children admired our father so much and always had such a close relationship with him. I was especially close to him. When I was a little girl, my brother and sisters would ask him, "Father, why do you pet Frommie so much?" His answer was, "Because Frances is named for your mother and because she looks like your mother when I married her." But I don't think he ever showed any partiality to any of his children, though he was especially fond of Laurie and me, maybe because we were the youngest. He never cranked up his car to ride over the plantations that we were not beside him. We enjoyed those outings so much. While he walked over the fields and talked with the farm hands, we would search for sweet gum trees and dig out the gum, or we would gather wild blackberries or huckleberries or find us a plum thicket. Sometimes we would run down to a fishpond and lean over the bank to look for the shadow of a fish. When a wild rabbit scurried by our feet, Laurie would scream, "I hear a snake. Let's scram!" When we started home, we looked at Father and worried because his face was beet-red after so much walking in the sun, and his bald head was drenched in sweat.

I think Laurie and I developed our lifelong love of the country on those trips with Father. I still enjoy drives in the country, seeing the roadside fields of brown-eyed susans, verbena, and red top clover. Such natural beauty puts my soul at rest. I even love the mournful coo of the dove, even though some people call it a sign of death. We have so much to be thankful for in this part of the world. I laugh when I think of the lady tourist from the North who passed through Alabama and asked, "Would anybody care if I picked some of those strawberries along the roadside?" She was told, "Those are not strawberries. They are clover."

Yes, honey, I have been all over the United States and into two foreign countries, but I've seen nothing to compare with my homeplaces. When Laurie was alive our greatest joy was driving the country roads around Omega. On weekends, while other people were going to Montgomery to a show or to Eufaula to see the boat races, we drove through huge tracts of pine trees, their heads reaching toward heaven. We loved the fields of peanuts tossing in the wind and fields of cotton white as though the Lord had sent us a heavy snow in late summer. And is there a more beautiful picture than white-faced cows grazing in a lush green pasture, licking and grooming the calves at their side? Since I was a girl I have loved the beauties of this world. How well I remember the fields and woods behind our house, where we gathered chest-nuts and chinquapins and muscadines and scouted the ridges for odd-shaped Indian arrowheads to add to our collection. The most wonderful pleasures of life are already in our laps.

My love of nature and God was a priceless legacy from my marvelous father, a man who was good not only to his family but to everyone. Here's a true story that will show you his goodness and generosity. One day it was snowing, a rare event for our part of the country. The ground was icy cold. Suddenly a man appeared on the porch of Father's store with no shoes on. Father looked down at his feet, then took his own shoes off and said, "Here, try these on for size." The man put them on and they fit. Father said, "Keep them. They're yours." Father then went inside the store, opened up a new box of shoes, got out another pair and put them on. That's the kind of man he was.

But Father's charity didn't stop with white people. One day a colored man came to the store with a fruit jar full of gold money. It must have been some that somebody buried during the war. He said, "Mr. Mac, I don't have any use for this kind of money. Do you want it?" Father said, "Sure, I'll buy it from you." And he did, even though it was illegal to own gold money. The jar was full of twenty-dollar gold pieces. After that, every Christmas we children each received a twenty-dollar gold piece with our other presents. When the accountant came after Laurie's death to make a list of everything she owned, he went to the bank to check her lock box. He took out a little leather pouch, opened it, and turned it upside down. Two twenty-dollar gold pieces fell out of it. She had kept Father's Christmas presents all her life. I also found in her lock box a five-dollar gold piece, and I'm thinking about having me a little pendant made out of it. It would be like having a little piece of Laurie with me everywhere.

When the time came for me to go to college, Father wanted me to go to the best college, so he sent me to Judson like sister Beulah before me. After I got to Marion, I began to have an odd feeling in my stomach that I had never experienced before. How can I describe it? Honey, have you ever had a severe stomach virus, one that hurt so bad you thought you were going to die—and wanted to? If you have, then

First Baptist Church, Union Springs, c. 1920.

you know about half as bad as I felt. It was plain old homesickness, and I thought I could not endure it until I got to come home for Christmas. But I did. Now, let me make one thing plain. I had never disobeyed my father. It was not done by anybody in my family. He was good to us but he expected absolute obedience. So I knew I was risking my father's anger and his belt when I said, "Father, I am not going back to Judson. I will go to a closer school like Troy." Well! Let me tell you something, honey. I had never seen Father's eyes flash so furiously or heard him raise his voice to a shout before. He shouted in a hard, stern voice, "Oh yes you are, young lady. Yes, you are going back to Judson. We are sacrificing to send you to the best woman's college in the South, and you go back!" I tried to calm him and reason with him. "Father," I said, "don't you think it's foolish for Judson girls to have to sit all together on one side in church with the Marion Institute boys on the other side?" I went on with other reasons for wanting to leave Judson, but I could see I wasn't very persuasive. "Don't you think Miss Brown, our dean, is too strict when she makes us undergo a military inspection before we can even go to church? Don't you think she goes too far when she pulls on my dress and snaps, 'You will have to polish these shoes again before you can leave this room'?" But I could come up with no argument that worked. Finally, I started crying. Then I committed an unpardonable act. I lost my temper. "All right, Father," I said angrily, "you asked for it and so I'll tell you what the main problem is. It's Beulah. I can't live up to her reputation. The teachers are comparing me to her, and I come up short. She was a straight *A* student and graduated *magna cum laude*. I just can't go back and be in her shadow!" Finally, I think Father understood my predicament and he showed a little sympathy. But I still had to go back. He said, "All right, Frances. I'll forgive your disobedience and your outburst. You must return to Judson, but I will try to visit you every month." So I went back and finally I adjusted to being

away from home and to being Beulah's little sister. After I was at Judson for two years, however, Father's health began to fail and he allowed me to transfer to Troy Normal School, where I completed my degree in art in 1934.

The school superintendent in Montgomery was one of my cousins, and he got me a position up there for the fall, but just before school opened, Father passed away. He just worked himself to death. He had so many family responsibilities and so many business interests. After Father's death, Omega just fell apart. It fell apart because Old Moneybags was gone. While he was alive, just about everybody in that end of the county did business with him. The Sorrells at Saco couldn't get ahead because Father had the business tied up. Without him, Omega began to dry up, and the Sorrells began to get rich.

Mother was helpless without Father, so she asked me if I would stay at home and help take care of his businesses. I said, "All right, Mother, I won't think about teaching." I went back to Omega and never taught a day. It became my job to try to do everything Father did. Uncle Bryant took over the store. I checked on the tenants. I kept the account books. I hired and fired hands. I knew I was no match for my father, but I held things together until 1941, when Mother bought this house I'm living in now from Sammy Cohn's half-sister Lakey, and Mother and Laurie and I moved permanently here to Union Springs. Mother lived here for two years and died in this house. In spite of her constant pain, she was the most remarkable and kindest person I ever knew. After Father died and times were so hard, colored people would come to the store and ask for food and be turned away. Then they'd come up to our house and say, "We're so hungry, Mrs. McLendon. Can you let us have a little something to eat?" Mother said, "Of course, I can. I've got a smokehouse full of meat. Tempie, get the key and give these people anything they want."

After we moved here, Mother didn't want to

confine Laurie and me, so she hired a nurse to look after her. We could get out and have dates and go around like other people. Yes honey, I had a string of beaux, but I always went with boys from out of town. I was once engaged to James Lee Reynolds, who I met when I was visiting my sister Lillian in Brundidge. James Lee worked with the Alabama Power Company, and he had already bought some furniture for housekeeping when I decided I didn't want to marry him. I gave him his ring back. Poor man, it liked to killed him! He went on and married somebody else, but he told me, "Frances, I will love you until the day I die." And I think he did. He died a few years ago.

I also went with another boy from Brundidge named Eldridge Leverette, and I came pretty close to getting engaged to him. Then I found out he was a heavy drinker, and I couldn't stand that. If I knew it, I would not go with a man who drank. Half of the reason I broke off with James Lee was that I found out that he occasionally drank. The other half? Well, I've come this far, so I might as well tell all my secrets. He asked me not to go out with other men, but I found out he was going with other women and not telling me. I don't play that way! So I gave him up. In later years I went with Hanley Harrison, who was a very outstanding attorney in Atlanta. I met him here in Union Springs while he was visiting his sister, Mrs. Winifred Rainer. But I couldn't marry him. I just couldn't marry him or any of my other beaux for one simple reason. I loved another man. I always had.

I knew the man I loved and finally married long before I moved to Union Springs, while I was still living in Omega. Mr. White was a farmer and cattleman and lived with his mother in Perote. I went with him for years, but his mother was feeble and didn't want to go to a nursing home. He wouldn't force her to go, so he said to me, "Frances, I just can't leave my mother, but I know it's not fair to you. It will hurt me deeply, but it's all right if you go with other men." Well honey, I tried. I really tried, but it didn't work.

You know, honey, you can't turn the heart on and off, can you? It's not a light switch. But we finally married in 1967, soon after his mother died, and he moved here to be with me here in this house. He lived only three years after we married. He dropped dead at my feet. He was a wonderful man, a wonderful man, a fine Christian man. We had waited for each other all those years, and it was worth it. We had such a beautiful marriage even though it was so short. But you know, honey, true love can't be measured in years. It's timeless. Mr. White left an undivided estate to me and his sister, and I managed his timber and cattle business for over thirteen years. Then a couple of years ago, I had some disagreement with his sister, and Judge Wallace gave me a permit to have a forced sale and we sold the whole works. It was sad but it had to be done. After that, my sister had all her heart attacks that left her blind and slightly brain-damaged. I got to where I could hardly manage all that stress and worry and responsibility. But I had to.

Now, here's something I haven't told you yet. Laurie and I married brothers, and we all lived here together in this house. We had a wonderful family life together. We had no children but we were a complete family. The brothers were very close, and Laurie and I had our special relationship all our lives. It was brought out at her funeral that the only time we were ever separated was when I was away in college. I don't

Abandoned store at Omega, 1998.

think there has ever been a relationship like ours. It's hard for me to talk about it even now. I gave her the best of care after she got sick. Our husbands were already dead, and we were sisters again, together in this house. For seven and one-half months I had nurses with Laurie around the clock, and I was up and down all night seeing about her. Just before she died, I was scheduled to leave on a cruise to Mexico, but Dr. Emfinger said to me, "Frances, you'd better cancel out that trip because Laurie's not going to be here long." But I had already seen that she was failing fast and had canceled my cruise. I can't imagine how I would have felt if she had died with me away from her bedside.

Since I lost Laurie, I've lived here alone. I'm alone for the first time in my life. I'm not afraid one bit. I have a Smith & Wesson long pistol right by the side of my bed, and I had it worked on yesterday. There have been some break-ins on this street recently, but I'm not scared. I know I'm being protected. When I get ready to go to bed, I say my prayers, "Lord, maybe I'm a little afraid, but I know You're going to take care of me tonight, just like You've always done." Then I turn over and go to sleep and don't wake up until Cindy rings the doorbell in the morning. Isn't that great? I don't worry at all.

Cindy is precious to me. She looks after my every need. She's been with me for sixteen years and was so wonderful to Laurie. She does anything for me I want done—cooks, keeps house, dresses me, waits on me. She's fifty now and lives just below Carter's Funeral Home. Like me, she's a widow but she's got five children, all married but two. She's got a marvelous mind. She is excellent, just excellent, and brilliant, just brilliant! I don't know what I would do without her.

I do have a lot of interests and I keep busy. During Laurie's last illness, I slacked off a lot of my activities, but I've resumed most of them. I've always been active in my church, First Baptist. For twenty-eight years I

was superintendent of the extension department of the Sunday School. For many years I taught a Sunday School class. Now I do whatever they want me to. I'm a member of the Wednesday Morning Bible Study. I'm active in the county historical society. I'm a member of the Smithsonian Institution—and the Mayo Clinic Letter Association! I bet I've pulled one on you now! I bet you've never heard of that one. Well, every month they send me descriptions of different illnesses, what to look for and what to do about them. Honey, I want to know about my body. Some people don't know their head from their toes, but I want to know it all. As a member of the Letter Association, I have the privilege of writing to the Mayo Clinic and asking about any health condition I want to know about.

I'm a big reader—always have been—and sometimes I read until three o'clock in the morning. I only read religious books, no trash. In my house I have every book that Helen Steiner Rice ever wrote, and I've read them all several times. I read a lot of good poetry, and I write it too, mostly religious. I watch religious programs on television. Before I go to church on Sunday, I get in about two sermons. I love Dr. James Kennedy from Ft. Lauderdale. He's wonderful, just wonderful. And I always try to watch Dr. Schuller from California.

I'm also a big traveler. I love to take tours and cruises, and I've been everywhere. You name it and I've been! I've been to Mexico twice and stayed six weeks one time. I've been to Nassau. I've been to California and Canada and Lake Louise. In October I'm supposed to go to Denmark, Sweden, and Norway. My family's chomping at the bits because of that plane that was hijacked, but I'm not afraid. When I get on that plane, I'll say a prayer and not worry. Next year I have reservations to go to England.

While I'm in England I want to go up to Scotland to see where my ancestors came from. Our clan motto, you know, was "As Sturdy as the Oak." I believe it's been a good guide for me and my family. Like an oak tree, I can't be shaken by the rough winds of life. I can't be swayed. And I know I can be stubborn and hardheaded when I think I'm right. Let me show you what I mean by telling you about my two cemeteries. The first cemetery is on my farm down near Post Oak. It was the cemetery of a white family and had a beautiful iron-grill fence around it. As long as my father lived, he said to the tenants, "Don't plow up near that graveyard. You've got to show respect for the dead." There are family cemeteries all over this county that have been plowed over, but not this one. Someone told me the other day that you can still make out where it is, and I'm going down to see it soon. I planted government pine trees all over that place, and they have more or less covered up the cemetery. But it's still there because my father wouldn't let it be plowed over.

My other cemetery is for colored people, and it's on my farm at Sellers Cross Roads, just below Ginny Green's house out from Omega. Back when Carl Green was road commissioner, he came to me and said, "Frances, we want to widen that road by your place, and we are going to cut into that cemetery up on the hill." I said, "Carl, you will over my dead body. I've got plenty of land over on the other side, and you can widen your road that way, but I will not allow you to cut up those dead people." I didn't care what color those dead people were, I was not going to let him dig them up. That would be terrible, wouldn't it? Would you want them to dig your people up? Nobody would! Well, I stood my ground, and Carl ran his road up on the other side and never bothered my cemetery. You can drive by that cemetery this afternoon and see a lot of pretty flowers blooming all over it. That's the kind of stewards the McLendons are.

Honey, I've lived a long time, and I imagine I've made some mistakes. But you know what: I can't think of anything I would change about my life if I could. Well, maybe there's one change I would make.

In college I think I would study journalism and writing instead of art and interior decorating. I love to write. I just love it! It's my greatest fulfillment. I have taken a one-year writing course by mail, and I've made a writing room out of my sleeping porch. I have a new desk and chair, two bookcases, and several hanging baskets. It is so attractive. I spend a lot of time now writing my column for the *Union Springs Herald,* but they just don't give me enough space to say what I want to. I put in some of my memories, some poems, and some funny stories. Here's an example: "I had a friend that put out a manger scene for Christmas. When her maid came to house clean after Christmas, she asked, 'Do you want me to put up this Jesus outfit?'" A lot of people tell me they love my column. I've been approached by the *Clayton Record* to write a column for them, and they'll give me more space. I may do it.

As a writer, however, my greatest passion is poetry. Here's a little poem I put in a column I wrote not long ago about Holmes Cafe. Wade and Curtis Holmes bought the old Jones Cafe in Union Springs in 1940 and made it a popular place to meet and eat. For years there was a coffee club for businessmen that met there every morning at five a. m. Curtis was famous for his pies. Here's the poem:

> If your stomach is so empty you could die,
> Go to Holmes Cafe for a slice of Curtis's pie.
> Wade can bring you a hamburger
> That can't be touched by another.

I've written a lot more poetry since I became a proud member of the Alabama State Poetry Society. Last year was my lucky year as a poet. Each lawful member was invited to submit a poem in the Gemstone Contest, and I never faintly dreamed I could win among so many talented members. But I did! I can't begin to tell you how very elated I was when the poet laureate of Alabama, William Young Elliott, announced that I had won a Recognition of Merit

Award. A beautiful golden heart pendant with a green stone was presented to me at the state convention. It was a great day for me. Sister Laurie said, "Frances, I know you will cry. You always do when you're so happy." And yes, I must confess that a few tears did fall. I don't know if I'll win anything this year, but the society meets this October at Arlington Mansion in Birmingham, and I plan to go. Now, I'll read you the poem I won my award for. You can judge whether I deserve it. The poem is called "Proven" and the inspiration comes from the Book of Isaiah, Chapter 66, Verse 1: "Thus saith the Lord, The heaven is my throne, and the earth is my footstool."

PROVEN
Did you ever see a rose bud,
From a bush buried deep in mud?
Did you ever see a dogwood tree shining with
    sprinkled snow
With blossoms so abundant the branches hung low?
Did you ever see a field of daises being tossed by the
    wind?
Did you ever see a fish with shining fin?
Did you ever see green grass,
After the long winter's passed?
Did you ever see a red bird
Or the song of a mockingbird heard?
Did you ever see the beauty of a white tailed deer,
Who sheds his coat, and puts on a heavier coat when
    winter comes near?
Did you ever hear the music of a talented choir?
Did you ever see a water lily rise above the mire?
Did you ever see a baby's smile?
If not, your life has not been worthwhile.
Did you ever see a sunrise,
After a night of sleep we prize?
Did you ever see a sunset,
After a day of unrest?
Did you ever see a prayer answered,
when in deep distress?
Did you ever see an Easter Lily on Easter Morn?

Did you remember who was resurrected
after wearing a crown of thorn?
If all this you have really seen,
Then surely you can't deny
That we have a Heavenly Father who lives on high.

Oh honey, you don't know how much pleasure it gives me to write poetry like that. Now, don't think that because I write religious poetry I'm some old stick-in-the-mud. I am a normal, funloving person. I'll even take a drink of wine as quickly as anyone else. You certainly won't find any wings on my shoulders. Like Helen Steiner Rice, I gain spiritual food when I write religious poems.

Before I get to heaven, I hope to publish a book of my poems. Do you think I ever will? Well, I'll think about that when I get back from Reno. I just get so excited thinking about my award. They'll present it to me in the afternoon in a big hotel, and Jayne Meadows will be there. Oh, I don't know what I'll wear. Whew, I'm going to be scared to death. They're giving so many awards I won't be asked to read my poem. I'm thankful for that. But I know I'll be shaking when I walk across the stage. Let me show you the two dresses I'm trying to decide between. You tell me which one. I'd better stop all this talking and take you all to the country club. They stop serving at 1 o'clock, and I think I've already said too much. Too much! Woooh-hooooooh!

POSTSCRIPT: Frances McLendon White did not have her wish granted to see the new century. In 1991, six years after our interview, she died at the golden age of eighty. Her real golden age, however, had been lived many years before when she was a girl and young woman in the security, warmth, and love of her large family. She had tried valiantly to adapt to the radical changes she had witnessed in her lifetime, but her death was yet another marker signaling the end of an era of Bullock County—and American—history.

JOSEPHINE BATES PRITCHETT

Woman of the Spirit

Josephine Bates Pritchett—we called her "Miss Josephine"—has been an old woman all my life. She was almost a generation older than my own mother and father. To a boy of ten, I suppose anyone approaching fifty is old. I remember her as a familiar though somewhat distant figure. She was a presence in her church at Mt. Zion and, after it ceased having regular meetings, at my own boyhood church, Liberty. Her younger son, Harvey, was a few years ahead of me in school and drove our school bus for several years. So far as I know, we are no blood kin, though it is likely that somewhere in the fringes of our respective bloodlines, there are some common genes. The house that she has lived in since I can remember was built by one of my Grider ancestors in the nineteenth century. Located about nine miles south of Union Springs, about half a mile north of Halls Cross Roads, her home is a double-pen frame structure, with an open breezeway or dog trot between the two sections. The sandy yard has no grass, but a number of flowering shrubs punctuate the hot summer air with color and fragrances. It is July 20, 1977, and we are talking on her porch while she waits for the mail carrier. She is 78.

Honey, did you notice if the mail rider has come yet? The *Herald* comes today and I've been expecting some other mail as well. I don't send pieces in to the paper any more, but when I was younger I did. Let's sit out here on the porch and wait for the mail while we talk.

Yes, bless your heart, I've had a number of items in the paper. In this scrapbook I've kept some of them. Here is a response I wrote back in the early 1930s to some religious pieces I read in the *Herald*. I called it "Consolation." I was trying to comfort people who were worrying about hard times by reminding them of what is truly important.

Soon our souls must meet eternity. Hadn't we rather go empty-handed than empty-hearted? Indeed, this depression is deplorable. But are we suffering from depression or lack of love of God in our hearts? Truly my heart was made glad when I saw a few items in our county Herald last week proclaiming the Christ. Why? Because I know the keynote of our condition is struck. We may stand near an electric current, though unless we are touched, nothing occurs. So are people here, living and dying, that are never touched by God's wonderful saving power. Those who wrote them, please continue praying and writing Christian literature. Give us food for Christian thought, for others reading your faith and work may turn to God for help. Yes, let us turn to the faith of our forefathers who braved stormy seas to reach this beautiful land of ours, which was then wild, that they might serve the one true living God. I, a subscriber and a sufferer of this trying time, ask each reader to go to Jesus with your tired, weary hearts. Have faith and work to help others. Unless we turn to God, our United States is doomed.

I signed it Mrs. Hogan Pritchett. And I really feel that's what's wrong with us today. It's not that we're so poor. Depressions and wars don't hurt us that much. They never did. I remember how awful it was during World War I when so many men were wounded and killed when the boys were fighting with France. We couldn't get flour or coffee and you had to make what you ate at home. I was too young to be married to Hogan at that time, but I remember when he and his brother Rex were soldiers. Not long after he came home—it was right after Christmas in 1919—we got married. I was twenty years old but I still thought I was a child. You know, honey, you feel with your heart and I never did *feel* grown until after I was married.

We married on the 28th day of December. I remember it well. I was living at the old homeplace right down below where Bessie and Benny Driggers live now, but the house is gone. My brother and Maggie and me and Hogan were on the way to Union

Springs to get married. It was a cold day and back then the cars weren't enclosed but had curtains. We stopped right out here in this front yard where there used to be a large hickory nut tree to put up the curtains. We never dreamed then that some day we would be living here. Riding in that car was something special. We had borrowed it from old Doc Boswell, who was a good friend to Hogan. At that time there weren't very many cars in this country. As it happened, there were two in Omega near where we lived, Clarence McLendon's and Doc Boswell's. Well, we put up the curtains, drove on into town, and got married. When we got back at Hogan's dad's just below Mill Creek, we found all our friends and family gathered there. There were so many presents. We didn't dream everybody would be there. There was never anything said, but I'm sure someone in the bunch had it all planned. We were a little embarrassed but pleased and happy.

Is that the mail rider out there? Oh, I see it's Sandy. He must be checking on some of his cows that got out.

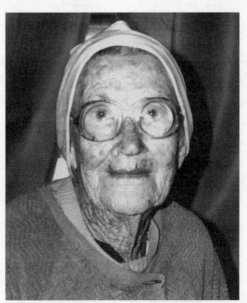

Josephine Bates Pritchett, 1977

Right after we married, we moved into a little house right up in front of where Mr. Pritchett lived and stayed there two years. The last time I noticed, the house was still there. Those were happy days and happy years, but they were hard times. It took us five years to pay out of debt. We had to buy almost all our furniture—and it wasn't much—but for every spoon and pot and skillet, we had to use borrowed money. That first year cotton was so cheap that people didn't even sell it. We kept ours a while in hopes the price would go up. The next year, 1921, was better. Prices were higher and we made a good crop, and Sandy was

born. That added one mouth to feed and we went on piling up debt, but we kept working. We enjoyed what little we had because we had to pay for it. In this day and time, children have it handed out to them on a silver platter and don't know how to appreciate anything.

We worked hard in the fields and around the house. I helped on the farm all my life and loved it. Back then people had what they called one-horse or two-horse farms. Hogan's was a one-horse farm, which was small but plenty for two people to work. I loved to get outdoors and work. I still do. The last time I went to see Dr. Emfinger in Union Springs was in February and he said, "Mrs. Pritchett, don't you stay out in the sun lots?" I told him I surely did. He said, "Well, whenever you get out, put something on your head and arms and legs." You know, I've tried that. It happened that last year was the Bicentennial and Alma English came out from town one day and said, "Josephine, I have something in the car for you." She brought out a bonnet she made for me. I was still wearing bonnets occasionally, but most of us thought we had outgrown old things like that—well just about everybody but Elma Lee and Beansie Hall. During the Bicentennial we were all wearing them again. They do provide wonderful protection against the sun.

I have lived in this house for more than thirty years. We bought this old place from Mr. John Grider, who got it from his father, old Uncle Toby Grider. Mr. John was getting old and his wife was dead and he said he'd rather we have it than anybody he knew. I'm pretty sure we moved here in February of 1946 right after the war closed, and we rented it for a few years before we bought it. At that time, no one was really picking up land around here, and it was pretty cheap. Hogan asked Mr. Grider to meet him in Union Springs on a certain day, and he would have the money ready. We owned some land right there where Wavey Brooks lives and we saw that we could sell it. With that money and a little cash we already had, we paid for it. When John Grider came down to talk to us about the place, he said Mr. Toby was born here in this house. So it must have been a hundred years old then. I asked him why the fireplace was so large in the front room. It is enormous! He said, "It's because there were so many of us children living here it had to be large enough so all of us could gather around the fire in the wintertime and get warm at the same time." He said they had later hooked on a room to the original structure and built a kitchen away from the house. I imagine it was all built out of lumber that you

A Bullock County tenant house.

could buy for next to nothing. Yes, bless your heart, I just love this old house with its open hallway and the wide planks. I imagine it's one of the oldest houses still standing in Bullock County.

Well, I don't understand why the mail hasn't come yet. There must be a substitute on today.

In this old scrapbook, I have some of the memorials I used to write and send to the *Herald* when somebody I knew and loved would die. Here's one to Hogan's father, and this one is about Uncle Sandy Outlaw, who was my granddaddy. If there ever was a Christian, I believe that old fellow was. He was Mama's daddy and all her people lived down in Geneva County, so I didn't know that side of the family as well as I knew the Bateses. But I knew Grandpa Outlaw because he came to see us every year. He lived out from Hartford, and when I was a tiny little girl, I went in a covered wagon with my mama and papa one time down to his place. I can just remember it. I'm sure we had to camp out going down and coming back, but those details are vague in my mind. After Grandma Outlaw died, he and Aunt Mary, his youngest daughter, moved into Hartford, and he lived there until he died.

Here is a memorial I wrote about my father, John Bates, who died Sunday, December 11, 1938. Papa was born in 1857 and was eighty-one when he died. Mama died eighteen years before him, and I know now that when she left him, a big part of his life was gone. I didn't realize it then because I was so young, but I know it now since I lost Hogan. Papa would try to be cheerful in front of all us children, but I know he went through so much. He was getting old, and he suffered with kidney disease. Back then, they didn't have a name for every ailment, and the country doctors didn't even tell you everything they knew. Papa had to go to Dr. Guthrie at Inverness so much, and finally we had to take him to Edge's Hospital in Troy. Of course, nobody had insurance, and we spent about all we had on Papa. Dr. Guthrie and Papa died the same year, and we've never had another doctor in this community.

Honey, I guess some people astonish the doctors. Not too long ago, I went to Dr. Emfinger and told him, "Since Dr. Guthrie died, you are the only other physician that has treated me." He hasn't been in Union Springs very many years and just couldn't believe me, but it is the truth. He gave me some medicine, but I don't take it like I'm supposed to. I don't feel any pain. When I take a headache, I get outside and do some work and get my mind on something that helps me forget my headache and it goes away. Sister Corrine takes medicine all the time, but I believe you can become too dependent on aspirin. The year that Dr. Guthrie died, we all came down with the flu—all four of us—but we fought it off without a doctor and ever since that we've felt fine.

When Mama died, the four of us children were still living at home—Andrew, Nora, and Douglas and I. I married soon after that and Papa stayed on with the three younger children. Then Nora married and the boys grew up and got jobs on the railroad. We all came up in an atmosphere of love. Did you know, honey, I've never hated anyone in my life? I just can't imagine how people can feel hate. From the time I can remember, I always knew right was right and wrong was exceedingly wrong. I can't stand lying. It's awful! I was taught there's not but two ways, the right way and the wrong way. I still believe that.

I can't imagine what's keeping the mail. It's way past time when it should be here.

Elma Lee told me the other day that Josie was looking bad. I said, "Well, when I saw her at church about two weeks ago, she looked the way she always did to me." Of course, Josie is old and wrinkled, like me, and walks with a stick, but you know she's been walking with that stick for a long time. I think she still gets around good for her age. You know, Elma Lee learns a lot about people, but I don't know where in the world she learns it. Just yesterday Corrine asked

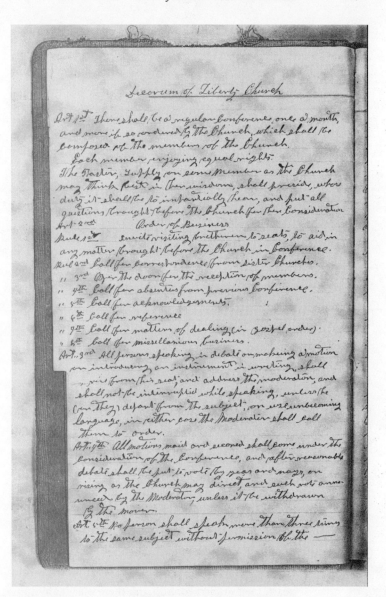

A page from the Liberty Baptist Church record book.

me if I'd heard about Eugene Cannon. She said Elma Lee told her that he was on his tractor and was stung by some yellow jackets and he jumped off with it running and it threw him and pulled all the ligaments in one of his legs and the yellow jackets almost stung him to death. Somebody managed to get to him and carried him to Union Springs, and Dr. Emfinger got him on to Montgomery and they operated on him. Corrine said Elma Lee said the doctor told him he'd never walk again. Now, I can't figure that because a doctor can't say that soon what will or will not be. You know, honey, we can hear something and every time it goes from one person to another, it gets larger. Elma Lee hears more than anybody I know. Well, people do like to talk.

Oh, here's a piece I wrote on Uncle Buddy Hubbard. He died July 25, 1940, and was Hogan's mother's baby brother. He was such a pathetic person. Back then the county had a poorhouse, and Uncle Buddy had to go there about ten years before he died. As long as he could, he lived and worked in Columbus, Georgia, in the cotton mills. Then he got to where he couldn't work and had to live on other people. I'm not sure who finally put him in the poorhouse, but it must have been some of his nieces and nephews. He had two daughters that lived in Montgomery, but they didn't care any more about him than a complete stranger. They were trying to live above their social standard. Their daddy was old and broken and unworthy, they thought, and they didn't want him around to embarrass them. Before he went to the poorhouse, he came down here to see us and said he felt like no one wanted him and no one loved him, and he couldn't go back to where he was staying. He cried all the time he was here. I gave him a little bit of money and a handkerchief and walked with him a piece when he left. Then I prayed for him. Bless your heart, I felt so sorry for him, but there wasn't anything more I could do. His wife had already left him, and he had no one in the world to look out after him.

The first time I was ever in the poorhouse, I went to see Uncle Buddy. It was several months after he moved there. The poorhouse was on the road going toward Columbus, right where the perpetual cemetery is now, up there on that hill. The poor people lived in three or four shotgun houses that were clustered around a big house where the superintendent and his family lived. Each little house had two doors and a porch. They had three Negroes in one of the

houses and the whites in the other ones. I don't know about the house for the Negroes, but the ones for whites had two rooms. In one of those houses Uncle Buddy was in one room, and an old Mrs. Sikes and her daughter from over near Stills Cross Roads were in the other one. When time came to eat, they would all go to the back porch of the big house with their little tin plates and spoons, and the superintendent's wife would put their meals in the tin plates. It was such a sad and anonymous life. Honey, it almost broke my heart to see those poor people. They were there day and night, alone with nobody to care about them.

Uncle Buddy just couldn't take it. He had always been so well-off before. He lived in that one room, with a bed and a chair furnished by the county. That was all he had. Just think: a chair and a bed and a few worn-out clothes and his tin plate and spoon. That was all. It bothered me to see him like that, but I knew I had to leave him there. There was nothing I could do to help him, but I felt for him so much. I went to see him because I know Jesus would have done it. You must ask yourself, "What would Jesus have me to do?" I'm sure He would have done it. You can always think in terms of what Jesus would have done. Yes, I'm sure Jesus would have visited Uncle Buddy in the poorhouse. Just before he died, he moved in with one of his nieces, and I would walk over there and cut his hair for him. He had once lived so well, but I guess he had spent everything he made. I don't know how he got into such a predicament. But when a person's in need, they're in need, no matter what they once had. You can't realize it now, honey, but it really was hard times back there. People just didn't have then like they have now.

I'm going to tell you something else that happened back then, about 1930. If she was living, I know Tress Waters would remember it. It was when Hogan and I were living in Union Springs. There was a rich, well-to-do family living in town named Singleton. The old man used to be probate judge. They had lived high. When the old man died, he left his widow and a son everybody called Bubba. I don't remember his real name, but he was like the Prodigal Son. He went to New York and lived until I guess he spent all he had and then came back home to Union Springs. He stayed there a while, and then left one morning on foot telling his mother that he was going back to New York. I don't know how many weeks passed, but there was a trestle on the way to Montgomery and up above it, there was a body found floating in the creek. Whoever it was had taken a rope and hanged himself. He had tied the rope to the trestle and then put it over his head and jumped off; and when the train came along, it cut the rope and the body fell into the water below. Evidently, it had stayed in the water so long it finally came to the top, but nobody could recognize it. Nobody could tell who it was because the body was in such awful shape. They brought it to town in one of those railroad carts and decided it must be a beggar or a railcar hopper. So they wrapped it up and put it in a plain box and took it out to the poorhouse and buried it in a pauper's grave.

I guess two or three weeks went by, and one day the sheriff was in Mrs. Ravencroft's drugstore showing her a pair of scissors and a cigarette lighter they had taken from the body, when a little Negro boy in the store said, "I know whose cigarette lighter that is. That's Mr. Bubba Singleton's. I know it." Well, that got the sheriff to thinking, so he took the scissors over to Bubba's mother and in casually talking to her, he asked about Bubba. She said she hadn't heard from him in more than a month. She said, "I haven't heard a word from Bubba since he left to go back to New York." The sheriff tried to keep from exciting her, but he asked, "Did you ever see these scissors before?" She examined them and said, "Yes, these look just like my scissors that I can't find." That's what led them to call up to New York and find out that Bubba had never got there. Then everything began to fall into place. One of the hardware men remembered selling Bubba

a piece of rope the morning he left Union Springs. Soon they knew whose body it was they had found floating in the creek and buried in a pauper's grave. They took Bubba up out of that poorhouse grave where he was buried in a box and put him in a vault and moved him in a flat-bed truck over to Oak Hill Cemetery, where he was placed with his family.

I can't imagine people doing things like that. I remember Papa telling about a man in Union Springs named Clyde Ellis, who ran his car into the building that is now the doctor's building but was then the Ellis Building and killed himself. He told somebody that he just could not live a poor man. He'd once been wealthy and had lost it all. Of course, we'll never know for sure why Bubba Singleton killed himself, but we do know that his people had once been rich and well-to-do. Honey, there's so many people who put their trust in the things of this world, and when they lose them, they have nothing to live for.

Oh, some people have such a hard time and want to live. Here's a memorial I wrote about poor old Georgia Driggers, Benny Driggers' first wife. "No silver or gold can obtain our redemption," I said. You know, honey, we can't ever see into a person's heart. We never can know what's really in there. It doesn't take silver or gold or prominence or popularity to save us. I had a feeling that Georgia had salvation, but we can't ever know for sure. She had cancer of the mouth. I know it came from all that snuff she had dipped all her life. It had eaten off nearly all her face. She first took sick when they were living in town on Conecuh Street. Then they brought her out here in the country to stay with Gilbert, her oldest boy, who lived in what they called the MacNeill House down between Mt. Zion and Boswell. When it got bad, they had to move her to Phenix City, and she died at her daughter's home there. Oh, the suffering she endured before she left this world! Now, Georgia had been a Norris and was the sister to Bessie Outlaw's first husband, Hardy Norris. So Hardy's widow and his sister Georgia's husband were brother and sister. When Georgia died, Benny married Bessie. I don't know how they kept their relationships straight. Of course, there weren't a lot of people around here that you could marry, and sometimes distant cousins married each other.

Oh, honey, I have seen a lot of people die, and I have worried about their salvation. Some people you just have the feeling are saved, and some you just wonder about. Now, here's a piece I wrote when Miss Lizzie Hall died. She was the sister to Mr. John Henry Hall and Miss Bessie and Miss Clyde. Her name was Lizzie but she was called Jennie. When Johnny Driggers's wife died, Miss Jennie stayed on there with them as a mother to Eugene and Eunice, and she died there. Everyone called Eugene "Fatty," and when he married L. A. Brooks he moved her in with his daddy. Johnny lived for a long time after that and died not too many years ago. When you think back on people like Miss Jennie and Miss Bessie and Miss Clyde, you have to be impressed. They were such fine women with good morals.

Mr. John Henry moved away and got married and then moved back here. I don't know where he'd been—maybe in Union Springs—but he brought back his two boys with him. In those days country people didn't know too much about what went on in Union Springs. It took a whole day to go to town in a buggy, and you didn't go unless you had to. James and Curtis were younger than I was, and I can remember those children when they were little. They lived with their daddy in a little log house down near where old U. L. Townsend lived below the cross roads. Mr. John Henry raised those boys all by himself, and that was something unheard of around here. You see, when he and his wife separated, he kept the two boys. I'm pretty sure they both finished school at Inverness.

I remember one time Curtis and Mr. Johnny Driggers went in and bought a piano for Liberty Church. The church had an old pump organ but this was the first piano we ever had. They got it from a widow woman—I *did* know her name—over in China Grove somewhere. She let them have it for fifty dollars, but way back then fifty dollars was harder to get up than five hundred dollars now. They asked me if I could help put on a play down at the Inverness School to help pay for it. I got in contact with Mr. Hamilton, who was principal then, and he said yes we could use the schoolhouse. We put on a good clean play called "What Can We Do with Aunt Sally?" Curtis was in the play and the Jones girls and Eunice and a lot of young people I can't remember now. We charged five cents and ten cents admission and didn't quite raise ten dollars, but that was a lot of money back then. It went a long way in helping to pay for that piano.

Yes, honey, these clippings bring back a lot of people who are gone now. There are not many people my age still living. I don't write memorials for the *Herald* any more, but when inspirational things come to me I still write them down and put them in the bulletin at Liberty. We don't have regular preaching at Mt. Zion, so I go to Liberty every chance I get. I have always loved church and Sunday School. When I was growing up, there were two things you did in our family and no questions were asked: you went to school and you went to church. We just did it. It was our life. There used to be churches all over this country—at Omega, at Mt. Zion, at Inverness, at Macedonia, at Indian Creek, at Liberty—and there was even a Methodist church at Post Oak. I love the Methodists, too. Of course, they sprinkle and we Baptists immerse—and I believe immersion is the Scriptural method of baptism—but it's not really essential for salvation. There's only one way to be saved, and that's to accept Jesus as your savior.

Years ago, we went to all the churches, especially during protracted meeting time in the summer. One time I remember going to a sacred harp singing school at Liberty. Every summer they had a singing school, and then on the third Sunday in August, after we had studied and practiced for about six weeks, we had an all-day singing and each of us had to lead a song. I thoroughly enjoyed it. Sacred harp singing is fa-so-la singing with shaped notes to indicate the name and the pitch. Our teacher taught us to sing first the notes and then the words. Mama especially wanted me to go, so Norma and Myrtle and I went, and Andrew would carry us on the wagon, collecting other people all along the road. By the time we got to Liberty, we had a wagon full. Not everybody who went attended the school. Most of them waited around outside or came in and listened to us practice.

I wasn't a member of the church then, but I've always felt close to the Lord. If you're saved you're saved, no matter which church you go to or how old you are. Some people try to discourage young people from joining the church, but I believe you should join whenever you feel like you're saved. I'm like the old preacher who said he thought you could do a lot of damage to a young person if you tried to keep him from making a public profession. He said when he was a boy he used to think church was only for old people, but he felt the call to preach and would sit on a rail fence and preach to the cornstalks. He said he wanted to be baptized but his parents wouldn't let him. They said he didn't know what he was doing. So he quit going to church, but when he was nineteen he went to a revival and got the same feeling he had as a little bitty boy and joined and was baptized. Soon he heeded the call to preach. He became a consecrated preacher and helped save hundreds of souls.

I believe I've been saved since I was a little girl. Back then we had Christian teachers who taught us the Bible. Miss Mittie was my teacher for five years and she taught us Jesus. She was my mama through the winter and my mother was my mama through the summer. I still love Miss Mittie though she's been gone a long time. I believe she influenced me to be saved, but I don't know when that was. I can't put an exact date on it. I know when I joined the church, but I was already saved by then. When I was almost grown and still not a church member, Miss Mittie wrote me and said, "Josephine, I've known you all your life, and I know you've been a Christian for a long time. Why don't you come out publicly on the Lord's side?" Her letter quickened my conscience, and I made my public profession of faith and joined at Mt. Zion. I was telling Preacher Butler's wife at Liberty the other day that some people can name the place, the time, and everything about it, but I don't really know when I was saved. As far back as I can remember, I've loved the Bible and the church and I've believed in Jesus. I've always enjoyed going to our country churches. My son Sandy and his wife Merle belong to the First Baptist Church in Union Springs, and when my other son Harvey came to visit last summer, he started going to First Baptist with his boys—and that is all right with me. But I do love our country churches. It's not *where* you go anyway; it's *where* your heart is that matters.

When I became church clerk at Mt. Zion in 1940, this record book that I have here in my hands was passed on to me. It's not complete because somebody has cut out part of it. You know, it used to be if you did something wrong, you would be kicked out of the church and couldn't be reinstated until you came before the church and confessed and apologized and asked forgiveness. I think somebody got a-hold of this record and cut out some pages they didn't want anybody to read. You can see in the minutes for a church conference held on July 16, 1916, there is mention of a committee that was formed to investigate "a delinquent member." It doesn't say what he had done, but you can be assured that he was voted out until he changed his ways.

The record book has a lot of names I remember so well, and some who came before my time. Here's John Driggers, who I believe was the daddy of Mr. Daniel and Mr. Marion Driggers. Here's J. W. Grider, Uncle Toby's oldest boy, the one we bought this place from. He must have gotten into some trouble because it says here the church excluded him in 1899, the year I was born. Here's a Mr. Frank Grider, who was received for membership in 1893 and later excluded for an unnamed reason. But it wasn't just the Griders, honey. A lot of people had church fellowship withdrawn from them in those days. I believe if the church was a little more strict like it used to be, it would be better off. We'd all be better off. Here's W. B. Grider and his wife Susan. They were the parents of Ada, who became Jeff Sorrell's mother. Jeff became one of the biggest landowners in this section of Alabama.

A lot of these people I don't remember since I've gotten so old. Oh, I do remember Christopher Grider, who joined, it says here, by letter in 1907, with his wife, Bettie Allen Grider. She died in 1909. He was a deacon at Mt. Zion, but they are both buried at Liberty. According to this record, all their grown children joined Mt. Zion with them. I remember Mr. Chris Grider so well, and Jack Hall, who is his great-grandson, really reminds me of him. Right here are the Hardens that used to live in that log house right in front of where Jerry Henderson lives now. And here is a Mr. Head, who was killed the day I was born in a sawmill accident. Here is Narcissus Hall, who was married to Mr. Ben Hall, and they lived right down by the bend in the road on the way to Mt. Zion. Oh, here is Miss Mollie James. She had a sister named Lady, and they were connected some way with the Griders. And here is Hattie Joiner. Bless your heart, I haven't thought of Hattie in a long, long time.

There were so many people who used to belong to Mt. Zion, but there's just three of us resident members left now—my sister, my niece, and me. But there's so many people that still love old Mt. Zion Church. One day I saw Martina Cogdell down at the cemetery, where all the Cogdells are buried. She was interested in getting up some money to repair the church, so I wrote over forty letters to members and former members and people with loved ones buried in

the cemetery and raised $1,680. Some had said, "She'll never do it." I didn't even know the complete addresses of some of the people I wrote—just the town where they lived—but every letter was answered. God blessed us.

You see, honey, I realized that with only three women we couldn't carry on as a church, but we could keep it preserved as a chapel with occasional services and gatherings. I stayed with the project day and night. I couldn't get away from it. I knew it was something I ought to do. I asked J. T. Bates if I got enough money could he get me a contractor to fix the church. I couldn't possibly have bossed anybody. He said he'd be glad to. The checks started coming in. Every day there would be something in my mailbox. I was so thankful and happy and every time the mail came, I'd cry. I called J. T. when I got up to a thousand dollars and he said, "I just can't very well believe it." The next week, when I got up to sixteen hundred, J. T. got Jack Hall to go and make an estimate. We had plenty for him to do. He fixed the roof, put in new windows, painted the floor and the inside and outside.

You know, honey, there's always critics. After all the work was done, some found fault with the color of the floor—it was chocolate red—and some said we should have put in shades. It was mostly people that came from up north that complained. A girl who lives in Washington State came here and found fault with just about everything. Her sister called me long distance from Montgomery and really blessed me out. I didn't boss J. T. and Jack while they were making the repairs and improvements, but everything looked nice to me. I hadn't found fault with the way it was done, but as long as we had some money left, I wanted the chapel to be the best we could make it. So J. T. went to town and got some different floor paint and some window shades. I wanted the people who paid for the work to be satisfied.

Mt. Zion was founded in 1850, and I believe the

present building is the original one. I think it's in good shape to be as old as it is. Jack made it look good, but an old building is like an old person. No matter what you do to it, it's still old. It may well be the oldest church building in Bullock County because so many of the old churches have been torn down. I loved the old building at Liberty. When they were tearing it down to build the new church, I went over there with Josie Hall, and believe it or not, the frame was pegged at the joints with lightwood pegs. They were tearing down a better building than they could build, but they wanted a smaller one they could heat and air-condition. I'm glad we still have the old church at Mt. Zion.

Not long ago I wrote a short history of the church that gives its origins, its pastors, deacons, and church clerks. I wanted that information to be a part of the permanent record. Since I became clerk, I've tried to keep a faithful record of the church—the membership, the preachers, the meetings, and the contributions. Here's where Cora Cogdell sent me twenty-five dollars to help with the church repair. I have everybody's name down and what they gave. It's good to have a record like that.

I'm old and won't be around much longer, and I want this record I've made to be protected. They want me to give this book to the state archives in Montgomery. I've never done anything like this on my own, so I won't give it until I ask our other two members and get their consent. We would be the ones to say. I know that in years to come there will be hundreds of people who will want to know what's in this book. It's the record of a few of the people who have tried to do the will and the work of the Lord in this community. What it represents is more precious than gold.

Well, I do believe the mail has finally come. It's an hour late.

POSTSCRIPT: In 1995 Josephine Bates Pritchett was still living at home alone at the age of ninety-six. She is feeble but able to look after herself and take a visitor on a tour of her yard.

*M*other's Day at Liberty Baptist Church, about 1950. The occasion was observed every year with a dinner on the grounds.

An Only Child

Like my grandmother, I always called my mother "Babe." Sarah Waters Hall (1917-1990) was my mother. Strangers often mistook the two of us for brother and sister. Small wonder. She was but sixteen when I was born. She had four more sons; and when the youngest started to school, she got a job as a clerk at Cohn's, a clothing store in Union Springs. It was her first job ever outside the home. It paid very little, but she loved the camaraderie with the other clerks and with the public. She was always shy and ill at ease with other people and uncomfortable away from home, but she loved the self-confidence and sense of independence that she began to develop. She blossomed even more after the death of my father in 1968 when he was fifty-eight. As an only child, she felt orphaned when her father died when she was only seventeen. Her mother's death in 1944 left her without a parent or grandparent. All her aunts and uncles had moved away from the home community, and she saw them infrequently on visits to Troy, Montgomery, Birmingham, Mobile, and Opp.

It is not easy to interview one's own mother—especially one as reticent as mine—but as we talked she opened up and spoke freely about her life and her relationship with my father. Indeed, I learned some things about her that she had never told anyone in the family. I was home on a visit in March of 1981, when we sat down for this conversation in her four-bedroom concrete-block home at Halls Cross Roads at the intersection of highways 223 and 14, about three miles east of where she was born sixty-four years before. Since my father's death thirteen years ago, she has lived alone, though within sight of three of her five sons and their families. A fourth son lives about three miles to the east, next door to the old family homeplace. I have lived in Kentucky since 1962.

My name is Sarah Elizabeth Waters Hall, but as I reminded one of my sons the other day, there's not an ounce of Hall blood in me. Hall is just my married name. I'm all Waters and Grider. I want to go to bed early tonight, but I'll tell you as much as I can remember about me and my family. I'm afraid it's not been a very eventful life.

I was born in Bullock County on June 14, 1917, in the same bed I sleep in now. Four of my five sons were born in that bed. Mama told me later that our family doctor, Dr. George Guthrie from Inverness, was with her. My mother was Tressie Grider Waters. She was born close by, up above Liberty Church, on the fifth day of June in 1881. She died on February 4, 1944. I have a postcard she wrote me two days before she died. She had been married to a Mr. Ellis for several years and was living near Opp, Alabama, at the time of her death. She was introduced to her second husband by one of her brothers who was living down there. I don't think I ever forgave my uncle for doing that. My father was born October 14, 1871, in Bullock County also. He lived here all his life. He died on November 25, 1934, about ten months after my first son was born. Daddy's mother, Granny Waters, lived with us for a while in the house he built for my mother. But in later years she moved in with Aunt Sallie, her daughter, a little piece down the road, and she died there.

I was an only child at a time and place when it was

unusual to be an only child. I never liked it. I can remember worrying my mother to go somewhere so I could find somebody to play with. Aunt Sallie had a son, my cousin H. T., but he was eight years older and he wouldn't play games with me. Uncle Till and Aunt 'Liza Outlaw lived just down the road, and when some of their grandchildren would come to visit, I'd go there and play. They were the Gause children— Estelle, Ruby, Moselle, and Helen—and they lived close enough to walk over with their mother, Miss Ethel. But I always wanted brothers and sisters of my own. Mama told me that the doctor brought babies in his black bag. So when one of us got sick and the doctor came with his bag and didn't leave us a baby, I'd say, "Mama, how come we didn't get a baby? Everybody else is getting a new baby. How come the doctor didn't leave us one too?" I don't remember what kind of tale Mama would tell me, but she wouldn't have said they cost too much. In those days you could pay the doctor with a little money or with a pig or a ham or some corn. There may have been some midwives in the community, especially for colored people, but I didn't know them. We always had plenty of doctors all around us at Boswell, at Inverness, and at Simsville.

I'm sure Mama and Daddy spoiled me because I was an only child. Lots of people thought I was fortunate not to have brothers and sisters to have to share with, but I didn't think so. When a family had six or eight children, naturally they couldn't give them very much. So I had just about everything I wanted, except brothers and sisters to play with. That doesn't mean that I had everything children have today. My grandchildren break and throw away more toys in one week at Christmas than I had during my entire childhood. Christmas was about the only time children got toys back then, and I'd get maybe a doll, a few children's books, and a ball and jacks. And Mama would also see to it that I got some apples and oranges and bananas and raisins—the kind with the seeds in them—and some hard candy. I never had an electric train. Of course, it wouldn't have done me any good because we didn't have electricity until after I got married. I never had a tricycle or a bicycle. My father wasn't dirt-poor but children then just didn't get many playthings at Christmas or any other time. I do remember that Daddy made me a skin-the-cat pole one time out of a small tree trunk with the bark removed. He placed it between two posts above four or five feet off the ground. I learned to do all kinds of tricks on that pole. One of the tricks was called skin-the-cat and it meant suspending yourself from the pole and pulling your body backwards through your arms. Sometimes I would fall and get the breath knocked out of me. Uncle Tom Brooks, Aunt Sallie's husband, was handy with his knife and he'd carve little animals and other objects out of pine bark and make whistles out of reeds and give them to me.

Most of the games we played were ones we made up and didn't require any special equipment. When the Gause children would come over this way, we would walk the steep banks along the roadside. We

Sarah Waters Hall.

would get a foothold and see who could walk farthest without falling down the bank into the gully. We played tag and crack-the-whip and other games, but we mainly just enjoyed being together.

My main enjoyment was reading. I read anything I could put my hands on, though books and magazines were not plentiful in our house. Daddy subscribed to *The Montgomery Advertiser* and enjoyed reading it. As a child, I'd look at his paper and think, "How in the world can anybody read this stuff?" After I started to school I could read it, but I didn't have any understanding of it. The only magazine we subscribed to was *The Progressive Farmer.* Mama, I'm sure, read at least some of it, but the only book I remember her reading was the Bible. I never saw her read a novel or any kind of fiction. She really didn't have time to read much because she was always busy with things that had to be done around the house and farm.

I think if I'd had brothers and sisters I wouldn't have felt so much like an orphan all my life. I grew up not having many close relatives living in the community. All of Mama's brothers and sisters had moved away from here by the time I came along, and they lived in places like Troy, Montgomery, Birmingham, Opp, and Mobile. She was the only one in her family to stay behind. We didn't visit relatives very much, and Mama kept in touch with her family with letters and post cards. One summer when I was about fourteen I spent a week with Aunt Florence and Aunt 'Rada in Montgomery. Aunt Florence took care of old people in her home, and Aunt 'Rada's husband, Uncle Paul DeMo, worked as a conductor on the streetcars. More than likely, when I'd see Mama's relatives, they'd be visiting us here in the country. Aunt 'Rada's children would sometimes come and spend a week or two with us. Aunt Emma O'Steen would visit from Troy with her children, Emma Jewel, Betty, and Edna Earle. Vashti, who was Aunt Della's daughter, also visited us from Troy. During the Depression, when I was in the ninth grade, Vashti lived with us for a year and went to school with me at Inverness. Times were especially hard for people in town, but we country people grew most of our own food and we had no utilities to pay, so we fared better. After one year with us, Vashti went to the Berry School over in Georgia, where she could work and pay her own expenses. I visited Vashti several years ago when she lived in New York state, but she has since moved back to Alabama, to Montgomery. She told me recently that she'd like to come and stay with me for a while, but she has a cat that she keeps inside the house, and I don't think I could stand that. I have a number of cats myself, but they stay outside in the yard. I never let them in the house.

J. T. Waters, Tressie Grider Waters, and infant Wade Hall.

Life was hard for everyone during the Depression days, but we got along pretty well. We had plenty of clothes to wear and food to eat. Of course, we produced most of our food. We had our chickens and hogs to kill, and we raised patches of corn and potatoes, sweet potatoes and Irish potatoes, and Mama always had a garden full of vegetables. She would can and dry peaches. And she canned tomatoes and beans and peas and she made jams and jellies out of pears, muscadines, and scuppernongs. During the winter we ate a lot of peas and beans that Mama had dried. We grew our own corn and ground our own cornmeal, and we grew sugar cane and made our own syrup.

About all we had to buy was flour, sugar, salt, pepper, and coffee. Sometimes we didn't even have to buy sugar. We'd use home-grown honey to sweeten our food.

All in all, I can't complain about what I had. I know our living conditions were a little better than many of the people around us. The house we lived in was considered good for country people. Our rooms had ceilings and our windows and doors had screens to keep out the flies and mosquitoes. Some houses nearby were not sealed at all and had wooden shutters at the window openings. Still, we weren't very comfortable by today's standards. About twenty years ago my husband Jabo built this concrete-block house that I'm living in, but he was only able to enjoy it for a few years before he died in 1968. Since then, I've lived here by myself, with four of my sons and their families living close by.

The house where I was born and grew up in is still standing, but it's been empty and neglected for years and is about to fall in. It's been going down fast since Jabo's sister Beansie and her husband moved out several years ago. If you have time, I'll take you on a memory tour of my old homeplace when it was having better times. We lived then on a dirt road about five miles from Inverness and about four miles from Boswell Crossing. The Conecuh River ran by Inverness and Boswell, and so did the railroad tracks of the Central of Georgia.

Our house was built by my father in the late 1890s. It was a one-story frame house with two large bedrooms, one small bedroom or lean-to on the back, a kitchen and dining room, a hall, and a front porch and a back porch. It was a high-pitched house and in later years we dropped the ceilings and made one large room upstairs. Each of the large bedrooms had two double beds, and at least four people usually slept in each room. When we added the room upstairs, we turned one of the old bedrooms into a living room. We also added a bathroom in the late '40s after we got an electric pump for the well. Before that, our toilet was a plain wooden structure with no sanitary facilities located next to the scuppernong arbor at the back of the yard. Mama always called it the bungalow. It was primitive but it was better than most people around us had. Some families had no toilet at all. They used the fields and woods. That was one reason we were usually asked to keep the visiting preacher or song leader during our protracted meetings each summer at church.

In addition to the bungalow, scattered all around the house were a number of other outbuildings. Our yard was enclosed by a paling fence to keep farm animals and wild animals from getting inside and destroying Mama's flowers and shrubs. In the fall after all the crops were gathered, most farmers would mark their animals and turn them out to forage for their own food until the next spring. Mama kept her yard cut clean of grass and weeds and swept clear of leaves and trash. I didn't like it, but I'd help her sweep when I had to. She had flowers planted all around—zinnias, petunias, marigolds, cosmoses—and several wisteria vines grew over the ends of the front porch. One wisteria started growing up a hickory nut tree in the back yard and eventually reached the top and covered the tree.

I enjoyed helping Mama plant bushes and flower cuttings we'd get from relatives and neighbors. We always had a porch full of potted plants—begonias, geraniums, ferns—that grew in old lard cans, buckets, and chamber pots. In the winter she kept them in a flower pit in the backyard. It was a large rectangular hole Daddy dug in the ground with several boards inside that we put the potted plants on. It had a large set of doors on top that we'd open on warm sunny

"Babe" and her father, J.T. Waters.

days. Sometimes we'd have a very cold spell that would kill a few of the plants, but most of them survived until spring, when we'd take them up, do some repotting, and put them back in their places on the front porch.

We had rose bushes and crepe myrtles scattered all around the yard, and a large cape jessamine next to the back steps. Around Mother's Day that bush would be filled with white blooms that made the whole yard smell like perfume. Sometimes we'd throw a bucket of water over the bush that would release the aroma. Every year we had a big homecoming service and dinner-on-the-grounds at the church on Mother's Day, and most people would wear a red flower, perhaps a rose, if their mother was living and a white flower if their mother was dead. A lot of people used to stop by our house to cut a cape jessamine to wear to church on that day.

We also had a number of oak and hickory trees all

Granny Waters's buttermilk pitcher.

around the place. There were white oaks, water oaks, pin oaks, and post oaks. Daddy planted some of the trees after he built the house, but some of them were already there. One of the oaks Daddy planted to the right of the front yard next to the calf pasture is still standing, although I noticed on my way to church the other day that it has a lot of dead limbs and a big scar where lightning has struck it. As a girl I remember when men would tie their horses to it when they came to visit. Our house was set back from the main road and a sandy drive ran up by the front gate. Between the drive and the county road we had a line of about half a dozen pecan trees. When the pecans began to ripen in the fall, we could walk out the front door and pick them up. We also had a larger pecan grove and several grape vines across the road. A little beyond the pecan grove and across the peanut field was our fishpond, where Mama and Granny spent hours and hours waiting for a fish to bite their hooks. I didn't claim to fish. I was too restless. Granny would say,

"Hush, Babe, I'm about to get a bite." So while they fished, I'd have to starve until they got their bait of fishing. Of course, I did like to eat the perch and bream they caught.

Daddy never fished much, but he liked to bird-hunt and squirrel-hunt with his old 12-gauge shotgun. Mama would fry the birds and squirrels he killed, but I didn't much like to eat them because they tasted gamey to me. Mama never went hunting but she knew how to use a shotgun, especially after Daddy died. She would shoot crows or hawks or snakes or anything that was crawling or prowling too close to the house. No two-legged intruder ever bothered her either because they knew she had a shotgun and wasn't afraid to use it.

Let's go now to the front gate, and I'll show you through the house and the outbuildings as best I can remember. The gate is weighted with an old broken plow point so that when you go through it closes behind you. We'll walk down the path to the front steps. Let's say it's June or July and on either side are beds of flowers and rosebushes. On the porch are several straight chairs and rockers and a swing on the right end next to the wisteria vine. I used to lie in that swing and watch the bumblebees bore holes in the porch rafters and dirt daubers build nests under the roof. Several of the straight chairs have cowhide bottoms that Daddy tanned and installed. The others have seats made out of oak strips. You can see Mama's potted plants all around the edge of the porch on the floor and on the long shelf that Daddy put up for her. If you turn around, you can see the dusty road in front of the house and the mailbox down to the right with its red flag up. Mama has probably written a penny post card to Aunt Florence in Montgomery.

We'll go on now through the screen door. The wooden door is closed only when there's a bad storm, and I don't believe it's ever been locked. I've never seen a key to it. We come now into the hall that runs from the front porch to the back porch. Our two large front rooms are both bedrooms. Granny's room is on the left and Mama, Daddy, and I sleep in the room on the right. The fireplace in each room provides us with the only heat we have in the wintertime. About the only furniture in Granny's room is a bed, a dresser, a chest of drawers, and several straight chairs. There is also a bed which we use when we have company. Across the hall in our room we also have a second bed for Daddy. Until I was a pretty big girl I slept with Mama, and Daddy slept by himself in the same room. Eventually, I got brave enough to sleep by myself in the little room off the back porch, but I was still afraid of the dark. I was scared every night. Sometimes Mama and Daddy and I would walk up to Aunt Sallie's and they would tell ghost stories. In those days they could tell fantastic stories which they said were true, and on the way home in the dark I'd be scared to death. I'd catch hold of Mama and Daddy on either side, but even then I'd think, "Well, I'm still not safe. Something could grab me from behind." Now that I live alone it seems strange that I was so scared.

On our bedroom walls are large pictures of Grandpa and Grandma Grider, and in one corner next to the window is Mama's Singer sewing machine. It was manually operated by a foot pedal, and it was the only "machine" that Mama had, and she always called it "my machine." She'd say, "Babe, stay away from my machine. You'll play with it and break my needle." Except for coats and an occasional Sunday dress, she made all our clothes as well as most of Daddy's. I always thought she was a good seamstress, but in those days every farm woman needed to know how to sew. Most of us girls preferred store-bought to homemade clothes because we thought it showed your family had a little money. Mama never taught me much about sewing, and I've never been a good seamstress.

As I said, Mama provided the power for her sewing machine with her feet. We didn't have anything electric until about 1940, when the Rural Elec-

Sarah and Jabo Hall

tric Cooperative started putting up lines to serve people like us in remote areas. The Alabama Power Company had a few lines up in the county, but they didn't get much beyond Union Springs. Of course, we didn't know what we were missing till we got electric power. I've always had trouble with the heat, and sometimes I'd almost pass out from heat prostration. But we didn't have air conditioning until years later. Many times on hot, humid summer nights it was hard for us to get to sleep. When it would get to be bedtime and the house would still be hot as an oven, Daddy would say, "Tress, make us a pallet on the porch so we can cool off." So Mama would lay some quilts and pillows on the front porch where we might catch a breeze, and we'd sleep until the house cooled off and then we'd go back inside to bed to finish out the night. We never slept on the porch all night long. We weren't afraid of being seen because nobody passed by late at night anyway. We also had our nightgowns on.

Although we lived in south Alabama, the winter nights could get very cold. Our fireplaces and the kitchen stove kept us warm. Daddy cut small logs for housewood about three or four feet long. If the logs were big, he'd split them open into smaller pieces with an axe and a maul. Stovewood was maybe a foot long and had to be cut into small pieces to go into the firebox. Green wood is hard to burn, so he'd cut housewood in the late summer or early fall to give it time to dry out before it had to be burned. We'd start the fires with lightwood splinters. We called them "fat wood" and found them in the woods and pastures where pieces of pine stumps and limbs had gotten hard without decaying. You could strike a match to a fat splinter and it would blaze up and singe your hair if you weren't careful. The fires would go out when we stopped feeding them with fresh wood. We were afraid to keep a big fire going while we were asleep because a spark could fly out and catch the house on fire. We knew of houses that burned down that way and burned up the people in them. So on cold winter nights after we had gone to bed, our main source of warmth was our quilts. The colder it got the more quilts Mama would pile on the beds.

Mama had inherited a few quilts from her mother, but she made most of the ones we had. She and Granny Brooks would take worn pieces of clothing or scraps left over from sewing and piece them into patterns for a quilt top. Then they'd set up the quilting frame and stitch the top to a backing with a layer of cotton in between. After a while, she got to

tacking her quilts instead of quilting them. Rather than make running stitches, she'd get two or three colors of heavy thread or yarn and run her needle from underneath to the top, then cut the strings and tie them together. Tacking a quilt that way was faster and easier but old-time quilting was prettier. I don't have more than two or three of Mama's quilts anymore. Most of them have worn out long since. Her quilts would be close to a hundred years old now, and that's a lot of wear and tear. They don't last forever if they're constantly used for pallets and cover and washed every year or two.

We'll leave our old bedroom now and go back into the hall and out the back door. We later cut a door between the bedroom and the dining room, but when I was a girl the only door out of the room led to the hall. Notice how Grandpa Grider's eyes seem to follow you around the room and out the door. I always thought he was watching me to make sure I behaved. Out here now on the back porch to the left is a smaller lean-to room, just large enough for a wardrobe, a small bed, and one chair. It's where I slept when I moved out of Mama's bed, and it's where, years later, we put our indoor bathroom. It was unceiled and you could see the wooden shingles covering the roof. After I started sleeping back here, I'd sometimes wake up during the night and get scared, but I'd be too afraid to leave my bed and run across the porch to Mama's room.

Leading off the porch to the right are two more rooms, the dining room and the kitchen at the rear, each with its door opening onto the porch. The kitchen has a woodburning stove, a safe where food is kept away from flies and a cabinet for dishes and pots and pans. On a ledge just outside the west window is the slop bucket, where Mama empties scraps of food and dishwater to feed to the hogs. Out the south window you can see the clothes lines strung between four trees where we hung our weekly washing. The ceiling in the kitchen was never completely finished, and people used to say they could hear ghosts and trace chains rattling up there and over the dining room. The dining room has one big table that will seat eight to ten people, several chairs and a smaller table in one corner where Mama keeps her jars of canned tomatoes, beets, corn, and okra. Women liked to show off and brag about how many jars of fruits and vegetables they put up each year.

Back here on the back porch are some more straight chairs my father made of hickory wood and cowskin seats. At the end of the porch is the watershelf, which has a waterbucket with a dipper in it and a washpan. This was our "bathroom." Every night we'd sit on the old quilt chest up against the wall or on the doorsteps and wash at least part of ourselves before we went to bed. Mama wouldn't think of letting us go to bed without washing at least our face, hands, and feet. A feedsack towel hangs on a nail by the kitchen door. To the left of the watershelf is the set of steps that lead into the backyard. Right below the watershelf on the ground is Mama's fishbait bed. It was always kept wet by water we'd pour on it from the dipper, the washpan, and the dishpan. Mama never had trouble finding worms to keep her fish hook baited. All she had to do was remove the boards on top of the bait bed, dig a couple of times with her hoe, and she'd have a can full of long worms.

Scattered all around the yard, inside and outside the paling fence, were the outbuildings and work places that every farm had to have. In the backyard to the right is our smokehouse, where we kept our salted and smoked pork. On the left is the syruphouse, which Daddy kept full of gallon cans of sugar cane syrup. Way out in the back beyond the garden Daddy had a cane mill, where he pressed juice out of stalks of sugar cane and boiled it into syrup. The syrup kettles had a shelter over them so that we could cook the juice

An old dinner bell.

even if it rained. When we made syrup, it was a gathering place for people in the community to come at night and sit around, visit, drink cane juice, and enjoy being together. Sometimes the women would sit around the quilting frame and work on one of Mama's quilt tops.

Daddy made so much syrup he would put some of it in sixty-gallon barrels and gallon cans to sell. We used a lot of the syrup ourselves—mainly at breakfast and supper to pour over hot buttered biscuits. We might also have ham or sausage and eggs and grits, but we always had buttered biscuits and syrup. I think syrup and honey were such important commodities for us because they were the only foods we made on the place that satisfied our craving for sweets. From time to time Daddy would keep a hive of bees, but Uncle Till Outlaw always had a row of bee hives, and we could get all the honey we wanted from him.

Just beyond and to the right of the smokehouse is the potato house, where we stored sweet potatoes bedded in straw. We also had a big potato hill outside the potato house covered with straw and dirt, but we'd have it used up by the time winter set in. Then we'd start using the potatoes from the potato house, and they'd last until the next year's crop was dug. Before we move to another location, look to the rear of the yard to the right of the bungalow. That's our scuppernong arbor. When I was a girl, I'd sometimes hide from Mama down there and play with my dolls and imaginary playmates. When the leaves were on the vines, it was like a little house with a roof and walls. Oh, the scuppernongs were so sweet and juicy when they got ripe. I remember one time Mama decided she'd try to make some scuppernong wine for medicinal uses. So she picked a big lard bucket full and set them in an old churn in the smokehouse to ferment. But as soon as she could smell the alcohol coming, she began to worry about it, and wound up pouring the whole batch in the slop bucket. I imagine we had some unsteady but happy hogs for a day or two. In addition to the scuppernongs, we also had a number of fruit trees—horse apples, which were small and hard and used mostly for cooking, large purple plums that one of Mama's brothers had brought her one time, a tall pear tree, several peach trees, and a pomegranate with fruit so sour we could hardly eat it.

Now we'll go over to the west side of the back yard, where our well and wash place are located. Here is the stand where Mama washed our clothes. There would be three wash tubs to soak and scrub the clothes in, a wash pot to boil the clothes in, and three tubs to rinse them after boiling. Mama washed with lye soap, which she made from grease and lye water made by running water through a hopper of ashes from the fireplace. She also had a battling block, where she'd beat the dirt out of real filthy work clothes with a battling stick. That was after she'd loosened up the dirt by boiling them in the pot. She'd also use the battling stick to poke down the clothes whiles they were boiling and to take them steaming from the pot to the battling block or the wash tub. In those days people worked hard in the fields and around the farm and didn't change clothes every day. So they'd get real dirty and it would take all that scrubbing and washing and boiling and beating and rinsing to get them clean. When she got ready to hang up her clothes on the line to dry, Mama would say, "Well, if there's any dirt left now, the sun will draw it out." It would take most of one day to do a big washing, and then it would take about as long to iron the clothes after they had dried. She used old sad irons which she'd heat in the fireplace or on the kitchen stove. That was a long and hot job I never liked! I'm afraid I wasn't as much help to Mama as I should have been. Sometimes she'd get a colored woman to help with the washing and ironing, but she usually did it all by herself. I've always believed that all the hard work Mama and Daddy had to do

contributed to their deaths when they were both not much over sixty.

Although we didn't have indoor plumbing, we did have a well in the yard. Some people didn't even have that! Some of Jabo's people had to tote water from a spring or open stream where animals drank and messed in it. They'd just dip it up, and there's no telling what might be in it. But we had a good well and it had a top over it too. It tasted good and was soft and easy to lather. Of course, at times we'd have to have the well cleaned out. That's when we'd draw out all the water and mud and silt and anything else that happened to be down there. Daddy would get a little man or a colored boy to ride the bucket fifteen or twenty feet to the bottom of the well, and he would fill the bucket until it was all cleaned out. Then he'd put in new curbing to keep mud and silt from running back in. After a few days the water would again be deep and clear. I never knew anybody to get hurt working down in our well, but I've heard of men being buried alive when the sides would cave in.

Our water was not treated, of course, and sometimes we'd get little bugs or wiggletails in it. If the bugs were too small to be seen, we'd not worry and drink them on down. We didn't know any different. They never killed any of us, and as far as I know, we never got sick from them. If the wiggletails got too thick, we'd throw salt in the well. That usually took care of them, but we'd have to haul our drinking water until the salt taste disappeared. To my knowledge, we never had any problems with lizards or alligators or frogs in our well, but one time we had a mad dog jump in. Somebody was working down in the well, when one of our dogs started having a fit and running around the house. Then he jumped up on the wellbucket shelf and fell all the way down to where the man was working. It must have stunned the dog so much he was harmless, and the man down there just put him in the bucket and somebody pulled him to the top. When the dog came to, he was all right.

Over there beyond the well to the west is the barn area, where we had a gearhouse, a lot, and a huge barn. The lot is in front of the barn, and that's where the horses and mules were penned when they were not in their stables. We usually had four or five mules to do the plowing and one or two horses for riding and pulling the buggy. To the left of the lot is the gearhouse, where Daddy kept the harness for the plow mules and the saddles and bridles for the riding horses. Daddy nailed a horseshoe to that post oak tree next to the gearhouse, and he used to tie his horse to it while he was harnessing or unharnessing him. If you look close, you can see it's still there but it's bedded deep in the trunk.

The barn has three corn cribs, a bean crib, and a big loft overhead where fodder and peanuts and hay were thrown up to dry. We had a stairway ladder made of planks nailed cross-wise that we used to climb up to the loft to throw down the feed for the stock. In the bean crib we kept velvet beans that Mama fed to the milk cows. Sometimes the beans would sting if you touched them without gloves, and most people didn't like to handle them. Daddy planted the beans next to the corn, and they'd run up the cornstalks where they were easy to find and gather. Daddy would usually have the Negro men on the place gather them. Right behind the barn you can see our calf pasture, where Mama penned and milked at least three cows twice a day. I'm afraid I wasn't much help there, either.

During the work season the horses and mules were kept in the lot and stables. People called their operations one-horse farms or two-horse farms or three-horse farms, depending upon how many animals they worked. We usually had one or two families that lived in tenant houses on the place and worked with Daddy on halves. They were sharecroppers who didn't have any land and worked ours. We had both white and black sharecroppers. It didn't matter to Daddy what color they were if they worked hard. He

Babe (left), her sons Wade and Jack, and her mother, Tress.

never had trouble with any of them. Daddy's main cash crop was cotton, and it took a lot of hands to work it. If a sharecropper had a large family, they would sometimes all be at work in the fields, hoeing or chopping or picking cotton. Sometimes he'd have eight or ten bales piled up in the sideyard already ginned. If he thought the price offered at the cotton gin was too low, he'd put the bales on his wagon and bring them home to keep until the prices went up. Of course, before the cotton could be ginned it had to be picked and stored in a cotton house in the field till Daddy had enough to take to the gin. Then he'd load up several wagons and haul it down to McLendon's gin at Boswell. The gin would separate the cotton seeds from the lint, which would be compressed into bales. That's what he would bring home if he thought the prices were too low. Of course, that meant he'd have to wait a while to settle his account at McLendon's store. That's where he bought his seed, his fertilizer, plows and plowpoints and anything else we needed for the farm or house.

You could buy practically anything you needed at McLendon's. Throughout the year Daddy would buy on account. Sometimes he'd just write a note and send one of his hands on a wagon or horseback to Boswell. It might say, "Let Sam Townsend have a fifty-pound sack of flour and ten pounds of sugar and a dozen Mason jars." Daddy would write down exactly what he wanted and Mr. McLendon would send it to him. October was usually the settling-up month. Daddy never had much cash during most of the year, but his credit was as good as cash.

Daddy owned maybe forty acres when he married Mama, and every time he'd get a little extra money, he'd buy more land. His homeplace, up where Aunt Sallie and Uncle Tom Brooks lived, was homesteaded by his grandfather, but most of the land he owned he bought one tract at a time, and when he died he owned several hundred acres. I don't think Mama completely trusted Jabo to keep the land in the family, and in her will she fixed it so none of the land could be sold until our youngest child was twenty-one. It was probably a good idea because Jabo had a reputation for buying and selling and wheeling and dealing, and he could have lost all my family's land.

In addition to the usual crops, we had cows and hogs and goats on the place. I don't know why we raised goats. It certainly wasn't for their meat or milk. I remember one time at a family reunion down near Opp, Uncle John Grider barbecued a goat, which I refused to eat. Maybe Daddy kept goats to keep the briars eaten down.

Mama did most of the work around the house, cooking and cleaning and milking. When Mama got the milk to the house from the cowpen, she would strain it in big pans and let the cream rise to the top. Then she'd pour the cream in the churn, let it turn and churn it till the butter came. To keep the buttermilk from ruining, she'd put it in a metal cooler with a tight-fitting lid, tie a rope to it, and let it down in the well to keep cool. We'd drink the buttermilk and Mama used it to make biscuits and cornbread. In later years we had an icebox to keep our milk in. It was then possible to keep our sweet milk from turning sour for

a few days. Sometimes on special occasions we'd buy an extra block of ice from the iceman and make ice cream in our hand-turned ice cream maker. That would be once or twice a year. During one period of time, Mama milked six cows and sold the cream so I could take piano lessons.

I took lessons when I was in the fifth and sixth grades. I didn't have a piano, but Aunt Sallie had an organ and I'd walk up there in the afternoons and practice. Daddy said he would buy me a piano and I'm sure he would have, but I lost interest and dropped music before he could get around to it. I took music from Miss Orie Weed at Inverness School. She later married Mr. Jake Cade, who owned a hardware store in Union Springs.

Oh, I mustn't forget our chicken house. It was in the back of the backyard. And we had a covered roost behind the syrup house. Sometimes we'd order pure-bred biddies like Rhode Island Reds from Sears and Roebuck, but we'd usually set our own hens and hatch out our own mixed biddies. We raised the roosters to eat when they were frying size, but we kept the pullets to lay eggs. When a hen got old and stopped laying, we'd boil and use her for chicken dressing or dumplings. Sometimes we'd swap a hen with Mr. Sam Katz, the fruit and vegetable man from Montgomery who came by our house every Sunday. We'd get some grapes or bananas or the Sunday *Advertiser* for the chicken, or a quarter in cash.

We also raised guineas. Daddy liked them because he said they sang so pretty. They'd go, "Pot rack, pot rack, pot rack." They hid their nests in a hole in the ground, and we might find fifty or sixty eggs in one nest. Daddy would get a spoon and dip the eggs out and put them in his hat and take them to the house. I know sixty eggs is a lot of eggs, but we had a bunch of guineas and they'd all lay their eggs in that one nest over a period of several weeks. Mama called that "stealing a nest," but it always seemed to me like we were the ones doing the stealing. There was also what she called it when a chicken hen would take over a nest where another hen was setting on eggs to hatch them. Anyway, Mama would use the good eggs—some of the old eggs might not be fit to use—to cook with. We could have eaten them as eggs, but we had plenty of chicken eggs and we preferred them. We would have eaten the guineas, too, but like their eggs, the meat was a little strong and we didn't care for it. We did eat turkey though, and sometimes Mama would raise them to sell. Mama and Daddy sold a lot of extra things around the place—eggs, chickens, turkeys, hogs, cows, milk, and butter. Daddy could sell his cotton and peanuts only one time a year, but it was convenient to have something to sell throughout the year to pay taxes and buy necessities like cloth that Mama used to make our clothes.

Across the backyard from the barn was the car house. Actually, it was first the buggy house, but when Daddy bought a Model-T Ford we started calling it the car house. When he bought the car, he didn't know how to drive it, so my cousin H. T. helped him learn. When they brought the car home the first time, H. T. backed it into the carhouse so Daddy wouldn't have to back it out. He bought the car from Mr. Eley in Union Springs and paid him about five hundred dollars for it. Daddy and H. T. were the only ones that ever drove it, though Daddy still preferred to go short distances on horseback. Mama never learned to drive, and I didn't learn until after I got married. Jabo tried to teach me, but he didn't have much patience, so I finally got off on an old dirt road and practiced by myself.

Daddy's car was one of the first ones in our community. After he got his confidence up, he would drive it to Boswell and Post Oak and eventually to Union Springs. One time he drove it all the way to Dothan. There was a group of four cars and we all drove down together and came back the same day. I remember that Grady and Ida Sellers went too and Grady took his car. It was the farthest we ever went.

Most of the roads were little more than wagon trails and we jolted and bounced all the way down and back. It was a long time before the roads to Troy and Montgomery and Union Springs were paved or graveled. Even after Daddy bought the car, Mama and I walked most of the places we went to. We'd walk when we went visiting or to church or to Post Oak.

We kept the old buggy a long time after Daddy bought the car. He kept it parked up against the big oak tree outside the carhouse. We used to say we had a lot of ways to get around. We could go on Pat and Bob, by which we meant our legs, or on the buggy, or the wagon, or on the Model-T. Mama would sometimes ride the train to visit her sisters and brothers, but neither she nor Daddy ever rode an airplane. I flew for the first time a few years ago, and I liked it fine. I only rode the train a few times, but I always loved to see them go by. When I would go visit Nell Tillery down near Boswell, her daddy, Mr. Cleve, would take us down to the depot to see the trains come in and the people getting on and off. It was always a highlight for me to see the train come in.

We didn't go to Union Springs very much, even after we got the car. Before that, Daddy would ride his buggy when he needed to go to town. It was only about twelve miles and he had plenty of time to get there and do his business and get home before dark. A lot of people rode their wagons to town. Even as late as the 1940s, the roads would be filled with wagons on their way to Union Springs on Saturdays. I heard Mama tell about Jabo's grandfather, who used to walk to town. He was a big tall man and when somebody would come along in a wagon and stop and say, "Mr. Rollo, do you want a ride?," he would say, "Thank you just the same, but I'm in a hurry. I'll just walk on."

There were a lot of grist mills around the community when I was a girl, but we didn't have one on our place until after I married and Jabo bought one and moved it here. He ran it with a tractor and ground corn into cornmeal for us and the neighbors. He took

Tress Waters, Sarah Waters Hall, and Wade and Jack Hall, about 1938.

a small toll of corn from each sack he ground. Daddy used to take his corn to a water-run mill down on the Conecuh River near Boswell.

I've already mentioned the outbuilding that was the farthest away from the house, our toilet that Mama called the bungalow. It was at the end of a path that ran downhill behind the house. It was a two-holer, though I never knew of two people to use it at the same time. Maybe the boys did years later. Country people around here were careful when they talked about bodily functions, especially women, and they would say they had to "step aside." We would say we had to go down to the bungalow, and we all knew what that meant.

I guess the bungalow is a good place to end this

homeplace tour. I haven't covered everything. I didn't mention the little store house we built after I married up beyond the car house on the main road. For several years Jabo operated a little business there, selling gas and oil and kerosene as well as canned goods and a few other groceries. But I wanted to tell you now about how things were at home when I was growing up in the 1920s. Now if you still have a little time, I'll take you with me to school.

I started to school at Inverness in 1923, when I was six. I rode the schoolbus driven by the Boswell family who lived over near Liberty Church. They had the bus route for this area. They would go first over to Post Oak and pick up the Sellers children, then come by our house and pick me up, and go up to Jenkins Cross Roads—which was near where Halls Cross Roads is now—and on up to Bread Tray Hill, where we'd turn on the quarter road and pick up the Davis children and then we'd be almost to the schoolhouse. All the roads were unpaved and could be bad when it rained, but the quarter road was the worst. That's where we always got stuck in the mud. We'd all get off the bus and push till we were muddy from head to foot. Sometimes when we couldn't make the bus budge, we'd just have to wait till somebody pulled us out with a team of mules.

When I started the first grade, Mama had to have help getting me on the bus. But after I got used to school, I didn't want to miss a day, even if I was sick. I liked my first-grade teacher very much. She was Miss Lawson and came from Josie. In those days you didn't know anybody out of your own community, and every place seemed a long way off. Miss Lawson spent the night with us one time. It was after we had a play at school, and Mynell Boswell played a colored girl and had her face blackened. After the play Mynell and Miss Lawson and another teacher, Miss Thompson, came home with us and stayed overnight. In my mother's time, the single teachers lived around with families that had children in school. But in my day teachers rented rooms or apartments and lived where they pleased.

Mr. Peacock was principal of the school when I started. The next one was Mr. Reagan. The last one was Mr. J. F. Hamilton, who was principal for more than thirty years. In my opinion, he was the best one anywhere. He kept good order and was well-liked and well-loved by everyone—well, just about everyone. He couldn't stand for any foolishness, and any boy who misbehaved was sure to get a sound whipping. He was head of the whole school, from the first grade through the twelfth. All five of my sons were fortunate to go to school to him.

My favorite subject in school was reading and literature. And I loved to write. I'd write letters to anybody I knew, and I kept a diary for a long time. After I got married, I read an article in either *Redbook* or *Ladies Home Journal* by a woman who'd moved with her family from one of the northern states to Alaska. I still remember the title, "I'm a Cream Puff Pioneer." I wrote her a letter and we started corresponding and exchanging photographs. That was during the Depression and they moved to Alaska for financial reasons, but I don't know if living conditions were any better there. It seemed like a hard life to me. But I do know that her letters about life in Alaska were very exciting and interesting to someone who'd never been north of Birmingham or south of Panama City, Florida.

When I was a girl, Mama was very protective of me. She never let me go to school barefooted, though I'd pull off my shoes once I got there. On cold days she'd make me wear long stockings and long underwear. I have a picture of Daddy holding me next to the yard fence, and I'm dressed like a little polar bear. I couldn't stand being watched so closely. I don't know why she was so concerned about me. Of course, I was an only child. I've often wondered if maybe she'd lost some babies before I was born. She and Daddy had been married for a number of years before I came

along. But in those days we didn't talk about things like that.

I enjoyed school so much. I liked my teachers and my classmates, and I liked the fun we had at school. One year I was elected May Queen and we all danced around the May Pole. Grace Grider nominated me and she got me elected at a penny a vote. Pennies were scarce, too. I had almost forgotten all about it until Eunice Hall showed me a picture the other day of a May Queen and said, "Do you remember, Sarah, when you were May Queen that one year?" Of course, I remembered then. It was the highlight of all my school years.

As much as I liked school, I didn't finish. I dropped out in the tenth grade to marry Jabo Hall. His real name was Wade Hall, but everybody called him Jabo, and so did I. A lot of the Halls had funny given names and nicknames—like Kinch and Kizzy and Beansie and Fraze. That was why I was determined that none of my children would ever carry a nickname. They would be called by their real names or none at all. We had so many "buddies" around here that no one knew which one you meant. There was

Inverness school pictures of, left, John Hamilton, son of the principal, about 1947, and John Hall, brother of the author, 1958.

Lou's Buddy and Charley's Buddy and Kinch's Buddy and this buddy and that buddy. I said, "We'll have no Jabo's or Sarah's buddy in this family." And we didn't.

All my children were boys and all their names have family connections. I named Wade after his daddy. Jack was named after Jabo's daddy. I also gave Jack my family name, so he's Jack Waters Hall. I named my middle son Jimmy Paul because I liked the name Jimmy and because I had Uncle Paul DeMo in mind. Donald's middle name was for Grandpa Christopher Grider. And John, my youngest son, was named for my father, John Thomas Waters, though everybody called him Ceif. I know I have two different sons named Jack and John, but I did the naming and that's what I wanted. Jabo liked all the names I gave them.

Well, here I am talking about my sons, and I haven't even told you about getting married. No, I was not a single mother! *All* my sons were born *after* I got married. Jabo and I had known each other all our lives. He was seven and a half years older than me, but he didn't have much formal schooling. His family sent him to school for a while over to Almeria and he'd usually play hookey—so he said. That was before the children in this community were bused to Inverness, and he'd have to walk or ride a mule to Almeria. So he'd decide to walk or ride his mule somewhere else. His parents didn't seem too much concerned about education, so they let him drop out when he was still in one of the lower grades.

Jabo started working when he was still a boy, and he'd held a number of odd jobs around the community before we started going together. The first time he asked me out was to go to a singing at Macedonia Church. And Daddy said, "No." But that didn't stop us long, and we had been going together for about a year when we decided to get married. Jabo was about twenty-two and I was fifteen, but I guess I thought I was old enough and smart enough to quit school. So

without telling Mama and Daddy, we ran off to Perote to get married. Jabo didn't have a car at the time, and he hired old Alex Allen, a colored undertaker, to carry us over there to the Methodist preacher's house. It seems to me like Alex had just been to Chicago in his hearse to pick up a body, and that's what he took us to Perote in! Of course, he'd already removed the body. The preacher's name was Jones and I'd never seen him before he married us, and I've never seen him since. His wife was one of the witnesses, and the other one was a friend of ours, Grady Sellers.

After the wedding Alex took us all over to the Brooks' house at Macedonia, where they were having a dance. Then somebody later carried us up to the little two-room shack that Jabo had rented for us up near Union Springs. I'd never seen the house before, but Jabo had already set up the furniture—such as it was—and the cookstove and had everything ready. I moved into that shack sight unseen. We had just the bare essentials, and sometimes not even that. One day I realized I didn't have a sifter for my meal and flour, and I had to borrow one from Hallie Youngblood, one of our colored neighbors. Hallie is now dead, but I saw Henry Youngblood last year, and I said, "Hey, aren't you Henry Youngblood?" And he said, "I sure am. Is that you, Mrs. Hall?" They were the best neighbors we ever had. She was so clean and helpful. Mama had never made me work much in the kitchen, so Jabo was a better cook than I was. He always said I learned to cook from him. Soon, with his and Hallie's help, I learned to fix things he always liked best— biscuits, ham, half-done eggs, and thin hoecakes of eggbread.

As I said, Mama and Daddy didn't know we were planning to get married. When we eloped I left a note, and I was kind of afraid to go back home. But Jabo wasn't. He had a lot more grit than I did. After a few days he got somebody to take us down to see them. When he didn't have a car, he always had a way to get somebody to carry us places. We got there and I went in the house and hugged Daddy and Mama and said, "I'm sorry if we ran away." Mama was crying and Daddy said, "Well, it's all right. It's been done. I reckon it had to be." But Jabo read the wrong meaning into what Daddy said, and he said, "No sir, it didn't *have* to be." Daddy meant, of course, that sooner or later we would have married anyway. Jabo thought Daddy meant I was in trouble. I always knew that Mama and Daddy were not too pleased that I married when I did—and I don't think they were too pleased that I married Jabo—but they accepted it.

Jabo didn't have much of a job when we got married, so we didn't have money to buy anything or go anywhere. We had so little furniture in our shack that I thought we were rich when we got our bedroom suite from Cade Hardware in Union Springs. It consisted of a bed, a dresser, and a chest of drawers—all of which I still have—and cost less than a hundred dollars. Jabo didn't tell me, but I know he bought it on time and paid for it a little each month. We couldn't afford a honeymoon and never took any kind of trip until many years later. Wade Henry was born less than a year after we married, and we soon had too many children to look after. After Jabo got his own car, we'd eventually go to a few places like Panama City or Mobile or Atlanta. Jabo never flew in an airplane, and I didn't either until after his death. After my first flight, I decided I liked it very well and have flown several times since then.

We lived a few months in that first house, then moved to another little house on the other side of Union Springs. Just before our first son was born and not long before Daddy died, we moved in with Mama. I guess by then they had completely forgiven us.

I've always gone to church at Liberty and became a member when I was about twelve. Mama and I went to church every time we had preaching, but Daddy didn't go often and I don't believe he ever joined. Jabo's people didn't go to church very much either,

and he was never baptized. No, it doesn't bother me that he was not baptized. Before he died in 1968, he had become a good and decent man and had accepted Jesus as his Savior. That's the only decision that is important in the long run anyway. Although he wasn't a member, Jabo would go to preaching with us from time to time. We didn't have services in those days but every fourth Sunday of the month. Sometimes we'd visit other churches, especially during their protracted meetings in the summer after all the crops were laid by. Our meeting at Liberty always started the fourth Sunday in July and ran twice a day for a week. Most of our new members would join during those meetings. I remember all the preachers we've had, but I think the most popular was Preacher Vickery, who would come over every month from his home in Hazelhurst, Georgia, to preach for us. He could fill our old church house to the rafters. He was a very emotional preacher and took in a slew of new members every summer. Even Jabo's family turned out when he came to preach!

All of my Grider relatives had been members at Liberty or Mt. Zion going back several generations. Most of my ancestors were originally from England and Scotland, but the Griders were from Germany, though they'd been in this country at least since the time of the Revolution.

There's a grave marker in the Liberty Cemetery of a relative named Benjamin Franklin Grider, who was buried there some time in the 1840s, not long after white people started moving into this part of Alabama and the church was started. My Grandmother Bettie Allen Grider had cut the church motto out of cardboard and sewed little pieces of cedar onto the letters that spelled out, "God Bless and Revive Our Work." I can still see those words arranged like an arch on the wall behind the pulpit. I don't know what happened to them when they tore down the old church house to build our new one. Grandmother Grider died before I was born and Grandpa Grider married a second wife we called Miss Dolly. His sister, Aunt Lady Jane, who lived over near Mt. Zion Church, built him a house over near her, and he moved his church letter there.

People used to tell me about hearing Grandpa Grider pray at Mt. Zion. A lot of people used to not want to pray out loud in church, but it never bothered any of the Griders. All my aunts and uncles were big church people, though some of them left the Baptists and became members of the Church of Christ. Uncle Tip Grider even became a Church of Christ preacher and preached all over south Alabama. He used to tell us that we had to be a member of that church to get to heaven, and he meant it. At our Fourth of July Grider family reunion one year, Aunt Florence said, "Brother Tip, our beloved Mama and Papa both died Baptists. They were good Christians and good people. Do you think they went to hell?" Uncle Tip thought for a minute and said, "Well, Sis Florence, I'm hoping they'll get to heaven on ignorance." I don't know where Grandpa's soul is today, but I know that his body is buried at Liberty Church. Grandpa lived to be an old man, well into his eighties, and when he died, it rained and the roads were wet and muddy. I remember very well that when the hearse started up Beaver Dam Hill to take his body to the church, it got stuck, and a Model-T with a high body had to go in front to make ruts.

Daddy died before Grandpa Grider. Mama stayed on the place after Daddy's death until she married a Mr. Ellis and moved to Opp about ten years later. She continued to make a little money with her cows and chickens and eggs, and she rented out some land. She never sold any of it and left it all to me and my sons when she died in 1944. Mama was always self-sufficient and never called on anybody for help. When she wanted to go somewhere, she'd walk or ride Daddy's old saddlehorse, Po Gal. She rode Po Gal everywhere, from Boswell to Post Oak. That was the gentlest horse you ever saw. I used to ride her to drive up the cows and to go horseback riding with other young people.

I always thought horseback riding was more fun than riding in a car. If Mama needed to go to Union Springs, she'd pay somebody a dollar to carry her. If she wanted to visit her brothers and sisters in another county, one of them would come after her or she'd take the train.

Daddy worked hard all his life. So did Mama. She kept the house and yards clean. She cooked and sewed and mended and washed and ironed and took care of the cows. She raised me as well as I would let her. She helped in the fields. She had very little free time. That's what made Sunday so special. It was a day of rest or visiting or going to church. People even worked all day Saturday, if there was work to be done. If Daddy had a hired hand who didn't want to work on Saturday, Daddy would say, "Well, I don't reckon I need you any more any time."

Life has not been easy for any of us. Jabo's lack of schooling and our large family limited what he could do. He did a little farming, he raised cows, he worked on the state roads, and he was in the storekeeping business off and on all his life. He dabbled around in a lot of projects, but he never really had a good job with a steady income. But all in all, I think he provided for us as best he could. I didn't have to marry him. I had other opportunities. But he was the one I chose.

I had boyfriends before Jabo. I even had one in the fifth grade. Not long after Mr. Hamilton became our school principal, two of his brothers, Winfred and Hiram, came over from Chambers County to live with him and go to school at Inverness. Winfred was in the sixth grade when I was in the fifth grade. That meant that we were in the same room. Well, back then Valentine's Day was a big event at school. We cut most of our valentines out of tablet paper and colored them with crayons, and we'd put our friends' names on them and drop them in the valentine box on the teacher's desk. Well, lo and behold, that year Winfred gave me a store-bought valentine. And he gave me not just one, but eight! I was overcome! I'd never seen so many fancy valentines! They were all made of crepe paper, the kind of paper that would stretch when you opened the card. I thought, "Boy, he loves me. I must be somebody!" And I guess I was that year. But oh me, the next year he transferred to the Berry School in Georgia. For a while we wrote letters to each other; then they kind of trailed off, and we stopped writing. But I hadn't forgotten him, and when I was in the ninth grade and Aunt Della and Uncle U. L. took my cousin Vashti over to the Berry School, I went with them. Vashti knew my old boyfriend was in school there, and they looked him up for me. I was bashful about seeing him, but they made me. I knew they were watching us, so we didn't say much. That was the last time I ever saw him. We wrote to each other again a little while after that meeting, and then we quit. Winfred wasn't as good looking as Hiram, but he liked me and that made him better.

Through all these years, he's always been in the back of my mind. Not long ago, I wrote to Mr. Hamilton's daughter Alice and asked about the family. I knew, of course, that Mr. and Mrs. Hamilton were both dead, but I wanted to know about their son John and the other daughter Anne. And I asked about Hiram and Winfred. She wrote me all the family news and then said that Hiram was living in Lanett, Alabama, but had a bad case of cancer. He's probably dead by now. She said Winfred had a family and was doing well and living in Florida. Of course, Alice never knew why I asked about Winfred. She didn't know he had once been my boyfriend, my first boyfriend.

A little later I had another boyfriend, Pearl Deason's son Wilson. He and I went around a little together, but we were never serious. You see, I had other opportunities, but Jabo was the only one I really cared about. He was the one I chose. Like everybody else, he had his faults. Sometimes he drank too much and became abusive. We had our ups and downs.

After we moved away from Mama's house, I'd sometimes leave my two oldest sons with her. Several times in those early years, I left Jabo and went home to Mama; but after a few days, when he came for me, I always returned with him. I always went back to him. Even during the bad times, I never regretted marrying him. He was he one I chose. He gave me five healthy, intelligent, good sons; and I only wish he was here now to enjoy our eight grandchildren.

That's all I have to say. I wish I'd taken more interest in my family background and asked Mama and Granny and my other relatives more about their lives and where we all came from. But it's too late now. They're all gone. And it's too late for me to be talking any more tonight. I still haven't done the crossword puzzle in the *Advertiser,* and I have to take my bath.

POSTSCRIPT: Sarah Waters Hall died April 28, 1990, at the Bullock County Nursing Home in Union Springs. For almost two years her sons and their families attempted to care for her at home; and as her condition—Alzheimer's Disease—worsened, they took turns nursing her in their own homes. She was finally taken to the nursing home when it was determined that she needed twenty-four hour care.

She was the first member of her family to have her body remain in the funeral home until the day of the funeral and burial. Several years before her death, she had remarked to one of her daughters-in-law during a visitation at the Gray Funeral Home in Union Springs how lovely and convenient it was for the body to remain there and not be returned to the family home for an all-night "sitting up" or wake. After her funeral at Liberty Baptist Church at which her favorite hymn, "What a Friend We Have in Jesus," was sung, she was buried in the church cemetery across the road between her husband and her mother in the family plot.

A Man of His Words

The Reverend John Butler became pastor of Liberty Baptist Church some ten years after I left home, but I got to know him and his wife well during my visits back to Bullock County. Like most of the pastors at Liberty, he was a non-resident, coming to the church community from his home in Montgomery County to preach and visit. Shortly after he became pastor in the early 1960s, the church voted to have "preaching" every Sunday, the first time in the history of the church. Hitherto, services were held only once a month, on the fourth Sunday. Like all his predecessors, however, he was not a full-time pastor. Until his retirement in 1979, he worked as a full-time employee of Appleton Wire in Montgomery. Most of the speakers in this book attend his church.

This monologue is based on a conversation taped on Sunday, July 24, 1983, at my mother's home at Halls Cross Roads on Highway 223, about three miles east of the church. It is about two o'clock in the afternoon following the morning church services and after a large dinner at which Mr. and Mrs. Butler were guests. The annual protracted meeting or revival will commence at the evening service with a guest preacher from Montgomery County. Preacher Butler sits at the dining room table surrounded by several of his male parishioners and guests as the women clear the table and wash the dishes.

He is a small, wiry man who speaks with the power and conviction of his high calling, whether discussing Biblical prophecy or a 1936 high school graduation. His narrative talents and his penchant for drifting from one story to another are reminiscent of Simon Wheeler, the yarnspinner of Mark Twain's "The Notorious Jumping Frog of Calaveras County," and other storytellers of the Old Southwest, an antebellum frontier region that included Alabama. Like many rural Baptist pastors of his generation in the Deep South, Preacher Butler has no college or seminary training.

Sarah, I really did enjoy that dinner. It was mighty fine. I believe you make the best chicken dressing of any lady in the church. No, I don't care for any more ice tea. I just want to get my pipe lit up before I start telling these fellows about myself. I want to save a little time for visitation before the evening service. I look forward to a good meeting this coming week, and there are some people living in the shadow of the church that I want to make sure come and respond to the messages of our visiting preacher.

To begin with, I've had a lot of good and a lot of bad in my life. In the beginning, it was mostly bad because I grew up like an orphan. I was born in Montgomery on the 29th day of August, 1917, on Plum Street next to the railroad tracks. I was only nine when my mother died. She had a miscarriage and died of blood poisoning. Oh yes, I remember her very well. She was a striking woman in appearance, over six foot tall and broad across the shoulders. She was from Sandy Ridge down in Lowndes County and was hard-fleshed because

Rev. John Butler.

she grew up hoeing and picking cotton and doing other heavy work around the farm. But she died young, leaving two girls and a boy.

My father was from Montgomery. I got my small size from him. When he was born, he was so puny they didn't think he would live. But Daddy was tough and smart and grew up to be a natural-born salesman. He made big money selling. He could sell anything people wanted. He told me a number of times, he said, "John, now don't try to sell people something they don't want, and be sure you get a good product." For years he worked with Texas Oil Company and he sold a lot of their products. When Jake Aronov went in business in Montgomery, Daddy sold him two carloads of roofing, but he lost his job because the

fellow that was the salesman there for roofing told him he was going to get the commission on the sale. Daddy said, "No, you won't get it. I sold that roofing and that commission is coming to me." They got into a big row and Daddy made his threat, **and the company** fired him—just run him off.

But Daddy went on to sell something else. He could sell anything. One time he sold shoes. You remember seeing men going around with a suitcase selling shoes? Well, Daddy would catch a train with his suitcase full of shoe samples and go to Selma or Prattville or Wetumpka and spend the day selling shoes and make plenty of money. Daddy liked to work and made good money, but he didn't take good care of his children. He married another woman just three months after Mother was buried, and he dropped us. He stopped supporting me and my two sisters and give us to my mother's people to raise. We were shifted around from one to another, but I lived with my grandmother most of the time. As soon as I got big enough, I helped out as much as I could. Every summer, I worked and made enough money to buy the clothes and books to carry us through the next school year. All I've ever known in my life is work, and I enjoy it now. If I can get out and do something, I'm happy. He didn't give us much out of his pocket, but I'm thankful I got that talent from Daddy.

Right after I finished high school, I went to the Navy recruiting office to enlist. The fellow there told me, he said, "Sorry fellow, you're too short and not heavy enough. We can't use you. Go back home and suck on a baby bottle to you get some size on you." I didn't like what he said, but I didn't say anything because I wanted to get in the Navy real bad. He was right, too, because even though I played football like the 180-pound boys did, I only weighed eighty-nine pounds. But still I wanted to go to the Navy because I had some buddies in there and I liked the uniform they wore. I also had a cousin in the Navy I hadn't seen since I was four years old, and I wanted to run him down. Well, about 1936 that was my big desire—going in the Navy.

When the Navy wouldn't take me, I went over to Columbus, Georgia, and worked in an automobile body shop where they repaired wrecked cars. I specialized mostly in trim work such as upholstery. I had an uncle who was in that line, and he's now got one of the best upholstery shops in Phenix City. I soon found out I didn't care for that work at all, and after about two and a half years I come back to Montgomery and got a job with Swift Packing Company. I didn't like that work either. They worked you for a while, then laid you off whenever they got caught up, so I finally told them shoot, I couldn't make a living like that.

That was before I got married, and I've never liked to live by myself. I toughed it out for a while, but one Saturday evening I got off from work and went down to my grandmother's place in Lowndes County and said, "Grandma, are you ready to go back to housekeeping?" She said she was, so I said, "Well, I got us a place." So we lived together on my farm for three years, from 1939 to 1942. That's when I got married. Grandma lived then with me and my wife for near about four years more until she got so bad off she said it wadn't her daughter-in-law's place to take care of her, and she moved in with one of my sisters.

No sir, I won't live by myself. If the time ever comes, I'll go live in the county jail just to be with somebody before I will stay by myself. I don't know about getting another wife because I don't expect I'll find another one like Nell. She said she had picked out her second husband in case anything happened to me, but he died. Then she picked out another one, and he died. So I said, "Well, I don't believe I'll pick out another wife or something will happen to her."

Yes sir, me and Nell have had a good life together for over forty years. We was married April 25, 1942. She was from Montgomery County, just a half a mile from where we live now and about twelve miles from where I used to live. We both went to Pike Road School together for three years. Then I moved back to Lowndes County and I went to Hayneville for a year and come back to Pike Road for what I thought was my last semester of high school. Down at Hayneville they had a professor that was one of the best teachers I ever set under. The only trouble was he didn't have a very good memory. He'd let things get away from him. For instance, he'd drive his car to the post office, go in to get his mail, then walk to the school two blocks away and leave his car at the post office running. Now, that's what I call absent-minded! Of course, some of us preachers are just about as bad. Well, when he sent my records over to Pike Road, he didn't send a complete transcript, and I lacked a quarter of a credit in physical education of having enough to graduate. They got me on that quarter of a credit. What was so bad was the principal didn't tell me until the night before graduation. You know I didn't like that. I wadn't a Christian then, and sure wadn't a preacher, and I let him know some things I shouldn't have said. So I had to go back to school another year and take a lot of courses over just to make up that quarter of a credit.

I finally graduated June 6, 1936, a year after I was supposed to. It was hot weather about like it is now. The stage we graduated on was surrounded with heavy wool curtains that didn't let in any air, and it was hot as blazes up there that night. It was the first time most of us boys had ever wore shirts with stiff collars—and they were stiff—and when I come off that stage I was just like a wet washrag. We was all just wringing wet with sweat. We was ashamed to get out there in the hall and let people pass by and congratulate us and shake our hands. All the girls had fixed their faces up and the teacher had fixed us boys' faces up with a little powder and rouge, and that sweat was just washing down in trenches. I tell you it was embarrassing.

When the war come on, I was in the dairy business that the government considered vital to the war effort. I was froze there on the farm, and the government wouldn't let me move to any other kind of work. I still wadn't married, and I still wanted to get in the Navy. I thought I might make it because I had got my weight up to 120 pounds. An article come out in the paper that said for the next fourteen days you could join any branch of service you wanted to, so I run down to my draft board. The clerk said, "What's the matter?" I said, "I want to join the Navy." He said, "Well buddy, I want to join the Air Force too, but they won't release me, so I know they won't release you." I said, "Anyway, it's worth a try." So I went back for a hearing and the board said, "What have you come for?" I said, "I want a release from the dairy farm because I got a chance to join the Navy." They said, "You go on back home. We'll let you know what you can do." I said, "All right." Well, I went home and waited and waited and finally I give up on the draft board and the Navy and got married. That was in 1942.

Nell and I was married for about three years and then Albert was born. An article come out in the paper about that time that if a man was married and had one child he didn't have to go in the service. All that time I'd been going back to the draft board every six weeks, and I had got tired of that mess. One day I told them, I said, "Why don't y'all move the draft board because I done wore out these steps." One day they called me in and said, "John, we're gonna let you in the Navy now. We'll give you six weeks to get all your bidness settled and everything straightened up, and we'll send you off." I said, "Sorry, it's too late. I ain't going." There was three people on the board, two farmers and the head was a town person who was a bookkeeper. He said, "Oh yeah, you'll go if we say so." I said, "No,

I ain't going." In six weeks I went back, and he said, "Well, Butler, you got your bidness straight?" I said, "I always keep my bidness straight. I don't go around with bidness undone." He said, "Good, because we're gonna send you off in two days." I said, "Sorry, I ain't going." Now, I knew the other two board members, one I went to school with and the other one I knew from way back. The bookkeeper was ready to get rough with me, when I just throwed down a birth certificate on Albert in his face. Albert was about six weeks old then. I throwed it down in that fellow's face and said, "You can keep this little piece of paper if you want to." He looked at it and his face got red and he soured up and give it to the other two members and they looked at me and laughed. I said, "Thank you, gentlemen. I'll see you later." Then out the door I went to Nell and Albert who was waiting for me outside in the car. I didn't hear any more from the draft board, and in less than three months the war was over.

During the war we'd listen to the news on the radio every day at twelve o'clock, and one day an amazing thing happened. There wadn't nobody home but me. Nell and Albert had gone to town or somewhere. I had a little old short-wave dial and I was dialing that thing and directly I heard something on there about the American forces invading an island in the southwest Pacific. Then this walkie-talkie way down yonder come in on that radio and somebody says, "Raise your fire five degrees, *Missouri*. I knew *Missouri* was a battleship and that they used a battleship every time they took an island. In a few minutes the voice said again, "Raise your fire ten more degrees, *Missouri.*" Then in about three minutes, it said, "Now lower your fire, *Missouri,* about three degrees." After that I didn't hear no more. I wondered what all that meant until I read the story of what the *Missouri* was doing that day. What else give that battleship a good name was when the Japs signed the surrender on it. That ship played an important part in the war, and I picked up one of its battles right here in Alabama on my farm.

While we was in the dairy bidness, I was also working with Appleton Wire. That was hard work and double duty—*eight* days a week with never a day off, and then Nell started having problems with her heart. When a woman has a light heart attack you know it's time to do something. Her doctors told her to get out of that dairy bidness and stay out. So after her second heart attack, I sold out at a big discount just to unload. We was milking forty-nine cows at the time, and overall we had about seventy-nine head. That last year we was in the dairy bidness, I bought twenty thousand dollars worth of cattle. What I had my eyes fixed on was going in the registered bidness, and I bought ten head of registered Jerseys at a sale in Montgomery. I didn't want all the Jerseys out of one herd. I wanted them out of ten different herds, where I couldn't get the same blood. Then I went up to Auburn and bought me one of those expensive Jersey bulls from up there. Even with all that investment, after Nell had her attacks, I told her, I said, "If this dairy is going to kill you, I'd rather have you than all them old cows." So I got shed of them.

I still had my work at Appleton Wire, but about that time I decided to quit them, too. The man that owned it, Mr. Buchanan from up in Wisconsin, called me in and told me, he said, "John I got a lot invested in you. You started off as a janitor and you've been moving up in this department. You've been here nearly three years and done a good job. But if you're quitting for more money, you'll have to go ahead because I ain't going to pay no more." I said, "Naw, I ain't quitting for more money. I just can't work the swing shift, changing my work schedule every week." He said, "All right, we can handle that. We'll give you a shift you can work." So they put me on the second shift, and I stayed with them. I'm glad I did. I had it made with them folks. I liked the work. They weave a screen wire that is very similar to your house screens,

only it's woven out of brass and bronze. That screen is used at the paper mill in the manufacture of paper. It's used in the process to separate your fluids from your pulp. They've changed over now entirely to plastic, but back then the screen was all brass lengthways and bronze crossways. That wire was very expensive, and there's no telling how much that scrap wire sells for now.

So I stayed on and before long I made top man in the brazing department. That was just a God-gift because I already knew how to braze before I went to work there. The work was all done through machinery, and you didn't see any of it with the naked eye. You looked at it through a microscope. We used oxygen and natural gas to get a hot flame, about twenty-five hundred degrees, to join those wires. Now if you let that hot a torch get loose from you and hit your meat, it'll go right through you. One time I got burned on my shoulder, and it was a nasty place there for a long time.

I was with Appleton Wire for twenty-four years and three months and I retired from them in 1979 in April. The last three years I worked in the box shop because I got to where I wadn't able to do heavy work and because of the death of our oldest son Albert. When he got killed, I was working second shift, and when I'd get home late at night Nell would have all his pictures and letters out looking at them, and I knew that wadn't good. Daytime she done all right, but I knew I had to be there at night. So I just told the boss, I said, "I've got to get another shift or quit or do something so I can be home at night." So he give me a day job and put me in the box shop running one of the biggest lathes in the plant. After the union come in, I had seniority and anything I wanted that come open, I could get it. But the trouble was I didn't want lot of responsibility, even if the new job paid a lot more money. One day when I turned down a job, the boss said, "Kid"—they called me Kid at work—"Kid, you can have this job. You got the seniority. You qualify for it. But you say you don't want it. What in the devil do you want?" I said, "Retirement."

With that new job I could have stepped on up and made around fifteen thousand dollars or more, but I didn't want anything to interfere with me and my family and my church. I didn't want to be on call at any time of the night or weekend. I had lived a long time on a lot less, and I figured I didn't need to worry about money because I had never suffered from want of anything since I'd been a Christian. I don't worry about nothing now. I have always worked hard, but the Lord has looked after me.

You know you live and learn, and I've learned a lot about getting along with people from the jobs I''ve held. But the most important lesson I've learned is the importance of a good woman and a good family life. You ain't seen me when I was sixteen. They tell me there wadn't nobody handsome as I was. Nell will tell you right now that I was a good looker and real sweet. I didn't mistreat nobody. I tried to be good to everybody because I was raised an orphan. You know an orphan's greatest desire is to have people care for him, to have somebody love him. The reason I love old people like I do now is because they are the ones that showed me love when I was young. Then Nell come along and she loved me, but we waited to marry. We didn't get married until I was twenty-five and she was twenty-six. I tell her that she was older than me but I still raised her. I said I wanted a good woman for a wife, and I had to raise her.

I have tried to take care of her and my family. If I saw something in a store window that I thought would look good on her, I bought it. It didn't make no difference about cost or nothing else. I thought she deserved whatever I got for her. Now, she was a good looker too when she was younger. Her hair ain't been that white all her life. When we was married it was coal black, except for a piece about as big as a quarter that was white as cotton. When I was going with her, she parted her hair on the side that covered up her

white spot, so I never knew she had it until we got married. But that was all right. The Lord has blessed us with three children. The oldest was Albert. He was in Viet Nam but got killed in a wreck after coming home from the war. My other two are Johnny and Ena Carol. She married Sonny Hall and plays the piano at church. We'll never get over Albert's death, but somehow it must have been the Lord's will to take him.

Having the Lord's will be done is the most important thing in anybody's life. I become a preacher because I believed it was His will. It was revealed to me like a vision. It was a calling of God, and His desire become my desire. It's only God that can call you into the ministry. There's some men that go around pretending to be preachers that are not called of Him. One time I worked with a boy at Appleton Wire that was going to school at Huntingdon College. He was a Methodist preacher and one day he made the remark that soon as he finished college he was quitting the ministry. "I'm in the ministry and going to Huntingdon," he said, "because the Methodist church is furnishing it. They're paying for it and I ain't." That's what he told me. I don't know what become of him, but I do know a true calling is a calling of God and not a way to get your college education paid for. I never went to college, and I believe my call is from God.

I accepted the call in 1960, but I had fought it for little over two years. I just couldn't answer it, and I got hard to live with. I got to the place I was fixing to leave my children, my wife, and everything—just give it all up and leave. I was like Jonah, trying to run away from the Lord's will. I didn't know where I would go or what I would do. I just wanted to get away and maybe the calling would pass over. That's what I *thought*. An old fellow that lived next door to me sensed what I was going through. He was a Methodist. He wasn't a preacher, but he was a man of God. One day he come over to the house and told me, he said, "Brother John, you better stop your foolishness and quit your running. The Lord done called you to preach and you might as well go ahead and accept it. If you don't you're going to make life miserable for yourself and your family, too." So I did. I went to church that Sunday, and I told them the Lord had called me to be a preacher, and they voted to license me.

We had been going to the Baptist church regularly all our married life, but I was raised up mostly in the Church of Christ. When I went over to Phenix City and was working in Columbus, I met a little red-headed girl who lived down the road from us, and she kept insisting I go with her to her church. You know it's not the nature of somebody in the Church of Christ to go somewheres else to church. She kept on inviting me and I got to where I wanted to go just to please her. To me she was beautiful. To everybody else, she was ugly. One time my wife and daughter saw her at a wedding over in Phenix City, and they said she was the ugliest gal in the state of Alabama. Nell said, "John, I don't know what you ever saw in her. You could have done a lot better—and you did!" I say it's not all looks that attracts you to another person. She was a good little old girl. I'll tell you one thing as a

warning: Bad girls is a dime a dozen. The worst thing you can do is hook up with some bad person, whether it's a man or a woman. The worst thing in the world for a man to do is to take up with these cheap women because they'll ruin you. In more ways than one, they'll surely ruin you.

Well anyway, one night unbeknownst to this little red-haired girl, I slipped into her church and set on the last pew in the back. After church was over, she saw me and we come on out together. So I got to going with her to the Baptist church. That first night I just sat there and listened. When the next Sunday night came around, I said, "I think I'll go back." So I went back and I kept going back. At first, I thought that old man in the pulpit didn't know what he was talking about. He wasn't a very good speaker. He was just a po' boy like me. But I kept on listening and finally I figured that well, that old boy did know something. Everything he said didn't set with me, of course, but I don't believe that every sermon preached has something in there that sets with everybody. I kept on listening to him and thinking and finally I decided well, I'm going to talk to that old man, and I talked to him several times about the Bible and the plan of salvation.

After my mother died, I went to live with my blood uncle and my aunt in Selma for about four years. She took the place of my mother. She was as good to me as she was to her own children. But she'd whup her children, and she's got the first time ever to hit me with a straw. They were members of the Christian Church, which is close kin to the Church of Christ. When the split come in their church, the Christian Church accepted instrumental music and the Church of Christ didn't. That's about the only difference. So my uncle and aunt were Christian Church people, but when I was in Phenix City I got to going to that red-headed girl's Baptist church and the more I heard and the more I talked with her preacher the more I liked it. I got to studying the Bible, and then Nell and I got to going together. I had to be goody-goody, I thought, because I was going with a little Christian girl, and I wadn't a Christian. I had to be just right. She was a old-line Methodist, and when people ask her today if she's still a Methodist, she says she's a Methodist made over into a Baptist.

God's people can be in any church. One of the main differences between a Methodist and a Baptist is in our mode of baptism. A Methodist preacher could just about baptize everybody in this room with this tea glass full of water, but it would take a pool full for me because I baptize them all the way under. I've baptized Nell and all three of our children. At Liberty I've baptized a number of people. We used to baptize in somebody's pond, but now we have an indoor baptistry in the new church. You remember how big Lindbergh Driggers' three boys were? Well, they all made a profession of faith at the same time, and when we had the baptismal service, the people out in the congregation got a little nervous. They looked at Donnie and he weighed three hundred and thirty pounds. They looked at me and I didn't go but one twenty—maybe a hundred and twenty-four pounds wet. They was thinking, "Is that little man going to baptize that big old boy?" Terry weighed two hundred and eighty-five pounds and he was scared to death. Steve just weighed a hundred and eighty-five, so I knew I wouldn't have any trouble with him. Because Terry was so scared, I said, "Terry, you do just exactly what I tell you. If you don't it's going to be bad." Now, I have a method I use of them holding me while I'm holding their nose. But when I get somebody scared or big like Lindbergh's boys, I change that method and let them hold their nose with a handkerchief while I hold onto their wrist. See, I know they ain't going to turn their nose loose. You try it and you can prove it to yourself. Before you take them down into the water, you make them take a deep breath and then you carry them down under the water with that deep breath in them, and it's easy to bring them right

back up. It's just like filling up a jug. You take a jug and put a stopper in it and drop it in the creek and you can't hold it down under the water. It's going to come back up. That's the way I work my baptisms, and I never have strangled the first person yet.

So I just took Terry down in the water and brought him back up. He had done quit trembling because his scare was over. After he went out, I said, "Donnie, you come on in." So Donnie come on in the tank, all three hundred and thirty pounds. He was just as calm as any man I ever saw. I told him what I was going to do and what I wanted him to do. Then I took him down under that water and brought him right back up. He went on out and Steve come in and I took him down and brought him up with no trouble at all. Them folks out in the church was looking at me by that time and thinking, "Well, Preacher Butler must be a muscle man."

Thirty years ago I was all muscle. I thought I was going to get to be a world champion cowboy. If a horse hadn't broke my back, I reckon I'd still be trying for it. Oh man, for fifteen to twenty years I used to pack leather every day, six days a week. That was when we had the dairy. I was running the dairy in the morning and in the afternoon I worked on the cattle farm. I did everything that come up. I'd help round them up and doctor them and vaccinate them and castrate them and take care of the baby calves, and get them ready to sell—just anything that come up.

When me and Nell got married, I had to go and buy her a horse. I got her a one-eyed, red and white spotted polo-type horse. She was a good saddle horse and would work anywheres you put her. You could just drop a saddle on that horse, put a youngun in it, and hand him the rein and that horse would move on just as smooth. The old man I bought that horse from told me, he said, "Brother Butler, I'm going to tell you something. I never have raised a colt out of that mare and I've tried for a long time. But you got to watch her. She's scared of trucks. A truck run into her and hurt her shoulder and knocked out one of her eyes. I don't believe she can ever have a colt." So I bought that horse for forty dollars, brought her home, and in seven months she dropped a colt. I went over there and told him, I said, "Mr. Carter, here's the horse you sold me. She's just dropped a colt." He said, "I can't believe it." I said, "Well, come on over and you can see the colt." He said, "Naw Johnny, I'll take your word. And you keep her. You got her fair and square."

A lot of people called me Johnny. Back when I was mechanicking up in Montgomery, me and Nell would be walking down Dexter Avenue on payday—fifty dollars for that week's work in my pocket—and people come along and said, "Hello, Johnny." I'd say, "Who is that? I don't know." I'd keep on walking and somebody else would say, "Hello, Johnny" and so on. I usually didn't know who it was talking to me—maybe somebody I'd seen out in the field while I was working on their tractor or hay baler. In a few minutes a lady come along—I mean she was a beautiful woman—and she said, "Hello, Johnny." I said, "Hello, ma'am." Nell looked at her, then looked at me and poked me in the ribs and said, "Well, *who* was that?" I said, "Believe me, sugar, I don't know who she was." I kept thinking and thinking about her, and when the boss sent me back to that woman's place, I knew who she was. I had been up there a month or two before and worked on their hay baler. They run a little dairy and sold butter and buttermilk and vegetables at the curb market in Montgomery. When I had finished my work, there wouldn't nothing do them but I had to eat dinner at their table. I said I had my lunch box out in my truck. But they said no, I had to come in and eat with them. Well, I didn't get to eat at all. They found out I was in the dairy bidness too, and they started asking me questions. By the time I answered one question, they'd ask another one. I didn't have no time to eat! I set there answering their questions and watching them eat. I lost my appetite. So when I went back out there, the lady come out and said, "Now

Johnny, you're going to eat dinner with us again today." I said, "No, I ain't lady. I'll be through in less than twenty minutes and then I'm fixing to leave." I got my job done and I left. I wadn't going to set down at no table full of food and talk myself to death and not get anything to eat. I will say she was a beautiful woman. No wonder Nell tapped my ribs when we passed her on Dexter Avenue! But I honestly didn't remember who she was or what her name was.

I never have been good on remembering names. It took me six months to learn all these Driggerses down here, let alone these Halls. That's mostly what you have around here. When we first come to Liberty, just about everybody in the church was either a Driggers or a Hall. If you called somebody a Driggers and he didn't answer, then you knew he was a Hall.

Talking about baptism, I just don't know how many people I've baptized at Liberty. I don't even have a record, but the church clerk would know. Larry Jones was the first, and then I baptized Jeanette Hall and the three Driggers boys. I have also re-baptized Ena Carol and Sonny Hall. I re-baptized them because it wadn't clear in their minds that they was saved. They made another profession of faith at a time when they were positive they was saved, and so I baptized them. That's what the Bible says do as an outward sign of your salvation: "He that believeth and is baptized shall be saved." I also baptized Louis Railey and his wife Jean. They all got saved in the same meeting with Jeanette and the Driggers boys. Louis told me, he said, "Preacher, I thought I was saved all these years, but now I know it for sure, and I want you to baptize me." I baptized all of them in the baptistry in the new church. I told the church when we was planning the new building, "If y'all will put a baptistry in this church, I'll pay for it myself." So I paid one hundred dollars to put it in. Before that, I had to baptize any place I could get. I baptized Larry Jones up here at Mrs. Pritchett's pond right in back of her house. I remember it had a lot of mud in it.

I don't know how many I baptized when I was down at Loflin Church. At Loflin I baptized in a little old shallow pool a man had built for a swimming pool. He built it out of blocks with a concrete bottom right up next to a bank. A spring of water come out of that bank and run in the pool. One time when I had a little teenager to baptize, I told some of the deacons to go over there and clean out that old slimy stuff called spirogyra and get it off the bottom so we wouldn't slip down on it. Well, we went over to the pool that Sunday evening for the baptism and when I stepped down on them steps going into the pool, I knew they hadn't done it. I had on socks but no shoes, so I just eased on down in the pool and took my feet and scraped out a place big enough for me to stand. When the girl started in, I told her, I said, "Now when you get in here, take your feet and scrub them backwards and forwards to get that green stuff up." She said, "All right, Preacher." But just when I took hold of her and had her about ready, her feet shot up and she went under. When she come up, I just pushed her right back down and brought her up in the name of the Father, the Son, and the Holy Ghost and she was baptized. I told the deacons later, "Well, y'all really played wild that time. You didn't come over and clean that pool bottom and you see what happened. It could have been a lot worse. Next time, I'm going down and clean it out myself."

Loflin is down near Josie right near the Bullock-Pike county line but still in the Bullock Association. I preached there about five years. See, I come to Liberty in October of 1962, and I went to Loflin in February of 1963 and left there in October of 1968. That was when we went to full-time preaching at Liberty. I didn't know anything about it, but the people at Liberty had been having prayer meetings about going full-time. Jesse Driggers told me, he said, "Preacher, you don't know it, but we've been meeting for prayer for three months to determine if it is the Lord's will that this church go full-time." I said, "Well, I know it

now." So I gave up Loflin to come to Liberty full-time. Liberty Church goes all the way back to 1837, and that was the first time it ever had preaching every Sunday of the month. That's how God works through people.

I've not always been sure the people of the Liberty community was doing God's will the way they should. It didn't seem to me that the people come to church the way they should. One time it got to me and I felt like, well, I ought to go on and resign and let somebody younger come on in and take over. One Saturday morning I was setting at home and I started counting the people up, and when I got through counting, I said to myself, "Well, who else is it to come? How many lives in the community? Everywheres you look—four ways, ten ways—there used to be a house here and a house yonder, but how many are standing now?" We had buried seven people in a mile or two radius of the church in a little over a year. Just name how many has passed away since we come here in 1962. Back then, you could go to that big old church on fourth Sundays and see that church near about filled with people. It was about forty foot by forty-six foot—a big church—and it would be full. I don't know how old that church house was, but it had rafters that was six inches square on the eave and three inches square on the corner. The way they architected those rafters when they put them together it didn't have any tendency to drop whatever. But the old building had a lot wrong with it and was hard to heat and cool, so we took it down the last of 1963 and the first of 1964. We borrowed five thousand dollars to build the new brick church. We sold the old church for four hundred and fifty dollars, and the man that got it didn't get anything because the termites had just about wrecked it. Well, he did get a hive of bees up there in a corner wall on the outside. You better not walk up there close when them bees was swarming or you'd get stung.

We had two ladies in the church, Miss Josie Hall

and Miss Ida Sellers, who hit the floor when we started talking about tearing the old church down and building a new one. "No sir," they said, "you ain't tearing down this church. My daddy helped do this and that and the other." But a majority ruled and we went ahead and tore the old wooden church down. Now let me tell you something: Those two women brought more money in to help pay for the new church than any other two members we had. They did. I could understand why they was attached to the old church, but they liked the new church once it was built.

One of my biggest problems as pastor is I live twenty-five miles away from this community up near Pine Level in Montgomery County. It's not been a real big problem but a problem nonetheless because if I lived on the field, I could see the people every day and not just every weekend. I could drop in any evening for a little fellowship. You take a preacher that the people love and that's living in the community, why there's no telling what he can do. I do what I can. I try to make people happy—I don't care who they are—church members or not, black or white. I try to get people in a good mood. See, if you are in a good mood and have a good attitude, everything works better for you. If you can get up in the morning and thank God you're living and on your feet, then you're going to have a good day. Even your arthritis won't hurt as bad! But if you get up all cross and mean with a filthy attitude, that's what you'll have all the day long. I can get up some mornings and my feet are so sore I can't hardly move, but when I say, "Thank you God, I'm still alive," it looks like it relieves everything.

You take my little grandson John. He's thirteen and lacks four pounds of being as big as me, and I'll soon be sixty-seven. That boy is a hard worker. He loves to have a garden and works in it like he's fighting a fire. He wants me to keep up with him in the garden, and I try to, but the next morning I'm so sore I can't hardly move—all in my back and arms and legs. But when I get up and thank God for what all I have and move around a little, all my soreness just goes away.

I'm getting to be an old man, but I still have a lot to look forward to in this life. Before I went full-time at Liberty, I wanted to write a book. It was going to be a sermon-type book. I knew I couldn't pay the price to get it published, so I went to town and bought me a mimeograph machine so I could sell it where people could afford to buy it. You know you can't have a book published for forty-nine cents a copy or even twelve dollars a copy. There ain't no way. But the more copies you make, the cheaper they come. So I bought that machine and anytime I want to I can use it to put out as many copies as I want to. Now that I'm retired from Appleton Wire, I want to get back to my book and do some other things to make use of my spare time. Within the last two months, I built me a double garage and done some other work around the place. I do a lot of studying too. I got about ten study courses from the Moody Bible Institute. My short-wave radio don't keep me as busy as it used to, but I stay occupied. If I'm doing something and somebody comes by and needs me, I drop what I'm doing and try to help out. I don't travel much any more. After my last operation, I had to give it up. When I'm driving around home, I don't pick up hitchhikers anymore. I had a bad experience one time when a fellow in uniform got in the car with me. I told him I wadn't going but about twelve or fourteen miles. We was riding along talking and I just happened to turn toward him and I saw him pull his hand out of his pocket. He did that a couple of times. I don't know what he had in his pocket—whether it was a knife or a gun—but I put him out on the highway before I could find out.

I don't even think about picking up women. You better believe it's dangerous. I had a buddy that pulled up to a country store and got out of his truck and went inside and got him some cigarettes and a soft drink. As he was going in, two girls was coming out, and when he got back to his truck, one of them was in the cab and the other was standing at the driver's door. He went up to them and said, "Hey, get away from my truck." The woman on the outside pulled a knife and stuck it in his ribs and said, "Now get inside in the middle. We're going to take you for a ride." When they found out he didn't have any money on him, they said for him to drive to his bank and get some. They pulled up to the bank and said, "You make one false move, and we're going to kill you." They all got out and walked up to the bank door. As they was going in, he saw a constable he knew, so he jumped inside and hollered, "Get them two women. They're thieves and robbers and they're holding me up." The constable pulled his gun and put handcuffs on both the women. When he saw he was safe, the fellow said he just fell out on the street—just passed out like somebody had hit him in the head. He said, "No sir, I don't let no strange women get close to my truck, and I don't ride nobody I don't know."

I knew another fellow that was home one night with his wife and somebody called him to the back door. He opened it and a man dressed in convict clothes told him, "We didn't come here to do you no harm. We was returning to Kilby Prison when our truck broke down, and we're trying to get somebody to take us back, or they'll penalize us." So the fellow said, "Yeah, sure, I'll be glad to drive you down to the prison." There was two convicts and after they got in the truck and got a piece down the road, one of the convicts pulled out a knife and stuck it in his side and told him to stop the truck and strip off his clothes.

He put on one of the convict's clothes and they left him by the side of the road and took off in his truck. He said he stumbled around all night lost and finally come up on a bunch of Negroes making syrup about two o'clock in the morning. One of them reached for his shotgun and held it on him, but he said, "Wait a minute. I ain't going to do you no harm. Some convicts stole my truck and made me swap

clothes with them, and I'm just trying to get back home to my wife. Can you tell me which way to go?" The man with the gun said, "The road out there goes this-away and it goes that-away. You can go any which way you want to. Just leave here." The white man said when he got out on the road, he turned back and the Negroes had took off and left the fire burning and the syrup cooking. He finally got down to a store and got some folks up out of bed and told them what had happened and asked them to call Kilby. The store-keeper held a shotgun on him while his wife went inside to call the sheriff. The sheriff told her that he was all right, that his wife had called to say he'd been kidnapped by some convicts. In a few minutes a state trooper come over and picked him up and carried him home. He said when he got home and walked up on his porch and saw his wife, he just fell out. They had to rush him to the hospital and it took him six days to get over that night. He said for a long time he'd just go raving when he went to sleep. Yes sir, them stories is a warning to be careful. I don't pick up nobody unless I known them and when I leave home in my van I lock all my doors. I sho' don't want to hurt nobody, but I'll hurt them if I have to before they can hurt me.

I've always tried to be good to people if they let me, and I believe they appreciate it. Some fellow up there in Union Springs asked Lillie Hall one day, he said, "Lillie, how did Preacher Butler stay down there at Liberty long as he has?" She said, "Two reasons. Number One: He loves everybody. Number Two: He gets out there among the people and tries to help them. He lets them know he loves them and he works with them. He takes care of his part, and we take care of our part." When I come to Liberty, I told them, I said, "I'm going to tell you exactly how it is. I'm going to tell you what the pastor expects of his church and what the church should expect of its pastor. It's a two-way street." Then I went on and spelled out what was expected of each side. Then I said, "If I take this church, the pulpit is mine. You're not going to tell me how to run it, what to put in it, who to put behind it. It's mine. I'll take care of the pulpit. Now, you deacons are supposed to seek out the needs of the congregation. You set down and talk about the needs and bring a recommendation to the whole church, and they can accept it or reject it. But you stay away from this pulpit. This pulpit is mine. I take care of the pulpit." And thank God, that's the way it's been all the years I've been at Liberty. We have all tried to work together to serve the Lord.

You know the day of Pentecost fell like the sound of a mighty, rushing wind. When the Holy Spirit begin to work on those people, Peter got up to preach in the Hebrew language, and everybody heard the message in his own tongue and understood. Some fellows walked up and said, "Peter, them folks up there are all drunk. Just look at them." Peter said, "Oh, they ain't drunk. They just got filled with the Holy Spirit." We know what later happened is they was all scattered abroad, and they went the world over preaching the Gospel. Just look at how the Gospel has spread to the four corners of the earth. That's just one of the signs of the end of time. If you don't believe time's running out, just read in prophecy. For four months we been studying Biblical prophecy, and we know the end is near. I don't know how many prophecies has already been fulfilled, and I don't know how many is left to be fulfilled, both in the Old Testament and the New Testament; but I don't believe there's many left. We studied about the people that's going to be saved during the Time of Tribulation. I've thought about that a long time, and I believe it's going to be the people of Russia. But there's plenty of people right around Liberty Church that needs to be saved, and the time is short. If you'd just stop and give God a chance to talk to you, all of you could have eternal life.

I don't know what's wrong with this pipe. If it keeps going out, I'll have to get a flambeau to keep it lit. Sarah, after I finish my pipe, I think I'll take a little nap and then go visiting. We want to fill up the church tonight. There's souls that need to be saved.

POSTSCRIPT: The Reverend John Butler retired as pastor of Liberty Baptist Church in 1991 and continued to live with his wife on their farm in Montgomery County near the junction of Highways 82 and 231. For a while he preached occasionally at funerals and revivals, but soon became so feeble he spent most of his time puttering around his yard and workshop and resting in his favorite reclining chair. He died on March 10, 1996, at the age of seventy-nine and was buried from the Pine Level United Methodist Church.

FINAL SERMON OUTLINE

Title: Psalm 95: 1-12 - 91: 1

Text: Matthew 11:28 - 30

Introduction: Known H. J. for several years and have had the occassion to talk with him many times. Found him to be the same each time I was around him. He had a lot of respect for me, never seemed upset always spoke kind and considerate. Went to see him in Veteran's hospital, seemed to lift Him up, enjoyed our company. Didn't want to see us leave. — Had many friends —

We are not here to judge the inner secret of any man's heart. We know not what emotions stirred his soul nor what secret communion he might have had with God. Neither do we come today to condone or condemn.

However, we do know this. That our God is a great loving God who never makes a mistake. He always looks on the

THE PULPIT WORKSHOP.   "a sermon outline se

Up From Poverty

Louise Hall Supple is my first cousin, the daughter of my father's brother Kinch and his wife, Maggie. Her first husband was killed in a store robbery in 1982, and three years later she married Jimmy Supple, a retired engineer for the state highway department. It is March 17, 1992, and we are talking on the patio of her four-bedroom brick ranch-style home in Hurtsboro, Alabama, on the county line between Bullock and Russell counties. A landscaped lawn surrounds the house, and an office-bathhouse overlooks the large in-ground swimming pool in the back yard. The house and furnishings suggest a lifestyle in sharp contrast to her humble beginnings sixty-seven years before, some thirty-five miles to the south on a tenant farm near Inverness. The cafe that has made her prosperity possible is located about a mile distant on the main street of Hurtsboro. It is a business she created out of will power and hard work. We have just returned from a funeral in Phenix City.

I've just come in from the funeral of my nephew Michael Hall, brother Charley George's thirty-four-year-old son. But I'm all right, and I need to talk. His death is not something I can understand, but we have to accept the Lord's will. The funeral was held at the Auburn Heights Baptist Church in Phenix City, and it was one of the largest and sweetest funerals I've ever been to. I've never seen so many flowers. They just covered up the front of the church. Mike hadn't had any warning, except he knew that all the Hall men have heart conditions.

He died in his sleep Saturday night. He has a place over on the Chattahoochee River, and Charley said he'd been there all day Saturday working on his boat and came home real tired and went to bed early, about nine o'clock. Charley is a deacon and he said he went to the church early the next morning to fix coffee for the deacons' meeting before Sunday School and church. When he got to the church, he found that somebody had broken in and tore the church up. He wanted to take some pictures of the damage before it was cleaned up and called Mike's house to get his camera. The middle child, Jimmie, who's nine years old, answered the phone. Charley told him he wanted to speak to Mike, so the boy went in to get his daddy up and came back to the phone and said, "Granddaddy, I can't wake him. He won't move." At that moment, Charley heard Jan, Mike's wife, screaming. So he dropped the phone and ran over to the house and found his son dead in the bed.

Mike had been married once before and had the oldest child by his first wife. The other two are by Jan. He worked with East Alabama Paving Company as a superintendent, and I hope he had a good insurance policy with them. I heard his boss say at the funeral that Mike was so important to the company it would be like starting over to lose him. I was especially close to all Charley's children because they used to live here in Hurtsboro when they were real little. Charley was working on a potato chip truck, and a lot of time the children would come to my cafe and I'd feed them. It was the same way with my sister Ellen Faye's children. You know Ellen was sometimes unpredictable and would just go off and leave them, and they'd come stay with me until she came back.

I've called Charley George by his given name, but we've always called him Sweet Thing or Sweetie for short. Our brother Buddy gave him that nickname. After Charley was born, Mama was real sick and had to go to Montgomery to the hospital. While she was gone, Buddy, who was almost two years old, would crawl in the bed with the baby and call him Sweet Thing to get his bottle. So we all picked it up from Buddy and started calling him Sweet Thing or Sweetie. I still call him Sweetie but his wife doesn't much like it and will correct you. "His name is Charley, and I wish you'd call him that," she'll say.

There were nine of us children born to Kinch and

Maggie Hall. Kizzie is the oldest, born in 1921. He's retired but used to make oak flooring at a plant here in Hurtsboro. Ned was born in 1922 and worked with the state highway department until he had to take early retirement after he had open heart surgery. Sarah Elizabeth was born in 1924 and worked as a hostess in a country club in Houston, Texas. She's also retired but still lives out there. She came home in November when Ellen died, and she was here for the family reunion the first week of December. I was born next, in 1925, and was named Mollie Louise after Daddy's mother, who we called Maw. I can remember her very well, especially her long dresses and long aprons, which she wore all the time. I think she would have felt undressed without her aprons. Elma Lee and Beansie, Daddy's sisters, wore those long aprons all their lives too. I guess they wore them to wipe their hands on and to keep their dresses clean.

James was born in 1927 and Sybil Mae the next year. There is a skip between her and Roy Dean or Buddy, who was born in 1932. Charley George was born in 1934 and named after two of Mama's doctors, Dr. Charles Franklin in Union Springs and Dr. George Guthrie in Inverness. The last born and the first to die was Ellen Faye. She was born in 1935 and died last November of a heart attack. Daddy and all of his brothers died of heart attacks. Their father, Papa Hall, helped push off the school bus one morning and came back to the house and fell dead. I was real little but I can remember him clearly. My cousin Jack Hall is named after him and is just like him.

Mollie Louise Hall Hughes Supple, 1938.

We were all born in different places around Bullock County. I was born somewhere near Inverness, but I don't have any idea where it was. It might have been on the old Lee Hall Place near Mt. Zion Church. I was old enough to remember where Sybil Mae and the younger ones were born. She was born when we were living on the old Norris Place on the Boswell Road, right where there's a trailer now. Daddy was born in Bullock County too, but I don't know where my people came from before him. Mama came from Pike County near Monticello. Her maiden name was Hughes, the same name as my first husband, but they were no kin. His people were from south Alabama around Brewton. Mama's mother and father died when she was just five years old and she was raised by relatives on a cotton and peanut farm.

We were a very poor family and came from a poor class of people. When I was a girl, we were so poor we sometimes didn't have enough to eat. Many a morning we'd wake up and not have anything in the kitchen to eat, so Mama would take some cornmeal and make little batter cakes for our breakfast; and that's all we'd have. We had a very large family and many mouths to feed and Daddy just couldn't make enough from the farm, even though we all worked hard. Of course, we raised chickens and hogs, but with so many of us it didn't take long to eat up all the meat in the smokehouse and the chickens in the yard. We just couldn't make the food we grew last all year long, and we didn't have money to buy any at the store. A lot of our food and clothes was given to us. Some of our clothes were from the Welfare Department, and Sarah Hall's mother, Miss Tress Waters, lived near us and would often give us food. Later, Sarah would help us out with food and clothes. She would get clothes from her relatives in Montgomery or Troy and bring them over to us. That's one reason she was so special to me all her life. She was my aunt by marriage but was only a few years older than me. I still appreciate what she did for us, and I miss her so much. I've never been one to remember many dates during the year, but I always remembered Sarah's birthday and sent her a card to tell her how much she meant to me. I know she didn't come from a rich family, but they had more than most people in our community. To us they seemed wealthy because they had some money and owned the land they worked. And they always had clothes and something to eat, and sometimes we didn't.

Sarah didn't have any brothers or sisters, and all her kinfolks had moved off by the time she was grown, so I know that after her father and mother died with her still so young, she felt like an orphan. Even after she married Jabo, Daddy's brother, I know she felt alone and lonesome because of the way he treated her. He would leave her and go off for long periods of time. At one time he ran a honky-tonk called The Paradise Inn a few miles out from Union Springs on the Montgomery Highway. They left their two little boys with her mother and lived in some back rooms of the honky-tonk. When he would get mad at her, he would bring her up to where we lived near town and leave her with us for days and weeks at the time. She stayed there because she didn't have any way to leave, and she didn't want Miss Tress to know how he was treating her. After he left Sarah with us, he'd go get one of his lady friends and move her into his place until he got tired of her. Then he would come and pick Sarah up and take her back to those rooms behind the honky-tonk. It hurt her so bad when he behaved like that, but she loved him so much she forgave him every time and went back with him.

I believe the way he treated her caused a lot of her sickness and her nervous condition. Sometimes she would get so weak she couldn't sit up. Several times they thought she was going to die, and I would be so sad and upset. But she survived, partly I think because she loved him so much and wanted to live and be with him. She was smart—I'd say brilliant—but she was trapped and afraid to go out and do anything on her own. She loved him until he died almost twenty-five years ago, and she grieved over him until she died two years ago. I miss her so much.

I think alcohol was a big part of Jabo's problem. It was also a problem in our family. When Daddy would drink, he would sometimes get violent and pick on Mama. I was scared to death he was going to hurt her real bad. I think that was a big reason she was sick so much and stayed in bed a lot of the time. Another reason was that she had too many children. She developed a bleeding ulcer and didn't do anything about it until she had to have stomach surgery. While Mama was sick, Elizabeth and I would do all the house work and look after the rest of the children. I can remember having to cook for the family when I was six and seven. I don't remember that Mama was ever really well until after Daddy died. Then she stopped staying in bed so much because I think she knew she had to take care of herself. I don't believe all her illnesses were real. She must have imagined some of them, but I always believed her when she said she was sick. Children didn't question their parents back then like they do now. They loved them and obeyed them. When Daddy told us to do something, we did it without question. It never occurred to us to do anything else. They were living on the farm near Brundidge when Daddy died of a heart attack at age sixty-three. Mama sold the house and land and was living with me when she died in 1983 at eighty-three.

I loved my father and mother. I knew they were probably doing the best they could for us, but I still resented our poverty. I think I resented it more than any of my brothers and sisters. It always bothered me that we didn't have anything. It caused me to grow up with an inferiority complex. I was withdrawn from other people and felt like they were better than I was. I thought they didn't want to have anything to do with me. We always worked other people's land. We didn't own any of our own until we moved to Pike County when I was in the eleventh grade. There we were able to make a little money from farming and then Daddy started working as a wage hand with the state highway department and he bought the place where we were living. That was the first house we ever lived in that had running water and an inside bathroom. It was the first time we ever had plenty to eat and to wear.

The Gholston Place we lived on at Bruceville when I was in the seventh grade had a nice house, but it didn't have many conveniences. At least the well was right on the back porch, so we didn't have to go out in the yard to draw the water. We lived then right across the road from where Elma Lee and Bootman and Maw lived. That was where Maw died. It was the best farm we lived on in Bullock County, with a lot of good bottom land where we could grow a lot of corn. Like all my brothers and sisters, I worked in the fields, doing whatever was needed—planting seeds, hoeing, pulling corn, picking cotton. I even learned to plow a mule, though women didn't usually do that.

In school I was a good student because I knew that education was my ticket off the farm. We all eventually left the farm, but I was the only one in my family to finish high school. Mama must have gone up to the seventh or eighth grade because she could read and write very well, but Daddy was just about illiterate. About all he was able to do was write his name. I never saw him read anything. Mama would read to him whatever he wanted read like letters and business papers. He was real smart and knew how to figure, but I doubt if he went above the second grade. All my brothers and sisters have done very well with-

Mollie Louise Hall Hughes Supple and a sister.

out much formal education. The Halls have always been smart even if they didn't have much education.

I think I loved school more than anyone else in my family. When Elizabeth and I would have to stay home with Mama when she was sick, I would cry because I had to miss school. We didn't have much time to study because when we got home from school, we'd put on our work clothes and go to work. Everyone of us had something to do, whether it was working out in the field or chopping wood or drawing water from the well or bringing in wood for the cookstove or fireplace or fixing supper. On Saturdays we girls did the family washing. About the only time we had to play was Sunday afternoon, when we might get up a game of softball.

The first school I went to was Inverness. My first

teacher was Mrs. Lola Waller, and like everybody else, I loved her. She was real strict and liked to use a ruler in your hand if you misbehaved. I was in the seventh grade and was taking math with Mrs. Campbell when we moved to Bruceville and I had to transfer to Union Springs. It was a painful experience. I didn't like the new school at all. I wasn't really scared of the school, but I felt completely out of place. We were the same class of people that went to Inverness, but in Union Springs it seemed like the people there thought they were better than us poor little children from the country. I didn't feel at home up there. I was in school there for about four years, and I never did feel comfortable. My clothes were not as good as theirs. I was shy about making friends. The few friends I had lived in the Mill Village, where their parents worked in the cotton mill. There was a definite separation of the people that worked in the mill from the rest of the town. We didn't have a large class, but I didn't get to know any of them very well. I do, however, remember who they were. If I tried, I think I could name all of them. There was Donnie Parker and Marge Springer and Adelaide Bale and Colleen Campbell. Colleen was from Fitzpatrick. There were the Paulks from Sardis. Moleen Johnson lived in the Mill Village.

Things got better when I was in the second semester of the eleventh grade. That's when we moved to the farm near Brundidge in Pike County. I graduated from the county high school in Brundidge. I felt great going to that school because I fit in better. We were all the same people. They mostly lived on farms and were poor country people like us.

I always tried to make good grades because I wanted to get out and get a job as soon as I could so I could start making some money to live on. I wanted to get away from home and away from the farm. I hated the farm. To me it meant working hard and having nothing. I didn't know what kind of job I wanted. I just wanted any kind of job to get me out from there. Mama's sister Aunt Mae was living in Montgomery,

so right after I finished school I went up there to stay with her. She didn't charge me a penny, but I only stayed with her about five weeks when Martha Jean Steed, one of my classmates from Brundidge, and I decided to room together. We started boarding with a Mrs. Carey, who charged us six dollars a piece for room and board. We both worked at Empire Rouse, a dry cleaning plant, and made twenty dollars a week. It wasn't much but it was the most money I'd ever seen. Of course, I didn't have much left after I paid my board and bought a ticket home almost every weekend to see Mama and Daddy and my boyfriend. What little I had left I spent on clothes. I never went to the picture show very much because I always considered them a waste of time and money.

Right at the end of World War II, I met and married J. T. Hughes. Although he was born in Brewton, his family moved to Montgomery when he was less than a year old. I met him through the family I was boarding with, and we married right after he got out of the service. I don't know what attracted us to each other because we were two different people altogether. He had a job as a short order cook at Perry's, a cafe in Montgomery that was famous for its hamburgers. He liked the country and drove me down to see Mama and Daddy several times before we married. He liked them and I think they liked him. After I started going with J. T., I broke off with my Brundidge boyfriend. He went on and married somebody else and now lives in Phenix City. He's a service man for Sears and Roebuck and came by and serviced my stove one time.

Almost from the beginning of our marriage, J. T. and I didn't get along too well, especially after he became an alcoholic. When he was in combat in Italy during the war, he was shot in the back with a machine gun, and he said he had real bad back pain most all the time. After J. T. was killed in a store robbery, the doctors found the bullets that killed him and then they found the bullet from his war wound laying on his spine. I realized then that he was in a lot more pain than we ever thought.

In 1950 we moved from Montgomery to Hurtsboro, where I've lived ever since. J. T. was in a real bad car accident and couldn't get a job. At that time Hurtsboro had about 750 people but didn't have a cafe, so a man decided to add a little cafe to the filling station he was building in town. My brother Kizzie was living here then and he talked J. T. into moving here and running the man's cafe. But J. T. didn't last long in the cafe. He began having trouble breathing inside. One of his lungs was closed by his war wound, and he couldn't take all the smoke and dust in the cafe. So he quit that job and worked for a stove company for a while; then he sold insurance.

Finally, in 1954 I started the City Grill. I had helped J.T. out when he ran the filling station cafe, and I loved the work. We needed some extra income because he wasn't making much money. I guess we could have lived on his disability from the government, but it would have been poor living. His pension got better, though, and when he was killed he was drawing almost six hundred dollars a month.

I went into the cafe business because I like to cook and I like working with people. I'd been cooking all my life, so I just started doing for pay what I'd been doing for free. Everything I learned about the cafe business I picked up on the job, and I managed to build up a real good business. My first place was on Main Street; then on April 1, 1981, while we were all asleep, a tornado came through and almost destroyed the whole town. A lot of people were injured and a few people were killed. Some people decided not to build their businesses back they were so discouraged. But I did. The wind took the top off the City Grill, but we repaired it and stayed open for business. J. T. bought the old filling station across the street from the cafe and said if I wanted to build a bigger place, he would give me the old brick from the station and help me finance the other costs. So I decided to take the risk

and bought a lot farther down the street from Steve Williams. We started construction and it was about half done when J. T. got killed. I was glad that it was far enough along that he could tell what it was going to look like. He had already opened up his own place, the H. & H. Western Store, out on Highway 26, and that's where he was robbed and killed in 1982. He was very supportive of my business. We both knew that we couldn't work together very well. He had his way of doing things, and I had mine. I've always been thankful that he helped me get the new restaurant. We moved into the new building the September after he was killed in July. It's been very successful. People tell me it's a first-class restaurant. We can seat about a hundred people and are open every day except Sunday.

Mollie Louise Hall Hughes Supple.

I'm completely retired now, and my son Don owns and operates it. When I owned it, I used to get to work by four every morning to make pies and cakes and prepare the menu for the day. By the time the doors opened at 5:30, we were ready for our first customers. We served regular dinners at noon every day and at night we had special orders for just about anything you'd want—steaks, chicken, seafood, sandwiches. We were open until nine every night, except for short hours on Saturday, when we were open from six to one. Those were long hours and hard work, but I always tried to leave about 1:30 in the afternoon to come home and do my housework and rest. Then I'd go back to help with supper. I couldn't have done it without a good staff of workers. Mrs. Elizabeth Coleman helped me serve and wait on tables for more than twenty years, and I had excellent help in the kitchen and behind the counter. Odessa Randolph, Helen Crawford, Viola Robinson, and Susie Jackson stayed with me for many years. Their loyalty and hard work made it easy for me.

Don has made a few changes since he took over, but he's running it pretty much the way I did. The menu is larger now than when we opened in 1954, but not much else has changed, except for the prices. In 1954 a regular dinner went for seventy-five cents, and that included meat, three vegetables, and a dessert. Now it's closer to four dollars, without the dessert. Don has a good range of food and drinks, but we've never allowed alcoholic beverages to be served. I didn't want to be around drinking if I didn't have to.

Our two sons, Ronald and Donald, were born about three years apart. Ronald works with the Alabama Power Company. I'm very pleased with what they're doing. It took Don a little longer to find himself, but I think he's now happy running the restaurant. He also has an antique auction here in Hurtsboro. Both of my sons seem to be happy; and if they're happy, I'm happy for them.

As I've said, I lost J. T. in 1982. Two men walked into his store one Friday afternoon to rob him and shot him five times in the face. He had a gun but didn't have a chance to get it before they shot him. When we found J. T., the cash register was open and there was blood from it to the telephone. The receiver was off and he was dead on the floor beneath it. J. T. and I had our ups and downs, but I did love him as my husband and the father of my two sons.

I have never liked to live alone, so in 1985 I married Jimmy Supple, who was an engineer for the state highway department for many years. His wife died of cancer. I've know him since we moved here, and he's a good, church-going man. I've been a Baptist all my life, but when we married, I joined the Hatchechubbee Church of Christ to be with him. He's so different from what I had. He's a good man. But I don't know if I had it to do over that I would marry anybody because of my sons. It's hard for them to see anyone coming in to take the place of their father. But Jimmy and I get along all right. We are both financially secure. We made a legal agreement before we married that everything I had before we married goes to my sons, and everything he had goes to his daughter. We like to travel together. On our honeymoon we went to San Francisco. For our first anniversary we went on a cruise to the Bahamas. We've also been on trips to Alaska and Nashville. When I was a girl, I never dreamed I'd get to go to those places and do things I've done. Since I retired, I have more time to do other things too. I've been working on my yard and cleaning out drawers in the house and doing things I've put up to do for a long time. I've started reading more—just about anything except history.

I've had health problems during my life, but overall I've been pretty lucky. When I was five years old and we were living on Mr. Lee Hall's Place, I had a bad case of pneumonia, and they had to go to Troy to get medicine. It was in February and they stayed up all night with me keeping a fire going. They thought I was going to die. Dr. Guthrie came to see me in his buggy and I guess he saved my life. Whenever we needed him, he'd come. Sometimes we didn't have money to pay him, but he'd come anyway. Whenever Daddy had cash money to pay him, it was usually because he'd done some bootlegging for one of his brothers who made whiskey. That was about the only way poor farmers could get money most of the time. In recent years I've had some pretty serious illnesses. I've had cancer, and I've had a bleeding ulcer. Like Mama, I had to have half of my stomach removed.

I've already lived longer and accomplished more than I ever dreamed I would. I have a comfortable home to live in. I sent both my sons to college and they are doing well. I've made good money as a businesswoman. I'm thankful for all my material blessings. But sometimes I get dissatisfied with myself and think I should have done better. I wish I had gone on to college, but back then I didn't know it was possible to work and go to school at the same time. I didn't have anybody to tell me about such things. I believe if I had gone on to college, I would have met someone I might have been happier with. Maybe I should have divorced J. T. after my first son was born and tried to make it on my own. I think I could have succeeded even then. The problem was I didn't know any woman of my class who had ever done it, and I didn't know anybody to turn to to back me up. I know I loved J.T. very much, but nobody can be happy with a person who drinks so much. I resented his drinking, but I endured it because I didn't know what else to do. Now, I don't see how I put up with his drinking and violence and beating me all those years. For a ten-year period, from about 1964 to 1974, he completely quit drinking, and we had a happy life together. Then he went back to drinking. When I asked him to leave it alone, he said he was in so much pain from his war wound that he had to have either alcohol or dope. He said he had to have something. Maybe he did, but it was hard on all of us.

If I'd been able to go on to school, I think I could have done office work or managed a clothing store or done something like that in business. I could have chosen something that satisfied me. I never thought I'd wind up cooking all my life for a living, but it was the only work I knew to do. As I say, I've done very well, but I think I could have developed myself in a lot more ways if I'd had the chance. I still have my feeling of inferiority. I still can't get up before a crowd and say a word. In Sunday School, when I'm called on to read the Bible, I can't even do that.

I know I could not have been a perfect person. I have my defects and shortcomings. Like all the Halls, I have a bad temper. I like to have things done a certain way. I can be impatient. But I've done some things right. I have some good points. I love to help people. I love to do things for them. Last week, I made some cakes and soups and took them to several older women in the community. It made me feel good to do that little bit of service for people who appreciate it. I've always tried to be generous with what I have. I guess I got that from Daddy. As poor as we were, he'd kill a hog and before he knew it, he'd given all the meat away and we had little or none for the smokehouse. Now, I can appreciate that kind of generosity, even if it meant we had to go without. It brings me closer to him and to my people who never had the opportunities that even I've had.

It helps me get ready for the day I'll join them all again. I'm getting along fine now, but I don't think I'll live to be very old. Mama and Daddy are buried at Bethel Cemetery in Pike County between Banks and Brundidge. It's the church Mama belonged to when she was a girl. I'll be buried here in Hurtsboro. I have a lot in the city cemetery and my stone is already up next to J. T.'s. Jimmy has his place set aside next to his first wife. I don't want to live long enough to be a burden on anybody. I want to take care of myself as long as I can. Then I'll be ready to go. I'm ready with the Lord whenever He calls.

POSTSCRIPT: In 1995 Louise Hall Hughes Supple still lives with her second husband in her home in Hurtsboro. She occasionally helps her son out at the City Grill.

INTERLUDE: YOUTH

*R*ight, the Inverness Consolidated School Beta Club, photographed on the front steps of the school, about 1952. From left: (1st row) Katie Frances Green, unidentified, Carol Roughton, Thomas Cameron; (2nd row) Allene Harrison, Nell Dykes, Carolyn Wilkinson, Willie Mae Pritchett, Martha Kate Braswell; (3rd row) Jeanette East, Sue Roughton, Mrs. Estelle Campbell, John Hamilton, Donald Scroggins.

Below, a group of boys from the community hanging out at Hall's cafe and store in the mid 1950s.

JEANETTE EAST HALL

A Dutiful Life

Jeanette East Hall is my sister-in-law, married to my brother Jack. She was raised some fifteen miles southeast in the Corinth community on the border between Bullock and Pike counties. It is July of 1984 and we are talking in the living room of the comfortable three-bedroom brick home Jack, a carpenter and contractor, built a few yards from the large frame home where he was born in 1935. They can see the remains of the older house across a small field now overgrown with briars and weeds but which used to grow bushels of sweet potatoes. The frame house was built by my Grandfather Waters for his bride, my grandmother, shortly after they were married. It has long been abandoned to wisteria, kudzu, and scattered patches of my mother's now wild zinnias, marigolds, and cosmos flowers. They have two grown children, Sharon and Gary, who are now married and live away from their parents. Gary and his family live across the road in a trailer. Sharon lives with her husband and three children just off the Boswell Road.

I've been married to Jack Hall since 1953, and I've been living in the Liberty community for over thirty years; but I was born in Pike County, right over the Bullock County line, on August 2, 1935. I'm two days older than Jack. A white woman from Pike served as the midwife. When I was still little, we moved just a few miles away to the Corinth community in Bullock County. Daddy had come originally from somewhere up in north Alabama around Double Springs. That's where he was born. I don't know why his people left and came down here—maybe looking for some place to settle that might be a little better than what they had. Some of his family had been in coal mining, but when they got to Pike County, they went into peanut farming.

Mother's maiden name was Culpepper. She was a native of Pike and was born near the same place I was born. She was an only child. Her mother died when she was about two years old, and her daddy couldn't take care of her, so he left the country. She was taken in by her grandmother who already had a drove of children. Mother said she never had a chance to wear any new clothes when she was a girl because she always got hand-me-downs from Grandmother Culpepper's children. I don't know where any of my people came from before they came to Alabama. When Mother's father died, some Culpeppers read it in the paper and wrote trying to discover their roots. I don't believe we ever established that we were kin.

Mother and Daddy married when she was about fourteen and he was twenty-four. By the time I came along, he was in the contracting business and my older brothers, Bruce and Charles, were doing most of the farming on our place. There were four of us children. First was Mary Evelyn. Then came Bruce, who was real black-headed. Then five years later was Charles, who was real white-headed. And I was the last one. When I was big enough to remember anything, Sis had already left home to get a job and help us out. During World War II she went to Florida to work at Wainwright Shipping Yards.

She soon found out she was real allergic to the sun and the materials she worked with, so she moved to Montgomery and got on with the Veterans Administration. She always seemed more like a mother to me than a sister, and she said she looked on me as her little girl. As a matter of fact, she provided me with most of my school clothes. Every summer she'd send me a bus ticket to Montgomery, and she'd take me shopping and buy me clothes and shoes for school. I would stay with her for a few days and then come back on the bus to Union Springs.

Charles is married with a family and is a contractor like Daddy. Bruce never married and stayed on the homeplace to farm. When Daddy and Mother moved to Corinth, they had about thirty acres of land, but he added on to it and had about one hundred and twenty acres when he died. Although we owned our land, most of the people around us were sharecroppers.

Nobody in the Corinth community had very much. We lived in a plain wooden frame house with five rooms; then Daddy added a den and a bedroom across the back and a screened-in porch before I left home. The rooms were ceiled with plain planks, which we painted. We had to move from where we were living in Pike County into the new house before it was finished. We only had it dried in. By that, I mean the outside walls were up and the floors were in and the roof was on, but there were no room partitions and no ceilings. It was just protected from the outside, so the rain couldn't get in. The first thing we did was to put up the bedsteads so we could sleep there at night. It was some time before we could use the kitchen. We had a wood-burning stove and had to build a flue up through the roof for the stovepipe to go out. Until we could get money to pay for that, we cooked on the stove outside in the backyard. It was fun to me because I thought it was like camping out. As Daddy got the money and found the time, he gradually got the house finished.

Jack and Jeanette on their wedding day.

But that didn't happen until a long time after we moved in.

In the wintertime the only kind of heat we had was from the fireplaces, but we had a lot of fun around the fire. That's where we'd shell our seed peanuts and corn that we'd plant the next year. Our fingers would get real sore from shelling peanuts, so we used a peanut popper, which is a piece of wood shaped like a U. We put a peanut in one end and mashed it to get the peanuts out.

When I was a girl we didn't have any indoor plumbing, so when we wanted to take an all-over bath, we bathed in a big old tin tub. We would draw water from the well and pour it into the tub and then leave it in the sun until it got real hot. Then we'd take it to the smokehouse, where we had two little rooms cut off from where we kept the meat. We used one of the rooms to take our tub baths. All of us used the same tub of water, and we started with the oldest and came down to the youngest, which was me. By the time I got to take my bath, the water wasn't much cleaner than I was. In the other room we kept a big box for ice we'd buy from Mr. Gwen's or Mr. Renfro's ice truck that came out from Union Springs once or twice a week. We'd buy a hundred and fifty or two hundred pounds of ice and pack it in the box with sawdust and cover it with old croker sacks that kept it from melting so fast. When we'd need ice for tea at dinner or supper, we'd take an icepick and chip off just enough for that meal.

We didn't have an icebox or refrigerator to keep our milk and butter in, so we'd put our sweetmilk and buttermilk in big tin cans and let them down in the well, and when we got ready for some, we'd draw the rope up. Mother warned us to be careful when we pulled the milk up because if we bumped the cans open we would lose the milk and ruin the well water too. Then she would have ruined our hide and sitting-down place!

We had enough cows to provide us with milk and butter for our own use, and sometimes we'd have enough to sell. A dairy company from Montgomery used to come around and buy all the milk we could let them have. They left big metal cans which we'd fill

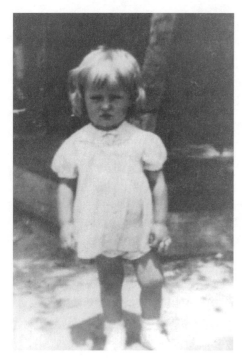

Jeanette East Hall.

and they'd take it back to the dairy for processing. Of course, we drank our milk straight from the cow. At one time Bruce and I each had four cows to milk twice a day by hand. That took a long time. Every morning and evening we took milk buckets to the cowpen, along with a small pail of warm water to wash off the cows' bag and tits. Sometimes the cows would be real dirty and muddy when they came up from the pasture. We fed them every time we milked, and they usually came up without any trouble, but sometimes we'd have to call them and go after them in the pasture and wouldn't get home until after dark.

Sometimes I'd still be down at the cowpen when Jack would come to pick me up for a date. If he got to the house and found nobody home, he'd take a seat on the front porch swing and wait for us. He knew where we were. We had good cows but sometimes they'd step in the milk bucket or try to kick us or swish their tails back and forth with cockleburrs in them. Many a time I've come up from the cowpen with a scratched-up face and arms and cockleburrs in my hair and smelling like a cow—and there would be Jack all dressed up ready to take me to the picture show.

No, I didn't really hate milking or doing anything else I had to do. Back then I didn't hate to do anything. I just didn't know any better. I didn't know there was any other way to do. I knew I had a duty to do and I did it. I never had a choice.

At home I was a tomboy. My brothers didn't want me to play with them, though I did some anyway. We didn't have many store-bought toys or games. We made our own checkers and checkerboard and would play at night around the fireplace. We did have a bought set of dominoes and a deck of cards that was so old you knew what each card was because of the way it was bent. One time my brother Charles made him a train set out of empty match boxes. He put a thread in the end of each box and filled it with sand. Then he connected all the boxes until he had a long string of them. He put up little sticks with strings between them to make light poles. We didn't have light poles out at Corinth, but he'd seen them on the way to town. He took real good care of his box-train and took it in the house each time when he was finished playing with it.

We also had a battery radio which we only played on Saturday night to hear the Grand Ole Opry. We turned the radio on when the Opry came on and turned it off when the Opry went off. We didn't want to wear out the battery. After Bruce was drafted for World War II, we started turning it on every once in a while to see how the war was going and to hear if it was over. One day, just before he was to leave to go overseas, Bruce was home on furlough and was down in the pasture trying to get some things done before he left. It was around noon that day and we turned the radio on, and it said the war was over. Bruce was half a mile away but he heard us whooping and hollering, and he came running toward the house to see what was wrong. We all ran out to meet him and hollered, "The war is over! The war is over!" Bruce had to stay out his two years in service, but he didn't have to do any combat fighting.

We lived in the country, of course, and raised most of the food we needed. In the summer we had our garden vegetables, and then for winter Mother canned peas and butterbeans and tomatoes. Sometimes she'd can some of the meat after we killed hogs.

We also beat out dry peas and ate them in the wintertime. We never knew what it was like to eat beef, but we had plenty of hogs and chickens to eat. Mother was a great cook. I've seen her take a chicken and wring his neck till it broke as smooth as you please. But every time I tried to twist his neck, I'd throw him down on the ground and he'd squawk and run off.

I never did learn how to wring a chicken's neck. Mother would cook the whole chicken, neck and feet and everything. Everybody wanted a leg or a breast or a pulley bone, but Mother teased us by saying if we ate the feet it would make us good looking. So we all fought over who would eat the feet. I don't believe I ever did! If there was a big dinner and not everyone could eat at the same time, us children waited outside until the old folks finished. And what Mother put on the table, we ate. We didn't say, "I don't want this" or "I can't eat that." We ate what was put before us and were thankful for it.

Mother always had something for us to eat after school. I could hardly wait to get home in the evening, when I'd walk straight through the house and through the kitchen door up to a nail on the wall, where Mother might have a flour sack hanging. If one was there, it would be full of tea cakes. That was my favorite thing to eat. If she hadn't cooked tea cakes, I'd look in the oven or warmer and get a biscuit and take off for the garden, where I'd get an onion and peel it and eat it with my biscuit. If it wasn't time for onions, I'd take my biscuit and head for the old storage house, where Mother kept huge jugs full of nine-day pickles, and get me a pickle and eat it with my biscuit. To this day there's nothing better to me than a cold biscuit with onion or pickle—unless it's tea cakes!

On special occasions we might have something different to eat. After we picked and sold our cotton in the late summer, the first thing we did was go to the store and get a pound of cheese, a can of salmon and several pounds of saltfish. We thought all that was real fancy food. Mother would take that can of salmon and put in enough eggs and flour and meal to stretch it to make fifty patties. It was something we looked forward to all year.

We went to town more than most people in Corinth because Daddy was in the contracting business. He did his work through a building supply company that was owned by Mr. Carl Green and Mr. D. Armor Caylor, who was the bookkeeper. The work was contracted through them because we didn't have a telephone and because Daddy could get materials and pay for them when a job was done. So when he had to go to town on business, Mother and Charles and Bruce and I would usually go with him, and it would be an all-day affair. We always took the Three-Notch Trail towards Union Springs. It comes up from Troy and runs through Blues Stand and cuts across and goes on through Smut Eye. We followed it until it cut off and went up through Three Notch, and then we took another road into Union Springs. All the roads near home were dirt, and it was hard to get out

A Fourth of July barbecue in the Corinth community. Jeanette East Hall is in the center of the photo, reaching across the table.

Bruce and Charles East, with their bird dogs, Corinth, Alabama, about 1952.

from there. None of our roads got paved until about 1953, the year I married and moved away. It was common to get stuck in the mud after a big rain. Or if it was dry, we might get bogged down in a big sandhill. It was real bad on hills after a rain. We had some hills that would bog a buzzard's shadow down if you tried to go up them. When we got stuck, we'd just get out and put sticks and limbs under the wheels and push to where we could back it up and start over. We'd get mud spattered all over our Sunday clothes, but we cleaned it off the best we could and went on to town.

Regardless of the bad roads, we managed to get to town about once a month, always on a Saturday. Daddy had an old GMC truck and Mother and Daddy and I would ride in the cab up front, and my brothers would ride in the back. When I was a girl, I thought Union Springs was a big place with lots of people. The streets were crowded with mostly black people all day on Saturday. In the 1930s and 1940s a lot of people still went to town on their wagons, and the roads would be clogged with mules and wagons. There was a place set off on a side street where they

would park and tie the mules to the wagons under the trees in the shade. The stores and sidewalks would be jammed. Most of the merchants had porches over the fronts of their stores and benches where the people could sit. There was so many people it could take you thirty minutes to walk from the Confederate soldier in front of the court house down to the picture show. Of course, not everybody came to town to trade or do business. Some people just came to have something to do and to visit with each other. The people who lived in Union Springs were nice and friendly enough, but I thought they were somehow different from me. I could see all the pretty things in the stores, and I knew that some people up there were rich enough to buy them.

We enjoyed walking up and down the street and seeing people we didn't get to see at home. When we got tired of walking, we'd rest on the benches in front of the stores. We'd usually go into a number of stores to do business or to buy small items. One of the stores was Bullock Hardware, where Daddy bought feeds and tools. Across the street was V. J. Elmore Five and Dime Store. That's where I'd get my ice cream cone. Even if it was freezing and we had on heavy coats, we'd still get that ice cream. They had strawberry and chocolate, too, but I always got vanilla. Nothing else seemed like ice cream to me. We'd go also to Mrs. Bonnefield's, which was a ten-cent store but also had some articles of clothing. We'd buy some of our clothes there because they were cheap. We never went into the Fair Company because we thought their clothes cost too much.

We'd also buy some clothes and shoes at Cohn's old store, where everything was piled up to the ceiling. It was a tiny little place with aisles so narrow two people couldn't hardly pass at the same time. Old man Sam Cohn would stand at the door and try to get people to come in and buy something. He'd say, "I've got just the dress or shoes or pants that will fit you—and they're cheap." Most of his customers were Negroes, but a lot of whites traded there too. Another store that had cheap prices was the Dollar Store, which had a sign out front that said, "The Store That Teaches Your Dollar to Have More Cents."

When we had the money to go, the main attraction for us children was the Lilfred Theater. It cost a dime for children to get in, and there would be a Western with somebody like Johnny Mack Brown or Lash Larue, and maybe a detective story, a cartoon, the previews of coming attractions, and a serial like "The Phantom," which continued from week to week. It was hard for us to keep up with a serial because we didn't get to go every week.

When we got hungry, we'd maybe get a banana or bunch of grapes from Mr. Sam Katz, who came to Union Springs every Saturday and parked his produce truck on the street next to the Jitney Jungle. If Daddy made enough money that week, we'd get a hot dog or a hamburger at Uncle Bish's little diner that was parked at the curb on a side street. They were the best hamburgers I ever ate! He had a couple of stools inside where you could sit, but most country people ordered through a little lift-up screen window outside. Uncle Bish would have two or three high school boys working there, and while they were cooking and selling hamburgers, he'd walk around the streets.

We never had much money to spend on anything when we went to town. It took everything we had to keep us going—and to keep our old GMC truck running. It had a short-drive that always kept breaking, and Daddy had to get it fixed for his business. We never had much left over. We had some neighbors that would eat every Saturday at Holmes Cafe. I always wanted to eat there just once to see what it was like, but it wasn't until after I got married that I had a chance to. You always think that people who have things you want are rich. We didn't have electricity

until I was eleven years old, and I didn't have a telephone until I married and moved over here to the Liberty community. A lot of times I tell Jack I married him because his family had electricity and a TV, and I thought he was rich.

Not many people lived around Corinth when I was a girl, and I'm not sure half as many live there now. You could just about count our neighbors on your fingers and toes. There were the Culpeppers, the Dykeses, the Langstons, and the Singletons. We never had anybody moving in, but we had a lot of families moving out. Most of the people were sharecroppers and during the Depression, they couldn't raise enough to support their families, so they began to move to Columbus and Phenix City, where they had the big cotton mills. People would go over there and get good jobs and come back and tell about how much they made and what they had, and more and more people pulled up and moved and never came back, except on weekends to see their kinfolks.

Most of our neighbors were friendly and helpful, but there was some rough people that lived near us too. When I was a little girl, there was this man that had some chickens that started dying on him. When they died, he'd throw them down in an old gully behind his house, and another man's chickens found them and started pecking on them. Whatever it was that killed the first man's chickens started killing the second man's. He got mad as the devil and went over to the man's house with his shotgun. When he got there, he saw the man down on his knees looking up under his house trying to pull out another dead chicken. The mad man raised his gun and it went "Boom," and that was the end of that man. The murderer said he believed in "an eye for an eye and a tooth for a tooth," though it seemed to me more like a man for a chicken. He went to jail for a while but soon got out. I was always scared to get too close to that man. One time he came through our yard and our dog started barking at him. While I was trying to

Jeanette East Hall, with her sister Mary East Lechner on a trip to Montgomery, 1945.

catch the dog and hold him, I saw the man pull out a knife with a blade about eight inches long. As I was holding my dog, he threw that knife at us and it just barely missed me. I was afraid of that man all my life.

I don't know what he did for a living, but he could have made moonshine whiskey, for all I know. It was a common thing for men around Corinth to do. That part of the county has some thick woods, and there are lots of little creeks and branches to supply water for the stills. The moonshiners would drink what they wanted and then sell the rest to contacts outside the county who would come and pick it up. The bootleggers would give them two or three dollars a gallon for the moonshine and then re-sell it for six or seven times as much.

Moonshining was a risky business because the revenuers were always coming through looking for stills, though most of them were never found. There was so many woods and hills and valleys the revenuers

couldn't cover it all. When they did catch somebody making whiskey, it was usually because somebody had turned him up and showed them where the still was. My granddaddy never got caught, and he made whiskey for a long time. He never sold any of his whiskey but made it for his own use. I think a lot of men thought they had the right to do that, and it was none of the government's business. His still was down in a valley between steep hills. One time he almost got caught. He was headed down the hill when he saw some revenuers hiding near his still so they could catch him when he came up. The revenuers didn't see Granddaddy, so he just took his seat and waited it out with them. So there he sat, watching them watch his still. They waited and waited. About dark they gave up and left. Then Granddaddy went in, took his still apart and moved it to a new location. When the revenuers came back the next day, there was no still there—nothing! It was long gone without a trace. Granddaddy kept on making and drinking his moon-shine and never got caught.

I guess a lot of the men drank for recreation. Some of our neighbors also loved to pull pranks and practical jokes. I remember a bunch of big old strap-ping boys about sixteen or eighteen that would get out on the side of the road at night, pull off all their clothes, and when some women would come by in a car, they'd jump out and say they were the highway patrol. "We want to see your driver's license," they'd say, and when the women could see they was naked, they'd run back into the bushes whooping and hollering.

There were very few cars in Corinth at that time, so the boys would have to wait a long time for a car full of women to come by. Most of the traveling was done by horse and wagon. I remember the Molen family that lived down below us in an old log house. The bedroom, living room, and sitting room were all in one big room up front, and across the back they had another big room for the kitchen and cooktable and the eating table. I thought that house was the prettiest I'd ever seen. The old couple that lived there was up in age, but they had a number of children that would visit them on the weekends and have a big dinner. Every Sunday we could see all the horses and wagons pulling into their yard with their children and their families. Nobody had much to eat back then, but this couple got commodities like prunes and coffee and peanut butter from the government. While the women were inside fixing dinner, the yard would be covered with horses and wagons and men and children and dogs, and then they'd all go inside and eat what was probably their only good meal of the week. Like us, they all got by and nobody starved.

The first school I went to was called Corinth. The school and the community were both named for Corinth Church, which was a little Baptist church. Mother belonged to Ramah, a Primitive Baptist church over in Pike County. That was the church that had the foot washings, but I never participated in that. In those days people took all their children to church with them and pacified the little ones with sugartits. That was a piece of cloth with sugar in it that babies sucked on. It kept them quiet—well, it did some of the time—while the preaching was going on. Sometimes school would be held in the church house, but Corinth School was separate from the church. It was really just one big room, with sliding doors that separated the first, second, and third grades, which were in one room, from the fourth, fifth, and sixth, which were in the other half. We also had another little room set off for a lunchroom. Our principal was Mrs. Anna Mae Gravel, Mr. George Gravel's wife. She taught the upper grades. My first teacher was Miss Ella Hardaway from Troy. Now, she was rough! When you did any cutting-up, she called you to the front of the class and said, "Give me your fingers," and when you held your hand palm up towards her, she took her ruler and raised a blister.

We weren't to say mean children, but sometimes we did get into trouble, as children will. One day some men were digging a well in the schoolyard, trying to get water for the school. They had piled up a lot of pretty red dirt, and at recess some of us got to playing in it. We got it all over ourselves and then we tracked it into the schoolhouse. Well, I can tell you, that didn't set too good with Miss Hardaway! So she said, "Everybody who played in that dirt, stand up!" Very few stood up. But I decided I was going to be big and brave, and I started up from my seat. About that time I saw the big paddle she had in her hand, and I eased back down. She whipped a few of the guilty ones, but she didn't get all of us who deserved it.

I'm telling you, that woman was in control. She wasn't afraid of anybody. She's even stand up to the men. One time I saw her stand up to a man whose children had involved in a nettle fight. A nettle, you know, is a weed that has a bloom that will sting you if you touch it. Well, we had this brother and sister that was real fond of pulling up nettles and whipping all the younger children to make them sting. One evening when we was walking to catch the schoolbus to go home, they started fighting the small children with nettles and making them cry. The next day Miss Hardaway found out about it and whipped that boy and girl until they cried. The next morning their daddy came up to the schoolhouse and said, "What did you whup my younguns fer? If they needs a whupping, I'm the one to do it." Well, we was all scared to death, but she stood right up to him, stuck her finger in his face and said, "Listen here, Mister, if you don't like it, you keep your children at home. When they're in school, they'll behave. And if they get into another nettle fight, I'll whip them again." I'll tell you, that man turned around and left without a word and never came back. His children behaved after that. He was one of Corinth's roughest characters, but he was no match for Miss Hardaway.

Miss Hardaway outlawed nettle fighting, but at recess we played other games that could be almost as hurtful. When we played springboard, we'd take a big old board and put it across a log, and one person would get on one end and one on the other and we'd jump up and down. While one person was up in the air, the other one was down. If you lost your balance and missed the board, you could get skinned up or have the breath knocked out of you. The boys played marbles. We climbed trees all around the schoolhouse. We played volleyball and dodgeball. In dodgeball we'd get a stick and draw a square and put everybody in it. Two players on each side would throw the ball and try to hit the ones in the square. It was a simple game but it was great fun.

Another thing we liked to do was walk about a mile and a half from the schoolhouse to Mr. Arthur Clyde King's store. If we had a few nickels and wanted to buy school supplies or candy, our teacher would let several of us take orders and go to Mr. Arthur Clyde's store. He would take a popsicle and split it in two, and if we had only two cents, that day he'd sell it for two cents. Or at another time, if we had three cents, he'd sell it for three cents. That was the kind of person he was. When we got everything we came for—crayons, paste, paper, pencils—we'd head back down the road to school. It was like a big adventure for us to go to the store.

In those days children did a lot of walking. We walked just about everywhere we went in the community. Our schoolhouse was too far for us to walk to, but we had to walk about two miles to catch the bus. Our school bus was just a big old wood body, with one long seat down each side and one seat down the middle. We sat on each side facing the middle and the ones in the middle faced each side. Each of us had a particular place to sit. Our bus driver was Mr. Aus Dykes, and we all just loved him to death. His wife was one of our teachers at one time. When the bus was loaded, he'd have a hard time getting up the hills. There was one long hill that was real bad when it rained. Even when it didn't rain, it was a hard hill for

us to pull up because our bus was so old. Mr. Aus was so funny when we'd come to that hill. He would rock forward in the driver's seat, trying to help the motor push the bus on up the hill. And he would tell us, "Now, y'all rock just like me and we'll make it to the top." Of course, we all believed him and would rock and rock, straining to get our bus up the hill. But sometimes we'd get almost to the top and stall. Mr. Aus would have to let the bus roll back down to where he could get another running start that would take us over the top. The hill was long and steep, with a bridge over a deep creek at the bottom. So we'd sit there scared to death, afraid we'd slip all the way downhill into the creek and get drowned. But the most trouble we ever had was getting stuck in the mud. We'd all unload and help push the bus over the top. If we couldn't push it out of the mud, we'd have to get a mule to pull us out. On those days when we got to school we might have big patches of mud all over our clothes, but it was something we all accepted.

The next school bus I rode was driven by George Dykes and it went all the way to Inverness School. There were about twelve of us in the sixth grade at Corinth, but only three of us came on to Inverness to start the seventh grade. The others just dropped out. They didn't have the money or the interest to go on. It cost thirty-five cents a week to eat in the lunchroom, and some people didn't have that much money to spend. Inverness was a much bigger school and had all twelve grades, and for a while I felt lost and alone. But I soon made friends and met the boy that became my husband.

I'd been living in the backwoods so long, I wasn't much attracted to boys. If there was an attraction, it was just so I could play ball with them. At Corinth we might have joked and called ourselves sweethearts, but we didn't know what that meant. In the sixth grade I remember one time kissing a boy through the glass pane in the schoolhouse door because somebody dared me to. But that was the closest I'd ever been to kissing a boy till I started dating Jack Hall in the ninth grade. The first time Jack came to my house to pick me up for a date, he got lost several times before he found the right way. But he soon had made some ruts in the road between his house and mine. Usually we'd go to the picture show in Union Springs. If he had a dollar it would be enough to get us in the show and buy two Co-Colas and a bag of popcorn. If he had any money left over, he'd put gas back in his daddy's pick-up truck. It didn't have a heater, but in the wintertime Jack was nice enough to bring a blanket to put over our legs to keep us from freezing.

Jeanette East Hall, Jack Hall, Dean English.

We both finished school in May of 1953 and married in October. Jack took a test to get a job on the railroad, but they never called him back. So we decided to go ahead and get married. When I was a girl, I wanted a job in Montgomery at the Veterans Administration like Sis. In fact, I took a secretarial course to prepare me to go and work up there. But when Jack couldn't get a job on the railroad, we both changed our plans and got married. Of course, I'd always wanted to get married some day and have children. When I was a little girl, I wanted Mother to have another little baby for me to have somebody to play with. I didn't know, of course, that she couldn't have any more children. She was thirty-two when I was born, but she had been told not to have any more children or it would kill her. She almost died when Charles was born, but I was lucky that she decided to have one more. Right after we married, we lived at Jack's old homeplace right across the field from where we live now, but we soon moved down to be with Mother and Daddy. That's when Jack started working full-time with Daddy in the contracting business and got started being a contractor himself. Daddy paid him five dollars a day, twenty-five dollars a week, and we thought we was rich.

After a few years with Mother and Daddy, we built this house and have lived here ever since. We've raised our two children, Gary and Sharon, here. Now they're both married and have moved out. Our house is a nice brick one. We just recently put in air conditioning. We have a TV dish outside and get dozens of channels. We have a telephone. In fact, the first time I ever talked through a telephone was when we got ours right here. I was in my twenties then, and I just couldn't imagine that you could say "Hello" and a voice would speak back to you. The only telephones we had in Corinth were two tin snuff boxes with a string between them that children played with and pretended they were telephones.

Life is a lot easier for us now, though there are things I miss about the old times. What I miss most is that back then we had more time for one another. Even with all the hard work we had to do, there seldom went a week by that there wasn't some big to-do around home—nothing fancy, just something for people to do to get together. Sometimes they were

Jack Hall.

work gatherings, like wood-sawings, when the men would go at night after work into the woods with their lanterns and saws and axes and cut down trees. They would saw the wood up in blocks and split it and haul it to the house to burn that winter. The wood-sawings would go around to every family so that everybody had enough wood to last through the cold months. While the men were sawing in the woods, the ladies would be inside the house making syrup bread or peanut brittle, which we'd all enjoy when the men came in. Back then, if you got sick, your neighbors would all come in and clean your house, cook your meals, milk your cows, and plow your fields until you were able to go back to doing your own work. Nobody ever thought of being paid. It was just something you did out of love for your neighbor.

I've held down a number of jobs since I married. I've driven a school bus. I've clerked at Cohn's store in Union Springs. I've worked in the school lunchroom at Inverness. For a while I went to a cosmetology

school in Eufaula, but I had to drop out because I found I couldn't hold out to go to school and work two jobs all at once. But the work I'm proudest of is raising two healthy, decent children and trying to be a good wife to Jack. We've had a lot of hard times, but we've had a good life together. Things could have been a lot worse. I don't have a lot of regrets. I'm not bitter about anything. Maybe Jack and I could have waited a little longer to get married. But it's turned out all right. We have worked together. We have shared together. We have loved together. We have hurt together. Sometimes I wish that Jack could have had a better job so he wouldn't have had to work so hard. But, all in all, I feel like the Lord's will was done.

POSTSCRIPT: In 1998 Jeanette and Jack Hall were still living in their home about two miles east of Liberty Church, where Jack is a deacon. Both their children live nearby with their families, and Jack and Jeanette see their three grandsons and two grand-daughters often. He continues to do construction work with a small crew. He also helps Jeanette with a new business, raising thousands of broiler chickens in state-of-the-art facilities about a quarter of a mile behind their house. When the chickens are big enough to be "processed," they are sent to the Wayne Poultry Company plant in Union Springs.

The wedding of Jimmy and Lillie Singleton Hall. Among the wedding party are, front row, second from left, Diane Singleton Hall; third from left, Jabo Hall; second from right, Mr. Singleton. Back row, John Hall, Donald Hall, Preacher John Butler, and, at far right, Jack Hall.

POSTLUDE: STATUARY, 1894

They come . . .

The women from the kitchen
Uncut roasting-ears in the dishpan
Unpoured buttermilk beside the biscuit tray
The safe open and swarming now with flies,
The cook stove fire covered in ashes;
Bonnets left hanging in the hall,
They stand on the steps in clean aprons.

The men, abruptly called from the fields
Cotton rows half laid by,
Upturned soil drying in the hot sun
Grass wilting in the plow's wake,
Bluejays feasting on an early dinner of grubs;
Their sun-creased faces stare from the center porch.

The children, too small to steady a plow stock
Or too young to trust with granny's churn,
From their games of crack-the-whip and playhouse;
Fretful at midmorning bath and Sunday clothes,
They pose stiffly before their mothers.

The old people from their fevered rest
In rockers shaded by the wisteria
Or rooms darkened to keep out the boiling light;
Impatient at disruption of routine and dinner's delay,
They find their seats in the front yard sun.

The neighbors from down the road
Seeing the wagon with the fancy words
Turn in at the Griders'
Stopped by to borrow flour or horseshoe,
At midweek, dressed in go-to-meetin' best;
Assured there is room for them as well,
They stand in family clusters on either side.

On the center step, a prim face in maiden innocence
Framed by auburn hair, lace neckband and medallion,
Looks wistfully across the years.

All is picture-ready, as
A hen strays unnoticed from under the house
A little girl in crisp bloomers picks her knee scab
A barefoot boy soothes his ground itch on a porch plank
A butterfly, unconscious of vanity,
Alights forever on a cosmos bloom.

From the lot, mules bray their approval of a week
With two Saturdays
While the headless stranger under the black cloth
Makes stone from flesh.

WADE HALL

INDEX

All placenames, unless otherwise indicated, are located in Alabama